Central Africa
a travel survival kit

Alex Newton

Central Africa - a travel survival kit
1st edition

Published by
Lonely Planet Publications
Head Office: PO Box 617, Hawthorn, Victoria 3122, Australia
US Office: PO Box 2001A, Berkeley, CA 94702, USA

Printed by
Singapore National Printers Ltd, Singapore

Photographs by

Eliot Elisofon (EE)	Bob Macke (BM)	Warren Robbins (WR)
Hal Frantz (HF)	Pamela Moffat (PM)	Karen Woodbury (KW)
Barry Hewlitt (BH)	Alex Newton (AN)	

Animal photos by Greg Herriman (GH)

Front cover: Pende Masked Dancers, Zaïre (EE)
Back cover: Lion (GH)

Cartoons by
Tony Jenkins

Thanks to Random House Inc for permission to qoute from David Lamb's *The Africans* (© David Lamb, 1984)

Published
May 1989

National Library of Australia Cataloguing in Publication Data

Newton, Alex.
Central Africa, a travel survival kit.

Includes index.
ISBN 0 86442 023 4.

1. Africa, Central - Description and travel -
1981-   - Guide-books. I. Title

916.7'04

© Alex Newton

Alex Newton

Raised in a small southern town, Madison, Georgia, Alex Newton spent time at Brown and Duke universities before joining the Peace Corps in the late '60s. Following almost three years service in Guatemala as an agricultural advisor and almost four years on Wall St as a lawyer, he studied French and development economics at the New School in New York and ended up again overseas, this time in Africa, where he has spent seven of his last eleven years working on development assistance programs. Travelling by plane, river boat, new trains and cockroach-infested ones, buses and pick-up trucks stuffed like sardines, and on top of lorries, he has been all over Central Africa and crossed the Sahara as well.

Since there aren't many guidebooks on Central Africa and since no class of traveller is spared the hassles of travelling in this area, Alex decided it was time to write a book that addressed the needs of all travellers. This is his second book. His first was Lonely Planet's guide to West Africa. An avid kayaker and now living in Quito, Ecuador, he bids travellers look him up and says on weekends he can be found most likely at the nearest squash court, running with the Hash House Harriers or scouting the rapids.

Dedication

This book is dedicated to Aunt T, the people of Madison, Georgia, and technicians like Jerry Johnson of SAFGRAD and Phil Serafini of ICRISAT who are spending their entire working lives abroad helping – and hoping – to find viable solutions to Africa's food problem.

Lonely Planet Credits

Editors	Peter Turner
	Mark Balla
Maps	Greg Herriman
Design & illustrations	Vicki Beale
Cover	Peter Flavelle
	Glenn Beanland

Thanks also to James Lyon for proofreading and Margaret Jung and Trudi Canavan for additional illustrations.

Acknowledgements

My foremost thanks go to Phil Jones, who spent endless hours reading and editing each chapter, and Olivier Leduc, who drew most of the maps and provided comic relief while I was slaving away on this book in Abidjan. I'm particularly indebted to the National Museum of African Art which provided a number of the photographs, as did Hal Frantz (Equatorial Guinea), Bob Macke (Gabon), Barry Hewlitt, (Central African Republic), Glenn Anders and Peter and Pamela Moffat (Chad). Special thanks also go to Buddy Roberts for sending me a computer, Steve Nelson for his advice on computers and the use of his office, Jennifer Ellingston for daily comic relief and stimulating conversations during the last gruelling months, Tim Farrell for picking me up a fantastic dictionary with the 'Queen's English', Kirk Talbott and Elizabeth Yates for information on slides of various countries, and those who sent comments on particular chapters – Denny Robertson (São Tomé), Micky Lang, Chris

Konarsky, Andy Sisson, Mrs Richard Podol and Katherine Montgomery.

And lastly, I'd like to thank the Lonely Planet team in Australia, particularly Tony Wheeler and Jim Hart who followed me around Africa by letter during our initial 'scoping out' period, Peter Turner and Mark Balla who undertook the arduous editing task, and Vicki Beale and Greg Herriman who did the artwork and maps.

A Warning & A Request

Things change – prices go up, schedules change, good places go bad and bad places go bankrupt – nothing stays the same. So if you find things better or worse, recently opened or long since closed, please write and tell us and help make the next edition better!

All information is greatly appreciated and the best letters will receive a free copy of the next edition, or any other Lonely Planet book of your choice.

Extracts from the best letters are also included in the *Lonely Planet Update*. The *Update* helps us make useful information available to you as soon as possible – it's like reading an up-to-date noticeboard or postcards from a friend. Each edition contains hundreds of useful tips, and advice from the best possible source of information – other travellers. The *Lonely Planet Update* is published quarterly in paperback and is available from bookshops and by subscription. Turn to the back pages of this book for more details.

Contents

Vitshumbi – Butembo – Beni – Mt Hoyo & Bunia – Mutwanga & Mt Ruwenzori – Central &
Southern Zaïre – Ishango – Lubumbashi – Kolwezi – Mbuji-Mayi – Kananga – Ilebo – Kikwit –
Northern Zaïre – Kisangani – Bumba – Buta – Epulu – Garamba National Park – Isiro –
Lisala – Zongo

Introduction

Travellers are drawn to East Africa by its incomparable wildlife and scenery. West Africa offers a real opportunity to experience the essence of black African culture – the art, the music, the markets. Central Africa combines the best of both worlds. Chad, northern Cameroun and northern Central African Republic, are clearly reminiscent of West Africa. The stunning costumes of the peoples of this region help to make the markets the most colourful in Central Africa. The people, mostly Muslim, live in hamlets scattered about the hot and dusty landscape, a bleak setting broken up by huge baobab trees which often appear to be growing upside-down.

Village life has changed very little over the centuries. Traditional roles are still very much a part of Central Africa, with decision making and hunting being left to the men,

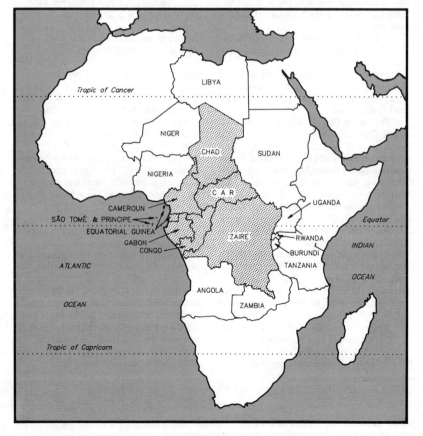

while the women tend to the children, work in the fields or prepare food. At night-time, the low beat of drums can often be heard, interrupted only by the occasional hyena calling his mate.

This is an area of stark beauty. Rumsiki in Cameroun, an area André Gide considered one of the 10 most beautiful on earth, has huge basalt outcrops creating a surreal, almost lunar landscape.

For a small fee the village sorcerer will predict your future in a ritualistic ceremony. Not far away is one of the better game parks in Africa, where during the hot season it is not unusual to see 300 or so elephants gathered around a single pond drinking to cool off.

The game reserves in the Central African Republic – sadly, the major big game hunting country in Africa – are even better. Further north on the edge of the desert at Lake Chad, you'll see fishermen tossing their nets being eyed by hippos wallowing in the cool muddy waters.

The rest of Central Africa is totally different. Thick rainforests are traversed by the worst roads in Africa. Small Pygmy camps crop up here and there throughout the jungle. Because of the incredibly dense vegetation preventing the growth of urban centres, this was the most primitive area in Africa at the beginning of the 20th century. This is Tarzan country, where Albert Schweitzer set up his famous hospital over 70 years ago. Just crossing Zaïre overland can still take up to three weeks or more. Gabon, the richest country per capita in black Africa, still has only about 400 km of asphalt roads outside the major cities and towns. The major cities, however, are some of the most modern in Africa, in part because three of black Africa's five richest countries (Gabon, Cameroun, Congo) are here. As is the case with many of the wealthier 'third world' nations, the relative affluence of these countries is oil based.

One of the most incredible sights is the snow-capped Ruwenzori mountain range in eastern Zaïre, with the third highest peak in Africa. What's unusual in this exceedingly wet area is the spectacular flora. At 3000 metres, giant heather plants grow up to a height of 4.5 metres (compared to only 60 to 90 cm in other parts of the world), flower stems as broad as a man's arm, blue lobelia plants over three metres high (five to 10 cm elsewhere), and an undulating carpet of brilliantly coloured moss which seems to grow everywhere. Eastern Zaïre and neighbouring Rwanda is also the home of the continent's last remaining gorillas. A gorilla family in the jungle mountains is an unforgettable sight.

For the African music buff, Zaïre and Cameroun are undoubtedly the places to be. The Latin-sounding Zaïrois Congo music is the most popular throughout Africa. Any night in Kinshasa, you can hear live bands, many of them internationally renowned. Cameroun's Makossa music is likewise heard all over West and Central Africa.

If it's African art you're interested in, you can't do better than Central Africa. The art of Zaïre, the Congo and eastern Cameroun is generally accepted as being among the finest on the continent. The Luba masks from Zaïre, with bug-like eyes and protruding nose and mouth, are so popular that they are sold all over West and Central Africa.

What is just as interesting, however, is simply mixing with people in the markets and villages. Africans offer a diversity of cultural identity which they have gained from mingling with bread women, cigarette vendors, town crazies or millet beer drinkers in mud bars and local markets. The best way to penetrate this culture is to make a friend. A friend will take you to his or her village, introduce you to the family, show you the bars with the best music in town, tell you when you're getting 'ripped off' and how to accomplish tasks in the best way.

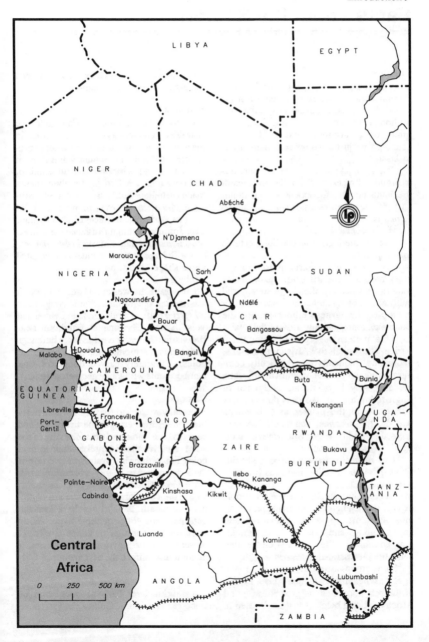

Facts about the Region

PEOPLE

One of the most startling things about Central Africa is the extent of ethnic diversity. Gabon, a country of little more than one million people, has 43 dialects and almost as many tribal groups. Most of the other countries are just as complex in their ethnic make-up.

The colonial powers chose to ignore this multitude of races, so that today the area of the Fang people, for example, constitutes part of three countries instead of one. Central Africa is overflowing with many such remnants of colonial days.

Such is the legacy of the Europeans in this respect that some countries have one or two tribes which clearly predominate, whereas other countries are made up of minorities which are often linguistically and culturally incompatible. In Cameroun, for example, the largest ethnic group, the Bamiléké, represent only 15% of the total.

This pattern is repeated throughout Africa. The result is that Africans of the same nationality frequently have difficulty communicating with one another. In many cases, the only way is by means of French or English, but a lot of Africans do not speak either. Go to the market in N'Djamena (Chad), for instance, and you'll be hard pressed to find a vendor who speaks the official language – French.

This makes governing exceedingly difficult. For the traveller, it makes life both interesting and frustrating. Each group has its own special characteristics. The Kirdi people of northern Cameroun, for example, are almost all farmers who are famous for their cliff dwellings and their intensive agriculture. The Fulani in the same area, on the other hand, are professional herdsmen.

Some groups are clearly more important, or at least better known, than others. Eleven of the best known ethnic groups in Central Africa are listed below. Most are located in one country; a few such as the Pygmy and the Fang are found in numerous countries.

Bamiléké

The largest ethnic group in Cameroun, the Bamiléké (bam-ee-lay-kay) are centred in the west around Bafoussam, the most densely populated area of the country. Best known for their art and as masters of expressionism, the Bamiléké are famous for their masks made entirely of beads and their wood carvings which, in contrast to more stylised African art forms, are recognisable by their freer forms and rough finishes. One of their most humorous dance masks is that of a person with huge oval eyes under an elongated glove-shaped brow, accompanied by a big toothy grin.

If you're in western Cameroun, don't miss seeing one of their chiefs' compounds (cheferies), the most elaborate in Central and West Africa. The one at Bandjoun near Bafoussam, for example, has large buildings with tall thin sculptured columns like totem poles, elaborately carved doorways, and bamboo walls with fancy geometric designs.

Bamoun

Especially renowned for their royal dynasty but also for their artwork, particularly wood carvings, the Bamoun (bah-moun) live in the same area as the Bamiléké, their capital being Foumban. The royal dynasty is one of the longest in Africa – 18 successive kings since 1394. Unlike so many African groups whose pre-colonial history is known only by word of mouth, the Bamoun have kept the personal belongings of the sultans dating back many centuries. These are well preserved in the Royal Palace museum, a major tourist attraction in Cameroun.

Fang

Constituting over half the population of Gabon and Equatorial Guinea, the Fang have a reputation for having had some of the best sculptors in Africa. The paradox is that while Fang artists were masters of form and capable of expressing sensuous humanism, the Fang warriors were among the fiercest in Africa, with cannibalism reputedly being practised by some. Unfortunately, with the onslaught of the colonial powers in the 20th century, the Fang soon lost their artistic talents almost completely.

Fulani
The origin of the Fulani (fou-LAN-ee), or Foulbé, is not certain, though it appears that they migrated centuries ago from Egypt and may even be of Jewish origin. They are usually tall, elegant and thin with aquiline noses, long dark hair, oval faces and light complexion. Some are so fair that they could be mistaken for Caucasian.

For centuries, the Fulani have been cattle raisers throughout northern Central Africa (and West Africa). While some combine farming with cattle raising, others are nomadic cattle herders who live in the pastoral zone and subsist entirely from livestock raising. A typical arrangement is for farmers to purchase cattle as a form of investment and turn them over to the Fulani to tend in return for occasional sacks of rice. Fulani herdsman can recognise every single animal in herds of 300 cattle and more!

Kirdi
The people inhabiting the rocky mountainous areas of northern Cameroun, the Kapsiki, Fata, Bata, Mafa, Guidar, Podoko, etc, are known collectively as the Kirdi (keerdee). Almost all farmers, they are a fascinating people.

For centuries they have lived on the sides of huge cliffs in round dwellings with tall pointed roofs covered with grass. From afar, their villages in the Mandara mountains (Mora, Mokolo, Mabas, Tourou) have a fairyland, hobbit-like appearance and are a major tourist attraction. They practise a type of animism in which priests and sorcerers play a particularly important role.

Kongo
The Kongo, the most numerous people in Zaïre, also live in Congo and Angola. At one stage they had one of the most powerful kingdoms in all of Central Africa, reaching its height around the mid-16th century, before being almost annihilated by the Portuguese.

Their dialect, Kikongo, is the most widely spoken language in western Zaïre, and their art is some of the finest in the Congo basin area. Kongo art is characterised by its realism and the typically natural poses of the human figures, usually with open mouths and often seated in relaxed positions.

A common theme is a mother and child. Fetishes, too, are extremely important in Kongo art – typically animals or human figures pierced with scores of nails or pieces of metal, giving the fetish its magical power and the sculpture a devilish air.

Kuba

The Kuba, or Bakuba, live towards the centre of Zaïre near Kananga, and are a tribe of virtuoso carvers whose artistic influence has been disproportionate to their small numbers. The Kuba kingdom flourished back in the 17th century during the reign of their 93rd king, Balongongo, whose ornate royal gown reputedly weighed 75 kg.

He became a cultural hero by introducing cassava, palm oil, tobacco, raffia and embroidery to the area. His wooden statue in the British Museum is the oldest art object from Central Africa. Kuba art is predominantly geometric and includes an unusually wide assortment of objects, such as masks with raffia cloth, a variety of wooden cups, boxes, game boards, tobacco pipes, combs, stools, charms, spoons and beds.

Luba

One of the largest ethnic groups in Zaïre, the Luba, or Baluba, is found in south-eastern Zaïre in the Shaba region, north of Lubumbashi. Many of the men working the all-important copper mines in Shaba are Luba, and their dialect, Tshiluba, is the most widely spoken language in southern Zaïre. They stand out in part for being the most prolific artists in Zaïre. Luba masks with huge bug-like eyes and ornate geometrical designs are sold all over Central and West Africa. It's almost as easy to find one in Abidjan as it is in Kinshasa.

Pygmy

Although there are not many Pygmies left in Africa, they are famous for their short stature (averaging about 120 cm (four feet) in height) and adaptation to life in the jungle. They are hunters and due to their basically nomadic existence, they are scattered in the tropical forests of Central Africa, especially the eastern areas of Gabon and the Congo, the south-western region of the Central African Republic, southern Cameroun and Zaïre.

Pygmies move about in small groups,

generally only settling in any one place for a short time. With a culture still largely intact, Pygmies are also known for their spontaneous dances, frequently at night around a fire.

Sara

In southern Chad, including the area of Sarh, the people are non-Muslim black Africans. The largest group is the Sara, accounting for roughly a third of Chad's population. While the majority are farmers, they also occupy most of the civil service and higher military positions. The practise of elongating the lips was common among the Sara women. The intent of this practice was not to enhance their appearance but rather to make themselves unattractive to the slave traders.

Toubou

In Chad's far north, the people are indigenous Saharans known as Toubou, numbering about 150,000. Like the Arabs with whom they are sometimes confused, they are Muslims, but unlike the Arabs, they do not consider themselves to be descendants of Mohammed. Rather, they consider themselves to be from a certain locality; Toubou means 'man from Tibesti'.

The Toubou are herders and nomads and not well educated. Fiercely independent, very clannish and heroic warriors, they started Chad's civil war back in the mid-'60s in part because they weren't well represented in the government. Libya became their ally and used this as an excuse to invade Chad, eventually taking over the war completely.

GEOGRAPHY

Central Africa has a little of everything – flat lands, vast rain forests, hills and mountains. The major mountains are the Tibesti range in northern Chad (after roughly 15 years, still off limits due to the war with Libya), 4100 metre Mt Cameroun in western Cameroun (the rainiest spot on the continent), all of Bioko Island in Equatorial Guinea, all of São Tomé, and the fantastic Ruwenzoris (rou-when-ZOR-ee) in remote eastern Zaïre, reaching over 5100 metres (third highest in Africa). In the rainy Ruwenzoris, known as the 'Mountains of the Moon', there are plants and flowers literally 15 to 20 times taller than similar varieties elsewhere in the world.

The principal hilly areas, typically rising to about 1000 metres and good for hiking, are the Bamenda and Buea areas of western Cameroun (the most popular areas for hiking), northern Cameroun around Rumsiki and Mokolo, including the Pic de Mindif south of Maroua (probably the most challenging rock formation for serious rock climbers), south-eastern Gabon around Franceville, and the lower areas of eastern Zaïre. Lubumbashi, in far southern Zaïre, is also a beautiful area, with rolling hills.

Above all, Central Africa is famous for its rain forests, the most extensive in the world outside the Amazon basin. Well over two-thirds of Gabon, all of southern Cameroun, most of northern Zaïre, north-eastern Congo and south-western Central African Republic is dense rain forests. This is Pygmy territory as well. Roads in all of these areas are virtually all dirt and invariably in horrendous muddy condition during the rainy season.

CLIMATE
Heat
Most people tend to think Central Africa is very hot. As the following chart of average temperatures (°C) shows, this is something of a myth.

	July	August
Washington	30	29
Rome	31	31
Tokyo	28	30
Singapore	31	30
Kinshasa (Zaïre)	27	29
Douala (Cameroun)	28	29
Lagos (Nigeria)	28	28
Cairo(Egypt)	35	35

In most of Central Africa, high humidity is the problem, not heat. The only area that gets really hot is near the desert (Chad, northern

Cameroun) – but not all year round. Only from March to May does it get noticeably hotter in these two areas. Put your face in front of a hair-drier and you'll know what it's like riding in a car with the windows down in Chad during this period. At least it's dry heat, however.

If heat (even dry heat) is really your bête noire, don't travel to Chad and northern Cameroun from March to May, when the climate there can easily get 20°C hotter. Nevertheless, many people prefer this to the humidity. Moreover, in the shade temperatures can be a good 10°C to 15°C lower. So if March to May is the only convenient time to travel, don't avoid Chad and northern Cameroun unless you are one of those who sit by the air-con all summer long.

Rain
While in West Africa the rainy season is fairly uniform (June to September), in Central Africa, the weather pattern is screwed up because of the equator, which cuts Central Africa almost in half – running just below Libreville, splitting Gabon in two, and through northern Zaïre near Kisangani and the Ruwenzori mountains. Douala, Yaoundé and Bangui are all about 4° north of the equator, while Kinshasa, Brazzaville and Pointe-Noire are roughly 4° south of the equator.

As a gross simplification, Central Africa has two heavy rainy seasons: May to October above the equator and October to May south of the equator (with the heaviest rains falling mid-January to May). In other words, the rainy season north of the equator is the dry season south of the equator. At or near the equator, rain tends to fall slightly more heavily and all year round, with a slight let-up in July to August in some areas, such as Libreville.

As an example of why this is a gross simplification, take the example of Yaoundé, which has two rainy seasons, March to June and September to November. It's fairly dry from July to August when you'd expect it to be rainiest. On the other hand, in Douala, only about 200 km due west, the rainy season is when you'd expect it – May through October.

If possible, avoid visiting these areas during the wet season. The sun rarely shines and most dirt roads, except for the main arteries, become impassable.

In Chad and northern Cameroun, it is not continually overcast during the rainy season (mid-June through September). Indeed, many travellers prefer the rainy season in these two areas. The sun is not incessantly beating down on you, and temperatures are a little lower.

The main problem during the rainy season is travelling upcountry. Whereas in West Africa most major roads upcountry are all-weather, in jungly Central Africa this is not the case. Many of the dirt roads, even major routes, are passable only with four-wheel-drive vehicles, and the driving times are doubled. Without a four-wheel-drive vehicle, you may have no hope of reaching some of those more remote spots you may have read about. This is true even in the dry areas, Chad and northern Cameroun. In late July on the edge of the Sahara, you can find yourself surrounded by lake-size 'puddles' of water that refuse to be absorbed by the lifeless soils.

People on tours shouldn't be concerned because four-wheel-drive vehicles are invariably used. Others who expect to do a lot of upcountry travel during rainy periods should bring patience, humour and a good book.

The Harmattan

December to February is the time of the Harmattan winds when the skies in northern Central Africa are grey from the sands blown south from the Sahara. On bad days, visibility can be reduced to one km, or occasionally even less, resulting in aeroplane delays or cancellations. Take a trip to the beautiful hilly areas of western Cameroun in December, for example, and you'll get none of the views that make them so popular with hikers.

The Harmattan usually begins in late November or early December and lasts several months. Thereafter, skies still remain slightly hazy until the first rains.

Fortunately, even during the peak of the Harmattan, some days are fairly clear, which is probably why most travellers don't get too upset by the Harmattan. People with contact lenses should be prepared for problems regardless. Photography nuts are going to be mildly disappointed to say the least, with somewhat hazy results a certainty. Professional photographers in particular will end up shooting themselves if they come during this period.

ECONOMY
The Bad News

Overall, the economic situation in Central Africa is pretty bleak. Five of the world's 36 poorest countries are here, including the world's poorest – Chad. The other four are Zaïre, Equatorial Guinea, São Tomé, and the Central African Republic, all with per capita GNPs of US$200 or less.

The situation is worse in Chad not only because there's a war still going on and the people are poorer, but also because the rainfall is so much more unreliable. A 50% drop in rainfall may mean a zero harvest; the same in rainy Gabon would not have nearly the same effect. The situation is so bad in Chad that many families cannot afford to have their only daily 'luxury' – a small glass of tea in the shade after a meal.

The problem is that the situation is not improving. To the contrary, despite assistance from Western Europe and North America, these five countries are all worse off now than at independence. The classic example is Zaïre, an 'upper middle income' country in West-Central Africa at independence, now near the bottom. Mobutu's well publicised excesses during the '70s are the reason.

With fairly decent prices in cotton, the country's sole major export, Chad wasn't doing so badly until the drought of the early '70s and the heating up of the civil war in the late '70s, culminating in the bombing of the capital, N'Djamena, followed by another drought in the mid-'80s and the world-wide collapse in cotton prices. Little wonder it's at the bottom of the totem pole.

Another economic disaster is Equatorial Guinea, due almost single-handedly to Macias Nguema, a little known African ruler who was demented and every bit the equal of Idi Amin, if not worse. Because of him, virtually every Spanish expatriate in the country left shortly after he took over in the late '60s, ensuring the country's economic demise.

Bokassa, the president who declared the Central African Republic an empire and spent over US$20 million on his coronation as 'emperor', put the country through a similar nightmare from which it is only slowly recovering. And, as in the case of Equatorial Guinea, São Tomé has never recovered from the full-scale exodus of the Portuguese following independence.

All five countries are net importers of food even though some of them were self-sufficient at independence. Except in the case of Chad, drought has had nothing to do with this because Central Africa is the rainiest area on the continent. Assistance from the west has had almost no effect either.

The Good News

There are some real success stories in Central Africa. Those of Gabon and Cameroun are the most well known. The three wealthiest countries in West and Central Africa on a per capita basis are all in Central Africa – Gabon (US$3650), Congo (US$1300), Cameroun (US$1100). Here's how the top 12 countries in West and Central Africa, based on per capita incomes, stack up now compared to several years after independence:

1963	1985
Gabon	Gabon
Liberia	Congo
Ghana	Cameroun
Ivory Coast	Ivory Coast
Senegal	Nigeria
Congo	Mauritania
Sierra Leone	Liberia
Zaïre	Senegal
Cameroun	Togo
CAR	Ghana
Mauritania	Guinea
Guinea	Benin

Oil is the reason these three Central African countries have done so well. However, with the drop in oil prices, all of the oil producing countries went into a significant slump during the first half of the 1980s and are only slowly recovering. What happens to these economies when the oil dries up is anybody's guess, but for the moment oil continues to fuel their economies.

During the '60s and '70s, the Ivory Coast, the 'economic miracle' of West Africa, had the model economy in Africa. Cameroun, however, has had the highest growth rate in Africa since independence and by the mid-'80s had surpassed the Ivory Coast in per capita income, at the same time replacing the Ivory Coast as the continent's model economy. Both are net exporters of food, the only two countries in West-Central Africa that can claim such.

Like the Ivory Coast, Cameroun's success has come primarily from agriculture (coffee, cocoa, rubber, timber, cotton) – and oil – the critical plus.

It is Gabon, however, that has big bucks, almost all from oil. In Africa, only Libya has a higher per capita income – South Africa is third. But Gabon has only 1.2 million people. If being in the Third World is primarily a matter of per capita income, it's not clear that Gabon deserves the title Third World country. However, when you look at its poor health care system, underdeveloped road system and high illiteracy rate, it's simple to see that oil money can't change things overnight.

MUSIC

Perhaps nothing is more interesting about African culture than the music and dancing. Because it takes some getting used to, few travellers get interested in this aspect of African life. It's too bad. After all, the origin of much of our pop music today can be traced back to Africa. Moreover, this is an area where Central Africa stands out above the rest of the continent. Africa-wide, the congo music from Zaïre is the most widely played. The music from Cameroun is right up there as well.

But travellers tend not to be interested because they don't know anything about it. Even if interesting, all the music over the radio may sound similar. Without knowing who is singing or from what country the music is coming, most travellers find the whole music scene incomprehensible.

One solution is to buy *The Music of Africa*, a brand new (1987), four-record anthology of modern African music by Hilton Fyle of BBC fame. This section may also help to demystify the music scene. It's followed by a reference section of the best-known recording artists.

If you want records of African music, don't expect to be able to find them outside Africa without great difficulty. The best stores by far for African music in New York, Washington, London and Paris are as follows: African Record Centre Ltd (tel 212-2812717) 2343 7th Avenue, New York, New York; The African Music Gallery (tel 202-4628200) 1722 Florida Avenue, NW, Washington, DC 20009 – Metro stop Dupont Circle; Stern's African Record Centre Ltd (tel 01-3875550) 116 Whitfield St, Covent Garden, London W1P 5RW; Afric Music (tel 01-45424352) 3 Rue Plantes, 75014 Paris – Metro stop Alesia.

In Australia, the proprietor of Out of Africa Imports (tel (03) 525 1536) 36 Chapel St, Windsor, in Melbourne claims to have the largest selection of African music in the country.

Traditional Music

Although there is a great deal of variety in the world of African music, there are essentially two veins – the traditional village music and the modern pop music. It shouldn't be surprising that the former is much harder for foreigners to appreciate than the latter. For one thing, very few of the instruments have scales and rhythm has precedence over melody. To the uninitiated, it may sound monotonous when in fact there is a lot going on.

Several things set traditional music apart from pop music. As custom would have it, traditional music in Central Africa has often been the prerogative of only one social group, sometimes known as *griots*. In some areas, they are not only the village entertainers but also the village historians and genealogists.

A second feature of traditional music is that it serves a social purpose. Not only does each social occasion have its own type of music but, in addition, there may be different kinds of music for women, young people, hunters, warriors, etc.

Unlike the pop groups with electrical guitars and the like, traditional musicians use

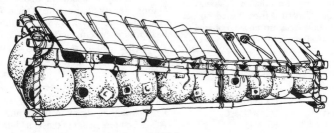

Balafon

only instruments that they themselves can make with local materials such as gourds, animal skins, horns, etc. Included in this group are, foremost, drums and stringed instruments. A quick visit to almost any museum in Africa will give you a good idea of the variety. Nowhere is there a more imaginative assortment of drums than in Africa – cylindrical, kettle and frame drums as well as goblet and hour-glass shaped ones.

There is a certain mystical aspect to musical instruments in Africa, as though they were alive with their own language of sounds. One reason, perhaps, for the variety of drums is that they serve not only as musical instruments but for communication as well. Some of these are made out of the trunks of trees that weigh several hundred kg.

Stringed instruments come in about as many varying shapes and sizes as drums, starting with a one-string lute. There are also wind instruments, including flutes made from millet stalks, bamboo and gourds, animal tusk horns, and trumpets made from gourds, metal, shells or wood. Again, they are found everywhere in Central Africa and take a slightly different form in each area.

One of the best new books on traditional African music is *The Music of Africa* by J H Kwabena Nketia (Victor Gollancz Ltd, 14 Henrietta St, London WC2E 8QJ).

Pop Music

Turn on the radio in Central or West Africa and if the song is African, there's a 50% chance that it will be Congolese-Zaïrois. The rest of the music likely to be heard is about evenly split between Camerounian music and local groups/singers. Upon hearing it for the first time, many people mistake it for Latin music. That's because there's a lot of Latin

influence in African popular music. Indeed, African pop music is an incredible mishmash of traditional, Latin and Black American music with elements of American jazz and rock.

The influence came from three sources. First, there were the Africans who were forced to become members of regimental bands associated with the forts. The music they played was typically European – polkas, marches and the like. Second, there was the impact of the Christian religious groups with their songs. Finally, with the increased trade with Europe came sailors from all over the world; they too brought with them not only their favourite ballads but also instruments such as guitars, harmonicas and accordions.

Ghana was the richest country in West-Central Africa and, not surprisingly, was where this influence was felt the most. What emerged was a westernised music called 'highlife'. Some was more westernised than others. The dance bands which played to the African elite in the cities, for example, were much more heavily influenced than those which played in the hinterland. The latter combined acoustic guitars with rattles, drums and the like and developed a type of highlife that was substantially different from that of the dance bands.

During WW II, Allied troops were stationed in West Africa resulting in the spread of more new musical ideas, especially the then-popular 'swing' music. One result was that after the war, there arose bands with sizeable repertoires, including calypso sounds. They began touring West Africa igniting the highlife fire everywhere, but at the same time continuing to assimilate foreign musical styles. Black music from across the Atlantic had a big impact, especially jazz, soul and, more recently, reggae.

In Central Africa there was another movement going on in Leopoldville (Kinshasa) and Brazzaville. During WW II, radio stations began popularising the early Cuban rumba stars, and new 'Congo-bars' were popping up offering not only refreshments but also dance music. The music was predominantly acoustic with solo guitars being accompanied by small brass ensembles. Bottles struck like gongs provided the rhythmic accompaniment.

A decisive turning point was the arrival of the electric guitar and amplification. Large orchestras emerged in the Belgian Congo (Zaïre), many elaborating on traditional rumba patterns. In 1953 *African Jazz*, featuring Dr Nico, was established, followed three years later by the famous OK Jazz. In the late 1960s when President Mobutu of Zaïre began his well known 'authenticité' movement, new orchestras began trying to remain more faithful to traditional sounds while at the same time experimenting with some of the North American rhythms. The result was enormously successful, bringing a deluge of new orchestras that have dominated the African musical scene ever since.

As a result of all this assimilation, a variety of musical styles are heard throughout Central and West Africa. African groups have incorporated African rhythms and developed their own unique sounds, with the result that African music is now having an impact on western music.

In Central Africa, the most popular music is Congo and Makossa music. Music from neighbouring Nigeria, particularly Afro-Beat and juju music is also quite prevalent. In northern Cameroun and Chad, you may hear popular Sahelian music from West Africa. Notes on these five major styles follow. Most of the stars are male.

Congo Music The Congo music from Zaïre and neighbouring Congo is at the top of all the 'pop' charts. For one thing, it's some of

the best dance music. The Latin influence is so strong that it's fairly easy to recognise. If it sounds Latin, it's probably Zaïrois. If not, the chances are very high that the music is from neighbouring Congo, CAR or Gabon.

Some of the biggest Congo Music stars/groups are listed here. Male: Tabu Ley, *OK Jazz*, *Langa Langa*, Samaguana, *Bella Bella*, M'Bongo, Papa Wemba, Dr Nico (deceased); Pierre Moutouari and Pamelo Mounk'a (both from the Congo); and Akéndengue (Gabon). Female: Pongo Love, M'Bilia Bel, Tshala Muana (all from Zaïre).

Makossa Music Cameroun has a distinct style of music that is second in popularity in Central Africa and very popular in West Africa as well. It all began in the early '70s with Manu Dibango's hit record *Soul Makossa*. Makossa music is a fusion of Camerounian highlife and soul. Like Congo music, the beat makes you want to dance which, of course, is part of the reason for its popularity. Recognising it, however, requires a little structured listening.

The biggest stars are all male: Manu Dibango and Sam Fan Thomas along with Sammy Njondji, Moni Bile, Tamwo, Toto Guillaume and Ekambi Brillant.

Afro-Beat A fusion of African music, jazz and soul, Afro-Beat along with juju is the most popular music today in Nigeria. Unlike Congo and Makossa music, there are so many variations that it's hard to classify. The undisputed king of Afro-Beat is Fela Anakulapo-Kuti.

Fela went to the USA in the 1960s and was highly influenced by James Brown. He took Brown's jazz and mixed it with the many cultural intricacies of his own African music and developed Afro-Beat. The instruments used by his orchestra are mainly non-African: guitars, trumpets, saxophones, and electric pianos as well as drums. Yet the sounds are substantially African inspired. His lyrics are always controversial and frequently political.

Other musicians whose music falls under

the general rubric of Afro-Beat include Nigeria's Mono-Mono, *Ghetto Blaster*, and Sonny Okosun with his 'jungle rock' music, Benin's popular *Polyrhythmic Orchestra* and Ghana's *African Brothers*.

Juju Music Juju music had its origins in Nigerian Yoruba music. As far back as the 1930s, the highlife bands began playing it. The Nigerian civil war gave rise to the popularity of juju music. Many members of the highlife bands went east to Biafra, leaving a dearth of entertainers in Lagos, so the people turned to juju. Today, it's one of the most popular music styles in Nigeria; outside of West Africa its popularity is rather limited but it is bound to crop up once in a while.

The leading singers are Ebenezer Obey and Sonny Ade, the latter being influenced by Afro-Beat and particularly popular with the younger crowd.

Popular Sahelian Music This is sort of a catch-all category of non-traditional music, played by groups from Chad to Senegal. What distinguishes this music is the greater use of traditional instruments, such as the 21-string kora and the balafon.

In Mali various dance bands, such as the Super Rail Band and Les Ambassadeurs du Mali and singers Boncana Maigo and Fanta Damba, make substantial use of traditional instruments in producing their rich, complex rhythms, not unlike music you will hear in Chad. Two musicians with heavy jazz influences are Touré Kunda, a Senegalese, and Mory Kanté, a Guinean and the undisputed king of the kora. But neither they nor other Senegalese recording stars, such as Thionne Seck, Youssou N'Dour and the group Xalam, are heard much in Central Africa.

One of the more interesting things to do while wandering downtown in any major city is to go into a record shop and ask to hear some of the local recording stars – giving the impression that you might buy something, of course. There's no better way to learn the different styles.

Records or cassettes typically sell for about US$10. You can get cassettes a lot cheaper at music stores in the business of making cassettes from their own records or from ones you give them. Bring your own good quality blank cassettes – the ones they use are invariably of cheap quality. Each country chapter lists the most popular local recording stars. Chances are they'll be the leading stars five years hence.

As for hearing live African music, the sad fact is that there are few groups which perform on a regular basis. Most of the nightclubs play recorded music. The best city in Central Africa for hearing live performances is unquestionably Kinshasa, where there are numerous clubs with regular bands. Other cities where groups play on a regular basis are Brazzaville, Bangui and, surprisingly, N'Djamena. Don't miss them. Some of your best memories of Central Africa will be of these lively clubs.

MANKALA

If you like games of intellectual challenge, one of the first things you should do upon arriving in Africa is to learn mankala – a game similar to backgammon. The game goes by many different names, including *mankala* in Zaïre, *woaley* or *awalé* in the Ivory Coast, *aju* in Togo and Benin, *ouri* in Senegal. For starters, buy a mankala board. Most are rectangular, about a half-metre long with two rows of six cups each. Some boards also have a cup at one or both ends for storing captured peas (48 come with the game).

Even if games aren't your bag, you won't find a better way to meet Africans, especially when there are communication difficulties. Mankala is a major pastime of Africans of all ages and has been since it originated in Egypt thousands of years ago. While it is designed for two people, teams are also possible. Finding an opponent is rarely difficult; opening the board amongst onlookers is usually all that's required.

The basics of play are not difficult, but mastering the game requires time. In Africa, one thing you will find is time, whether waiting for a bush taxi or simply cooling off in a bar or under a shade tree. There are several versions of the game played by different ethnic groups and varying in complexity. So don't be surprised if your opponent's rules are slightly different from those explained here.

Rules

1 Moves are always left to right, anticlockwise.

2 A move is made by picking up all of the pieces in a chosen cup and dropping them one by one (and only one) in each consecutive cup to the right, starting with the cup to the right of the cup from which the peas are taken.

3 You can initiate a move by picking up peas from a cup on your side of the board only.

4 A move may be made from any cup on your side that has peas. (In some versions, a move can only be made from cups containing at least two peas.)

5 You are entitled to only one move at a time. (In some versions, play continues until you 'capture' a cup.)

6 In some versions, if there are so many peas in the cup that you go completely around the board dropping peas back to the original cup, you skip the original cup.

7 Peas may be 'captured' from either side of the board. (In some versions, the initial captured cup – always the last cup in a move – must be on the opponent's side.)

Starting Play

All mankala boards have 12 cups and 48 peas. Four peas are placed in each cup. Either player may start. The first player picks up all the peas in a chosen cup (from the player's side only) and drops one at a time in each consecutive cup, anticlockwise. Captured peas are put to the side. Then the opponent does the same, and so on.

Capturing Peas

A player scores by capturing peas; the winner is the one with the most captured peas at the end of the game. A player captures peas only when the last pea dropped falls in a cup containing one or two peas (ie, two or three peas after the move).

In a well-executed move, a player may capture several cups of peas at a time, but only if they have three peas or less after the move and are in a row immediately preceding the last cup.

For instance, if the last pea falls into a cup with two peas and, say, the three cups immediately preceding it each contain three peas or less after the move, the player would capture the peas in all four cups (including the peas he/she put into them). On the other hand if, after moving, the second last cup contained two peas and the third last cup contained more than three peas, he or she would capture the peas only in the last two cups.

End of Game

The game ends when one of the players has no peas left on his/her side and the other player must play at least twice consecutively in order to reach the opponent's side of the board. It is against the rules to prematurely end a game by not moving to the opponents side of the board if it is in fact possible to make such a move. Ending up with no peas does not mean you win the game, although it is beneficial in the scoring.

Scoring

Each player counts the peas he/she has captured plus any peas remaining on the opponent's side of the board. Since there are 48 peas, any peas over 24 constitute a point. If, for example, your total is 30 peas (your opponent will have 18 peas), you will receive six points and your opponent zero. A match is whatever you decide – three games, 100 points, two hours, etc.

RELIGION

Before the Christians and Muslims began making inroads into Africa about 500 and 1000 years ago respectively, the only religions in Africa were the traditional ones, virtually all of which are animistic and involve ancestor worship.

Now, Christianity is the major religion in every Central African country except Chad, where Islam holds a slight edge over animism, and the Central African Republic, where Christians and animists are of roughly equal numbers. To some extent, this is a little misleading because many adherents of Christianity follow at least some animist practices as well.

Outside the northern two-thirds of Chad and northern Cameroun where Muslims predominate and pockets of northern Central African Republic, you'll find almost no followers of Islam in Central Africa. That's why it's so unusual that the president of Gabon, a country with a Muslim population of less than 1%, professes to be a follower of Islam.

Animism

Each ethnic group in Africa has its own religion, so there are literally hundreds of traditional religions in Central Africa. However, there are some factors common to all of them. Virtually all are animistic, accept the existence of a Supreme Being and believe in reincarnation.

The Creator is considered to be too exalted to be concerned with humans. There are, however, numerous lesser deities with whom one can communicate, typically through sacrifices, along with deified ancestors. There are no great temples or written scriptures. Rather, beliefs and traditions are handed down by word of mouth.

The lesser deities, who act as intermediaries between the Creator and mortals, are frequently terrifying, corresponding to natural phenomena or diseases. Africans pray to these deities in order to gain good health, bountiful harvests and numerous children. Many of the village celebrations are in honour of one or more of the deities.

The ancestors play a particularly strong role in African religions. Their principal function is to protect the tribe. They are also the real owners of the land, and while it can be enjoyed by the living descendants, to sell the land would be to incur the wrath of the 'real owners'. Ethnic groups are usually broken down into clans, which include all individuals who can trace their origins to a particular ancestor. Each has its own taboos in relation to its protective genies.

Magic is another element common to native African religions. Good magic keeps away evil spirits. The medicine men or sorcerers are the ones who carry around bags of fetishes, dispense charms, tell fortunes and give advice on how to avoid danger. The charms worn around the neck are called *grigris* (gree-gree) and are found in northern Central Africa and all over West Africa. If it hasn't been blessed by a medicine man, it's worthless.

Islamic Customs

If you'll be visiting northern Cameroun or Chad, keep in mind the following. First, whenever you visit a mosque, take off your shoes. There are some mosques which do not admit women; others may have a separate entrance since men and women pray separately. Second, if you have a taxi driver or guide for the day, he may be in need of doing his prayer ritual, which occurs five times a day. Be on the lookout for signs he may express indicating he wants a few moments off, particularly around midday, late afternoon and sunset (three of the five prayer times).

Third, you may have heard that some Muslims drink like fish. Even so, it's impolite to drink alcohol in their presence unless they show approval. Fourth, if a Muslim man refuses to shake hands with a woman, remember he's only following the Koran; so don't take offence. Finally, there are some important Islamic holidays, during which time little gets done.

FESTIVALS & HOLIDAYS

A consideration in planning an itinerary is the special events throughout the year. The more important ones are listed below and discussed more fully in the country chapters.

January

1 New Year's Day is celebrated all over Africa.

26* Mt Cameroun Race. On the last Sunday in January, this race up and down Mt Cameroun is the continent's toughest.

April

3-4* Brazzaville to Pointe-Noire Car Rally. This is Central Africa's biggest auto race.

May

5* Feast of Ramadan. Estimated 1989 date – moves back 11 days every year. This is the second major Islamic holiday, celebrated primarily in Chad, northern and western Cameroun, and northern Central African Republic following the annual 30-day Muslim fast. Especially interesting are the celebrations in Foumban (western Cameroun).

20 Cameroun's National Festival, the country's major non-religious holiday.

June

15 Closing of most game parks in northern Cameroun and the Central African Republic.

15 Beginning of best period for visiting Virunga park (through September) and climbing the Ruwenzori mountains (through mid-August) in eastern Zaïre.

July

14* Tabaski. Estimated 1989 date – 11 days earlier every year. This is the major Muslim holiday and is celebrated in Chad, northern and western Cameroun, and northern Central African Republic. Tabaski is particularly interesting in Maroua (northern Cameroun).

August

15 Congo's Independence Day, the country's major holiday.

17 National Festival of Gabon, the country's major holiday.

November

5 Opening of the game parks in northern Cameroun and the Central African Republic.

15 Beginning of best period, lasting three and a half months, for climbing Mt. Cameroun.

December

15 Beginning of second best period, lasting one and a half months, for visiting Virunga park and climbing the Ruwenzoris mountains in eastern Zaïre.

25 Christmas is celebrated everywhere.

* approximate dates

Islamic Holidays

There are some very important Islamic holidays, when almost all of northern Central Africa's commercial life comes to a stop. Since the Islamic calendar is based on 12 lunar months, with 354 or 355 days, these holidays are always about 11 days earlier than the previous year. The exact dates depend on the moon and are only announced about one day in advance.

End of Ramadan (Id ul Fitr) Ramadan is the ninth month of the Islamic lunar-based calendar (the year is usually 354 days). During the entire 30-day month, Muslims are supposed to fast during the daylight hours. Muslims who fast (many do not, particularly those living in the cities) are usually weak during the afternoon because they are not allowed to eat or drink (except for athletes, pregnant women, and a few other exceptions) from sunrise to sunset. Also, work hours typically end around 1 or 2 pm.

It might be expected that people would lose weight during this period, but some actually gain weight because of the huge meals served after sunset and before sunrise. In general, it's a very festive time, something like the Christmas season, and people go more frequently to the mosque and visit friends at night. For 1989 the fast is expected to begin on 7 April and for 1990 on 27 March.

The end of Ramadan is the second most important Muslim holiday – celebrated by a big feast, known as the Feast of Ramadan or the Small Feast, beginning on the evening of the 30th day. The main attraction is usually a roasted sheep, or possibly a goat. The estimated dates for 1989 and 1990 are 6 May and 25 April.

Tabaski (Id al Kabir) Also known as the Great Feast, Tabaski is the most important celebration throughout northern Central Africa. This is the day that Muslims kill a sheep to commemorate the moment when Abraham was about to sacrifice his son in obedience to God's command, only to have God intercede at the last moment and substitute a ram instead. It also coincides with the end of the pilgrimage (hadj) to Mecca. In the preceding two weeks, sheep prices can jump 50% or more.

One-third of the sacrificed animal is supposed to be given to the poor, one-third to friends, and one-third for the family. Those who cannot afford a sheep are really embarrassed; most will do anything to scrape up the money.

If you can manage to get an invitation, you'll be participating in what is for African Muslims the most important and festive day of the year. It's mainly lots of eating and visiting friends following several hours at the mosque. It's an official government holiday only in Chad and Cameroun, usually lasting two days. The estimated dates for 1989 and 1990 are 14 July and 3 July – 69 days following the Feast of Ramadan.

The Hadj Ask a farmer in northern Cameroun what he's going to do with any profits from a development assistance project and he's likely to tell you that he'll use it to finance a pilgrimage to Mecca. Many other Muslims would say the same. All Muslims who are of good health and have the means are supposed to make the pilgrimage at least once in their life.

Those who make the pilgrimage receive the honorific title of Hadj for men, and Hadjia for women. For some, this can involve a lifetime of savings, typically several thousand dollars. It's not unusual for families to save up and send one member. Before the invention of the aeroplane, it used to involve a journey overland of a year or more, sometimes requiring stops on the way to earn money.

SOCIAL CUSTOMS
Greetings *(les salutations)*

One of the basic social customs in all of Africa is a long greeting. Sometimes this ritual lasts up to half a minute. A typical greeting might start with 'Peace be unto you', 'Do you have peace?', 'How are you doing?', 'Is your body in peace?', 'Thanks be to God'.

African greetings generally go into all kinds of inquiries about the family, one's health, work, the weather, etc. Even if somebody is at death's door, the answer is always that things are going fine.

In the cities, the traditional greetings may give way to shorter greetings in French or English. In either case, it's a social blunder to get down to business immediately or to walk past an adult in a house without greeting them. Those who do are likely to run into hostile or negative attitudes from people with whom they're doing business.

The emphasis on greetings makes the handshake important. It's a soft handshake, not the western knuckle cracker. Not to shake a man's hand when entering and leaving a social or business gathering is a real gaffe. In social settings, you must go around the room, greet everyone, and shake hands with the men. You do the same when leaving.

In most areas, men and women don't shake hands unless the woman extends her hand. This takes a little getting used to at first, but eventually it becomes natural. In the French-speaking countries, the thrice-kissed cheek greeting (starting with the left) is the norm for friends and even casual acquaintances of the opposite sex.

Women have traditionally been considered inferior to men, and for this reason they tend to show deference to men in their greetings. As noted, they usually don't shake hands, but African men usually shake the hands of western women. In Chad and northern Cameroun, women may encounter elders who, in strict compliance with the Koran, refuse to shake hands.

Another consideration is eye contact. Usually it's avoided, especially between men and women. A boy does not look his father in the eye. If he does, his father will be suspicious. Don't think that because a women avoids eye contact she's being cold. Some eye contact is perfectly OK as long as it doesn't develop into a gaze. So if you're accustomed to looking people in the eye and associate this with honesty, remember that this is not the case in Africa.

Begging

Beggars need to be seen in a different light in Africa than they are in other parts of the world. In Africa the only social security system for the great majority of people is the extended family. There will be no government cheque to help the person who is out of work, sick or old. Many beggars are cripples or lepers. Nevertheless, because of the effectiveness of the extended family in providing support as well as the general respect that Africans give to their elders, there are remarkably few beggars considering how poor Central Africa is.

For travellers, a point to remember is that Africans do not look down on beggars. Almsgiving is one of the pillars of Islam, something to remember in Chad and northern Cameroun. Travellers with foresight will do everything possible to keep small change on them for this purpose. They're not asking for a lot, usually a coin equivalent to five or 10 cents US.

Gifts *(les cadeaux)*

One thing foreigners tend to notice immediately is how many people come up to them asking for handouts. This is not seen as begging. Kids are going up to foreigners all the time with their hands out saying,

'Cadeau, cadeau'. A guy will take you a block to point out the place you're looking for, and then ask for a cadeau. The girl at the bar may want a cadeau for just talking. Everybody's looking for a cadeau. The reaction of many foreigners is negative.

In African societies gift giving is a highly structured and extremely important social ritual. You are expected to give gifts to those above you in the social hierarchy, or to respected people. If someone's mother-in-law comes for the day, a gift to her is in order.

There's less sense of reciprocity; rather, it's more that if the spirits have been good to you, you should be willing to spread some of it around. Since foreigners are thought to be rich, they're expected to be generous. It's something worth keeping in mind everywhere you go.

In Chad and northern Cameroun, for example, tobacco is prized by the men, and both men and women are pretty keen on perfume. In the deep jungle, scarce items such as matches may be greatly appreciated. Similarly, the smart businessperson will bring small items from the States or Europe to show his or her appreciation. One of the best gifts of all is a photograph, and it may even be worth bringing a cheap polaroid as a second camera.

Dress *(les costumes)*

In general, Africans place great importance on clothing, giving a huge portion of the non-food budget. Western informality is definitely not the norm, although it is making a few inroads with the young in the bigger cities.

In Chad and northern Cameroun, both men and women often wear long *costumes*. For men, this is an embroidered robe-like garment reaching the ground, with pants and shirt underneath. The woman's *boubou* is similarly regal, long and embroidered.

For more everyday wear, women wear a loose top and a length of cloth (*pagne*) around the waist for a skirt; this is made from the colourful cotton prints that can be found everywhere in Central Africa. The same wax or wax-like cloth is used in making men's casual clothes, which look like pyjamas.

With clothing such as this, it is not surprising that in the more traditional areas, especially in Chad and northern Cameroun, shorts and tight pants worn by women are considered offensive. This may seem like a double standard because African women often go bare breasted in the villages, yet they would be ridiculed for wearing tight pants. It's all a bit confusing, but women should keep in mind that clothes should not be revealing or suggestive. For men, standards are less strict.

In the big cities such as Libreville, standards are different; you'll see the latest Parisian fashions, but shorts are not worn by either sex (unless jogging). As for the villages, women would do well to purchase some colourful wrap-around *pagnes*, or wear very loose fitting long pants with socks.

A week without a shower in the jungle, and come a short rainstorm one is out in the droplets maximizing surface area...

Cameroun

Along with nice clothes, Africans are particular about cleanliness. A bucket bath is a morning ritual for the great majority of Africans. In this respect, it's interesting to note that many Africans think that most foreigners stink.

Eating Traditional Style

In the villages and in many city homes, food is eaten with the hands. Visitors will usually be offered a spoon if there is one. A bowl of rice and a bowl of sauce will be placed on the ground and those eating will sit around on a mat and dig in, but never before washing their hands. The head of the household will distribute meat and vegetables to the visitors.

Take a handful of rice or other staple and part of the sauce or meat, then form a ball – this is the hard part – and eat. Don't shy away; it's usually a lot of laughs for everyone. It won't be pleasant the first time getting your hands all gooey but remember, a wash basin is always passed around afterwards. You may even grow to like this way of eating because of the increased 'family' feeling that it fosters.

Particularly in the north, only the right hand is used in forming the ball of food because of the ancient practice of using the left hand for personal toiletries. A violation of this rule will cause a silent turmoil. Just because you're a tourist won't make much difference. Eating with the left hand would be as offensive to Africans as a stranger drinking from your glass would be to you. Never wanting to create a scene, they'll continue eating while wondering just how 'developed' the western world really is.

Social Events

Much of African life centres around special events, such as weddings, baptisms, funerals, holidays and village celebrations (*fêtes*). If you get an invitation by all means accept. Just be sure to bring your dancing shoes because except at funerals, there will probably be dancing. At baptisms, guests bring gifts for both the mother and father; a small amount of money is perfectly acceptable.

There will be a ceremony followed by a meal.

Village celebrations (*fêtes*) may be for any number of reasons, from something fairly common, such as celebrating the end of the harvest, to something a little different, such as honouring the dead. There's usually traditional African dancing in a circle, in which case any foreigners present generally have to be content with watching. If there's modern African music, you can expect to do some dancing. Each fête is a little unique; elaborate dances with masks are typical. If you get the chance to see one, don't pass it up.

GAME PARKS

The main problem with game parks in Central Africa isn't the lack of animals; it's their remoteness. The best ones – in the Central African Republic – are two days drive from Bangui, for example.

You can see elephant, lion, giant eland, buffalo, wart hog, baboon, monkey, crocodile, birds galore, various species of antelope and hippo in many of these parks – even gorilla families in Zaïre, and giraffe in the Central African Republic, Cameroun and Zaïre (Gambara park). In Waza National Park in northern Cameroun, herds of up to 300 elephants are frequently found at the principal water holes in the hot season (March to May).

The first four game parks in the following list are good even by East African standards. Most are in remote locations.

Waza National Park in northern Cameroun, is open 15 November to 15 June, and is a 90-minute drive from Maroua, which has daily flights from Yaoundé and Douala.

Bamingui Bangoran National Park and nearby St Floris National Park and André Felix National Park in north-eastern Central African Republic, is open November to May (one or two days by vehicle or chartered plane).

Virunga National Park in eastern Zaïre, is more accessible from Rwanda than from Kinshasa (the dry season, June through September, is the best viewing time).

Kahuzi-Biega National Park is a gorilla sanctuary in eastern Zaïre (an hour's drive from Bukavu).

Okanda National Park is in central Gabon (a five-hour train ride from Libreville).

LANGUAGE

Of the eight countries in Central Africa, French is the official language in six (Cameroun, Central African Republic, Chad, Congo, Gabon, Zaïre), English in one (Cameroun – along with French), Spanish in one (Equatorial Guinea) and Portuguese in one (São Tomé).

Some say it's an awful legacy of the colonial period that the official languages are non-African. At the same time it must be recognised that any attempt to pick one of the many local languages for the official language would be politically disastrous. Moreover, few would be able to speak it.

Facts for the Visitor

VISAS

Exemptions

Travellers of the nationalities below are not required to have visas to the following countries:

French CAR, Chad, Gabon, Zaïre. While visas to the Congo are not required in principle, they are required in practice.
West German CAR, Chad, Gabon. While visas to the Congo are not required in principle, they are often required in practice.
Swiss CAR.

Visa Requirements

In addition to anywhere from one to four photographs, some embassies (Cameroun, Gabon) require that all travellers possess an airline ticket with a flight out of the country (showing proof of intention to leave the country). What they neglect to tell the intending visitor is that they will accept a photocopy of the airline ticket and that sometimes they'll accept a letter or guarantee from a travel agent instead of a bank.

A one way ticket to Africa is the same as a one way ticket to a headache – some countries won't issue visas without a bank statement or guarantee (*caution bancaire* in French) showing proof of adequate funds to return (ie at least the price of a return airline ticket).

African embassies in Europe and North America are stricter in enforcing these requirements than those in neighbouring countries in Africa. Many people travelling on the cheap try to procure the majority of their visas in Africa for this reason. It's worth keeping in mind.

One quirk is that some embassies will issue visas of only very short duration. Don't get upset. In every case, it's relatively easy to get an extension once inside the country. Also, in the Congo, everyone must get an exit visa except those transiting within 72 hours.

Another peculiarity is that every so often an embassy will not issue you a visa if you could have obtained one in the country of your residence. This problem is most likely to be encountered with embassies of Zaïre. Canadians, for example, cannot get visas at the Zaïre embassy in Washington.

Still another oddity is that most African countries refuse to issue visas in passports with South African visas. If yours has one, most countries including the USA will recognise this as justification for issuing you another passport. South African border officials used to insert removable visas if requested. They no longer do this.

Finally, in Gabon, some border officials

27

(not those at Libreville airport) still insist on proof of a hotel reservation. One recent traveller reported that the officials at Cocobeach insisted on this and would not give in, requiring him to return to Cameroun. (The Gabon Embassy in Washington says that this old requirement initiated during the country's boom years has been dropped.)

Multiple-entry Visas

In addition to single-entry visas, some embassies issue multiple-entry visas. It's amazing how many visitors to Africa think that they can take the four-hour trip from Maroua (Cameroun) to N'Djamena (Chad) and re-enter Cameroun using the same visa. Sorry. Once you've left country, another visa is needed to re-enter. This may seem senseless, but ask an African about the ordeal of getting a visa to the USA – you may be a little more understanding.

Multiple-entry visas are almost always more expensive than single-entry visas. Most embassies won't tell you about the availability of a multiple-entry visa unless you ask. Once they are in Africa, many tourists regret that they didn't obtain such visas, even if their itinerary didn't include re-entry. Plans always change.

Obtaining Visas In Africa

Most people advise getting all the visas you can before leaving. This is generally good advice. Still, there are some countries for which visas are easily and quickly obtainable in Africa, and others for which this is not the case. If you don't have time to get all the visas you need, be selective and get the ones that are more difficult to obtain in Africa. The list follows:

Difficult São Tomé (tourist visas still not issued), Gabon (takes three to four days in most African cities), Zaïre (has many embassies but they often refuse to issue visas if you could have obtained one at home).

Easy CAR, Chad (both obtainable from French embassies).

Central African Diplomatic Missions Abroad

In the cities below, you'll find diplomatic missions of the following Central African countries:

Bonn Cameroun, CAR, Chad, Congo, Gabon, Zaïre
Brussels Cameroun, CAR, Chad, Congo, Gabon, Zaïre
The Hague Zaïre
London Cameroun (visas for UK residents only), Gabon , Zaïre
New York Cameroun, Chad, Congo, São Tomé
Ottawa Cameroun, CAR, Gabon, Zaïre
Paris All countries except São Tomé
Rome CAR, Congo, Gabon, Ghana, Zaïre
Stockholm Zaïre
Tokyo CAR, Gabon, Zaïre
Washington All countries except São Tomé

In Australia the only place where a visa to any (though not all) of these countries might be obtained is through a French diplomatic mission, whether it be the embassy in Canberra or one of the consulates in Sydney or Melbourne.

Visas to Ex-Colonies

French embassies have the authority to issue visas to Chad and the Central African Republic except in the few countries where those countries have their own diplomatic missions. Portuguese embassies do not have authority to issue visas to São Tomé.

Visa Agencies

If visas to a number of African countries are needed, it'll take a little time tripping around to all the embassies. In Britain and the USA, there are businesses that specialise in visa hunting. In the telephone directory, they're listed under the heading 'passport' or 'visa service'.

Some are apparently better than others. Five among many are Perry International (tel 202-9661760) 4327 Harrison St, NW, Washington, DC; Embassy Visa Service (tel 202-3871171) 2162 California St, NW, Washington, DC 20009; Travel Agenda (tel 212-2657887) 119 West 57th St, Suite 1008, New York, NY 10019; The Visa Service (tel

01-6297276) 411 Oxford St, London W1R 1FG; and P & O Passport & Visa Service (tel 01-8311258) 77 Oxford St, London WC1.

Travel Agenda, for example, charges US$10 to US$20 per visa depending on the country plus the embassy's fee. Total charges range from US$11 for the Ivory Coast to US$38 for Gabon. The Visa Service charges £7 per visa, plus the embassy's fee. They will send out application forms which must be returned with passport, photographs and, for some countries, a health card.

Businesses rely heavily on these agencies, and many travellers who have used them wouldn't do it any other way. It is not really worthwhile for anyone wanting less than three or four visas.

EMBASSIES & CONSULATES

The following non-communist countries outside Central Africa have embassies and consulates in Central Africa:

Belgium Cameroun, Congo, Gabon, Zaïre.
Canada Cameroun, Zaïre.
Egypt Cameroun, CAR, Chad, Congo, Zaïre.
France All countries except São Tomé.
Germany Cameroun, CAR, Chad, Congo, Gabon, Zaïre.
Italy Cameroun, Congo, Gabon, Zaïre.
Ivory Coast Cameroun, CAR, Gabon, Zaïre.
Japan CAR, Gabon, Zaïre.
Netherlands Cameroun, Zaïre.
Nigeria Every country except São Tomé.
Senegal Cameroun, Gabon.
Sweden Zaïre.
Switzerland Cameroun, Zaïre.
Sudan CAR, Chad, Zaïre.
UK Cameroun, Zaïre. Consulate: CAR.
USA All countries except São Tomé.

Australia has no diplomatic representation in Central Africa. UK and Canadian embassies will look after the needs of Aussies in the event that they require help of some kind.

MONEY
CFA

One French franc equals 50 CFA. This is a fixed rate. So if the French franc and the US dollar are trading, say, 6 to 1, you'll get 300 CFA for US$1.

Of the eight countries in Central Africa, only Zaïre and São Tomé don't use the CFA. By tying the CFA to the franc and exchanging it freely with the French franc, France has given Central Africa perhaps its greatest gift – a hard currency. This means you can go from one CFA country to the next without exchanging money.

However, exchanging CFA in other countries isn't easy. In East Africa, the banks act like it's funny money. In the USA, even major banks won't accept them. In short, the CFA is hard currency only in West and Central Africa and France. So don't get caught with excess CFA. If you're returning home via France – no sweat – CFA can be exchanged for French francs at Charles DeGaulle airport in Paris.

One hitch is that there are actually two CFAs – the Central African CFA (used in Cameroun, CAR, Chad, Congo, Equatorial Guinea and Gabon) and the West African CFA (Senegal, Ivory Coast, Mali, Burkina Faso, Niger, Togo and Benin). While there's usually not too much difficulty exchanging one for the other at a bank or at a major hotel, don't expect the man on the street to do the same. So avoid getting caught on the weekend with the wrong kind of CFA; you may go bananas trying to exchange it!

Black Market

The black market scene in both Central and West Africa has changed dramatically since 1983. At that time there were nine countries with black markets; the differences in rates were enormous. Now, Equatorial Guinea has the CFA and Zaïre has a floating exchange rate, leaving in Central Africa only São Tomé with a substantially over-valued currency. While Zaïre still has a black market (or 'parallel market'), the official rate is almost as favourable. However, inflation, which almost invariably follows a devaluation, is out of control in Zaïre.

Changing money on the black market is

of course illegal. Sometimes, there's no way to avoid it. If you're travelling overland by bush taxi, you're not likely to find a bank at the border. How do you pay for the onward taxi? You purchase currency at the last town before crossing the border and hide it on entering.

As for the logistics of black markets, you'll find money dealers in a number of places. Sometimes it's very open, typically near the border stations in Zaïre and around the markets. Sometimes it's very secretive, with taxi drivers in the business themselves or acting as conduits.

Importing Currency

Limits on the amount of foreign currency that you may import into a country are not particularly tight, but if you intend to import a very large quantity it may be worth making some enquiries prior to entering the country or countries in question.

Bringing in local currency is another matter. In CFA countries, there's no problem bringing in CFA. In Zaïre and São Tomé, it is either prohibited or severely restricted, typically limited to the equivalent of about US$10. In Zaïre any violation of the restrictions can cause major problems, so be careful!

Exporting Currency

CFA Countries The rules for exporting CFA are unclear and unevenly enforced. In many CFA countries, tourists are theoretically supposed to be able to take out more than local business people, and the limit is supposed to be higher if travelling to another CFA country. However, most border officials don't seem to know exactly what the rules are.

Only in the Congo is the rule crystal clear and strictly enforced. The limit there is CFA 25,000. In all other CFA countries, taking CFA out of a country is almost never a problem if you don't have more than about CFA 75,000. If problems arise, playing the ignorant tourist should help. When it comes

to exporting other currencies the story is much the same as with importing.

Non-CFA Countries The rules in Zaïre and São Tomé are quite different. Tourists are never allowed to take out more than the equivalent of about US$5 to US$10 in local currency, and on leaving it is not possible to reconvert it into foreign currency. There is basically no limit on the export of other currencies.

Exchanging Money at the Airport

There are banks at only a few of the airports (Kinshasa, Douala, Brazzaville), and even these banks are sometimes closed. So expect to change money at the banks or hotels. If the banks at the airport are open, don't hesitate to exchange money there – the exchange rate is invariably as good as the in the banks downtown.

There are always taxi drivers who'll accept dollars, French francs and frequently pounds, but don't expect the best exchange rate in town. In non-CFA countries, drivers may actually prefer to be paid in hard currency. Keep in mind that any currency declared on arrival in the country must be accounted for on departure.

Credit Cards

The most widely accepted credit card is American Express (AE); Diners (D) is second. Although increasing in usage, Visa (V) and Carte Blanche (CB) are much less widely accepted, and Master Charge (MC) and Eurocard (EC) are all but worthless. As for restaurants, only the fairly expensive ones accept credit cards, and even then usually only American Express or Diners.

Travellers' Cheques

Take American Express – more banks accept American Express cheques than other kind, and they can be replaced faster if they are lost. American Express travellers' cheques are accepted at almost all major banks in Central Africa, but not always at banks upcountry.

In southern Chad, for example, don't expect to be able to exchange money (cheques or bills) unless the cheques are denominated in French francs because they won't have the foggiest idea what the day's exchange rate is on anything else. Anticipate this problem in any town or city outside the capital city.

As for Thomas Cook, Citicorp, Barclays and Bank America travellers' cheques, it is unlikely that any problems will be encountered in the largest capital cities but elsewhere, many banks simply do not accept them.

Make photocopies of the travellers' cheque purchase slip with numbers and put them in various bags and pockets and give one to your travelling companion. This will greatly expedite replacement of lost cheques. Also, bring a good amount of cash in small bills (preferably US dollars and/or French francs) for emergencies.

Wiring Money

Wiring money can take weeks, and problems are often experienced. The bank may deny receiving money which has actually arrived. So don't rely on money being wired. If money is wired, arrange for the forwarding bank to send a separate confirmation with full details. You can then go into the African bank with the much needed proof that your money has been sent.

Foreign Banks

Citibank Kinshasa, Port-Gentil
Barclays Kinshasa
Chase Manhattan Douala, Yaoundé
Chemical Brazzaville

COSTS

Central Africa is the most expensive region in Africa – particularly Gabon and the Congo. In Libreville or Port-Gentil (Gabon), finding a hotel room for less than US$25 takes heroic effort.

If you're travelling on the cheap, plan on staying the minimum time possible in the major cities, and budget at least US$15 a day,

higher in the principal cities of Gabon and the Congo. This includes the cheapest lodging in town, eating on the street or in the cheapest African restaurants, and using the least expensive means of transportation – and nothing else.

As for restaurants, they're a luxury for most Africans. Most places deserving the name restaurant serve continental cuisine, and they're usually not cheap, particularly if some of the ingredients are flown in from Europe. Eating relatively modestly can easily run to $US10 or US$20 a meal, and sometimes a lot more. On the other hand, with a little effort it is possible to find inexpensive restaurants everywhere. The risk of getting stomach problems will be greatly reduced if you stick to things like meat and rice and stay away from raw vegetables and fruits.

People travelling on the cheap usually eat on the street or in 'stalls', frequently near the markets, paying around US$1 for African food. Street food is often just as good as or better than that served in cheap restaurants and usually safer if eaten African-style with the hands. And remember this – food served on the street is invariably fresh, something few restaurants can claim.

TIPPING

Tipping is a problem in Africa because there are few clear rules applicable to all people. Africans are not in the habit of tipping, but as they move up the economic ladder, a small amount of tipping is expected from them.

Tipping to most Africans is related to the concept of a gift (*cadeau*); rich people are expected to give cadeaux. Almost all foreigners appear to be rich, therefore a cadeau is expected unless the person obviously looks like a hitchhiker. Anyone going to a fancy hotel would be expected to tip, for example, but there would not be the same expectation from a backpacker in a cheap hotel.

Everyone, even Africans, is expected to tip 10% at the better restaurants, but check the bill closely to see if service is included. It frequently is at restaurants and hotels in

French-speaking Africa. At the other end of the scale are the African restaurants with almost all African clientele – no tipping is expected from anyone.

There's a grey area between these two classes of restaurants. Tipping at these restaurants is rarely expected from Africans and those who are obviously backpackers, but tipping is expected sometimes from local expatriates, and almost always from wealthier tourists. Even the wealthier Africans will sometimes tip at all-African restaurants, not so much because it's expected but because it's a show of status.

As for taxis, generally speaking, tipping is not the rule but well-heeled travellers are expected to tip about 10%, except for rides in shared cabs where tipping is almost unheard of. In bigger cities with numerous foreigners such as Kinshasa and Douala, the taxi drivers are becoming more like those in New York every day. A small tip may still be hoped for even from backpackers.

From the Africans' perspective, tourists and well-dressed people should tip more because they can obviously afford it. Africans do not think of tipping in fixed percentage terms or as applicable to all persons equally. So if you are travelling on the cheap and look like it, less tipping is expected.

CONCERNS OF BUSINESS PEOPLE
Business Cards

It is a good idea to bring lots of *cartes de visites* to Africa. Without them, you have no legitimacy at all. Be generous with the distribution of the cards; all Africans like to think they have a sugar daddy in the USA or Europe who's going to send them a plane ticket to deliver them from all this mess. It seems people never have them when they need them. They're even useful when the police decide to stop a cab full of tourists who have left their passports back at the hotel.

Social Customs

Greetings and shaking hands are extremely important to Africans, more so than to Europeans and Americans. Never start a conversation without first greeting the other party. This means that when you go to the airline reservation office, for example, you make some small talk before getting down to reserving your flight. For getting appointments, this means being very friendly with the person's secretary. Those who fail to follow this custom are going to find it difficult to get things done.

Another thing to keep in mind is that the handshake is much more important in Africa than in the USA or Europe. The firm grip used by Americans is definitely not the style. In social settings, greet everybody when entering and leaving no matter how many people are in the room. In many countries, men and women do not customarily shake hands unless the man extends his hand first; if in doubt, shake hands because it's never in bad taste.

The thrice kissed greeting and leave taking (left cheek first) is practised between friends and even casual acquaintances of the opposite sex in French-speaking countries. It may seem awkward at first to go around the room and establish contact with each person individually, but it is very important to do so and gradually it becomes automatic.

Regarding dress, Africans are fairly formal. This means that dress for business meetings in Africa is no different to that expected in western nations. For social gatherings, at homes of Americans and Europeans, informality usually governs. At Africans' homes, dress is more formal. For women, the long African dresses go well in either setting.

Law Firms

The only American law firm with offices in Central Africa is Duncan, Allen & Mitchell, a Washington, DC based firm (tel 202-2898400, telex 440106), 1575 Eye St, NW, Washington, DC 20005, with offices in Kinshasa (tel 243-30659, telex 21340) BP 12368, Kinshasa, Zaïre. They are involved primarily in commercial law, helping companies set up operations and the like. Working with local lawyers, they will provide similar services in neighbouring countries on a case by case basis when required by the client.

GENERAL INFORMATION
Post
Mail service in Africa bears the brunt of many jokes, but the reality is that the service is fairly reliable in most of Central Africa – it just takes a while getting there. From the USA the typical delivery time is three to six weeks depending on the town's size and remoteness.

From Europe, the delivery time is slightly less. However, delivery times considerably longer than this occur just frequently enough to make it impossible to rely on the mail for matters involving critical time-constraints.

Contrary to what you may hear, it's only rarely that governments open the mail. Courier service is an alternative; DHL, for example, is located in many of the major cities of Central Africa.

Telephones
Telephone connections between Africa and Europe/USA are much better than one might think. First-time users are invariably surprised by the good quality of the reception. That's because international calls now usually go by satellite. Calls between African countries, however, are frequently relayed through Europe, in which case the reception is usually bad – if you can get a call through.

Calling from the USA or Europe to Africa is usually easier, and always less expensive, than vice versa. Direct dial is possible to a number of African cities. Between 5 pm and 6 am, the direct dial rate from the USA and Britain to most of Africa is about US$0.75 a minute. This is also the easiest time to get a line. If you call during business hours in the USA or Europe, you may find it very difficult to get through – after 5 pm your chances increase significantly.

Calling from Africa to Europe or the States is sometimes problematic. It's about seven times more expensive and there are no reduced rates at night. Second, the waiting time can be minutes or hours depending on the locality and time of day. Third, in several countries, calls to the USA must still be relayed through Europe so the reception is highly variable.

Electricity
The electricity supply throughout Central Africa is 220 volts. Plugs are usually two round pins like those in Europe and different from the USA or Australia.

HEALTH
Medical kit
Bring Lomotil (only for cases of severe diarrhoea), Pepto-Bismol (better for ordinary diarrhoea), prescription drugs (stored in two separate bags in case one is lost), malaria tablets and mosquito repellent. It is also a

good idea to include antiseptic ointment (Bacetracin is widely used) and iodine or halazone tablets for purifying water, though halazone is not readily available in Africa.

Vaccinations

Everyone must carry an International Health Certificate with a record of vaccinations. Sometimes it is possible to get into some Central African countries with as few as two (cholera and yellow fever) and in many cases they are only required if you arrive from an infected area. These two are essential if you will be travelling extensively, but take them regardless to avoid hassles by border officials.

The average traveller will also need to have hepatitis and typhoid vaccinations. It is also advisable to take anti-malarial tablets once a week starting two weeks prior to departure. In addition, vaccinations for TB, tetanus, meningitis and polio are recommended for those planning to live in Africa a while, and those travelling on the cheap who may encounter fairly unsanitary conditions.

Yellow Fever Required by all Central African countries. Some of them waive the requirement if you're not coming from an infected area and intend to stay less than two weeks – but how many airport officials know this? The yellow fever shot is valid for 10 years, and the injections should be started about three weeks prior to departure.

Cholera Required in Equatorial Guinea, Zaïre, Chad, Gabon, Congo. Also required in the Central African Republic if you're coming from an infected area. It must have been taken within the past six months.

It's a well-guarded secret that the vaccination against cholera is not very effective. Rather than waste the effort, a number of doctors will simply stamp your card as having received it. If there are no crooked doctors in the neighbourhood then it is probably a good idea to have the vaccination rather than risk being stabbed with a dirty needle at an airport or border station.

Hepatitis The gamma globulin shot is given for hepatitis and should be taken just before departure because its effectiveness decreases rapidly. Moreover, it does not prevent hepatitis but only reduces the severity of the disease. Some doctors shrug off the efficacy of the gamma globulin shot, but some protection is better than none.

Typhoid This is the last of the four vaccinations that every traveller should have. If you've had a booster shot within the last three years, you won't need one.

Other Vaccinations There are four additional recommended vaccinations – polio, tetanus, meningitis and TB.

Polio is still common in developing countries but not a major problem. Most people will require only a booster shot. Tetanus is more likely to be a potential problem for those travelling on the cheap. Again, a booster shot is probably all that will be needed.

Type 'A' and 'C' vaccine for meningococca meningitis is recommended for people planning more than a short visit. As for TB, short-term visitors are very unlikely to get it. So forget about it unless you'll be staying a while and/or likely to drink a lot of locally made yogurt that is not sold in containers.

Finally, smallpox has now been completely eradicated (the last case was reported in 1977); vaccination is no longer required anywhere in the world.

Malaria

Malaria is probably the most serious disease in Africa, affecting about one in five Africans yearly (and yearly killing about one million people worldwide). Nevertheless, in general there is no need for short-term travellers who take their malaria suppressant tablets religiously to get worked up over this somewhat mysterious tropical disease.

There is a rare type of malaria that is fatal and death can occur in a day or two. So anyone not taking their tablets regularly is playing with death except in northern Chad where mosquitoes are almost non-existent.

Despite what you may have heard, malaria is usually not fatal and frequently only lasts a few days. Someone not taking preventive medicine may contract it many times during the year. When someone told me for the first time that their child had malaria *last night*, I responded: 'What do you mean *last night*.' I thought the kid must be at death's door. You learn that these things happen all the time, especially with the Africans who can't afford the daily or weekly treatment. It puts you on your back and a typical African farmer may have malaria 25% of the time. The problem for travellers is that unlike cholera and typhoid, no vaccine exists, only anti-malarial tablets which suppress it.

Diagnosing malaria is not easy because it can mimic the symptoms of other diseases – high fever, lassitude, headache, pains in the joints, chills. As a rule, the onset is sudden, with a violent, shaking chill followed by a rapid rise in temperature. Headache is common. After several hours of fever profuse sweating occurs.

Even Peace Corps nurses who have seen it many times have difficulty diagnosing malaria, so you should be a little skeptical if some Joe Doe is 100% certain someone has it. The only sure way to diagnose malaria is by thorough examination of blood smears, and it's not everywhere that this can be done.
· To avoid contracting malaria, take a malaria suppressant such as aralen or chloroquine once a week, starting two weeks before you arrive and continuing four weeks after you leave. In Africa, aralen is not easily obtained.

An equally effective substitute is nivaquine, which contains chloroquine but must be taken every day. Chloroquine only acts to suppress malaria; it does not prevent it. If you get malaria, the treatment is the same for prevention, only in higher doses. Moreover, once you get malaria, traces remain in the blood so that you can never again donate blood. Also, if you've taken aralen, you shouldn't donate blood for a period of three years from the last pill.

There is a strain of malaria (plasmodium falciparum) with varying degrees of resistance to chloroquine. This is found in East Africa, the eastern regions of Zaïre and the Central African Republic. If travelling to these areas, in addition to chloroquine (aralen or nivoquin), Paludrine or Fansidar should be taken. The latter is stronger but not recommended for pregnant women or people sensitive to sulphur. Moreover, some people frequently suffer very bad side effects from Fansidar, including rash, fatigue and retinal damage. For 99% of all travellers to Central Africa, however, chloroquine is sufficient.

Drinking Water

Whether or not the water is impure, foreigners can easily get sick from drinking the local water. For travellers on the cheap, the best solution is to take iodine or halazone tablets (not available in Africa), and avoid fresh vegetables and unpeeled fruits. In a pinch, you can use clorox/ammonia, but it's not as effective. Filtering water, by the way, clears the water but does not sterilise it.

For those with a little money, the solution is to buy bottled water, available in every capital city in Central Africa (except possibly São Tomé) and quite frequently even in the smaller cities and towns. The cost is not prohibitive, ranging between 50 cents and US$1 per litre in most places (supermarket prices that is, because the hotels will sell it for three times that amount).

It's easy to avoid drinking bad water. The real problem is taking in bad water through other means, most commonly when eating raw vegetables or unpeeled fruit. The only solution is to avoid salads and the like altogether no matter how tempting they are or how fancy and modern the restaurant may be. It's an extremely rare restaurant that soaks its vegetables in an iodine solution. Hotels like the Intercontinental simply import their vegetables from Europe, but this doesn't avoid potential contamination through handling. So just bring along some vitamin tablets if you're a health nut.

Fortunately, most water in African cities and towns comes from potable sources. The problem is that the water can become contaminated in the pipes. African water systems operate under low pressure, so that seepage of sewerage and the like into the pipes is quite possible. This is a much bigger problem during the rainy season, so consider this if faced with drinking untreated water.

Dysentery & Diarrhoea

You may think that diarrhoea is inevitable, but there are in fact many short term visitors to Central Africa who never get it. It's water that has by far the greatest likelihood of causing diarrhoea, not meat, African dishes and staples such as noodles and rice. But it's not just drinking water – your Coke and fries may be safe but not the glass or utensils.

In certain ways, eating at restaurants may be more risky than eating on the street with your hands. (The opposite is true when street food is eaten with plates and utensils.) Street food is usually safe because the ingredients are purchased daily. The same certainly cannot be guaranteed of restaurant food.

If you are very careful about the water and still get diarrhoea, it doesn't mean you've got dysentery; it's probably caused by the change in food and a change of bacteria in the intestines. The treatment is simple – starve it out for at least 24 hours and drink plenty of unsugared liquids such as tea, bouillon soup and bottled water.

A nourishing preparation containing salt, potassium, and water is: the juice of one orange and a quarter teaspoon of salt together with 10 ounces of water.

Adequate replacement of fluids is essential; becoming dehydrated is no solution to the problem. Moreover, the flow of fluids will help wash out whatever is down there. As improvement occurs, one or two days of soup and bread or soda biscuits or unsugared oatmeal (easy to find) should follow.

In general, drugs are not recommended. Lomotil, however, will help to reduce the symptoms of diarrhoea if not the cause. If this doesn't work, a very effective French drug available locally that some people swear by is ercefuryl. If that's not available, try centrecine.

If plagued by a really bad case of diarrhoea which doesn't respond to any of the standard treatments, there's always a chance that it's dysentery. If this is the case, visit a doctor. Be wary, however, of needle-happy doctors. Africans tend to have an overly high regard for medicines taken by needles; most doctors comply. In most cases, medicine taken through pills is just as effective as that injected.

If there are no doctors in the region, avoid dehydration at all costs. This means drinking lots of fluids. Drinking also helps wash out the system. Finally, if the diarrhoea is accompanied by severe stomach cramps, drinking tea or fruit juice with salt will help to relieve the pain.

Sexually Transmitted Diseases

To hear the doctors talk, the only way to describe STDs in Africa is rampant. There are about 12 kinds, however, and many aren't so terrible. In Gabon, non-gonococcal urethritis (NGV) is so prevalent that it's virtually certain to strike at anyone who is sexually active.

AIDS

A virus very similar to one carried by green monkeys, AIDS ('SIDA' in French) has been traced back as far as 1959 to a case in Zaïre. Still, it is only conjecture that it originated there. As of 1988, the following twelve African countries were the worst hit by the AIDS epidemic: Tanzania, Uganda, Zambia, Rwanda, Burundi, Kenya, Angola, Zimbabwe, Malawi, Central African Republic, Zaïre and the Congo. While only three of the 12 are in Central Africa, the disease is spreading rapidly.

What is not commonly realised is that the risk is many times greater in the cities than in the rural areas. In Africa, AIDS is primarily a disease not of homosexuals but of, as a Nigerian newspaper phrased it, 'women of loose virtue'. Avoiding sex just with prostitutes is not enough, however, because Africans from all walks of life are known to carry the virus.

The following additional information on AIDS in Central Africa was supplied by the Traveller's Medical and Vaccination Centre in Sydney:

In Central Africa the spread of AIDS is mainly through the heterosexual population with male to female transmission being more infective than the reverse. The carrier rate in certain parts of Central Africa is significantly higher than in developed countries with reports of between five and 10 percent of the general population being infected.

These figures are probably conservative since accurate prevalence figures are difficult to obtain due to poor diagnostic facilities, unreported cases and political reasons (ie tourism is a major source of revenue). The problem is almost certainly far greater than we think.

Sexual intercourse whether heterosexual or homosexual with anyone in Central Africa could be extremely dangerous. In certain parts of the region up to 80% of prostitutes are carriers. Unless one can be certain from the social and sexual background of a new sexual partner that the risk of infection is unlikely, the best course is to abstain.

Should sexual intercourse occur, a condom will provide some protection. However, condoms are not a fail-safe method of preventing infection, as even when used correctly they can tear or slip off.

Regarding blood transfusions in Central Africa the rule of thumb is quite simple: unless the situation is one of life and death, blood transfusions from local donors should be avoided. Possible alternatives to receiving potentially infected blood would be:

1 To receive blood from a fellow traveller (if compatible).
2 To have prior arrangements for emergency evacuation to home country in the event of serious accident or injury.
3 To avoid injections unless you know that the needle/syringe is new. Many people carry their own syringes and needles although the possible consequences of this should be carefully thought out before following this course of action.

Weird African Maladies

You may have heard that it is unwise to go swimming in lakes or rivers because they are chock-a-block with weird African diseases, one that over a period of time ages you about 20 years, and another that causes blindness. It's no joke. The first is called bilharzia or schisto(somiasis) and the other is called oncho(cerciasis). Oncho, however, is not a major problem in Central Africa.

Bilharzia – Schistosomiasis Bilharzia or 'schisto' is a disease caused by tiny blood flukes (worms) which enter the veins and lay eggs. It is spread by snails which live just at the edge of lakes or slow moving rivers. Anyone in the mud or shallow water along the edge is susceptible to having these microscopic worms penetrate the skin; labourers in irrigation ditches are particularly susceptible. A strong case of the disease is mildly painful and can have a very debilitating effect over the years.

The symptoms are blood in the urine and intestinal pains. For a mild case, there may be no clear signs at all, which is why anyone living overseas for a few years must get checked for schisto upon returning. Until recently, the only cure was a dangerous treatment with strong dosages of arsenic, which killed the worms but, hopefully, not the

patient. Now it's just a case of taking pills for a week.

Tumba Larva Another major nuisance is the tumba larva. A wet piece of clothing hanging outside to dry is the tumba fly's favourite place to deposit her eggs. If they are not ironed, or dried in a clothes drier, the eggs will become larvae. After that there is very little that can be done to stop them boring into the skin.

Often a small white spot can be seen at the site of the lesion. Fortunately, the larva always stays just below the surface. Yet even many old African hands don't know how simple the treatment is – put vaseline over the wound to suffocate the worm. It'll come out, although a little push may be necessary. Left untreated, these worms become the twice the size of a rice grain from eating juicy human flesh and are quite painful.

Sleeping Sickness Another weird malady caused by biting insects in Africa is trypanosomiasis (sleeping sickness), one of the symptoms of which is physical and mental lethargy. It is caused by the tsetse fly, which is about twice the size of the common house-fly. The main problem is that it kills horses and cattle, leaving large areas of Central Africa with few or no such animals. Fortunately, the risk of infection to travellers is virtually nil, and the cure for the disease is effective.

THEFT & SECURITY

Central Africa stands out as being one of the safer places in the Third World, and certainly safer than most large cities in the USA if not Europe as well. Of course there are problems, but compared with the atrocities in Uganda, the rioting in South Africa and the civil wars in Angola and Sudan, the Central African countries have got it good.

Still, Central Africa in general is not as safe as the Sahelian countries of West Africa. One reason for the difference is that Central Africans, excluding those in Chad and northern Cameroun, drink so much more alcohol.

Warding off sometimes belligerent drunks is a major problem in Zaïre, Gabon, Central African Republic and Congo.

In reality, though, thieves are the major concern. Travellers are continually being robbed on trains in Zaïre, for example. Walking around Douala at night is tantamount to inviting theft. The worst that usually happens, however, is a loss of money and papers. It's still fairly rare to hear of thieves carrying guns, but when they do, the news spreads like wildfire.

On a scale of one to 10, many South American cities would rate about an eight in terms of danger versus three or four for Douala, Libreville, Brazzaville and Bangui, and less for the remaining cities.

Kinshasa (Zaïre) is a special case. On the same scale it might rate a 10. If safety is a concern, avoid Kinshasa. This includes changing airlines in Kinshasa because even taking a cab downtown at night is risky. It's much safer to change airlines in nearby Brazzaville. Many business people simply do not go out at night in Kinshasa. Travellers on the cheap are almost as vulnerable.

Theft

Petty theft is the main problem. Women are naturally more vulnerable. They have been robbed while jogging alone on seemingly safe beaches and had their purses and jewellery snatched while leaving the grounds of hotels and elsewhere.

Most thefts are due to the traveller's lack of foresight. The most common error is forgetting what you've got on. Avoid the temptation of wearing that new gold necklace or watch.

Even seasoned veterans in Africa slip up, going in risky areas with jewellery and watches, even passports bulging out of their shirt pockets. Frequently, it's because at the beginning of the evening they didn't expect to end up in the hot district of town.

Purse snatching in markets and near the entrances to restaurants and nightclubs is fairly common in major cities. At nightclubs, leaving a purse at the table only invites theft.

The best advice is to leave your purse or wallet behind. Either hide your money, take a small pouch bag which can be worn at all times, or wear clothing with lots of pockets – and leave most of your money, passports, IDs, credit cards, even watches at the hotel. It's surprising how few travellers use hotel safety boxes!

If the police hassle you for not carrying a passport, the worst that usually happens is having to fetch it or bribing the policeman. Better that than to risk having the passport stolen. It's a rare expatriate, for example, who carries around a passport except when going upcountry.

Carrying a photocopy of the first few pages of your passport will appease most policemen. If you do that make sure that you have copied your visa or entry stamp too.

A final suggestion is to hire a guy to accompany you when walking around a risky area. It's usually not too difficult to find a kid hanging around who wouldn't mind picking up a few shillings by warding off potential molesters.

Sexual Harassment

A frequent complaint of western women living in Africa, particularly single women, is sexual harassment. The problem is greater in Central Africa than in West Africa because men drink so much more in the former. Unfortunately there are always the 'admirers' who won't go away and the border officials who are into verbal abuse. Rape, on the other hand, is a very infrequent event, perhaps in part because Black African societies are not sexually repressive.

One reason for such harassment is that western women are frequently viewed as being 'loose'. Dress is sometimes a factor. Although African women in the larger, more modern cities often wear western clothes, most still dress conservatively, typically with skirts to the ground. When a visitor wears something significantly different from the norm, she will draw attention. In the mind of the potential sexual assailant, she is dressing peculiarly. He may think she's asking for 'peculiar' and aggressive treatment.

In general, the problem of dress is easy to resolve; look at what other women are wearing and follow suit. Long pants are usually not a problem but long dresses are much better. If you want to wear shorts, bring along a wrap-around skirt to cover them when you're in public.

If you're in an uneasy situation, the wisest thing to do is stick your nose in a book or invent an imaginary husband who will be arriving shortly. If you are travelling with a male companion, introduce him as your husband. Cultures have enough different customs with names that having two different surnames does not usually pose a problem.

PHOTOGRAPHY
Permits & Limitations

There are a few peculiarities about photography in Africa. The main one is that a photo permit is required in Chad, Congo, Equatorial Guinea and, in practice, Cameroun. In no place but Chad, however, does this take more than 24 hours.

As for video cameras, most countries treat them like regular cameras. However, in a few countries, you may run into problems. The governments' concern is that you may be a commercial film maker, in which case special permission is required virtually everywhere. If you wear a Hawaiian shirt and look like a tourist, you may be more convincing. Alternatively, contact the country's embassy and ask them to cable for clearance. Don't expect the embassies to know the precise rules.

A second peculiarity is that in almost no country in this book may one photograph militarily sensitive installations. This includes most or all government buildings (even post offices!), airports, harbours, the presidential palace, ministry of defence buildings, dams, radio and TV stations, bridges, railroad stations and factories. In short, any photos that might aid a potential coup d'etat.

Photographing policemen or military personnel is a major blunder. The problem for tourists is that prohibited areas are rarely put in writing or stated in specific terms. When in doubt, ask first.

In Cameroun, an extra limitation is that you cannot photograph anything potentially embarrassing to the government, such as beggars and deformed people. Other countries prohibit photographing of native religious services. The rules change from country to country. In 'progressive' Cameroun, for example, taking a photo of the presidential mansion, would probably result in confiscation of the offending camera followed by a couple of days of intense interrogation for the photographer.

Photographing People

Every respect must be shown for local customs and beliefs. In some places, the camera's lens may be seen as taking away something personal. As for objects, some are sacred and should be treated as such. The golden rule is to ask permission – and take 'no' for an answer. In some instances, dress may be important. Wearing long pants and removing your shoes in mosques, for instance, may make it more likely that a potential subject won't object.

Usually, Africans enjoy being photographed, especially if the photographer is friendly. There are very few things more valuable to Africans than photographs of the family, relatives and friends. A promise to send them one will be taken seriously, moreover, it is one of the most appreciated, and yet inexpensive, ways to express your friendship. The great pity is that maybe only one in 10 travellers actually send that promised photo.

A great way to make a hit in Africa is to bring along a polaroid camera as a second camera. Despite the poverty everywhere, a nice photo is worth much more than money. In some instances, it may be the only photo that they have. Just be sure to let them know that there's only one shot remaining other-wise everyone in the village will want their picture taken.

When it comes to paying for pictures, there's no simple answer. Some people recommend having some candy ready to give children who have been the camera's subject; others believe it only encourages begging. When taking photos of a craftsperson, the answer is clearer – it's only fair, and expected, that a small purchase be made afterwards. Fortunately, there are so few tourists in Central Africa that rarely do people demand money for photos.

Special Concerns

Film in Africa is expensive – anything from US$5 to US$20 a roll – and only the most widely used film is sold. Also, light conditions vary widely. So buy all the necessary film in a variety of ASAs (100,200,400) before heading for Central Africa. Once on the dark continent, 100 ASA film and some 200 ASA are readily available, but there is virtually no 400 ASA film.

During the rainy season, 200 ASA film is more useful and 400 ASA is probably the best in the jungle areas. If the gorillas in eastern Zaïre are on your itinerary, bring a roll or two of 1000 ASA film.

As for equipment, bring everything along, especially extra batteries and cleaning equipment. Dust and dirt can get into equipment, making it filthy in no time. A filter is also a good idea.

For two or three months starting in December, the Harmattan winds cover the skies in northern Central Africa with fine dust particles from the desert. Visibility can on occasion be reduced to one or two km. If photography is a primary reason for visiting Africa and northern Central Africa is of particular interest, pick a time other than between the beginning of December and mid-February. In eastern Zaïre, the hazy dry period is June to mid-September.

All too often, pictures of Africans come out with the faces too dark, with little or no detail. Black faces have to be compensated for. If you use a light meter, the general rule is to open up one or 1¹/₂ stops from what the meter reads.

Finally, older model x-ray machines for checking baggage at airports can damage undeveloped film. With the newer models, this is not a problem. Since it is never possible to be certain that a particular machine is safe, bring some protective lead bags – they're fairly inexpensive. While customs officials will usually allow film to be carried separately, this isn't the case in all countries.

FOOD & DRINK
African Food
African food is written off by many tourists as being too risky and seemingly unappetising. For people who cannot tolerate hot pepper, it's probably wise to avoid it. The rest will be missing an interesting experience.

Don't think that the food served up in restaurants or on the street is the best available. It often takes a few years in Africa to learn that good African food has many more ingredients than that which is normally dished out in a local chop house. In cities, Africans are accustomed to eating street food, but they rarely eat at restaurants. When they do, they

tend to prefer simple things such as braised chicken or fish. For this reason, there are few restaurants serving really good African food.

The best place to find good African food is in somebody's home. Africans eat very well if they have enough money to buy a lot of interesting ingredients. If you happen to make friends with someone who then invites you home for dinner, you might offer to pay for the ingredients. This would almost certainly add quite considerably to their usual food budget. You could be certain of a terrific meal and at the same time feed not only yourself but your host's entire family.

The best way to satiate an interest in African ingredients and spices is undoubtedly to accompany an African woman when she goes shopping – this is about the only way to learn what all that weird food at the market is. Most African food is quite hot, but as you get closer to the desert, the dishes become less spicy.

If someone tells you they don't like African food, it's more likely to be due to the texture or excessive pepper than to the taste. The pepper is sometimes controllable; the hot sauce is frequently put to the side. As for the texture, a number of African dishes are made with okra; the result is a distinctly slimy concoction.

In rural areas you may be eating in the same way as the locals – with your hands – in which case it's like dipping your hand into a bowl of raw eggs. There are any number of staples with which any meal can be eaten. One is *bidia* in Zaïre, which is basically a glob of mashed corn. You grab a small chunk, form a ball, and dip it in the sauce or make an indentation in it with your thumb, and use it to scoop up the sauce.

If you're turned off by slimy okra, you won't be the only one. Lots of people who love African food aren't particularly fond of it either. No matter, there is a much greater variety of African dishes than is commonly known by foreigners, even those who have been around for quite some time.

African food consists typically of a staple plus some kind of sauce. The preferred staple everywhere is rice; it is also more expensive because most of it has to be imported. In northern Central Africa sorghum and millet are common staples. Corn and cassava are the principal foodstuffs in the rest of Central Africa.

Grain is placed in a wooden receptacle and pounded, sometimes for several hours – not exactly most people's idea of a fun way to spend the afternoon. African villages are too small to support the mills seen in most towns and cities, and even in the cities many people cannot afford the extra cost of the service. (It's close to slavery. Ask a group of women in a small village to make a wish list, and a mill will be at the top of most.) The pounded grain results in a white mound that hardly makes the juices run – but neither is plain white rice. Eaten with a tasty sauce, it can be surprisingly good.

Sauces & Recipes

Sauces are the heart of African cuisine and each country has its own specialities. The spices commonly found in Cameroun, for example, differ more from those in Zaïre than is commonly realised. One of the most popular dishes in all of sub-Saharan Africa is groundnut stew, which varies slightly from country to country. As for desserts, they are not a part of the traditional African cuisine, however, fresh fruits are sometimes eaten after a meal.

Many of the African sauces are difficult to duplicate outside Africa for lack of the proper spices. Three recipes which require no special ingredients are listed below.

Spinach Stew (CAR)

2 lb (900 grams) spinach
2 small onions, finely chopped
2 peeled tomatoes
1 green bell pepper, chopped
2 chilli peppers, or 1/2 teaspoon cayenne pepper
1/3 cup peanut butter
2 dessertspoons oil
1 teaspoon salt

Sauté the onions in oil until golden brown then stir in remaining ingredients, except for peanut butter, and simmer for five minutes. Thin the peanut butter with several tablespoons of warm water to make a paste, then add to the pot and cook another 15 minutes or so. If it begins to stick add small amounts of water. Serve with rice. Serves six.

Groundnut Stew (Central Africa)

1 chicken, cut into pieces
3/4 cup peanut butter
2 large onions, chopped
1 pint (600 ml) chicken stock
1/3 cup oil
3 or 4 fresh tomatoes
2 cups okra
1 teaspoon salt
2 hot chillies, crushed, or 1 teaspoon cayenne pepper
1-inch (2 1/2 cm) piece ginger, crushed

Cut the chicken into cubes. In a large heavy pot, brown chicken in hot oil, then add stock, onions and seasonings, cover and boil for 20 minutes then reduce the heat. In another pan, boil the tomatoes and okra. Then add this and remaining ingredients to the stew and bring to a boil, stirring vigorously to avoid sticking. Reduce the heat and simmer until chicken is well done. Serve with rice. Serves four.

Okra & Greens (Gabon)

16 okra
1 lb (450 grams) turnip/collard greens
1 finely chopped onion
1/2 cup palm (or pine) nuts
4 finely chopped/crushed chilli peppers or 2 teaspoons cayenne pepper
2 dessertspoons oil

This is a hot dish; you may want to reduce the peppers. Any greens will do. Sauté onions until golden brown. Add remaining ingredients plus 1/4 cup water. Cover skillet and simmer until tender (roughly 20 minutes). Serves four to six.

Beer

While African cuisine is not everybody's cup of tea, everybody agrees that African beer is good by any standard. It is certainly better than the watery stuff in the USA and cheaper than that in Europe. And it's even good in remote places, such as Chad. There may be a war going on there, but the Gala brewery keeps putting it out. In all there are roughly a dozen different beers brewed in Central Africa, about half coming from Cameroun.

In Zaïre tourists say that Primus is as good as or better than what they're accustomed to drinking at home. Part of the reason may be that the brewery in Zaïre is partially owned by Heinneken. While everyone has their own favourite beer, the best in Central Africa are reputed to be Gala and Primus.

Unfortunately alcoholism is a serious problem in Central Africa, especially in Gabon and Equatorial Guinea, where you're likely to be drunk under the table. Gabonese spend an estimated 12% of their disposable incomes on alcohol and it appears to be even higher in Equatorial Guinea.

In Zaïre, Central African Republic, Congo and southern Cameroun beer halls are everywhere. In Central Africa, being able to hold your liquor is the first thing every Peace Corps volunteer must learn. And you've got to learn to start drinking at 8 am!

Home-made brew is popular everywhere, even in Muslim areas. Palm wine is drunk in villages in the jungle areas. You'll see it sold along the roads. This is the juice tapped from the palm oil tree. It contains yeast and is allowed to ferment overnight. Closer to the Sahara where the climate becomes too dry for palm oil trees, it's the cheap millet beer that gets the men wasted in the villages.

There's one non-alcoholic drink, loosely called 'ginger beer', that is consumed so much throughout all of Africa that it could almost be called the continental drink of Africa. It is made with so much ginger that it burns the throat and most foreigners find the burning sensation too strong. In remote villages they may have nothing else to offer you. If you drink the local water (most travellers should definitely not), look for this ginger drink on the streets, frequently in old soft drink bottles. The name changes from place to place.

BOOKS & BOOKSTORES

The following list of books is short and selective. All are in paperback and can be obtained through the mail. Only two are out of print. At the end is a list of bookstores specialising in Africana, travel and maps. If you only have time to read one book and are looking for something informative and entertaining, it's hard to beat David Lamb's *The Africans*.

History

The Story of Africa by Basil Davidson (Mitchell Beazley London, 1984). This is a superbly illustrated and engaging book which was published to accompany Davidson's eight-part documentary series on the history of Africa for British TV.

A Short History of Africa by J D Fage & Roland Oliver (Cambridge University Press, Cambridge). This is also a very good, less expensive book.

Africa Since 1800 by Roland Oliver & Anthony Atmore (Cambridge University Press, Cambridge, 1981). This is the last of a trilogy, the others being *Africa in the Iron Age* and *The African Middle Ages 1400-1800*. The book has three parts: the pre-colonial period up to 1875, followed by the partition and colonial rule, thematically rather than by region, and finally the roads to independence taken by different African territories, plus the post independence decades.

Modern Africa by Basil Davidson (Longman Ltd, Harlow, Essex, England; or Longman Inc, White Plains, NY, 1983). This book focuses on African history since 1900.

Social History

The African Genius: An Introduction to African Social & Cultural History by Basil Davidson (The Atlantic Monthly Press, Waltham, Maine, 1969).

Art

African Art in Cultural Perspective by William Bascom (W W Norton & Co, London or New York, 1985). This is an excellent paperback, but out of print, focusing solely on sculpture and covering West and Central Africa region by region.

African Art by Frank Willett (Oxford University Press New Jersey, 1971). Out of print. Almost 400 pages long, the book offers an in-depth discussion for those with a keen interest in the subject. Several other good paperbacks, such as *African Sculpture* by Fagg and Plass, are also out of print.

African Arts, a quarterly published by the African Studies Centre, UCLA. This is an excellent magazine with good photography and articles.

Novels

Cameroun is the only country in Central Africa that has produced any well-known novelists. Two of them are Mbella Sonné Dipoko and Kenjo Jumbam. Dipoko's *Because of Women* is a delicately told story of a river-man who quarrels with his pregnant wife over another woman. Jumban's *The White Man of God* is about a boy growing up in a Camerounian village which is seriously divided when a white missionary arrives. Both are available from Heinemann Educational Books (New Hampshire or London).

Ask Heinemann for their free 'African Writers Series' catalogue of paperback books. They have about 270 titles by African authors.

For other novels about life in Africa, refer to western writers or to those from neighbouring Nigeria, such as:

A Bend in the River by V S Naipaul (Random House Inc, Maryland, 1979). Set in Zaïre, it is an excellent selection for those wanting a novel on rural life in Central Africa. V S Naipaul is a Pulitzer Prize winner.

Talking Drums by Shirley Deane (John Murray Publishers, London) is a novel about Cameroun. She focuses on village life near Yaoundé.

Things Fall Apart by Nigeria's Chinua Achebe (Heinemann Educational Books, 1958) is the most famous novel by an African writer. This classic has sold over a million copies and is definitely worth reading. The tragic story takes place in the mid-1890s at the time of the colonial take-over. The main character is a powerful tribal figure who is divided between the past and the present during rapidly changing times. Achebe's historical imagination coupled with a mastery of the English language have led critics to compare him with Conrad and the like.

Politics & Economics

The Africans by David Lamb (Random House, New York, 1984). A portrait of modern-day Africa which is rich in political and social detail, this book gets rave reviews from travellers. Lamb, who has been twice nominated for the Pulitzer Prize, spent four years travelling to 46 countries, talking to both guerrilla leaders and presidents, and catching midnight flights to coups in little-known countries collecting information for this startling work.

Africa: The People and Politics of an Emerging Continent by Sanford Ungar (Simon & Schuster, New York, 1986). This guide to the present-day political, economic and social realities of Africa, makes sense out of a complex continent and is highly readable and entertaining. Although the sections on Nigeria, Liberia, Kenya and South Africa take up half the book, there's a section on every country in Central Africa except São Tomé.

The Political Economy of Africa edited by D Cohen & J Daniel (Longman, 1981). This gives a left-wing viewpoint.

Ecology

Africa in Crisis by Lloyd Timberlake (Earthscan, Washington DC). This book focuses on the political and environmental factors contributing to drought and famine in Africa, particularly the roles international aid organisations and African leaders have played in recent environmental disasters.

Cookbook

The Africa News Cookbook by Africa News Service Inc (Viking Penguin Inc, New York, or Middlesex, UK, 1985). This appears to be the only African cookbook in print. It's quite good, covering the entire continent, with a few recipes from Central Africa. Each recipe has been carefully chosen to ensure that all ingredients can be obtained in the west.

Magazines

Jeune Afrique (in French), (Le Groupe Jeune Afrique, Paris). This popular weekly magazine covers both Central and West African and world events, always with an African perspective.

New African, (IC Publications, London). This monthly has a reputation for accurate and balanced reporting, with a mix of political reporting, financial and economic analysis, features on social and cultural affairs, plus regular country and topic surveys.

Political Publications

The best in terms of giving the inside scoop is, unquestionably, the twice-monthly *Africa Confidential* (Miramoor Publications, London).

Commercial Publications

There are several annual publications. *Africa Review* (World of Information, Essex, UK) is an annual publication providing a concise and up-to-date digest of economic and commercial data on African countries, along with general information on the African business environment.

Africa South of the Sahara (Europa Publications, London) is a well-known annual publication containing similar but more detailed information.

Africa Contemporary Record (Holmes & Meier, London), published annually, is even more detailed.

You'll also find a number of monthly publications. *Africa Business* (IC Publications Ltd, London) is a monthly magazine providing a wide variety of news items, commentaries and feature articles.

Africa (Africa Journal Ltd, London) is a monthly magazine covering business, economics and politics.

The best weekly is *Economic Digest* (Middle East Economic Digest, London), a report providing business news, economic analyses and forecasts.

Maps

The best regional maps are by *Michelin* – No 153 West Africa including Chad and Cameroun, and No 155 for the rest of Central Africa. The *Bartholomew* maps are not as good.

Bookstores

Bookstores in Central Africa are listed under each country. Don't expect to be able to pick up any interesting reading in English outside Cameroun except with great difficulty. Books in French, however, are abundant. For specialist books on Africa, it is better to buy them at home.

London *Foyle's* at 113 Charing Cross Rd, London WC2H OEB, is one block from Cambridge Circus and may be the world's largest bookshop. Ask for their Africana section. Their travel section is not good. *Waterstone's*, next door to Foyle's, is much better for maps and travel guides.

Even better for maps, with a fairly good selection of travel guides as well, is *Stanfords* (tel 01-8361321) 12 Long Acre St, Covent Garden, London WC2P. They even have maps of individual countries in Africa.

Several blocks away, the *Africa Book Centre* at the Africa Centre (tel 01-8361973) 38 King St, Covent Garden, London WC2 8JT, has a small bookshop, and is a good place to get practical first-hand information on Africa.

Operation Headstart in West Green Rd, London N15 5BX, has books exclusively on Africa, including a section on African cookery. *Knightsbridge Books* at 32 Store St, London WC1E 7BS, specialises in African and Asian studies.

USA In New York City, the two stores with the best Africana sections appear to be *Liberation Book Store* (tel 212-2814615) 421 Lenox Avenue, corner of 131st St, Harlem, and *Barnes & Noble* (tel 212-8070099) 5th Avenue at 17th St. For maps and travel guides, your best bets are *Travellers Bookstore* (tel 212-6640995) 22 West 52nd Avenue, *Complete Traveller Bookstore* (tel 212-6859007) 199 Madison Avenue at 35th St, and *Scribner Book Store* (tel 212-7589797) 597 Fifth Avenue, near 49th St.

In Washington, DC, the best store for travel books and maps is *Travel Books Unlimited* (tel 301-9518533) 4931 Cordell Avenue, Bethesda, MD. Downtown, *The Map Store* (tel 202-6282608), 1636 Eye St, NW, carries Michelin maps of Africa.

Travel Centres of the World (Box 1788, Hollywood, CA 90078) specialises in very detailed maps and travel guides. Write for their catalogue.

Europe In France, try *L'Astrolabe* (tel 1-42854295) Metro stop Chaussée d'Antin) 46, Rue de Provence, 75009 Paris. They specialise in books and maps for travellers and may be the best of that type. *Gilbert Joseph* (tel 01-43255716), 26, Boulevard St Michel, 75006 Paris, (Metro stop St Michel) has an excellent selection of maps and travel guides. *Hachette*, one block away, has some books not found at Gilbert Joseph. Several blocks from Gilbert Joseph is *Presence Africaine* (tel 01-4326588) 25 bis, Rue des Ecoles, 75005 Paris, which specialises in serious books on Africa, many by African authors, but has no travel guides.

In Holland, your best bet may be *Geografische Boekhandel* (tel 020-121901) Overtoom 136, 1054 HN Amsterdam.

In West Germany, try *Daerr Expeditionservice GmbH* (tel 089-9031519) Hauptstrausse 26, D-8011 Kirchheim/Munich, Ortsteil Heimstetten.

Australia In Melbourne the *International Bookshop* (tel 03-6142859), 2nd floor, 17 Elizabeth St, probably has the largest selection of books on Africa. In Sydney it would be worth trying *Gleebooks* (tel 02-6602333), 191 Glebe Point Rd, Glebe.

SPORTS

One of the secrets of meeting people in Africa is to look for activities in which they're involved. Sports can be a key in this respect. You've got to be a little selective. You're not going to find Africans sailing and deep sea fishing or, to any great extent, on sail boards or on the golf links. Tennis, squash, football (soccer) and basketball, on the other hand, are favourite African sports.

If you want to meet the entire spectrum of expatriates, run with the Hash House Harriers or head towards the nearest tennis club.

If you're a pretty decent tennis player, there's hardly a private club in Central Africa that will not invite you to play at least a game or two. If you can give one of the club's top players a battle for his life, you're in, win or lose. If you're not quite that good, you can still probably finagle a temporary membership if you're friendly and buy lots of drinks.

One way to enter is to arrange a game when the courts are empty; the local African pro is the guy to approach because he wants your business hitting the ball even if non-members are not technically allowed. Become friendly with him, and he may come to be your 'in', in addition to becoming a friend.

Basketball & Soccer

These two sports win the sports popularity contest hands down. Bring along a deflated football (soccer) for a village family, a boy or a group, and you'll be the hit of the day. Seeing a game of football is easy as there are games almost every Sunday in the major cities. They can get as rowdy as anywhere else on the globe.

The biggest sports event in Africa is probably the Africa Cup football matches held every even year in the spring. People are glued to their radios and tubes. If you want to play, the universities and municipal stadiums are by far the best places to find a game.

Tennis & Swimming

There are tennis courts and swimming pools in almost all cities over 100,000 in Cameroun as well as in Chad (N'Djamena), Gabon (Libreville, Franceville, Port-Gentil, Lambaréné), Congo (Brazzaville, Pointe-Noire), Equatorial Guinea (Malabo) and Zaïre (Kinshasa, Lubumbashi). Most of these facilities are at major hotels and even if you're not a guest, you can usually use them – for a small price, of course.

Squash

There are courts only in Gabon (Libreville, Port-Gentil) and Zaïre (Kinshasa).

Hash House Harriers

This is a jogging group of sorts which started back in 1939 when a bunch of Aussies in Malaysia with nothing better to do than drink beer began meeting to run through rice paddies and anywhere else so as to build up a thirst for drinking still more. It's now an international organisation; in Central Africa there are groups only in Cameroun (Yaoundé, Bamenda and Garoua).

The runs, typically once a month on a Saturday, are not so tough as to prohibit non-joggers from participating. They run through African villages, through corn fields and in the hills, sometimes on city streets – anywhere. Since the starting point changes each run, the only way to find the Hash is to ask around the expatriate community. But beware – the beer drinking rituals afterwards are as important as the run.

Foot Races

The gruelling 27 km race up and down Mt Cameroun sponsored by Guinness every January (last Sunday) since the mid-1970s is a major race that attracts runners from outside the continent; most of the winners have been British or Camerounian. It's so steep that runners must carry poles – a 'must see'

if you're in the area. There's also a shorter distance race in Yaoundé.

Mountaineering-Hiking

By far the most popular mountain for climbing is 4070 metre Mt Cameroun, an hour's ride from Douala. A greater challenge, however, is the snow-capped Ruwenzori mountains in remote eastern Zaïre, the highest mountain range in Africa. Elizabeth Peak, 5119 metres, is the third highest in Africa (Kilimanjaro and Mt Kenya are higher).

Nearby are the active volcanoes of Nyiragongo (3470 metres) and Nyamulgira (3056 metres). They offer some truly spectacular sights because of the snow-capped peaks just above the tropical forests; that's part of the reason why the Ruwenzoris are nicknamed the Mountains of the Moon. The other major volcano is 3106 metre Mt Malabo in Equatorial Guinea (government permission is required before it can be visited).

The best place for technical rock climbing is probably Mindif in northern Cameroun. There's a huge rock 'La Dente de Mindif' jutting up out of nowhere that is so difficult to climb as to attract, reportedly, a TV network from as far away as Japan to film an ascent (by a Japanese team of course).

Golf

The best course in Central Africa is in Yaoundé; the 'greens' are dark sand but the mountainous setting is quite impressive. The only other cities with golf courses, all with sand greens, are Libreville, Brazzaville, Kinshasa and Bangui.

Sailboards

Sailboards are available for rent only in Libreville (Gabon) and Pointe-Noire (Congo).

Sailing

There are sailing clubs in some cities along the coast, but renting a boat is virtually impossible except in Pointe-Noire, where Hobie cats are available from the local club.

Fishing

The countries most deep sea sports fishermen head for are the Congo and Gabon. Tarpon is the major attraction. Charter boats are available in Libreville and Pointe-Noire. The season for tarpon in Gabon and the Congo is December to February.

The major agencies offering special fishing trips are located in Paris:

Jet Tours (tel 01-4602-7022 and 4705-0195) Departement Chasse et Pêche, 19, Avenue de Tourville, 75007 Paris. They offer one-week fishing trips to Gabon. Prices range from about 10,000 to 20,000 FF depending on the numbers (one to four).
Au Coin de Pêche (tel 01-4227-2861/4168) 50, Avenue de Wagram, 75017 Paris. Their prices are lower.
Orchape (tel 01-4380-3067 and 4754-7857, telex 640771) 6, Rue d'Armaille, 75007 Paris.

Cycling

Cycling expeditions are virtually non-existent in Central Africa, in large part because of the muddy interior roads. Cameroun would be the best country for attempting such because the major roads upcountry are paved and the climate is drier. Wherever, the only appropriate time would be the dry season. Be prepared for some long distances between major stops.

THINGS TO BUY

For anyone interested in art, particularly wooden carvings, Central Africa is bound to please. Some of the best art work on the continent is found in the centre. You can buy silver and gold jewellery, a fascinating assortment of spears, musical instruments, agricultural tools, etc. African art, like wine, is an acquired taste.

Two suggestions: before arriving, buy a book on African art (see Books & Bookstores) and, after arriving, go to a museum or good art shop. In Yaoundé, for example, pass by the Museum of Camerounian Art at the Benedictine monastery near the Sofitel; it has the finest wooden carvings in Central Africa. In Libreville, see the museum near the US embassy. Then you'll have some standard of comparison.

There's a maturing process regarding taste; what you may find interesting at first may not appeal to you later. You're likely to get tired of the cheaper mass produced items very quickly. So when travelling, it's a good idea to save shopping for the second half of the trip.

Knowing the context in which an object is used is important in terms of both appreciation and in detecting artificially used or aged pieces. Unlike western art, almost all African art has a use. Masks, for instance, are for dances. A knife may seem like any other knife until you learn that it's used only for circumcision. The use of any piece is at least half the interest.

No one likes to lug around souvenirs. So mail them back. Shipping is actually fairly reliable. Purchases not exceeding US$25 in value that are mailed to the States enter duty-free, and you may bring with you goods worth up to US$400 in value without paying duty. The US$400 includes all purchases mailed as well.

Australia prohibits the importation of ivory and some other products. Anything made from animal or plant matter is synonymous with the plague to Australian customs and any items made from these materials will certainly be fumigated, if not confiscated. It is wise to check the customs regulations first.

Wooden Carvings

Masks are sold all over Central Africa and are not cheap unless mass produced. Other objects in wood include charms, African game boards, carved doors, latches, figurines and boxes. Each area has its own specialities.

Art which is authentic and valuable cannot be exported under the laws of most African countries. However, since very little art purchased by non-experts fits this description, it's more a matter of being

hassled by the police than doing something illegal.

Don't expect to travel upcountry and find something really valuable. Most of the museum quality stuff has already been purchased. Also, knowing the difference between the real thing, ie old and used, and a forgery requires seeing and handling thousands of pieces. No book or sixth sense will enable you to by-pass this process.

Africans are extremely clever when it comes to artificially ageing wooden objects and making them appear used. Even museum curators can be fooled by a mark made by sandpaper rather than normal wear. Furthermore, after learning that 'old' for most wooden objects usually means nothing older than 40 to 50 years (they deteriorate rapidly in Africa unless specially protected), you may wonder why all this fuss over age anyway.

What's old and used will invariably bring a much higher price than what's new. But that doesn't mean all pieces made today are aesthetically inferior (although most are); they just don't have the wear.

Prices of the better pieces, like all art, can

be pretty subjective. As for mass produced items, the prices are a little more uniform and you can certainly be 'taken'. The only way to learn the price range is to ask knowledgeable natives or expatriates, or visit a fancy store and then bargain for about half the price at the local market (beware, however, the quality may be inferior).

Two major concerns with all wooden objects from Africa are cracking and beetles. Buy a new wooden carving, and you may find it cracked by the time you get home. New wood must be dried slowly. Wrapping in plastic bags with a small water tray enclosed is one technique.

If you see tiny bore marks with white powder everywhere, it means the powder post beetle (frequently confused with termites) is having a fiesta. There are two remedies – stick the piece in the freezer or cover it with lighter fluid.

Ivory

Elephants are an endangered species and are being slaughtered by the thousands in Africa, mostly by poachers. In early 1987, for example, police investigating a traffic accident in central Tanzania discovered 476 elephant tusks hidden in a secret compartment of a single trailer! Elephants have been entirely killed off in some countries, and are rarely seen elsewhere except in game parks.

While many say that they believe African countries don't have the resources or determination to stop the killings, more often than not they seem to be simply groping for reasons to justify their purchases. Certainly such purchases only drive the price still higher, encouraging poachers to take even greater risks.

Quite simply, those with a conscience do not purchase ivory. There's nothing illegal about it, however. In the USA, you can import small amounts of ivory in the form of jewellery and the like, but not for commercial reasons. On the other hand it is absolutely not allowed to import ivory in any quantity or form into Australia.

If you are toying with the idea of purchasing ivory, why not first check out the readily available substitutes? One is bone and another is wart hog tusk; both age very nicely. Unfortunately, the bone is often from an elephant, which makes it just as bad.

Another substitute is plastic; it is almost indistinguishable from ivory, even to experts! The only sure way to tell the difference is to put it under a flame or, better, touch it with a lighted cigarette. Plastic will melt and bone will be scorched. Ivory, on the other hand, will not scorch but can be discoloured if the flame is left too long.

In addition, there is the beautiful green malachite jewellery from Zaïre sold throughout Central Africa. With all these alternatives, it takes a heartless creature to buy ivory.

Gold & Silver

Instead of ivory, why not buy gold? Almost all gold and silver is sold by the gram, the art work being included in the price. The art work is decent but not exceptional. Most people are more than pleased with the workmanship and the prices, which in the CFA zone are approximately US$15 to $17 (CFA 4500 to CFA 5000) a gram for gold and US$1.70 to US$5 (CFA 500 to CFA 1500) a gram for silver, depending on the quality. Prices vary little from country to country.

Quality is not a serious problem with gold. Getting cheated with the carats is fairly rare. The jewellers want you to return, and just because you don't speak French doesn't mean they won't believe you're a long-term resident. Some countries have laws which allow people to return gold if they have been cheated.

With silver quality is a major problem, and a major reason some people prefer to stick with the more expensive gold. The problem is that silver is not sterling. It tends to tarnish quickly, so that it has to be cleaned fairly regularly.

Paintings

Painting is not a native African art form. Nevertheless, in Kinshasa and Brazzaville, there are several well-established schools of art where you can pick up some fairly interesting oil paintings by young students. The country chapters give the specifics.

Beads

Beads can be found all over Central Africa. In the markets, they are sold by the string, with only one type of bead per string, while in the shops you can sometimes find ready-made necklaces with a variety of beads. Several hundred major bead styles are sold in Africa, including a variety of glass beads and shells. Prices vary considerably. Most travellers don't realise that they can sometimes make their own necklace by asking the vendor to string them on the spot. It's more interesting this way as well.

Baskets

Because of their bulkiness, baskets are not a hot item with travellers. Some of the best are found in western Cameroun.

Sandstone

Sandstone is not something you'll find in most of Central Africa. However, in Gabon there's tons of it, sometimes fairly well carved.

MARKETS

The markets in northern Central Africa are far more interesting than those the south. Some of the best are those in N'Djamena, Maroua and Yaoundé. All the same don't let this be a reason for missing some of the lesser markets. Those in small towns are often more fascinating even though they may not have anywhere near as great a variety.

Bargaining, of course, is the name of the game. Most travellers expect the initial price to be three times the 'real' price. This is usually true, but not always. With African cloth sold by the yard, for example, you can expect little or no lowering of the price. If the vendor tells you the price and you come back with an offer one-third that amount, don't be surprised if he or she becomes extremely ticked off, folds up the material and refuses to talk further. You'll feel like a real fool.

The best way to shop in the markets is to try to get a feel for prices beforehand. Ask knowledgeable locals or check out one of the hotel shops; prices in the market are typically half those in the stores.

Thieves are not a major problem in most markets in Central Africa. Still, the best way to avoid being the unlucky victim is to dress as if going horse riding – leave watches, jewellery, passports, most of your money, etc locked in your pack at the hotel, or better still, in the hotel's safety deposit box. Hide any other money on you or hold your bag firmly. Pants with lots of pockets are advantageous, especially if the pockets have zips or buttons.

WHAT TO BRING
Clothes

Travel light. For one thing, the aeroplane baggage limit is 20 kg, not two pieces of luggage as in the States. Travelling light will give you space for souvenirs, while permitting you to buy the loose-fitting African clothes. Two tips: clothes which can serve a dual purpose (eg a blouse which can be worn with both jeans and fancier outfits in the evening) will help you pack lighter. Also, bring clothes you can leave behind.

As for dress codes, in East Africa you'll see travellers in safari outfits, pith helmets and all. In Central Africa, you'll get laughed at if you show up like this. Keep things simple to avoid standing out like a sore thumb – and being easy prey for hustlers.

Central Africa is an ideal place to pick up clothes as you go. Women, for instance, can leave long dresses at home and buy the long, flowing African dresses sold everywhere and popular with foreigners. Business people, on the other hand, should expect to dress for meetings as in the west, ie jacket and tie for men.

Shorts are great for the tropics, but women should not expect to wear them anywhere in public, even in modern cities such as Kinshasa. One suggestion is to bring several wrap-around skirts to put on over your shorts as needed. While western men have the prerogative to wear shorts anywhere, this will only accentuate the differences between them and the locals.

Pants worn by women are acceptable everywhere. But in the rural areas, western women often find it easier to develop a good rapport with African women if they wear similar clothes, ie long skirts of African material.

Essentials

Medical kit See the health section.

Tampons, pads and contraceptives They're often impossible to find outside major cities.

Suntan lotion You'll use less than you think. It is frequently available but usually not the kind you want.

Extra photos Bring lots. You'll need two or three for every visa and visa extension, and one or two for a photograph permit in countries where such is required. Visa-type photos are readily obtainable everywhere if you run out.

Recommended Items

Alarm clock Hotels cannot always be relied upon for waking you up.

International Drivers' License Sometimes required to rent cars.

Credit cards American Express is the most widely accepted, followed by Diners, with Visa a distant third. Others are almost worthless. Cards are required by most rental agencies and are useful for hotels and emergencies.

Pocket purifier This is an ingenious device that purifies water on contact and works like a straw. Filters up to 50 gallons. Available at better camping stores or send US$16 to Handsome Rewards, 19465 Brennan Ave, Perris, CA 92379.

French phrasebook Don't expect to find one easily in Africa.

Books Good books in English are hard to come by.

Small mirror & flashlight Note that even in good hotels, room lighting is occasionally poor. Plastic bags and a washcloth are useful too.

Business cards Calling cards are important in Central Africa. Africans like to make friends; giving someone your card is an indication you want to keep in contact. Those on the cheap take note – they can even be useful in dealing with policemen and other officialdom.

Gifts Some businessmen pack things like solar-powered calculators and microrecorders to give as presents to colleagues.

Especially for Budget Travellers

Cassettes Africans love music from the west with a good beat. Hard-core blues and complicated jazz go over like a bad joke. You can be sure bus and taxi drivers and many other Africans with cassette players will, for a change, want to hear your music. And cassettes make great gifts to leave along the way.

Plastic rain poncho This can double as a ground mat, and it's easier to carry than an umbrella.

Camping gear Consider leaving camping gear behind. It is useful only if you'll be travelling in your own vehicle, hiking considerably, or crossing the Sahara. Except for those with vehicles, camping is not as popular as in East Africa. Who wants to lug all that equipment around when there are invariably cheap places to stay? Plus there are only a handful of camping spots in all of Central Africa.

Student ID In Zaïre, you can get substantial discounts on the river boats and on flights within the country. If you'll be crossing the Sahara, those under 26 years of age can avoid having to change 1000 dinar (US$200) at the Algerian border by bringing a student ID and a letter from the school attesting to their enrolment. Within Africa, Nigeria Airways also gives 40% student discounts. Other than this, you'll find student ID's rarely useful.

WHEN TO TRAVEL

Rain is the major factor to consider in choosing a date to travel to Central Africa because the upcountry roads, mostly dirt, become extremely muddy, making travel difficult if not impossible. Because the equator runs through the middle of Central Africa, the rain pattern in the south tends to be just the opposite of that in the north. In other words, the best time to travel in northern Central Africa tends to be the worst time to travel in southern Central Africa.

In Chad, Cameroun, Equatorial Guinea and most of the Central African Republic, the best time to travel is November to April. You should be aware, however, that in Chad and northern Cameroun, midday temperatures over 40°C (104°F) are the norm in March to May.

In Gabon and São Tomé, where it rains virtually all year round, with a slight dry spell in July and August, try to avoid the heavy rain season from January to May.

In most of Zaïre and the Congo, there's a dry spell from June to September and sometimes a very short dry spell around Christmas time, making these the best times to travel. The time to avoid is February to mid-May, the heavy rainy season everywhere except in the far north, where rain tends to fall all year round. Near Bangui (furthest point north), the dry season is November to February.

Game Parks

Another consideration for some people is whether the game parks (for viewing animals, not hunting) will be open. Those in Cameroun and the Central African Republic open around 15 February, and close around mid-June (the roads become too muddy). In the rest of Central Africa, the parks are open all year round. In Zaïre, the best viewing time for most parks, including Virunga, is from June to September.

PLANNING AN ITINERARY

There are a number of factors to consider in planning an itinerary, particularly if you have some choice of countries. Basically, there are two environments – the hot tropics which cover most of the area and the dry savannah area of northern Cameroun, the southern half of Chad, and northern Central African Republic.

Cameroun and the Central African Republic are the only two countries with both environments. Although there is desert in northern Chad, starting just north of N'Djamena, most people don't see it because of the lingering conflict with Libya. Also the great distances to be covered in getting there are, to say the least, daunting.

Things to See

While the most interesting aspect of Central Africa is its people and their cultures, there is certainly an abundance of natural beauty which rivals anything in East Africa. The following list includes some of those places most appreciated by visitors to the region. Admittedly these places are more over-run by tourists and travellers than are other parts of Central Africa, but they are, nevertheless, too good to miss. More information on these and other attractions can be found in the relevant country chapters.

Virunga Park-Ruwenzoris mountains of eastern Zaïre

Lake Kivu area of eastern Zaïre, including Kahuzi Biega gorilla sanctuary

Rumsiki and Mora area of northern Cameroun

North-eastern game parks of the Central African Republic

Western Cameroun, particularly Foumban and Bamenda

Lubumbashi area of southern Zaïre

Mt Cameroun-Limbe area

Waza park, northern Cameroun

Lake Chad

All Pygmy/rainforest areas (that of south-western Central African Republic is the most accessible from a capital city).

Getting There

FROM NEW YORK
Routes

There is no direct service from New York to anywhere in Central Africa. You have the choice of flying via Europe or West Africa. Most people prefer flying via Europe because connections are usually faster, the selection of airlines and routes is much greater, and the price is the same.

The only two airlines with direct service from New York to West Africa are Air-Afrique (tel 800-2372747) and Nigeria Airways (tel 212-9352700); they offer flights to Dakar, Monrovia, Abidjan and Lagos, where you can change for a connecting flight to any Central African capital.

Air Afrique has two flights per week from New York to Abidjan (Ivory Coast) via Dakar (Senegal). Nigeria Airways has two flights a week to Lagos (Nigeria). Both also stop once a week in Monrovia (Liberia). Air Afrique is more professionally run than Nigeria Airways, moreover, Abidjan and Dakar are far better places to change airlines than Lagos, with its high crime rate and notorious airport hassles.

Chad, São Tomé and Equatorial Guinea are unique in that there are clearly preferred routes. For Chad, the cheapest route is via Paris, connecting with one of the two weekly flights to N'Djamena on UTA or Air Afrique.

The most convenient way to get to São Tomé is flying to Lisbon and connecting with TAP Air Portugal's twice-weekly service to São Tomé. Otherwise, you'll have to make two airline changes, the second being in Libreville (Gabon), with at least one night's stopover there.

For Equatorial Guinea, the most convenient way is on Iberia (tel 718-7933300), which offers a weekly service from New York to Malabo, changing planes in Madrid. Otherwise you could fly to Casablanca and connect with Air Maroc's (tel 212-9743790)

Monday evening flight to Malabo. (That flight continues on to Libreville, Gabon.)

Fares

Regular listed fares from New York to Central African capital cities are all the same and are not cheap – US$1352 one-way economy and US$2078 return excursion (US$2183 during the high season, 15 May to 14 September). So even though Kinshasa (Zaïre), for example, is over 1000 km further south than Douala (Cameroun), the fares are the same, and it makes no difference whether you go via Europe or West Africa.

Flying within Africa is also expensive. Brazzaville/Bangui (about 1000 km), for example, is US$255 one-way (US$357 return excursion).

The airlines offer three special return fares – excursion, APEX and youth fares. The excursion fare is about 25% less than the return economy fare.

APEX fares are cheaper still, but are not available for any Central African destinations. However, there are APEX fares for flights from New York to many West African cities, including Lagos (Nigeria), which is only 700 km west of Douala. The APEX fare New York/Lagos is only US$1264 (US$1375 high season), and the return fare Lagos/Douala is US$246 (US$162 one-way) – a savings of US$568 compared to the low-season excursion fare (US$2078) to Douala.

Return fares from Lagos to other Central African cities are not much higher. Lagos/Brazzaville, for example, is US$380 excursion.

With both excursion and APEX fares, there is a compulsory minimum stay of 13 days and the return ticket must be used within 45 days. The date of return cannot be changed without a 25% penalty. (Excursion fares within Africa have slightly different conditions.)

APEX fares have two additional conditions: reservations must be made at least 30 days in advance, and stopovers are not allowed. An excursion ticket, on the other hand, can be purchased up to the last minute, and you are allowed one or more stopovers.

Travellers under 24 years of age can take advantage of the youth fare, which is US$1354 return to all capital cities in Central Africa. The big advantage is that there are less restrictions – a minimum advance purchase requirement (at least five days) and no 45-day return restriction.

Nigeria Airways does not offer a youth fare from the USA, but within Africa they offer a student fare (as does Air Afrique), eg up to 40% off from Dakar to Brazzaville – a huge saving but the flight is still not cheap. Moreover, within Africa the cut-off for eligibility is 27 years, not 24 years, but you'll have to produce a student ID.

Special Agencies

Most travellers will find that the cheapest way of getting to Central Africa is using one of the following travel agencies, all of which advertise in the *New York Times* Sunday travel section:

Maharaja Travels (tel 212-3910122 and 800-2236862) 518 5th Avenue at 44th St, New York, NY 10036.
Travelow International (tel 718-4458429 and 800-2315561) 136-75 37th Avenue, Flushing, NY 11354.
Lan-Si-Aire-Travel (tel 212-8895478) 303 5th Avenue at 31st St, New York, NY 10016.
Pan Express Travel (tel 212-7199292/2937) 25 West 39th St, Suite 705, New York, NY 10018.
Citt (tel 212-3552488) 20 East 49th St, New York, NY 10017.
Airlink Travel (tel 212-8677770) 50 East 42nd St, Suite 211, New York, NY 10017.
Discount Brokers International (tel 415-3988462) 275 Post, Union Square, San Francisco, CA 94108.
CES Travel (tel 212-6875388 and 800-5417667) offices in New York, Chicago and Washington.
Travel Sales International (tel 800-2332585 and 203-8667137).

These are New York's equivalent to the London 'bucket shops', discussed in the next section, and appear to be equally legitimate.

Maharaja, for example, has been around for many years. These companies offer special return fares to cities in Central Africa for at least one-third less than the excursion fare. Pan Express Travel, for example, offers return flights New York to Douala for US$1120, while Citt offers New York-Brazzaville for US$1400.

All flights are on regularly scheduled airlines. The restrictions are usually identical to those of APEX; the big difference is that sometimes you must return within two weeks instead of 45 days. If you want to stay longer than this or pay less than 30 days in advance, call all of them. You will find that they're not all sticklers for the rules.

Only if you must stay longer than 45 days does it pay to fly to London or Amsterdam and buy a ticket from a bucket shop or, alternatively, fly to Paris and buy a ticket there. However, with the demise of Le Point and the fall in the dollar, this has become less advantageous for Americans than in previous years.

The other advantage of buying a ticket in Europe is that an African trip can be combined with a visit to Europe. Unfortunately, some bucket shops are too understaffed to respond to mail, but you can always call. The only way to make a reservation is to pay for the ticket, which can be done by mail. Except during the Christmas holiday season, you'll be taking little risk by waiting until you get to London or Amsterdam to buy a ticket; the chances of getting a flight within a day or two are usually good. The wise will call first, however.

FROM LONDON

Full fare economy tickets to Central Africa are ridiculously high. London/Douala, for example, costs £1408 return. Excursion fares are also available for all Central African destinations, but they limit the passenger to a stay of 30 days. APEX fares are not as freely available. The excursion fare London-Douala, for example, is £936, 19 days minimum and 30 days maximum stay. Return London to Lagos is considerably less

– £972 economy, £851 excursion and £768 APEX. So unless you're purchasing a ticket through a cut-price travel agency, flying through Lagos may be cheaper.

Another anomaly is the London/Kinshasa (Zaïre) flight. It is significantly cheaper than the flight from London to Brazzaville (Congo) across the river.

Going through a travel agent is usually cheaper than buying from the airlines directly and the savings can be as much as 50%. In London (and Amsterdam), there are two distinct kinds of travel agencies. The first kind are the well-known ones like Thomas Cook which offer virtually no fare reductions unless you go on one of their all-inclusive tours.

The second group, known colloquially as bucket shops, offer rock bottom prices on European and African airlines. These travel agencies are small operators (typically three to five people) and for the most part are quite reliable. They get their name from the fact that the airlines sell them a 'bucket' of tickets at a discount, and the savings are passed on to the passenger.

Typical return fares offered by bucket shops from London to coastal Central African cities range from £420 to £540 (ie about US$750 to US$970). There's no advance purchase requirement and return dates can be changed.

Aeroflot is the cheapest – £420 return London to Brazzaville (Congo) or Bangui (Central African Republic) – but you'll have to spend at least one night in Moscow (at the airline's expense). Aeroflot also flies once a month to Douala (Cameroun) and Malabo (Equatorial Guinea).

Unless you buy your ticket through a bucket shop, Aeroflot is no cheaper than any other airlines. So if you're in Central Africa looking for a way to get back to Europe, don't expect Aeroflot to be cheap.

If you insist on flying on a European airline, it'll cost you around £50 or so more than if you take an African airline. Something else which effects the price of the ticket is the length of stay. Return tickets with a 30-day maximum return restriction (typically £400 to £440) are about £70 to £100 cheaper than those with the return portion valid up to one year (typically £470 to £540). Bucket shops also offer cheap one-way fares.

Some people think that because the tickets are so cheap, there must be something fishy going on. It's not true; the great majority of bucket shops are quite reliable. The problem is that every now and then one goes bust, giving their reputation a black eye. Shopping around for the better ones takes time but some of them are listed here.

It's important to see at least three or four agencies because they don't all deal with the same airlines. Some refuse to deal with Aeroflot, saying it's only marginally cheaper than other more direct flights. Consequently, you'll find a wide variation in prices and availability of flights to a particular destination. Warning: Tickets from bucket shops sell out much more quickly than for flights in December and January than during the rest of the year. Also, reservations cannot be made without payment.

As for youth fares, *STA Travel* (tel 01-5811022) 74 Old Brompton Rd, London SW7, offers special fares to those under 26 years of age, but the fares aren't any lower than those offered by the bucket shops.

The following bucket shops appear to be the most reliable; most of them will even respond by mail to inquiries:

Trailfinders Ltd (tel 01-6031515) 46 Earls Court Road, London W8 6EJ. You cannot find a better agency than this one. They deal with most airlines except Aeroflot. Ask for a copy of their magazine *Trailfinder*.
Euro Asean Travel Ltd (tel 01-4996615/4408) Gucci House, 27 Old Bond St, London W1X 3AA. An agency that will respond immediately and informatively by letter to inquiries, but they do not deal with Aeroflot.
The World Sports Supporters Club (tel 01-9359107) 40 James St, London W1M 5HS. Equally well-known and reliable, this agency offers return fares that are about £100 more expensive than most of the others. They are unique in that they sell tickets on flights originating in Africa.
African World Travel Services (tel 01-7347181/2/3) Radnor House, 93 Regent St, London W1R 7TG. They are agents for almost all airlines serving West

Africa from London. As an example of their fares, London-Accra return on Ghana Airways is £470, valid for one year. Like many, they also offer one-way fares.

Tourtrav Ltd (tel 01-4091868) 22 Old Quebec St, London W1. They are well-established agents for almost all airlines serving West Africa.

Hogg Robinson Ltd (tel 01-8714455) 84 Bishops Bridge Rd, London WC2. Not a bucket shop but a major travel agency, they offer equally cheap fares if you use this special telephone number.

Additional bucket shops which are well established and seem reliable are: *Afro-Asian Travel Ltd* (tel 01-4378255/6/7) Linen Hall, 162 Regent St, London W1R JTB; they are agents for most airlines serving West Africa. *Allied Air Travel* (tel 01-7346080) 90 Regent St, London W1R 5AP; the entrance is at 29 Glasgow St. *Economic Air Travel Bureau* (tel 01-3871211) 93 Judd St, London WC1H 9NE. *Super Fare Travel* (tel 01-7347927) 231 Oxford St, London W1. *Levitas Travel* (tel 01-4390880) 147 Oxford St, London W1. *AZAT Travel* (tel 01-5804632/3) 61 Charlotte St, London W1; they are agents for most airlines serving West Africa. *African Travel Systems* (tel 01-6025091/2) 6 North End Parade, London W14.

FROM PARIS

Most airlines offer excursion fares with a 30-day return restriction (compared to 45 days from the USA), plus UTA and Air Afrique offer a youth fare (ages 12 to 23) with a one-year return restriction for about 40% less than the regular economy return fare (ie about 4300 FF Paris-Douala).

The special fares offered by travel agencies in France are, in general, slightly cheaper than those offered in London. However, most of them limit you to a maximum stay of 30 days. Some agencies offer special return fares valid for a year; the typical price is about 25% higher than that with the 30-day restriction.

One company, however, is unique – *Le Point Mulhouse* (tel 01-47632258) 2, Place Wagram, 75017 Paris or, on the Left Bank, 54, Rue des Ecoles, 75005 Paris. Until Le

Point went bankrupt in 1988 they were even cheaper than the bucket shops, with flights from Marseilles to Bangui (CAR) and Ouagadougou (Burkina Faso) with the return portion valid for up to a year. Since they might start up again, the details are included.

There are two flights per month to/from Bangui and five to eight flights a month to/from Ouagadougou. Return fares to Bangui and Ouagadougou are about 3200 to 3800 FF (US$615 to US$725) and 2800 to 3100 FF (US$550 to US$600), respectively.

Connecting flights Paris-Marseilles on Air-Inter are only 170 FF (US$30) one-way. The return fare is about 340 FF (US$60) more if you travel during the high season (summer and Christmas). One-way with Le Point is about 65% of the return fares.

Le Point also has special fares to Douala (Cameroun) for about two-thirds the normal excursion fare, but this flight offers much less flexibility – the typical 30-day return restriction, with no one-way or Africa-origin options.

The problem with Le Point is that reservations must be made well in advance and only upon full payment. You cannot make reservations by phone or pay by wire, which means that travellers from North America and Australia cannot make reservations until arriving in Europe.

Still, calling can be useful to find out what's available and also the names of travel agencies in Europe which have special arrangements with Le Point for receiving payment. The wise will give alternative departure dates. There's a fee for changing departure dates, and notification of the change must be made well in advance.

Flights are frequently full a month or more in advance, especially during the summer. Reconfirmation is required in person; one day in advance of the flight is usually sufficient even though they say three days, the only problem is that Le Point sometimes cancels a flight with numerous vacant seats and/or late reconfirmations.

Other French travel agencies offering special fares are:

Nouvelles Frontières (tel 01-42732525) 74, Rue de la Federation, 75015 Paris, offers return fares to Douala (Cameroun) and Brazzaville (Congo) for about 5000 FF and 7200 FF, respectively. A four-week return limitation applies, and there are limited cancellation rights.

Jeunes Sans Frontières (tel 01-43293550) 31, Quai des Grands-Augustins, 75002 Paris, offers similar fares with the usual 30-day return restriction and limited cancellation rights.

Uniclam (tel 01-4321236) 63, Rue Monsieur-le-Prince, 75006 Paris, has unbeatable return fares to Bangui (on Le Point) and Brazzaville (on Aeroflot) – about 3500 FF and 5200 FF, respectively. The return portion is valid for up to one year. Flights during peak periods, such as Christmas time, have a surcharge of about 700 FF.

GO Voyages (tel 01-42661818) 22, Rue de l'Arcade, 75008 Paris, has fares that are not quite as attractive. They offer 20 to 25% reductions on the normal seven to 30-day excursion rates, plus return tickets valid up to a year for 25 to 50% more. Departures are from Paris, Brussels, and some from London.

OTU (tel01-43291288) 137, Boulevard St Michel, 75005 Paris, is a university tourist organisation offering special fares to students and young people.

FUAJ (01-42855540) Federation of Youth Hostels, 10, Rue Notre Dame de Lorette, 75009 Paris, offers special fares to young people as well as organised tours.

FROM BRUSSELS

Travel agents to try in Brussels include:

Uniclam (tel 02-2185562) 1, Rue de la Sablonnière, 1000 Brussels, offers the same fares as Uniclam in Paris.

Nouvelles Frontières (tel 02-5118013) 21, Rue de La Violette, 1000 Brussels, offers the same fares as Nouvelles Frontières in Paris.

Acotra (tel 02-5125540/8607) Rue de la Montagne, 38, B-1000 Brussels, offers special prices to teachers, students and recent students under 31 years of age. Central African destinations include Brazzaville and Kinshasa. The return price to Kinshasa is 44,750 FB (about US$1300). The return portion is valid for up to a year. All flights have a one-way option which costs 55 to 65% of the return fare.

FROM MUNICH

In Munich, *ARD* (tel 089-7592609/45) Konigwieserstrasse 89, 8 Munich 71, is a travel agent specialising in Africa.

FROM AUSTRALIA

There are no direct flights from Australia to Central Africa. The basic options are to fly via East Africa or Europe.

The only direct flight to continental Africa is with Qantas to Harare but at around A$2300 return from Sydney or Melbourne this is one of the most expensive options. From Perth you can fly direct to Harare for A$1850 return, but there are no cheap flights to Central Africa from Zimbabwe.

A better option is to fly to Nairobi and then pick up a return ticket to Central Africa from there. This usually involves flying to Singapore and connecting with another flight to Nairobi. PIA (Pakistan Airlines) seems to have the cheapest flights and you can pick up a return Sydney/Singapore/Karachi/ Nairobi ticket for around A$1700. A slightly cheaper alternative is to fly via Manila and connect with a PIA flight there.

If flying with PIA doesn't attract you, other carriers fly from Singapore to Nairobi but they are usually more expensive. One interesting alternative is to fly Air Mauritius from Singapore to Nairobi with a stopover in Mauritius for about A$1800 return from Melbourne or Sydney.

Internal flights in Africa are not cheap,

however, Nairobi is the one of the best places in Africa for airline tickets. Whilst Nairobi travel agents don't compare with London bucket shops, they should be able to undercut the scheduled fare and sell you a more flexible ticket.

The high cost of flying to Africa makes flying via Europe a viable alternative. A low-season ticket to Europe costs around A$1600 return and you can then buy a bucket-shop ticket to Central Africa in London or Paris.

The most important thing is to shop around. Travel agents offer different flights and prices, airlines occasionally have special deals, and it is best to get as many quotes as possible before deciding. A good place to start looking is STA (Student Travel Australia) which has offices in all Australian capital cities.

ADVENTURE TRIPS

Most of the agencies specialising in African adventure trips skip over Central Africa. *Sobek* (tel 209-7362666) Box 1089, Angels Camp, CA 95222, offers a 12-day adventure in Zaïre's Ruwenzori mountains looking for gorillas. In the UK, you might try *Ecosafaris* (tel 01-3705032) 146 Gloucester Rd, London SW7 4SZ, which has wildlife safaris to Zaïre among other places.

In Paris, your best bets are *Le Point Mulhouse* (tel 01-47632258) 2, Place Wagram, 75017, or 54, Rue des Ecoles, 75005, (tel 01-47632258); the much more expensive *Visages du Monde* (tel 01-45870404) 26, Rue Poliveau, 75005; and *Explorator* (tel 01-42666624) 16, Place de la Madeleine, 75008, which is involved in a wide assortment of adventure trips.

Elsewhere in Europe, you could try *Explorado* (tel 02-6482269) 61, Avenue Legrand, 1050 Brussels, which specialises in isolated adventure trips; and *Sliva Expeditionen* (tel 089-294336) Postfach 548, 8000 Munich 33, Germany, which conducts expeditions in various West African countries, possibly expanding to Central Africa as well.

OVERLAND EXPEDITIONS

There are numerous companies in Britain and some on the Continent which take travellers across the Sahara desert to Kenya via West and Central Africa. The trucks typically go through Niger, Nigeria or Chad, Cameroun, Central African Republic and Zaïre on route to Kenya.

These trips take four to five months and are not for everybody by a long shot. Breakdowns and border closings requiring drastic changes in itinerary are warnings that shouldn't be taken lightly. The overland vehicles are almost invariably huge trucks with seating down the sides and a capacity of 10 to 15 people. Clients are typically in their 20s, rarely over 40.

The prices are very reasonable considering the distance covered and the time involved – about £1500 to £2750 (depending on the company) including the food kitty and one-way airfare. Guerba's 21-week trip from London to Nairobi (and vice-versa), for example, costs about US$3350 including the kitty, plus airfare.

Hobo Trans-Africa runs a four to five-month trip once a year to Nairobi and Johannesburg for about £1500 including food but not airfare (about £300).

Long Haul Expeditions conducts five or six overland expeditions a year to Nairobi via West Africa; five months costs about £1050 plus airfare.

Tracks charges about £1350 plus airfare for its 15-week overland expedition from London to Nairobi.

These trips offer the opportunity at a very reasonable price to see just about every kind of environment that Africa has to offer. The disadvantage is that they involve a lot of time in a pretty slow truck. A group that I saw passing through Cameroun had just passed near Rumsiki, an area with spectacular almost knife-like mountains jutting out of the ground. There's hardly a tourist brochure on Cameroun without at least one picture of the area, yet neither the trip leader nor anyone in the group had even heard of it.

Since the quality of the guides varies

greatly, be sure that you meet your trip leader before signing up; a bad one can ruin the whole trip. What these trips offer is a cheap price and an unforgettable adventure for those with a little time to blow.

Most of the British companies offering such trips advertise in *Time Out, LAM, TNT* and in Saturday's *The Guardian*. There are about 10 or 20 small travel companies in England offering such trips; some last only a few years. In Germany, they advertise in *Abenteuer & Reisen* and *Tours*. The following are the most established and well-known.

British Companies

Guerba Expeditions (tel 0373-826611) 101 Eden Vale Rd, Westbury, Wiltshire BA13 3QG, UK
Encounter Overland (tel 01-3706845) 267 Old Brompton Rd, London SW5, UK, or c/o Adventure Centre (tel 415-6541897) 5540 College Avenue, Oakland, CA 94618
Exodus Expeditions (tel 01-8700150) All Saint's Passage, Department LM, 100 Wandsworth High St, London SW18 4LE, UK, or c/o WestCan Treks (tel 403-4390024) 17 Hayden St, Toronto, Ontario M4Y 2P2
Hobo Trans-Africa (tel 09867-3124) Wissett Place, Halesworth, Suffolk IP19 8HY, UK
Long Haul Expeditions (tel 01-4401582) 56 Bohun Grove, East Barnet, Herts, UK
Tracks (tel 01-9373028) 12 Abingdon Rd, London W8 6AF

American Companies

Himalayan Travel (tel 203-6220055) Box 481, Greenwich, CT 06836
Overseas Adventure Travel (tel 800-2210814) 6 Bigelow St, Cambridge, Mass 02139
Adventure Centre (tel 800-2278747; 800-2288747 for CA only) 5540 College Avenue, Oakland, CA 94618

European Companies

Jerrycan Expedition (tel 022-469282) Rue Sautter 23, 1205 Geneva, Switzerland
Explorer (tel 0211-379064) Huttuttenstrasse 17, 4 Dusseldorf, Germany
Travel Overland (tel 089-272760) Barerstrasse 73, Munich 78, Germany (represents Guerba and Exodus Expeditions)
Lama Expedition (tel 069-447897) Roderbergweg 106, 6000 Frankfurt, Main 60, Germany

BY FREIGHTER

From North America, there is no longer any company that offers regularly scheduled passenger-carrying freighters from anywhere in the USA to West or Central Africa. There are only vessels chartered for a particular shipment. While they might accept a passenger or two, you'd have to go down to the docks to find out about them; in other words – forget it.

From Europe, there are still a few romantics who occasionally hop a freighter. It is only for those with a few extra shekels. A typical trip from Europe, say Antwerp, takes about nine days to Senegal, 13 days to the Ivory Coast, and 17 days to Zaïre.

Of the lines serving West Africa, you cannot do better than the Swiss *Nautilus Line* (c/o Keller Shipping AG, Holbeinstrasse 68, 4002 Bale, tel 061-237940; Douala c/o Socopao, Quai de la Marine, 5; Abidjan c/o Transcap). Their freighters which are reportedly quite clean, leave from Genoa and Marseilles to Point-Noire (Congo), stopping at Dakar (Senegal), Tema (Ghana), Lagos (Nigeria) and Douala (Cameroun).

Nautilus charges about 2200 Swiss francs (about US\$1500) one-way to the Congo (about 875 SF to Dakar); the price includes meals. If you're shipping a vehicle, count on paying about 50 to 75% extra for the vehicle, depending on its length and weight.

From Antwerp, *Compagnie Maritime Zaïroise* or *Compagnie Maritime Belge*, both offer service to Zaïre, stopping in Dakar and Abidjan (Ivory Coast). From Hamburg or Rotterdam, there's *Polish Ocean Lines* (c/o Gydnia America Shipping lines Ltd, tel 01-2539561), 238 City Rd, London EC1; or c/o Pakhold-Rotterdam BV (tel 302911) Box 544, Van Weerden Poelmanweg 25-31, Rotterdam, which has a service twice a month to the Congo, with 10 stops.

From Britain, there appears to be no service to Central Africa. However, you can get as far as Nigeria. *Nigerian Shipping Lines* has a freighter once a month from Liverpool to Lagos, stopping in four West African cities along the way. The one-way cost for the owner's suite/1st class is £594/504 to Lagos, including meals. The trip takes about one week to Dakar and another week to Lagos. Contact Nigerian Shipping Lines' agent, Brown Jenkins & Co Ltd (tel 01-5911700) Dunster House, Mark Lane, London EC3.

For more information, consult the monthly *ABC Shipping Guide*, available in some libraries and from World Travel Centre (tel 0582-600111) in Dunstable, UK LU5 4HB. Or, better, contact *Carolyn's Cruises* (tel 415-8974039) 32 Garner Drive, Novato, CA 94947 or *Freighter Cruise Service* (tel 514-4810447) 5925 Monkland Avenue, Montreal, Quebec H4A. Both specialise in passenger-carrying freighter service. Freighter Cruise publishes a free newsletter thrice yearly with freighter schedules. They can tell you all about *Compagnie Maritime Belge*, for instance, which costs US$3890 to US$4980 for a 38-day return to Zaïre.

You can also get leads from the *Freighter Travel Club of America* (Box 12693, Salem, Oregon 97309). The US$16 membership dues include a question-answer service as well as a monthly magazine.

Getting Around

AIR
Confirming Reservations

Reservations must be confirmed in person before the flight. If this is not done there is no way that a seat can be reserved even if the ticket says 'OK'. It is not possible to reconfirm by telephone because all tickets must be stamped. The regulations say to reconfirm within 72 hours of the flight – that means not later than 72 hours. You can usually reconfirm up to a week in advance, sometimes more. If someone else is going to reconfirm for you, don't forget that they'll need the ticket. Flight schedules change frequently, so maybe it's just as well that tickets must be reconfirmed.

If you're put on the waiting list, don't panic. African airlines usually don't overbook, so your chances of getting on are fairly good. It's usually not how far up the waiting list you are that counts, but who gets to the check-in counter first. The standard check-in time is two hours before flight departure; get there even earlier if you're on the waiting list. The check-in line will probably resemble a rugby scrum, so be prepared.

African Airlines

African airlines have been described by readers of the *African Economic Digest* as frightening, unreliable, dangerous, unpleasant, unpredictable, uncaring, overbooked, impertinent and dirty.

Service varies greatly even with the same airline, but to be fair it can be excellent. On the other hand it can be as organised as a cattle car. There's some correlation between service and safety, but not always. The real concern is the quality of the maintenance operations. Foreign pilots operating in Africa say it varies greatly. Most of the airlines are serviced routinely in Europe; many have contracts with foreign airlines which provide the pilots and maintenance personnel. There is, then, an element of control.

So despite the horror stories you may hear, in general you need not worry about flying on African airlines. There's no reason, however, not to try taking one of the better airlines. In many instances, however, there is no choice. If an ambassador wants to get from Libreville to São Tomé, he or she will take the local airline, and so will you.

Don't be terribly surprised if, on occasion, you have to wait at the airport a half day or so (never go to the airport without a good book and several magazines), or during the flight they're doing things to keep the door from coming off, or the luggage is stuffed in the back prohibiting an emergency exit. These things happen every now and then on airlines like Air Tchad and Air Equatorial Guinea.

When you do have a choice, the list of airlines below in descending order of quality (safety and service) is intended to give you some basis for choosing:

1 *Ethiopian Airlines*, *Air Afrique*, *Air Gabon* and *Cameroun Airlines* – the order in which the readers of *African Economic Digest* in 1985 rated the African airlines serving Central Africa.
2 *Lina Congo* has the best reputation of the airlines offering primarily in-country service.
3 *Ghana Airways* and *Nigeria Airways*. Between these two, Ghana Airways (seemingly improving every day) wins hands down in terms of service. Nigeria Airways' service is good only within Nigeria. On its intra-Africa routes, Nigeria Airways has one of the worst reputations of any airline in Central and West Africa. It's the type of airline you board without knowing whether there's really a seat for you.

In terms of safety, however, Ghana Airways and Nigeria Airways seem to be on an equal footing and superior to those in category four. There have been, apparently, few or no accidents on either airline. This is no proof, however, that their maintenance operations are adequate.

4 Most other African airlines operating in Central Africa, such as *Air Tchad*, *Scibe Zaïre*, *Zaïrean*, *Equatorial International* and *Equato de Guineana de Aviación* are almost entirely local operations and are at the bottom of the barrel, but you may have no choice. Foreigners take these airlines all the time.

Air Zaïre's international flights should be avoided because repair problems and delays are frequent. It has the worst reputation of any airline with international flights in Central Africa. However, within Zaïre, don't avoid *Air Zaïre*; it may be a tad bit more reliable than the other two Zaïrian airlines mentioned above.

Changing Tickets

Tickets written by Nigeria Airways and Ghana Airways are not accepted by other airlines unless written outside Africa (ie paid for in hard currency).

Hassles at the Airport

For all too many travellers, the most harrowing experiences in Africa are at the airports. Kinshasa and Brazzaville airports have the worst reputations. Checking-in can be a nightmare. You don't have to have been in Saigon the day it fell to know what it was like getting on the last plane out. In Africa, it's like that on every flight.

It's rare that the good guy who respects the queue doesn't get on the plane, but it's just frequent enough to cause many people, Africans and foreigners, to lose their civility. There is a way out of this, however.

Find one of the enterprising young men who makes a living by getting people checked in. They rarely rip you off. If they take your baggage, they're not going to run away because they know they'll be nabbed by the police the next time they show up for work. This doesn't mean you should go have a - *pastis* (a popular drink in Central Africa) while they perform their magic. The point is

that they are there to earn an honest living – even if they give you the line that they're only being your friend.

It will only cost you a dollar or two, more when you don't have a confirmed seat, and don't be surprised if the guy behind the counter insists you show your appreciation to him as well. So don't worry about these guys; it's the taxi drivers who are much more likely to rip you off.

Airport Tax

In Cameroun, Gabon, the Congo and São Tomé, the airport tax is included in the ticket price. In Equatorial Guinea, the Central African Republic, Chad and Zaïre, the tax is levied at the airport when you're leaving. If you're not prepared, you may have to cash a US$50 bill to pay a US$10 tax.

Costs of Flying

Fares tend to be expensive in Africa because the standard excursion fare, which requires a minimum seven-day stopover, sells at about two-thirds the economy fare. This is as cheap as fares get. However, in countries with a healthy black market, it can often be cheaper to fly between cities than to travel overland as it can literally take days to cover just a few hundred km. It will, of course, only end up being cheaper if you choose an airline which will accept payment in local currency.

BUSH TAXIS *(taxis de brousse)*

There are a number of types of overland transport that could come under the title 'bush taxi'.

Car

One of the most frequently used cars, especially in Cameroun, is a Peugeot 504 station wagon. All of them are assembled in Nigeria and are quite comfortable when relatively new and not packed like sardines (more than eight including driver). Usually, all it takes to change a nightmare to a pleasant ride is to buy an extra seat. Even then, the price is usually very reasonable. Throughout the CFA zone in Central Africa, the average cost of a seat in a car bush taxi is about US$4 per 100 km.

It is not true that the waiting time is always long. For the most well-travelled route, Douala-Yaoundé, the average waiting time is five to 10 minutes. For other well-travelled routes, such as Yaoundé-Bafoussam, Douala-Bafoussam, Libreville-Lambaréné, and Malabo-Luba, the waiting time is typically no more than 20 minutes to an hour.

On the other hand, going on less travelled routes, such as Yaoundé-Ngaoundéré, could involve a half day's wait or more, especially if you arrive at the wrong time. In most cases, 6.30 to 8.30 am is the best time to catch bush taxis. If you get there late, say after 10 am in Libreville and Bangui, chances are good you won't find a ride in any direction.

As for where to locate them, they are almost always located at a bush taxi station (*gare routière*). Just remember that some of the largest cities have several, one for each major road leading out of town.

While expatriates tend to ridicule bush taxis, most have never set foot inside one. What you hear about them isn't always true. One thing for sure, however, is that they can be quite dangerous. The better the roads, the more the danger. That's because it allows the drivers to drive like maniacs, which they all do. Don't sit there like most people with your eyes shut; pay him extra to go more slowly or say you have a heart problem.

For the adventurous and those on-the-cheap, bush taxis are the only way to travel. Travellers on higher budgets should not write them off. If a well-driven route is chosen, such as Libreville-Lambaréné, chances are that the experience will produce a few good stories to tell back home and some cherished memories. (My first vehicle to Lambaréné broke down about a third of the way there, and I ended up back in Libreville at one of the passenger's homes for the night, boozing away as they all do and learning where all the hot spots were.)

If you want to charter a bush taxi car all to yourself, the price is easy to calculate if all you're doing is going from A to B and back.

Take the price of one seat and multiply it by the number of available seats; do the same for the return portion. Don't expect to pay a cent less just because you're saving him the time and hassle of looking for other passengers – time is not money in Africa.

Small buses

At many bush taxi parks, you may find no cars but only small buses (or both). Slightly less expensive, they are not necessarily less comfortable, particularly if the cars are being stuffed to the hilt. The big disadvantage is that they are always a little slower and have longer waits at the numerous police checks because of the larger number of passengers to search.

Pick-ups *(bâches)*

With wooden seats down the sides, covered pick-ups are definitely second class, but sometimes the only kind of bush taxi available. These trucks are invariably stuffed with not only people but probably a few chickens as well, and your feet may be higher than your waist from resting on a sack of millet.

The ride is guaranteed to be unpleasant unless you and your companions adopt the African attitude, in which case each time your head hits the roof as the truck descends into yet another big pothole, a roar of laughter will ring forth instead of a cry of sympathy. There's nothing like African humour to change an otherwise miserable trip into a tolerable, even funny experience.

Trucks

You'll find yourself taking trucks a lot more in Central Africa than in West Africa. While not falling under the general title of bush taxi, they are frequently the only mode of transportation available, such as in Chad, many parts of eastern Zaïre and northern Congo – wherever the bitumen ends. Drivers almost always demand payment and the amount will be about what you'd pay for a bush taxi. The chapters on the individual countries give the details.

The chances of getting stuck in the mud

on a jungle road are excellent but then that's what travelling overland in Central Africa is all about.

BUS

Bush taxis are usually preferred to buses because the latter are usually slower. Most don't have fixed schedules, so the waiting time tends to be longer as well. The advantage of buses is that they are usually cheaper. In many instances there is no choice, buses being the only transport available.

No part of Central Africa has a well-developed bus system with fixed schedules and deluxe buses like those in some parts of West Africa. In Chad there are no buses at all. Those leaving from the bus station in Bangui almost have fixed schedules but they are hardly comfortable.

As for local buses, you'll find them in the largest cities, particularly Kinshasa and Brazzaville. Kinshasa is so large that taking the bus will save you considerable money. In Brazzaville taxis are not cheap, so again taking the bus is a good idea. In Libreville, Douala and Yaoundé, shared taxis tend to take the place of local buses. In N'Djamena, Malabo and São Tomé, plan on hoofing it.

TRAINS

Most people on the Central African cocktail circuit ridicule the African trains to the extent that you may conclude the idea is best forgotten. You're likely to find, however, that your informant has never taken one. Most of what you hear is second-hand and third-hand information. Moreover, the stories of the good rides rarely get told. In Pointe-Noire, for example, you may be told the Brazza Chou-Chou never arrives on time. Many travellers, however, are more than pleased with the service, especially if they have a bed (*couchette*).

Cameroun, Gabon, the Congo and Zaïre all have trains. Gabon's *Transgabonais*, Libreville to Franceville, is brand new with air-con and a restaurant but without *couchettes* (the train arrives in the evening). Both Cameroun's and the Congo's trains have *couchettes* with fresh bed linen. The Cameroun train usually doesn't have a restaurant but the Congo's does, only it's usually too crowded to get a seat.

The dilapidated trains in Zaïre are another matter. Robbery is a major problem on all of them. But if you want to travel overland in Zaïre, taking the train may seem like a luxury compared with going by road. Distances are so long in Zaïre and the trains so slow that you may literally be on one for four or five days. Taking a truck could be slower still and more expensive.

Following is a summary of the major trains in descending quality; the country chapters give the specifics.

1 Gabon (Libreville-Franceville) 17 hours
2 Congo (Brazzaville-Pointe Noire) 13 hours
3 Cameroun (Ngaoundéré-Yaoundé) 12 hours
(Yaoundé-Douala) 7 hours
(Douala-Kumba/Nkongsamba) 5 hours
4 Zaïre (Kinshasa-Matadi) 7 hours
(Ilebo-Kananga-Lubumbashi) 5 days
(Lubumbashi-Kamina-Kalemie) 4 days
(Lubumbashi-Kamina-Kindu) 5 days

DRIVING

The only places where there are fairly decent roads are Cameroun, Bioko Island (Equatorial Guinea), the Central African Republic between Bangui and the Camerounian and Chadian borders, Gabon between Libreville and Lambaréné, and in Zaïre between Kinshasa and Matadi, the port. Chad, for instance, has virtually no paved roads outside N'Djamena. Some dirt roads are all-weather while others are not. Those in Gabon are fairly well maintained while those in Zaïre are not.

Few travellers drive as far south as Brazzaville or Kinshasa because you cannot get from there to the Central African Republic or eastern Zaïre except by river boats (which carry vehicles), and driving south-east to Lubumbashi is tougher than crossing the Sahara.

As for travelling times, the major routes/times are given in the following list. 'One day' means seven to 10 hours driving time in a private vehicle, eight to 14 hours in a bush taxi.

Yaoundé to Douala (three hours), Bangui (three days), Maroua (2½ days), Libreville (two days, three by bush taxi), Bata (two days), Lagos (three days).
N'Djamena to Sarh (1½ to two days), Maroua (four hours), Maiduguri (six hours), Kano (two days).
Brazzaville/Kinshasa to Libreville (four to five days, longer in the rainy season), Pointe-Noire (two days, 13 hours by train), Lubumbashi (two weeks), Kisangani (by boat only – 10 to 12 days).
Bangui to Sarh (1½ days), Ngaoundéré (1½ days), Kisangani (four to five days if road is not too muddy), Goma (nine to 12 days if the road is not too muddy – a big if).
Bukavu to Goma (one day), Kigali (one day), Bujumbura (five hours), Nairobi (four days).

TAXIS
Taxis at the Airport
Taxis in Central Africa do not have meters *(compteurs)*, so bargaining is almost always required at the airport and at major hotels. Typical fares are given in the country chapters. Fares do not go up annually so be a little suspicious if the quoted price is much higher than that given in this book.

If you can't speak French, be content if you pay no more than a 25% premium. The price always includes the luggage unless you have a particularly bulky item. Also, fares invariably go up some time between 9 pm and midnight; the country chapters specify the time. Don't be surprised if the driver tells you an earlier hour.

The fare at most airports into town is fixed by law. Not all the drivers receive their training in New York – some are honest and will quote the correct fare. All the same it is wise to ask an airport official before throwing yourself to the wolves.

Taxis Downtown
Prices are usually fixed under law but sometimes negotiable in reality. The zone system operates in all cities, only it's never clear where they begin and end. The locals always know. Frequently, the quoted price will be the correct one.

Keep in mind that there are two bases for calculating taxi fares – one when you hop in a cab with other people going in the same direction, and another when you charter one to yourself, called a *déplacement* in many French-speaking countries. In Libreville, for example, your driver may tell you that the fare to the airport is two déplacements, one being CFA 1000.

From the hotels, the rate is always the déplacement rate, moreover, there's usually a 50 to 100% premium on top of that to cover their waiting time. When you hail a cab on the streets downtown, you'll almost certainly be quoted the déplacement rate; drivers usually do with foreigners. You'll have to know the shared rate and going in a fairly popular direction before you'll ever get the driver to accept the shared rate.

If there are already others in the car and you know the shared rate, the best tactic is usually to say nothing. The driver will assume you reside there and accept your CFA 100, or whatever the shared rate is.

As for the ease of finding taxis, in N'Djamena, Malabo and São Tomé, it's like looking for shooting stars. In Yaoundé, Douala, Libreville, Kinshasa and Brazzaville, they're plentiful except after dark. In some cities there are *taxi gares* where taxis wait for people wanting a charter, and/or there will be certain streets which are heavily travelled by taxis. Stand a block away, and you may lose your diplomatic cool.

The major hotel in town is invariably a place to pick up a cab. The problem is that it may take an exhaustive walk to get there. All too many visitors to Africa are so intimidated by Africans or the language barrier that they don't make use of people willing at every step of the way to make your stay much more pleasant – at a cost of less than the price of a doughnut. And you don't have to speak French to say 'taxi' to a young kid – he'll usually get the message.

CAR RENTAL

There are car rental agencies in every capital city except Malabo and São Tomé. All you have to do is go to the city's major hotel to find one. There is little difference in price between car rental agencies except in large cities where you're likely to find a number of small operators.

If the small operators charge less, it's usually because the vehicles are older and sometimes not well maintained. While you can sometimes get a good deal, the problem is that you can never be sure about the car's condition. If you can't afford to get stuck in the middle of nowhere with a broken-down vehicle, stick with Hertz, Avis and Eurocar.

As in Europe and the USA, you will usually need to have a credit card to guarantee payment, or put down a sizeable deposit. Nowhere in Central Africa may you take a rental car across a border or leave it in another city.

While Hertz, Eurocar and Avis are not the only car rental agencies, they are all well represented in Central Africa.

Hertz Bangui, Brazzaville, Douala, Garoua, Kinshasa, Libreville, Pointe-Noire, Port-Gentil, Yaoundé.
Avis Brazzaville, Douala, Franceville, Kinshasa, Libreville, Lubumbashi, Port-Gentil.
Eurocar Brazzaville, Douala, Kinshasa, Libreville, Pointe-Noire, Port-Gentil.

Before renting a car, consider whether it might not be better to hire a taxi on a daily basis. First, if a rental car breaks down, it's your problem instead of the taxi driver's. Second, the chances of finding a remote spot or the African nightclub that you're looking for may be slim, especially if you don't speak French. More important, if you get a friendly driver, chances are he'll show you some things you'd never otherwise see.

For those on a limited budget, the major consideration will be cost. If you add all the costs up, the price of renting a car will easily be double that of an all-day taxi. Moreover, in virtually every city you'll be required to take a driver with a rental car if you go into the countryside – another CFA 4000 or so a day.

One problem with hiring a taxi is that it is more likely to break down than a rental car. More than one weekend trip has been ruined when the taxi broke down miles out of the capital city and couldn't be quickly repaired. Naturally in such a situation there is no refund. The lesson is to inspect the car beforehand; if there is a lot of rattling, choose another.

Another problem with hiring taxis by the day is that many taxi drivers have never done it before and may not understand the terms. Negotiate a price and agree to pay the petrol bill separately, otherwise you'll be asking for trouble. He'll reduce his speed to a slow trot and complain incessantly every time you take even the most minor detour. His attitude will ruin your trip, no joke.

Getting the driver to agree to a fixed rate plus petrol takes the guesswork out of his calculations. A change in itinerary won't matter to him because he's not paying for the petrol. Still, it's not always easy to negotiate because many taxi drivers do not speak English or French very well. The solution is to go to the nearest major hotel and explain to the doorman what you want and then have him explain it to the driver. Once this is settled, the only other problem is calculating the petrol usage. If the petrol meter is not working, there is bound to be an argument at the end of the day. Get another driver!

Cameroun

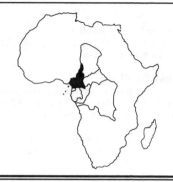

Twenty years ago, eight countries in West and Central Africa had GNPs higher than Cameroun's. Now Cameroun is third, behind Gabon and the Congo, surpassing even the Ivory Coast. Some of this wealth comes from oil – but only some. Agriculture is the cornerstone of the economy and Cameroun is one of a handful of African countries that feeds itself. Sound economic policies are the reason. You won't find many 'show' projects here – mundane matters like education count.

Travellers are in luck. In the north, there are hobbit-like villages perched on rocky cliffs, each house like a miniature medieval fortress. Nearby is the land of the Kapsikis with its great basalt outcrops. Then visit Waza National Park, one of the best game reserves in Central Africa. If you are the blood-thirsty type you could join a hunting safari – Cameroun follows only the Central African Republic as the best place for hunting in Central Africa.

In the south-west, you could climb Mt Cameroun, the highest mountain in Central Africa outside of the Ruwenzori mountain range in eastern Zaïre. It's also easily accessible. Other possibilities include hiking in the scenic mountains around Bamenda, and relaxing at a mountain resort in Dschang, which at 1400 metres has an average temperature of 22°C, making it a sort of Camerounian Baden-Baden.

In Foumban you can see the unusual Royal Palace of the Bamoun tribe displaying the personal belongings of 18 consecutive royal dynasties dating back to the 14th century, then browse through more than 20 artisan shops.

Finally there is the beautiful coastal region around Kribi where there are long, isolated beaches of squeaky, white sand.

HISTORY

During most of the colonial period, France and Britain split up Cameroun, causing severe problems of unification when independence came. There's not even a single official language; Cameroun is unique in Africa in that both French and English play that role. This, plus the fact that ethnically Cameroun has one of Africa's least homogeneous populations, makes it all the more amazing that today, Cameroun has one of the most stable governments in Africa.

Little is known about Cameroun before 1472 when the Portuguese arrived, exclaiming 'Camarões, Camarões' in amazement at the large number of giant shrimps – hence the country's name. It is known, however, that Hanno the Carthaginian visited the region in the 6th century from his description of an active volcano – apparently Mt Cameroun – as a 'Chariot of the Gods'.

Until the mid-19th century southern Cameroun's history, like the rest of coastal Africa's, revolved around the slave trade. Northern Cameroun, by contrast, was a battle ground for control by various great empires, first the Kanem-Bornu in Chad, later the Fulani. When the Germans arrived in the late 19th century the whole of 'feudal' northern Cameroun was under the control of the Fulani empire in Sokoto (Nigeria).

Colonial Rule

In 1856 one of the chiefs of Douala signed a commercial treaty with the English, and later wrote to Queen Victoria inviting her to estab-

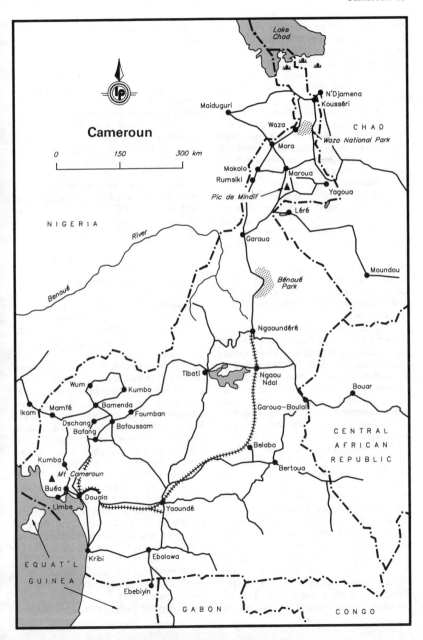

lish a protectorate over the area. A response to that letter and repeated other requests would have changed Cameroun's history. When the British consul finally arrived in 1884 with a favourable reply, he found that the Germans had beaten them to it by only five days.

The Germans were active. They built schools, wharves along the coast, a railroad from Douala towards Yaoundé, and 1000 square km of plantations around Mt Cameroun. But German rule was harsh. At one plantation the death rate of the labourers in one year was 20%.

After WW I Cameroun received new masters. The League of Nations gave the French a mandate over 80% of the territory and the British a mandate over two non-contiguous areas, one in the south-western highlands (Southern Cameroons) and one in the north (Northern Cameroons, now part of Nigeria), thereby dividing what was considered one country into three under two tutor nations. This was hardly conducive to later unification.

The British neglected the British Cameroons, focusing their attention instead on neighbouring Nigeria from where the territory was governed. Within five years they had sold the plantations back to their former German owners. By 1939 the Germans, consisting of about 300 settlers, were again solidly entrenched, only to be divested of all their belongings and repatriated following the outbreak of war.

The French, in contrast, completed the railroad to Yaoundé (using forced labour, prohibited by the mandate), developed cocoa and palm oil plantations and exported timber, causing a fivefold increase in the value of the territory's trade between the wars.

As the Cameroons were merely a 'mandate', the French private sector never established itself in Cameroon as it did in parts of West Africa like the Ivory Coast and Senegal. Today, for this reason, there aren't as many French shopkeepers in Douala and Yaoundé as in Abidjan and Dakar. This fact has been taken advantage of by Greek and Indian merchants who are relatively plentiful in the region.

Independence

During the '50s, two political parties espousing independence arose in French Cameroun – the Union des Populations du Cameroun (UPC) supported by southerners, particularly the Bamiléké and the Bassa; and the Union Camerounaise, led by a northerner and ardent Muslim, Ahmadou Ahidjo.

Ahidjo's party gained the upper hand in the new assembly, formed in the mid-'50s, which was naturally resented by the southerners. In 1960, following independence, the Bamiléké started a full scale rebellion in the west around Bafoussam. It took five battalions of French troops and a squadron of fighter bombers eight months to suppress the Bamiléké uprising (it wasn't until 1975 that you could visit the Bamiléké area without a special pass). Thousands were ruthlessly killed.

Elections were held for the assembly in the same year. The Union Camerounaise won the most seats and Ahidjo became president. British Cameroons continued to be administered as part of Nigeria.

In 1961 both parts of British Cameroons held a referendum to decide whether to join in what they thought would be a loose federation with the new country. Southern Cameroons voted in favour of federation while Northern Cameroons voted against, preferring to become part of Nigeria. For the next 11 years, French Cameroun and Southern British Cameroons existed as East Cameroun and West Cameroun, with two assemblies. In 1972 they voted to merge as a single 'republic' with one assembly.

Ahidjo remained as President and was re-elected in 1975, the year Paul Biya, a southerner and a Christian, was installed as the country's first prime minister. Ahidjo gave other southerners important positions in the government but power rested with a small clique of northern Muslim 'barons' close to him.

Ahidjo had forged a nation, but this time

without strong-arming the trade unions. The state of emergency declared during the rebellion remained in effect even though the threat of armed rebellion had long since gone.

Economically, Ahidjo acted cautiously, avoiding the massive borrowing that today is sinking the economies of so many developing nations. Instead of investing in show projects and putting most of the money in infrastructure, he stressed agriculture and education. Today the school enrolment level is 70%, one of the highest in Africa. After years of investing in agriculture, Cameroun has become a model for other African countries and is self-sufficient in food with a wide range of agricultural commodities for export. Admittedly Ahidjo did have some luck on the way. In 1978 the country began pumping oil, making major investment initiatives possible.

Then suddenly and unexpectedly in 1982 Ahidjo announced his resignation. His hand-picked successor was Paul Biya. Biya was his own man and started weeding many of the old 'barons' out of the government. Ahidjo may have had second thoughts. In 1983, he was accused of master-minding an unsuccessful coup attempt, forced into exile and sentenced to death in absentia.

In 1984 the northern barons, seeing their protected interests slipping away, recruited a group of northern army officers to stage a coup. The surprise was so great that they almost succeeded, but after two days of fighting and 70 casualties Biya was back in control.

Today

Most of the credit for Cameroun's healthy economy today must go to Ahidjo, who was, after all, in power for over 20 years. Biya is following the same conservative policies. During the '80s, real growth has averaged around 5% to 6%; average per capita incomes are now about US$1070. Oil production spurred the economy until 1986 when oil revenues dropped 55% because of low prices and reduced production.

Fortunately, Cameroun has a strong

agricultural sector to fall back on. It is the world's fifth largest producer of cocoa and the earnings from coffee are frequently even higher. One reason for the health of these two crops is that the government has significantly raised prices paid to producers.

Major projects are underway to regenerate the coffee plantations. Cotton is the north's only export crop, but low world prices have hurt production. Revenues from wood, the country's third major resource, are on a steady upward trend. One result of this superior economic record is that the government has finally been able to improve its roads. Both the southern and northern regions now have a complete asphalt road system. All that remains is to connect the two.

PEOPLE

The array of ethnic groups and languages in Cameroun is bewildering. With more than 130 ethnic groups, it may be the most artificial country in Africa. These tribes are not being overwhelmed by the 20th century. Strongly hierarchical, some are tenaciously managing to hold on to their traditions. Tribal leaders are not just called *chef* (chief). With the Bamoun, it's *sultan*; with the Bamiléké, *fon*; with the Fulani, *lamido*.

The Bamiléké, centred around Bafoussam, are the most populous group in the western highlands. The Bamoun, another well-known tribe, are in the area around nearby Foumban. Around Yaoundé you'll find mostly Ewondo, and in the north mostly Fulani and Kirdi.

Traditionally the Bamiléké women do the hard farm work, while the men tend to the animals and look after the cocoa and coffee plantations. Today the men are perhaps more famous as traders and so many have migrated to Douala that the Bamiléké constitute over a third of the city's inhabitants, more than the city's original inhabitants, the Douala. Forming a middle class of transport entrepreneurs and heavily involved in the import-export business, the Bamiléké control the city's economy.

In their homeland, you'll get a different picture – a people with a strong sense of tradition and a complex socio-political structure centred on independent chiefdoms. Unlike the Bamoun who give allegiance to a single person, the sultan, the Bamiléké have about 80 *cheferies*, each strongly independent and very hierarchical. Below the *fon* is a council of dignitaries called the *mkem* and each member has responsibility for a secret society, such as the *kamveu*, which in turn is responsible for preserving the rituals. You can see these *cheferies* in the highlands, the one in Bandjoun being the most photographed.

For more about Cameroun, read Shirley Deane's new book *Talking Drums* (John Murray Publishers). She gives some insight into village life near Yaoundé.

The north is Muslim Fulani country. Whereas the south has been in contact with the western world for over 500 years, until the 20th century the north was part of quasi-feudal Fulani kingdoms centred in Nigeria and tradition and resistance to outside influences remain strong. If you're in Cameroun at the time of Tabaski, head for Maroua. You'll see how strongly the Fulani hold to tradition. Partially for this reason, development here is going more slowly, eg far fewer children are in school.

Most northerners, however, are neither Muslim nor Fulani. These people are known collectively as Kirdi, the Fulani word for pagan. They are the tribes the Fulani drove into the inhospitable rocky areas near Nigeria. You'll see them when you visit Rumsiki, Mokolo and Mora. They are even more alienated from the rest of Cameroun than are the Fulani of the north. Life expectancy among the Kirdi is less than 30 years.

GEOGRAPHY

Forming the boundary between West and Central Africa, Cameroun is about the size of Spain, with a population approaching 10 million.

There are three major zones: the northern savannah area, the southern and eastern rain-forests, and the smaller western hill region near Nigeria that was once British Cameroons. In the west around Bafoussam and Bamenda, the rich volcanic soils have permitted much higher rural population densities than elsewhere. This is coffee and cocoa country. In the north are the major game parks, rocky escarpments including the Mandara mountains to the west of Maroua, and the broad Benoué River flowing by Garoua and eventually into the Niger River.

The south is covered with thick rain forests. Because of the underdeveloped road system below Yaoundé and Bertoua, few travellers venture there. In remote pockets, there are still small hunting bands of Pygmies and, hopefully, a few remaining gorilla families.

CLIMATE

The extremes in rainfall are astounding – from barely enough rainfall to support agriculture in the extreme north near Chad, to over 5000 mm (200 inches) in the southwest around the 4070-metre Mt Cameroun. There is no single rainfall pattern. In the north the rainy season is June through September. In the south and around Douala, light rains in March and April are followed by heavy rains from May to mid-November. There is less rainfall in Yaoundé than in Douala but the pattern is the same except that in July and August, when Douala is being virtually flooded, Yaoundé has a dry spell.

LANGUAGE

Both French and English are the official languages. French is by far the more widely spoken of the two. You won't hear much English, for example, in Douala or Yaoundé. Most government personnel, however, understand both. English is the principal non-African language in only one-tenth of the country – the far western area bordering Nigeria, including the towns of Bamenda, Mamfé and Limbe.

Cameroun has more African languages than just about any country in Africa. Four of the major ones are Bamiléké (spoken in the western highlands and around Douala), Ewondo (around Yaoundé), and Fulfulde and Arabic (in the north). Some basic greetings in Ewondo are:

Good morning	bem-bay keh-REE
Good evening	bem-bay ahn-gouh-GEE
How are you?	oun-VUOY
Thank you	ah-boun-ghan
Goodbye	oh-kell-em-VUOY

VISAS

Everyone must get a visa. To get one, you must produce a roundtrip ticket or a letter from your bank showing not only sufficient funds to buy a ticket, but a little extra to tide you over. Beware: police at Douala airport are extremely strict in enforcing all rules. If you arrive there without a visa, you'll be forced to leave on one of the next flights out unless you can prove that you're residing in a country without a Camerounian embassy. They enforce this rigorously. Chances are good they'll also ask to see your roundtrip ticket or bank statement even if you have a visa. You need no visa if you're merely transiting within 24 hours to another flight and you have a ticket and confirmed reservation.

As there is no Camerounian embassy in Chad, the border post next to N'Djamena issues Camerounian visas; at all other border posts you will be denied entry if you don't have a visa. Once you're in the country, you can obtain a visa extension at any of the regional capitals, usually without problem (except in Yaoundé where the hassles are much greater).

In Yaoundé you can obtain visas to all six neighbouring countries. The Gabon Embassy will probably insist on sending a cable to Libreville; you'll have to bear the cost, up to CFA 6000 for a telex! The process can easily take five days or more. For the other five countries it should not take more than 24 hours. Zaïre visas take about four days to process.

The French Embassy issues visas to Togo and Burkina Faso, and the British Embassy issues visas to Kenya, Ghana and Sierra Leone. France and Britain have diplomatic missions in both Yaoundé and Douala.

Diplomatic Missions Abroad

Addis Ababa, Algiers, Bangui, Bonn, Brazzaville, Brussels, Cairo, Calabar, Kinshasa, Lagos, Libreville, London, Madrid, Monrovia, New York, Ottawa, Paris, Rio de Janeiro, Rome, Washington.

MONEY

US$1 = CFA 296
£1 = CFA 570

The unit of currency is the Central African CFA. West African CFA can easily be exchanged at the banks for Central African CFA. The major hotels in Yaoundé and Douala will accept them too, but hotels elsewhere usually will not unless pressed. If you have money wired to a local bank, you must get permission from Customs to receive it in foreign currency, otherwise, you'll have to take it in CFA.

Banking hours: weekdays approximately 8.30 to 11.45 am and 2.45 to 4.15 pm; closed weekends.

GENERAL INFORMATION
Health

A yellow fever vaccination is required. For emergencies, Clinique St Marthe (tel 223109) is the best in Yaoundé. You'll find several good pharmacies on Ave Kennedy in Yaoundé. The best, however, is Chuss (tel 230659/221751).

In Douala, the best clinic is Polyclinique de Douala (tel 421840). The best pharmacies are Pharmacie du Centre (tel 421430) at 38 Blvd de la Liberté and Pharmacie des Portiques (tel 421444) on Blvd Ahidjo.

Security

Security is not a major concern except in Douala where a lot of foreigners, including sailors, pass through and get robbed. If you walk around Douala at night, the risk of getting your purse or wallet stolen by pickpockets is quite high.

Police officers can be a pain in the neck in Cameroun, bothering you with rules and red tape. They throw up road blocks everywhere, even inside cities. If you don't have your passport, don't be surprised if they detain you while someone else goes to fetch it. It is a good idea to carry your passport (or at least photocopies of the first few pages) everywhere.

Business Hours

Business and government: weekdays 8 am to 12 noon and 2.30 to 5.30 pm; Saturday 8 am to 1 pm.

Public Holidays

1 January, 11 February, Good Friday, 1 May, End of Ramadan (6 May 1989, 25 April 1990), 20 May (National Day), Ascension Thursday, Tabaski (14 July 1989, 3 July 1990), 15 August, Mohammed's Birthday, 10 December, 25 December. The country's major holiday is National Day. In the north, especially Maroua, Tabaski is the major celebration.

Photography

Taking photographs in Cameroun is a problem. Photo permits are not required except for specialised photography. However, policemen frequently insist on seeing an authorisation or a slip of paper saying you don't need one; some will undoubtedly be looking for bribes. You risk little in rural areas out of sight of the police, but in cities and towns you risk getting your camera confiscated. People have been detained just for enquiring, which is why local expatriates suggest that you ignore the official rules, and simply be very aware of who is watching when you take a photo.

The safest route is going to the Ministry of Information & Culture in one of the regional capitals (valid for that region only) or in Yaoundé (valid for the entire country) and getting the slip of paper saying you don't need a permit. Alternatively, get a Cameroun

photography regulation sheet from them or a tourist office so that the police, who rarely know the rules, can't bully you around.

Even with a permit, you may not photograph government buildings or personnel (ie anywhere the flag flies), airports, harbours, bridges, railway stations, industrial installations, ethnic ceremonies or 'anything embarrassing to the government'. The problem is that the government interprets these restrictions so broadly that it's difficult not to break the law.

Time, Post, Phone & Telex

When it's noon in Cameroun, it's 11 am in London and 6 am in New York (7 am during daylight savings time). If you're getting mail sent to you via poste restante, you'll receive it quicker in Douala than in Yaoundé. In Douala, the post office has about 15 booths for placing international calls, and one for calls within Cameroun!

If your hotel doesn't have a phone, try Hôtel Arcade near the Douala post office. They charge CFA 700 for each successful in-country call. Getting a Douala-Yaoundé line during working hours is very difficult. The international telex centre in Yaoundé is very efficient; most major hotels have telex facilities as well.

GETTING THERE
Air

There are no international flights to Yaoundé, only to Douala, with one exception – Libreville/Yaoundé. From Europe, there are direct flights to Douala from Brussels, Frankfurt, London, Marseilles, Paris and Rome. The cheapest flights from London are on Aeroflot with a ticket purchased from a bucket shop. The cheapest alternative used to be Le Point's flight to Bangui (CAR).

From the USA, you could take Air Afrique or Nigeria Airways from New York and transfer in Dakar, Abidjan or Lagos. From East Africa, you can fly direct from Addis Ababa (Ethiopia) on Ethiopian Airlines. Cameroun Airlines flies from Douala to Malabo (Equatorial Guinea) four times a week. Between Douala and Yaoundé, there are flights about every 90 minutes until 10 pm, so don't worry if you miss a connection to Yaoundé.

As for Cameroun Airlines, you have to wonder whether they couldn't have come up with a better symbol than something that looks like a paper aeroplane. Regardless, its international service is good; by reputation it's one of the four or five best airlines in black Africa.

Car

Motorists must have a carnet de passage. The route from Lagos (Nigeria) to Douala (1250 km) or Kano (Nigeria) to Douala (1360 km) via the southern border crossing at Ekok (Cameroun) both take two or three days. The road is paved the entire distance within Nigeria. In Cameroun, the scenic (jungles

HANDS IDLE FOR ONCE!

Traffic Cop
Douala, CAMEROUN

and mountains) Mamfé-Kumba-Douala road is not paved between Mamfé and Kumba (181 km). However, it is in much better condition than the 205 km Mamfé-Bamenda road, which becomes impassable during the rainy season, from June to September.

The drive south from N'Djamena (Chad) to Ngaoundéré takes 1 1/2 days on an asphalt road. From there it's another 1 1/2 or two days to Yaoundé or Douala via Bertoua.

Yaoundé to Bangui (CAR) is 1200 km and takes about 2 1/2 days. Half the distance is paved; the remainder is an all-weather road.

Yaoundé to Libreville (Gabon) via Oyem is also 1200 km and takes the same amount of time. The road to Gabon is the same as that to Equatorial Guinea. The road splits at Ambam, a few km north of the border. Either way you must cross a river just below Ambam by ferry. Beware – it breaks down frequently. In Gabon, be prepared for some very muddy roads from October until May; bulldozers keep them passable year round.

Bush Taxi

Trucks make the trip from Douala to Maroua/N'Djamena in three days. Bush taxis take longer – up to three days just for the N'Djamena-Ngaoundéré section. Most travellers take the train for the Ngaoundéré-Yaoundé stretch. You'll find a bridge crossing over to N'Djamena; the Chad border closes punctually at 5.30 pm.

Going to or coming from Nigeria, you'll find many taxis on the Maroua-Maiduguri stretch in the north. Once inside Nigeria, taxis fill up in minutes and go like the bomb was about to drop. The most popular crossing, however, is in the south via Ikom and Mamfé. The road between Mamfé and the border is so bad in the rainy season that drivers sometimes demand more money than usual.

If you're headed to the Central African Republic, you can take the train from Yaoundé to Belabo and catch a bush taxi from there to the border, or take an uncomfortable 18-hour bus from Yaoundé to the border (Garoua-Boulai). Once you're in the CAR, roads are good and connections are fast.

Those headed to Gabon or mainland Equatorial Guinea should go to the Gare Routière du Centre behind the post office in Yaoundé and get a taxi to Ebolowa and on to Ambam near the border. There, the road splits, the left route going to Libreville via Oyem (Gabon) and the right route to Bata (Equatorial Guinea). Each road crosses the river just south of Ambam at a different point. If the ferry is not operating, there are always canoes (*pirogues*). The price of a pirogue is CFA 500 but don't be surprised if they ask CFA 2500. From the other side of the river, the best, if not the only way to get to first major town in Equatorial Guinea, Ebebiyin, is by truck.

Boat

Douala is the best port in Central Africa for catching freighters (expensive!) and other water-bound transport to Europe. For a berth, contact the maritime travel agency Camatrans (Douala tel 424750) or Cameroun Shipping Lines in Douala (tel 420038/428103, telex 5615) 18 Rue Joffre, and Paris (tel 1-42935070, telex 640016) 38, Rue de la Liège, 75008 Paris, or their European agent, Unimar Seatransport GmbH (tel 30060, telex 2162116) Box 106226, D 2000 Hamburg 1.

GETTING AROUND
Air

Cameroun Airlines offers good service from Douala and Yaoundé to all major towns, including daily flights to Maroua and Garoua. To charter a plane, call Air Affaires Afrique (Yaoundé tel 231423) or Avia Service (Douala tel 423892).

Bush Taxi

Bush taxis cost CFA 10 to CFA 15 a km depending on the quality of transport. Douala-Bamenda is 390 km and costs about CFA 5000 in a Peugeot 504, plus 10% extra for any luggage. Especially in the north, they leave early in the morning. Between Douala and Yaoundé you can get them any time of the day, and there's little waiting time. The trip only takes 2½ hours.

Car

The road system in Cameroun is good and improving. Most African countries have given high priority to road building, reasoning that the lack of good roads impedes development. In Cameroun, the powerful railroad lobby won the day, arguing that railroads were more efficient than vehicles. While neighbouring Nigeria spent enormous sums developing the best road system in Africa outside South Africa, Cameroun put paving roads on the back burner.

When Cameroun started pumping oil, however, the economics began to change. In the mid-1980s, the most critical link in the country, Douala-Yaoundé, was finally paved. Today, it's the Nigerians who are looking for work in Cameroun, not vice versa. You can't buy development with roads.

Having wisely invested its limited resources, Cameroun can now afford to develop a topnotch road system. The major arteries in the north and the south-west are paved and you can now drive from both Yaoundé and Douala to western Cameroun on excellent roads. All that remains is the 800-km road between Yaoundé and Ngaoundéré. Until then, driving from Yaoundé and Douala to the northern part of the country will remain time-consuming – two days from Yaoundé to Maroua. Most traffic between Douala and the north passes through Yaoundé, not Bafoussam. You can also put your vehicle on the Yaoundé-Ngaoundéré train for about CFA 70,000.

Car Rental

Hertz has representatives in Douala, Yaoundé and Garoua, while Avis and Eurocar are represented only in Douala. In Douala and Yaoundé, there are also a number of local rental agencies.

Train

If you're travelling to the north, consider taking the *Transcamerounais*. It's cheap, quicker than driving or taking a bush taxi, and fairly decent. Just don't expect air-con or a dining car. Two trains leave daily in each direction. If you take the day train, you cannot be sure there'll be a 1st-class car. On the night train, you may be offered a choice between a two-berth and a four-berth cabin. The former is only slightly more expensive. Pillows, blankets and linen are provided.

Reservations for a berth (*couchette*) on the night train can only be made on the day of departure; reservations for the day train are not necessary. You can buy drinks and snacks from vendors. Second class is crowded and uncomfortable; get to the train station two hours in advance to be guaranteed a seat.

The Douala-Yaoundé stretch takes seven hours compared to 2½ hours by bush taxi, so most people take only the Yaoundé-Ngaoundéré section, which costs CFA 11,135 for 1st class (CFA 1500 extra for a couchette) and CFA 7000 for 2nd class. (Douala-Yaoundé costs almost exactly half this.) Trains leave punctually, but they usually arrive an hour or two late. Trains depart Yaoundé (tel 224433/230455) at 7.45 am (arriving 6.30 pm) and 7.30 pm (arriving 8.30 am). They depart Ngaoundéré at 7 am (arriving 6 pm) and 7.20 pm (arriving 6.45 am).

If you're headed to Yaoundé from the Central African Republic, you can save time by heading north-west from the border crossing (Garoua-Boulai) and catching the train at Ngaoun Ndal (250 km by good road) instead of heading south-west from the border to catch it at Belabo (350 km by bad road). Most Africans catch it at Belabo because the train fare is about 40% less. If you're staying overnight in Bouar (CAR), you'll have to leave at the crack of dawn to catch the night train which passes Ngaoun Ndal around 9 pm or so.

YAOUNDE

Set in hills some 750 metres above the sea, Yaoundé was a clear choice over Douala for the 'honour' of colonial capital. Its cooler, almost European climate was more amenable to the newly transplanted Parisian overlords.

Many people feel that Yaoundé isn't active enough. This may well be true, but then Yaoundé is smaller than Douala and, even with over half a million inhabitants, it still can't seem to shake off its small town reputation.

First-timers to Yaoundé are usually a little baffled by the street pattern, or lack thereof. Sprawled over undulating hills, the city has only a few streets that aren't snake-like, all in the compact downtown section which can be covered on foot. The tall Concorde building, Ave Kennedy and the market are useful landmarks.

Ave Kennedy is a major hub of activity. At one end is the Artisanat, the large tent-like structure where you'll find all sorts of Camerounian handicrafts. The high point for many French expatriates is Thursday night with the arrival of fresh seafood from France at Le Cintra, a stone's throw from the Artisanat. One of Yaoundé's oldest restaurants, Le Cintra's sidewalk tables are a fashionable place to have a drink and watch the crowds. Another Yaoundé institution is the deluxe Mt-Fébé Sofitel set on a hill over 1000 metres high on the outskirts of town, with a golf course below. The climate there is delightfully cooler and the view of the city is unbeatable.

Two of the liveliest African sections are Messa and Briqueterie, sometimes known as *le quartier*; both are several km north-west of the centre, about half a km beyond the hospital. It is an area full of dirt cheap lodgings, good street food and small bars with names such as 'Chasse-cafard' and 'La Parole de Dieu'. The unlicensed 'chicken houses' in le quartier serve the best grilled chicken this side of Abidjan (Ivory Coast).

Information

Banks Chase Manhattan, Banque de Paris et des Pays-Bas, BIAO, Charter Bank, Banque pour le Commerce et l'Industrie (BICICI).

The last one, in the heart of town near the intersection of Kennedy and Ahmadou-Ahidjo, charges no commission when changing travellers' cheques.

Embassies Addresses of some of the embassies include:

Canada
    (tel 220203) Immeuble N Stamatides, Ave de l'Indépendance near Chase bank, BP 572
France
    (tel 221822) Plateau Atemengué, BP 1071
West Germany
    (tel 230056) Ave Horace-Mallet, BP 1160
Netherlands
    (tel 220544) Immeuble Le Concorde, Ave 27 Août, BP 310
Switzerland
    (tel 222896) Route du Mt-Fébé, BP 1169
UK
    (tel 220545/220796) Ave Churchill near Hôtel Indépendance, BP 547
USA
    (tel 234014/221794, telex 8223) Rue de Nachtigal, BP 817

Other embassies include: Algeria, Belgium, Benin, Brazil, CAR, Chad, Congo, Egypt, Equatorial Guinea, Gabon, Greece, Italy, Ivory Coast, Liberia, Morocco, Niger, Nigeria, Senegal, Spain, and Zaïre.

The Belgian, CAR, Congolese, Gabonese, Italian, Spanish and Zaïrese embassies are all in Bastos, a chic area named after the cigarette factory between the centre of town and the Mt-Fébé Hôtel, while the Ivory Coast Embassy is in Nlongkak right before Bastos. The Nigerian Embassy is downtown near the Renault and Mercedes dealers on a side street leading off Ave Vogt (near Cameroons Airlines).

Bookstores & Supermarkets The two best bookstores are *Librairie Moderne* on Ave Kennedy and *Librairie Integrée* on Ave Foch a block or so from the Capitole cinema. For books in English, go to *Ebibi Books*.

Yaoundé has four large supermarkets; two of them are *Score* at the end of Ave Kennedy and *Prisunic T Bella* on Ave de

l'Indépendance, two blocks from the US Embassy.

Travel Agencies The best are Intervoyages (tel 231045) near the Hôtel de Ville and Transcap-Voyages (tel 231296), BP 153. Among other things, they arrange package tours to Waza Park and nearby Rumsiki. Cameroun Airlines does the same. Camvoyages is not recommended.

Musée d'Art Camerounais

Don't miss this museum at the Benedictine Monastery, a five-minute walk from the Sofitel. The quality of the art is somewhat higher than in most African museums. Despite its small size, the museum has one of the best collections of Camerounian art in the world. The pieces have been collected by the monks over the years; most of the items are Bamoun and Tikar from the north-west. It's open Thursdays, Saturdays and Sundays from 3 to 6 pm. If the door is shut, just ring the bell and wait; the monks will come eventually.

Palais des Congres & Palais Présidentiel

On the road between town and the Mt-Fébé Sofitel is the modern and impressive Palais des Congres, built by the Chinese. The Presidential Palace is visible in the distance. The latter is modern and impressive, with peacocks walking around, but strictly off-limits as are all the roads around it. Paratroopers will nab you if you so much as try to set a foot in that direction.

Mass in N'Djong Melen

If you're in Yaoundé on a Sunday morning, don't miss the open-air mass at the Catholic Church in N'Djong Melen, several km west of the city centre on the other side of the lake from the Hôtel des Députés and just north of the university. Take the No 2 bus to the Place de Melen. The mass, which is recited in Ewonde, takes place every Sunday from 9.30 am to noon and is a fantastic blend of African and western culture, with African music,

drums, dancing and a women's chorus –
highly recommended.

Places to Stay – bottom end

The *Mission Presbyterienne* in Djongola
(bus No 4), sometimes called the Mission
Protestante, welcomes travellers and charges
CFA 2000 for a bed (four to a room) and
about CFA 500 for camping. You can't beat
it, but it's fairly far from the centre of town.
Hôtel des Nations is also cheap and near the
Mission.

As for other hotels, the best for the price,
about CFA 4500 for a clean room, may be the
small *Hôtel Idéal* (tel 220304) just north of
downtown at Carrefour Nlongkak on the
road to the Sofitel. *Hôtel Aurore* (tel
230806), about two km from the city centre
at the intersection of Briqueterie and Sebas-
tian (the road to the Grande Mosquée in
Briqueterie), is a bigger, well-known hotel
with a sterile atmosphere. It costs about CFA
4400/5700 for singles/doubles.

If you care about quality, check out *Hôtel
de l'Unité* (tel 222022), probably the best in
its price range, with singles/doubles for CFA
5500/6000. A Peace Corps favourite, it's at
the Place de l'Indépendance, several blocks
from the US Embassy, within easy walking
distance of downtown. If you don't care
about quality, try *Hôtel de la Paix*, 400
metres behind the central post office on the
road to the airport (Blvd de l'Ocam). At CFA
3300 a room, it is likely to be full. If you are
particularly set on this one, it might pay to
book ahead (tel 233273).

Places to Stay – middle

Hôtel les Boukarous (tel 223746, cards AE,
D) is downtown two blocks from the US Embassy, with 20 rooms (CFA 8200) and one of
Yaoundé's most popular restaurants. It
stands head and shoulders above other
medium-priced hotels despite its occasional
bedbugs. There's no air-con, but in Yaoundé
many people don't want it.

If the Boukarous is full, as is often the
case, try *Hôtel Indépendance* (tel 222924),
near the city centre. It is a pretty uninspiring

place which is very much over-priced at CFA
13,000 for a room with air-con. The somewhat dingy *Hôtel Central* (tel 233611), near
the central post office, has similar quality
rooms with balconies for the same price.

Moving down the ladder, you can get
decent singles/doubles without air-con for
about CFA 8000/9000 at the *Terminus* (tel
230011, telex 8282), 300 metres from the
post office. They have a lounge room with a
TV. Nearby, half a km behind the post office
you'll find the *Grand Hôtel* (tel 230477),
with rooms for CFA 9000 (CFA 12,500 with
air-con) and, across the street, the rundown
Impérial (tel 223566), a rip-off at CFA
11,000/13,500.

If you'd rather be in the African section
of town, try the *Hôtel le Progrès* (tel 224906)
facing Marché de Mokola. With 60 clean
rooms for about CFA 7700 (CFA 1500 more
with air-con), it has a decent reputation.

Places to Stay – top end

Yaoundé has only two topnotch hotels. The
renowned *Mt-Fébé Sofitel*, perched on a hill
on the outskirts of town and overlooking a
golf course and the city, is the best. The
cooler altitude is worth the price difference.
Hôtel des Députés is only a small notch
down. About two km from the heart of town,
it's such good value that getting a room is
nigh impossible without a reservation.

Mt-Fébé Sofitel (tel 234002/224224, telex 8263), CFA
24,000/30,000 for mountain view/town view rooms,
pool, tennis, golf course, TV/video, nightclub, cards
AE, D, V, CB.
Hôtel des Députés (tel 231363/230155, telex 8341),
CFA 17,000/19,500 for singles/doubles, small pool,
two tennis courts, nightclub, cards AE, D, V, CB.

Places to Eat

Cheap Eats The cheapest places to eat are
naturally in the popular African sections,
such as Briqueterie and Messa, particularly
around the markets. Look around for
Yaoundé's speciality – Ntomba Nam, with a
peanut based *pâté* and meat.

Downtown, *L'Ane Rouge*, next to the
Artisanat, serves excellent brochettes for

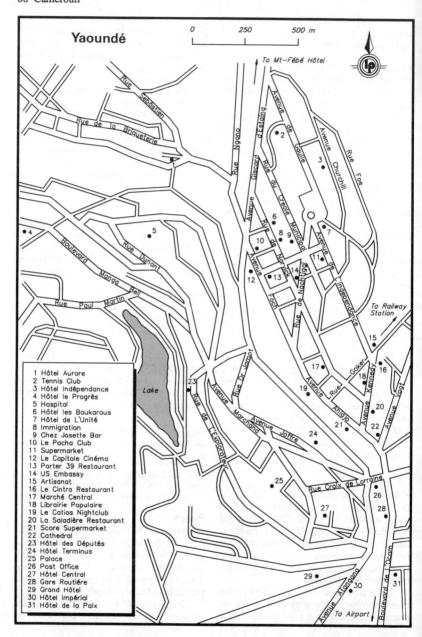

1 Hôtel Aurore
2 Tennis Club
3 Hôtel Indépendance
4 Hôtel le Progrès
5 Hospital
6 Hôtel les Boukarous
7 Hôtel de L'Unité
8 Immigration
9 Chez Josette Bar
10 Le Pacha Club
11 Supermarket
12 Le Capitole Cinéma
13 Porter 39 Restaurant
14 US Embassy
15 Artisanat
16 Le Cintra Restaurant
17 Marché Central
18 Librairie Populaire
19 Le Catios Nightclub
20 La Saladière Restaurant
21 Score Supermarket
22 Cathedral
23 Hôtel des Députés
24 Hôtel Terminus
25 Palace
26 Post Office
27 Hôtel Central
28 Gare Routière
29 Grand Hôtel
30 Hôtel Impérial
31 Hôtel de la Paix

Top: Typical Houses, Kapsiki Area, Northern Cameroun (AN)
Left: The Crab Scorcerer, Rumsiki, Cameroun (AN)
Right: Men's meeting place, Rumsiki, Cameroun (AN)

Top: Royal Palace of the Bamoun People, Foumban, Cameroun (WR)
Bottom: Typical housing compound, Northern Cameroun (AN)

CFA 100 – a favourite eating and drinking place for Peace Corps volunteers. Near the French Embassy, *L' Oasis* is a licensed chicken house ('une maison de poulet braisé') which serves braised chicken and fish, typically for about CFA 2500 a plate.

There are many other unlicensed and unmarked ones, with only a number of cars outside to suggest that a place is a restaurant, not just a home. Your taxi driver should know one. Downtown on Ave Foch across from Cinéma le Capitole and on the second floor, you'll find *Marseillaise*, where you can get a full meal and drink for less than CFA 2000. The menu is extensive and includes Chinese food.

Lebanese The popular *Hôtel les Boukarous*, open every day and highly recommended, is primarily a Lebanese restaurant, but serves pizza and a variety of Italian and French selections. The ambience is special – tables set in several *boukarous* (African huts) which encircle a charming tropical garden complete with a fish pond. The food is good, especially the Lebanese bread which must be the best in Central Africa. Prices are moderate – CFA 3500 for most main courses.

Various Cuisines The new *Le Romain*, which serves excellent Tunisian and Continental meals, is highly recommended, as is *Porter 39*. The latter is excellent value for money, with good food (including hamburgers) and service. It's open all day and is two blocks behind the US Embassy on Ave Foch. *Mimosa Pâtisserie* across the street is a good place to have pastries and coffee.

La Saladière, on Ave Kennedy, is another good lunch spot and they have interesting salads for CFA 1700 to CFA 2200. Pizza, croque-monsieur and ice cream are also among their specialities.

Asian *Aux Baguettes d'Or* (tel 223929), closed Monday, offers good Vietnamese food and service at reasonable prices in a pleasant setting. Heading towards the airport, it is just beyond the Dauphin on the right, next to the Total station. Others prefer the slightly more expensive *La Paillote*, across from Apartement du Soleil. The service and the food are excellent. For Chinese cuisine, try the new reasonably priced *Le Grand Muraille* next to the German Embassy.

French *Le Dauphin* (tel 221254), on the road to the airport, is the most expensive and elegant restaurant in town, with excellent service and superlative cuisine. *Le Cintra* (tel 223388), downtown on Ave Kennedy and closed on Mondays, is a French style bistro run by a friendly Corsican. Fresh seafood flown from France arrives on Thursdays; reservations are needed. The *Mt-Fébé Sofitel* has an excellent four-star dining room, and is also noted for its CFA 6500 Sunday luncheon smorgasbord.

Entertainment & Sports

Bars The three best places for a drink and watching people are all in the same area – Ave Kennedy. *Le Cintra* and *La Saladière* both have terraces. La Saladière has a jazz group on Tuesdays, Thursdays and Fridays starting around 7.30 pm. For a rustic atmosphere, head for *L'Ane Rouge*, across the street from Le Cintra. It is open until 10 or 11 pm. For small African bars with cheap beers, head for Messa and Briqueterie.

Nightclubs *Chez Josette* bar, one block from the US Embassy (open every night), is where it all starts in the evening, about 10 pm, peaking 11 pm and dead an hour later. After finding a partner, everybody used to head for *Club St Hilaire*, which has closed. Nowadays *Les Caveaux*, near the gare routière, gets most of the business. Drinks are CFA 3000 on weekdays, and CFA 4000 on Saturdays. Couples prefer *Sanza*, near the train station.

The Sofitel's *Les Balafons* is ultra modern and best on weekends; the cover charge is CFA 4000, which includes a drink. *Le Pacha Club*, downstairs in the Hajal Massad building on Ave Foch, one block from the

Capitole theatre, is a modern disco with a large dance floor.

Cinemas Le Capitole (tel 224977), downtown on Ave Foch, is Yaoundé's best. Shows are at 9 pm. Cinéma Abbia, two blocks away, is another.

Sports The Sofitel and Députés have pools open to outsiders for CFA 1000 or so, but on Sundays the Sofitel's is closed to outsiders after 10 am.

For tennis, there's the Sofitel (open to members and hotel guests only) and Hôtel des Députés (open to outsiders for about CFA 2500 a game). If you go by the Tennis Club of Yaoundé, near the Hôtel de Ville, or the American Club on the western side of town, you may find someone looking for a game. The latter has four lighted courts and temporary memberships available. Or check out the new sports centre in Yaoundé bearing the name of Cameroun's famous tennis star, Yannick Noah. (France claims him too because his mother was French.)

Joggers can join the Hash House Harriers; the marines at the US Embassy should be able to tell you the time and location. The most popular place for jogging is on the boulevard leading to the Sofitel. Warning: don't jog towards the nearby Presidential Palace. You could get shot. At a minimum, the police will ask for your passport. If you don't have it, you may spend the night in jail.

Down from the Sofitel is the 18-hole golf course. You'll find clubs for rent at the club house. While the course is not tournament quality because of the sand greens, it is in a beautiful setting and is undoubtedly the best course in Central Africa.

Things to Buy

Markets The city's two major markets, the Marché Central downtown and the Marché de Mokolo four km away are both worth checking out.

Artisan Goods Anyone looking for artisan goods should first check out the Artisanat at the end of Ave Kennedy. You'll find handicrafts in wood, brass, leather and fabric. The leather goods, including handbags and wallets, are an especially good buy. The Mission M'Volié also has a shop. For top quality items, however, the Museum of Camerounian Art can't be beaten. They sell items they don't want or need.

A word of caution – exporting antiques is forbidden and bribe-hungry customs officials have been known to declare obvious tourist art as antiques. Protect yourself with receipts from handicraft stores or certifications signed by a museum chief.

For inexpensive African fabrics, try the Marché Central downtown. If price is of no concern, try Mouna Mboua Tie-dye Shop next to Hôtel Impérial. They have a large selection of women's and children's clothing in tie-dye fabrics.

Le Fétiche next to Electra on Ave Kennedy sells expensive gold and silver jewellery. Especially interesting are the rings and pendants done in gold with elephant hair, the gold Ashanti doll pendants, the silver bracelets with Abbia stone trim and the ivory tusk necklaces.

The Ivory Carver has a large workshop where you can watch the ivory carvers at work and they also carry pieces in ebony and a few unusual items such as ostrich egg lamps. It's on a street running perpendicular to the street on which the Boulangerie Française is located.

Getting There & Away

Air There are flights from Douala to Yaoundé with Cameroun Airlines every 90 minutes or so until around 10 pm.

Bush Taxi Bush taxis headed for western Cameroun (Bafoussam, etc) from Yaoundé now leave from the Gare Routière du Centre. They are plentiful throughout Cameroun, so you should have no problem getting to Yaoundé from anywhere in Cameroun.

Getting Around

Airport Transport There is no airport tax. The

Yaoundé airport has a restaurant, Hertz and several local car rental agencies. The SOTUC Bus No 9 goes to the airport about every half hour. The taxi fare from the airport into town (4 km) is CFA 1000 to CFA 1500. Fares increase by CFA 500 at 10 pm. Bargaining is required. Going to the airport can be considerably cheaper from the centre of Yaoundé in a shared cab, for instance.

Bus Buses operate until 9 pm.

Taxi Taxis are supposed to have the official prices on the window. Fares for a shared cab are CFA 100 to CFA 200 depending on the distance. A *course* in a taxi to yourself is CFA 500 (CFA 600 after 10 pm), more for long distances (CFA 1500 to the Mt-Fébé Sofitel). Count on paying CFA 2000 per hour even though the official rate is CFA 1000, and about CFA 12,000 plus gas per day. Prices increase after 10 pm. Taxis are fairly plentiful but they don't have meters. They are all yellow.

Car Rental In Yaoundé, you'll find Hertz (tel 234002, telex 8263) at the Mt-Fébé Hôtel, Inter-Auto (tel 220361, telex 8371) near the Hôtel de Ville, and Delta Voyages (tel 221532; telex 8374) at the airport.

AROUND YAOUNDE

For getting away on weekends, some locals like to stay at *Luna Park* (tel 231754), 40 km to the north on paved a road, two km from Obala. Surrounded by forests, this complex has 16 African style huts (*boukarous*) for about CFA 7000 each, a restaurant, pool, tennis, mini-golf and poorly-kept animals. If this doesn't appeal, you might want to see Nachtigal Falls instead (best to visit in the rainy season). It's 28 km north of Luna Park.

DOUALA

Called the 'armpit of Africa' by some, Douala has an image problem. Many short-term visitors will tell you all they can remember is seeing some ordinary architecture and feeling like a wet sponge. Lacking the class of Abidjan, the beauty of Dakar and the soul of Lagos, Douala has its admirers nevertheless. They like its vitality. With 850,000 inhabitants, Douala is as big as Dakar, yet much of the activity is conveniently centred in one area – Akwa.

The old Hôtel Akwa Palace in the heart of town on the main drag, Blvd de la Liberté, is the place to have a drink in the late afternoon and haggle with the local vendors. Across the street is the famous Harry's Bar. Or take in La Jungle, a unique African cabaret that's been in operation since 1960, which is highly unusual for Africa.

Whereas in much of Africa getting good local cuisine in a restaurant (as opposed to the streets) is difficult if not impossible, Douala has one of the best authentic African restaurants in Africa. The famous Porte Jaune is not far from the Akwa Palace, and crocodile and boa constrictor are on the menu.

Those with boats at the Marina spend their weekends sailing. During the dry season, others head for the beaches at Limbe or Mt Cameroun for a cool relaxing time at a delightful old hotel, or to climb one of Central Africa's tallest peaks. Both Limbe and Mt Cameroun are only an hour away from Douala by bush taxi. For a more secluded beach area, you can head south through the jungle for three or four hours to Kribi.

Information

Banks Chase Manhattan, Banque de Paris et des Pays-Bas, BIAO, Charter Bank, BICICI. The last one charges no commission on changing travellers' cheques.

Consulates The following eight countries have consulates:

Belgium
(tel 424750)
Equatorial Guinea
(tel 422611)
France
(tel 426250/425370) Rue des Cocotiers near the Meridien, BP 869

Italy
(tel 423601) Rue de l'Hôtel de Ville
Nigeria
UK
(tel 422177/422245) Rue Alfred Saker off Blvd de la Liberté, BP 1016
USA
(tel 425331/426003) 21 Ave du Général de Gaulle, BP 4006
West Germany
(tel 423500/428600) 47 Blvd de la Liberté

Bookshops & Supermarkets The best bookshop is Aux Frères Reunis at the Akwa Palace. Another good one is Aux Messageries on Blvd de la Liberté, a block from the Cathedral.

Also on Blvd de la Liberté, you'll find La Soudanaise, a big supermarket that sells a little bit of everything including photographic supplies.

Travel Agencies The three major travel agencies are Camvoyages (tel 423188/422544) 15 Blvd de la Liberté, BP 4070; Transcap Voyages (tel 429291) Bonanjo, Rue de Trieste, BP 4059; and Delmas Voyages (tel 421184) Bonanjo, Rue Kitchener, BP 263. Among other things, they arrange package tours to the north. Cameroun Airlines is the agent for Norcamtour, which has its headquarters in Maroua and specialises in group tours of Waza Park and Rumsiki.

Hôtel Akwa Palace

This famous old hotel, newly renovated, is the city's major attraction. In the morning, you'll see travellers having coffee and croissants on the terrace of the hotel and watching the activity on the city's major street, Blvd de la Liberté. Again, in the late afternoon, activity at the Akwa picks up. Walk down Liberté towards the post office and you'll find several places to pick up African art.

Musée de Douala

Continue on in the direction of the post office to the Hôtel de Ville (town hall); the Musée de Douala (open weekdays 8 am to 12 noon and 2.30 to 5.15 pm, Saturday 8 am to 1 pm) is on the second floor. It has some old photographs of Douala and examples of Bamoun and Bamiléké art, enough to allow you to distinguish on the street between what's good and what isn't.

Place du Gouvernement

Nearby, at the Place du Gouvernement, you'll see a curiosity building that looks like a Chinese pagoda. It was built by the local African ruler, Rudolf Douala Manga Bell, who was executed by the Germans in 1914 for refusing to cede certain land.

Places to Stay – bottom end

If you want to camp, the Father at the *Foyer Protestante*, downtown one block behind Le Lido and the Foyer des Marins, usually has no objections, but he'll warn you that the chances of getting ripped-off are high.

You'll do better paying CFA 3000 to CFA 4000 for a bed (two to a room with air-con) at the *Procure Générale des Missions Catholiques* downtown on Rue Franqueville. There's a pool and you can eat there as well. If it's full, which is often the case, especially on Thursdays, there's usually room at *Le Centre Baba Simon*, a big building on the main drag, Blvd de la Liberté, opposite the cathedral. The cost is about CFA 3000 a person for a dormitory bed, and twice that for a room with air-con. The mission is friendly and serves meals.

For hotels, it's hard to beat *Hôtel du Littoral* (tel 422484) on Ave Douala Manga Bell in Quartier Bali, about two km from the centre of town. The very decent rooms are CFA 5000 (CFA 5500 with air-con), and the hotel has been spruced up a bit. Several blocks away is the well known *Hôtel de Douala* (tel 425478), with rooms for CFA 5000 (CFA 6000 with air-con). The mattresses sag, and the hotel in general is much worse unless you like the sounds of a boisterous crowd at the bar and outside the hotel. Most people will find the nearby *Cameroun Hôtel* (tel 428153), four blocks from the Douala and next to Cinéma l'Etoile,

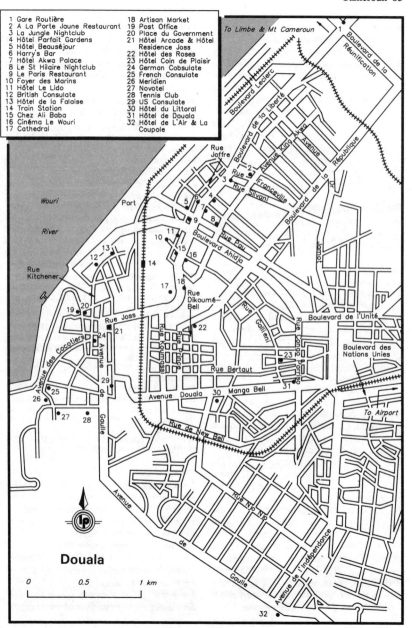

1 Gare Routière	18 Artisan Market
2 A La Porte Jaune Restaurant	19 Post Office
3 La Jungle Nightclub	20 Place du Government
4 Hôtel Parfait Gardens	21 Hôtel Arcade & Hôtel
5 Hôtel Beauséjour	Residence Joss
6 Harry's Bar	22 Hôtel des Roses
7 Hôtel Akwa Palace	23 Hôtel Coin de Plaisir
8 Le St Hilaire Nightclub	24 German Cobsulate
9 Le Paris Restaurant	25 French Consulate
10 Foyer des Marins	26 Meridien
11 Hôtel Le Lido	27 Novotel
12 British Consulate	28 Tennis Club
13 Hôtel de la Falaise	29 US Consulate
14 Train Station	30 Hôtel du Littoral
15 Chez Ali Baba	31 Hôtel de Douala
16 Cinéma Le Wouri	32 Hôtel de L'Air & La
17 Cathedral	Coupole

Douala

a better buy at CFA 5610/6115 for singles/doubles with air-con.

If every shekel counts, try the newly painted *Hôtel Coin de Plaisir* (tel 426970) on Rue Gallieni, which is the street behind the Douala. The tiny clean rooms with fans are CFA 4180 (CFA 5225 with air-con).

For a little luxury, try *Le Foyer des Marins* (tel 422794) at CFA 7000/8500 for singles/doubles with air-con. You don't have to be a sailor or male to stay there. They have a pool and a restaurant. It is a very friendly place in the centre of town not far from the train station.

Places to Stay – middle
Hôtel de la Falaise (tel 424646, telex 5625, cards AE, D), not to be confused with Résidence la Falaise, is an older hotel near the heart of town matches the best hotels in quality but is medium priced. It is excellent value for money at CFA 12,300 a room. There is a pool and a good view of the port.

The seven-floor *Beauséjour* (tel 420522, telex 5255), with singles/doubles for CFA 10,000/11,100 and only a block from the Akwa Palace, has a pool and a popular top floor restaurant, but it's a little run-down.

It's hard to beat *Résidence Joss* (tel 423646, telex 5546, Cards AE, D) for value. It costs CFA 9265 a room with air-con and is in the heart of town. From the outside, it looks like the higher priced three star hotels, but inside it's a little worn. Another good buy is the *Hôtel de l'Air* (tel 428159) on Ave de Gaulle several km from downtown. Singles/doubles with air-con go for CFA 7214/8422. The bathrooms are fairly clean, the bar is popular, and there's a pizzeria a block away.

If you prefer to be downtown, try *Le Lido* (tel 420445), where decent air-con rooms are CFA 7665. It is a block from the Foyer des Marins, a block off Blvd de la Liberté. For a more African ambience with an inexpensive restaurant, try *Hôtel des Roses* on Dikoumé-Bell in Bali, about one km from downtown. The rooms are quite decent and cost about CFA 8000 to CFA 9000 with air-con.

Places to Stay – top end
There are three deluxe hotels. The *Meridien* and *Novotel* are both top quality and next door to each other, near the heart of town. At the centrally located *Akwa Palace*, which has a little more character but is less peaceful, you'll find a delightful street-side terrace for drinks and an older section where prices are about one-third less.

In addition, there are four three-star hotels, with as much character as a Wendy's hamburger joint. Of the four, the *Ibis* has the most sparkle and activity, however, it's about a km from the heart of town. The other three are all on the main drag in the centre of town: the *Parfait Gardens* is next to the Akwa Palace, *Résidence La Falaise* is several blocks away, and *Hôtel Arcade* on Rue Ivy is near the post office.

Meridien (tel 426136/429324/429135, telex 5822), CFA 25,270 a room, pool, TV/video, disco, Hertz, tennis next door, cards AE, D, V, CB.
Sawa Novotel (tel 429044, telex 5822), CFA 25,270 a room, pool, TV/video, sauna, Avis, tennis next door, cards AE, D, V, CB.
Akwa Palace (tel 422601/429410, telex 5322), CFA 28,000 a room (CFA 19,000 for rooms in the older Akwa I section), long pool, shops, Mattei car rental, cards AE, D, V, CB.
Hôtel Ibis (tel 425800/17, telex 5558), CFA 16,840 a room, pool, cards AE, D, V, CB.
Résidence Hôtelière La Falaise (tel 420445), CFA 16,845/18,500 for singles/doubles, no pool, cards AE, D.
Hôtel Arcade (tel 14,950), CFA 14,950 a room, pool, Hertz, cards AE, D, V, CB.
Hôtel Parfait Gardens (tel 426357, telex 5716), CFA 13,475 a room, no pool, cards AE, D, V, CB.

Places to Eat
Cheap Eats Braised chicken and fish with the local speciality, *ndole*, are primarily what the cheaper African restaurants serve. One of the most popular and well-known is *Restaurant du Wouri* in Quartier Congo.

The atmosphere of those in the centre of town doesn't match the Wouri's. *Cabane d'Eva*, for instance, is several blocks from the Porte Jaune, behind the Parfait Gardens, has a tranquil atmosphere where you can dine under straw huts. One of the cheapest downtown is *Chez Theresa* on Blvd de la Liberté across from Hôtel Arcade; a platter of grilled chicken goes for CFA 1700. Two others, near each other, are *Restaurant les 3 Veuves* and *Hôtel des Roses* in Quartier Bali on Rue Dikoume-Bell, about one km from downtown.

Downtown near the mission, you'll find all manner of stews, meats, fish, etc with rice sold on the streets for CFA 250 to CFA 350. Beers go for CFA 150, bananas three for CFA 50, and chocolate pâté at CFA 125 for a small tube.

For de luxe hamburgers and croque monsieurs (not particularly cheap) head for *Croque O'Burger*, like a fancy McDonalds, on Blvd de la Liberté about one km north of the Akwa Palace. *La Gourmandise* at the Akwa Palace and *Délices*, about a block away, seem to have the best ice cream.

African *A la Porte Jaune* (tel 429854) is one of Douala's most famous restaurants, a place where you can have an entire zoo on your plate – porcupine, crocodile, boa constrictor, ant-eater and antelope. The food is good but over-priced. You'll find it behind the Akwa Palace on Rue Franceville. Camerounian food is also the speciality of the less expensive *Le Touristic* (tel 424088), at the intersection of République and Réunification (three km from the Akwa Palace), where you can dine outdoors.

Seafood Three of the city's best seafood restaurants are all within a block of the Akwa Palace. Highly recommended is *Plein Ciel* at the top of Hôtel Beauséjour. The panoramic view of the city is as much an attraction as the good seafood and moderate prices. If you just want the best seafood and don't care about the view, try the moderately expensive *La Marée* (tel 421429) between the Beauséjour and the Akwa Palace. Seafood is also the speciality of *Le Paris* (tel 421289), a very good French restaurant on Blvd de la Liberté. It's open for lunch and dinner every day except Sunday, and prices are moderately expensive except for the special two-course menu for about CFA 4200.

French *L'Auberge* (tel 423623), closed Sunday, is one of Douala's two finest and most expensive restaurants – one that most people save for a special occasion. It's on Blvd de la Liberté about two km north of the Akwa Palace. The other is the luxuriously decorated *La Gitane*, on the same street but in the opposite direction towards the cathedral.

If you're looking for a more moderately priced French restaurant downtown, some people recommend *Le Lido* (tel 426206), a block off Blvd de la Liberté near the Foyer des Marins. Cheaper still, *L'Agip*, downtown at the Station Agip next to the Place du Gouvernement, serves a decent full meal for CFA 4200, as well as à la carte selections and sandwiches.

Asian For Chinese food, *Restaurant Chinois* (tel 421426) near the Novotel, and *Aux Baguettes d'Or* on Rue Franceville near the Akwa Palace, get the best reviews, but *Hong Kong*, near the Hôtel de la Falaise and closed on Thursday, is cheaper and a better buy. Vietnamese food is the speciality of *Le Dragon d'Or* (tel 427488, closed on Thursdays) which is across from the Akwa Palace.

Various Cuisines What's most unusual is *Tandoor & Teppanyaki*, which serves Indian and Japanese food. No other restaurant in Central Africa serves these types of food. It's half a block from the Akwa Palace in the direction of the Beauséjour and is definitely worth a try. For Lebanese fare, there's *Mille et Une Nuits* (closed on Tuesdays) downtown across from Hôtel Arcade.

For the price and quality of the food, it's hard to beat *Le Refuge* (tel 424232), an Italian restaurant with a Swiss atmosphere. One block from Hôtel de la Falaise and open every day, they serve a four-course set menu for about CFA 4200. They also have pizza.

Entertainment & Sports

Bars The sidewalk terrace of the Akwa Palace is by far the most popular place for a drink. Another is the beautiful pool-side terrace of the *Beauséjour*, one block away.

Nightclubs Most of the nightclubs in Douala are fairly crass. There are several exceptions. The plush *Harry's Bar*, across from Parfait Gardens, is probably Douala's best known nightclub. It's more for drinking and listening than for live entertainment and dancing. Expatriates still like *La Jungle*, a cabaret strip-tease that has been in business for over 27 years. You'll find it a block from Croque O'Burger, off Blvd de la Liberté (on Rue Sylavani). For dancing, *Le St-Hilaire* behind the Akwa Palace is fairly respectable and popular. You might also try *Safari Club* (tel 426199) on Rue de la Motte-Piquet; let a cabbie find it for you.

For dancing with more local colour, you have a choice of at least five places in Akwa. Leave your valuables behind. One of the most popular is *The Night Spot* directly behind the Parfait Gardens. *Kaissa*, another disco with strobe lights, is nearby.

Around the Cinéma le Wouri, a few blocks down from the Akwa Palace, you'll find three more. *The Scotch Club*, two blocks from the Wouri, reportedly has live music on occasions. One and a half blocks from the Wouri, on Rue Gallieni, you'll find *Le Macumba*, which plays a mixture of African and disco music and has an almost entirely African clientele. Likewise, you'll probably find only Africans at *Queen's Club* on Blvd de la Liberté between the Akwa Palace and the Wouri.

For those on the cheap the 'bar-dancing' places for ordinary folk are certainly more affordable and probably more interesting. Akwa and, further out, in New Bell are the places to find them.

Cinemas The two best cinemas, both with air-con, are Le Wouri (tel 421947) on Blvd de la Liberté several blocks from the cathedral, and Le Paris. The ventilated Le Toula, a block from the Hôtel de la Falaise, is cheaper, with two studios and numerous US films.

Sports For tennis try the Tennis Club next to the Novotel, a private club used by the hotels. For swimming you'll have to choose one of the hotel pools. The closest beach is at Limbe, an hour's drive away. Sailors might check out the Marina, about five km beyond the Novotel area. There are no boats or windsurfers for rent.

Things to Buy

Markets There are five markets; the most interesting is probably the Marché de Lagos, at its most animated on Saturday morning but it is nothing special by West African standards. You'll find it in New Bell, the most heavily populated African section.

Artisan Goods If you're looking for high quality art, try Alain Nyang Ouman across from Hôtel Coin de Plaisir on Rue Gallieni. Le Fétiche on Ave de Verdun is another. If you want good quality items, a wide selection and reasonable prices, head for Ali Baba in the city centre, half a block from Blvd de la Liberté and a block from the cathedral. The hours are 8.30 to 11.45 am and 3.30 to 7 pm every day except Sunday.

If you're prepared to bargain hard, you can get better prices, but often inferior quality, at the Artisanat, an open air craft market across from the cathedral. You'll find wooden pieces, musical instruments, leather items, ivory, ebony and malachite jewellery. Remember to keep your sales slips because otherwise customs officials may hassle you on leaving, arguing that you're carrying valuable antiques.

Music For records of Camerounian music, one of the better places is at the airport. You might also enquire at Son et Musique facing Le Paris restaurant on Blvd de la Liberté. Cameroun probably has more hit singers than any African country besides Zaïre and South Africa.

Cameroun's biggest star, Manu Dibango, came out in the early '70s with a still popular album entitled *Soul Makossa*. Since then Makossa music, which is great for dancing, has become a major style of modern African music. Some of the big names are Sam Fan Thomas, Sammy Njondji, Moni Bile, Ekambi Brillant, Toto Guillaume, Tamwo and Samson – all male and all very popular throughout Central and West Africa.

Getting There & Away

Air You can fly direct to Douala from Brussels, Frankfurt, London, Marseilles, Paris and Rome. Connections from West African coastal cities are also good. Cameroun Airlines has flights every 90 minutes or so to Yaoundé until 10 pm.

Bush Taxi Bush taxis for Yaoundé and Bafoussam leave from the gare routière in the Yabassi area. Those for Buea and Limbe leave from a small auto gare in Deïdo on Blvd de la Réunification near Wouri bridge, two km from the Akwa Palace Hôtel.

Car If you're headed to/from Nigeria, the quicker route is via Kumba and Mamfé. From June to September, you'd better ask about conditions because the road can become so muddy that driving via Bafoussam can sometimes be faster.

Train If you're in Douala and looking for kicks, catch the train headed north for Kumba or Nkongsamba. You can also take it to Yaoundé, but it'll take about seven hours.

Getting Around

Airport Transport There is no airport tax. The Douala airport is one of the best in Central and West Africa; it has a bank, a restaurant-bar, and Avis, Hertz and Eurocar agencies. You'll find a SOTUC bus stop if you walk in the direction of the freight building (to your right leaving the airport); get off at Carrefour St-Michel, where you can a take a shared taxi in any direction. A taxi from the airport into town (10 km) is CFA 2000; fares increase by

CFA 500 after 10 pm. Bargaining is required. Going to the airport, you can get a taxi for less if you hail one on the street.

Bus Buses operate until 9 pm.

Taxi Fares for a shared cab are CFA 100 to CFA 200 depending on the distance, while a cab to yourself (a *course*) costs CFA 500 (CFA 600 after 10 pm).

Car Rental You'll find Hertz (tel 429918, telex 5532) at the Novotel, Avis (tel 429748/426136, telex 5622) at the Meridien, Eurocar (tel 421878/9) facing the Akwa Palace, Locauto (tel 422601) at the Akwa Palace, and Auto Joss (tel 428619) at 2 Rue Philips. The first three all have booths at the airport as well.

LIMBE

On weekends during the dry season, beach lovers in Douala head for Limbe. Bush taxis from Douala take an hour and leave from a small station on Blvd de la Réunification near the bridge. The beach in town is too rocky for swimming, so the locals go to the black sand beach at Mile Six; it's on the asphalt coastal road leading north-west towards Idenao. Any closer to town you're likely to find oil on the beach.

During the week you'll have Mile Six beach to yourself. On weekends it's crowded; the restaurant is open as well. Getting ripped-off is a distinct possibility, so pay the gate attendant to guard your things. For a taxi, wait in front of the stadium near the Miramar hotel. Those looking for a more secluded beach should head further out to Mile Eight, Mile 13 or Mile 20; don't expect to see any signs.

Places to Stay – bottom end

Downtown you'll find three cheap hotels on the same block. The renovated *Bay Hotel* is not a hotel but a restaurant, bar and nightclub. CFA 1000 will get you stuffed. You'll find street food and several dirt cheap restaurants on the same block. The *Victoria Guest House* next door is no cheaper than the Miramar (discussed in the top end section) and several hundred metres from the ocean. At the *Mansion Hotel*, you can get a double for about CFA 1500 to CFA 2000. Rooms upstairs are CFA 300 more, but they are quieter and the showers and toilets work better.

Some travellers have camped in the Botanical Gardens surrounding the *Park Hotel Miramar* (tel 332333, telex 5845), a 10-minute walk from the centre. If you do, find someone to guard your stuff. The Miramar has the same telephone and telex as the Atlantic Beach Hotel because both hotels and the Bay hotel in the city centre have the same owners. It's good value – a bungalow costs about CFA 3200/4700 for one/two people; breakfast is CFA 300. The pool is relatively clean, but the nightclub is closed. With air-con, the rooms cost an extra CFA 1000 to CFA 4000. The Miramar serves meals only when they feel like it, ie when there are a number of guests wanting to eat.

Places to Stay – top end
The picturesque *Atlantic Beach Hotel* (tel 332333, telex 5845) is several hundred metres down the beach from the Miramar and closer to the centre; it's the only really good hotel in town. The price of an air-con room with breakfast is CFA 12,000 to CFA 20,000. The pool is pictured in all the travel brochures – the ocean waves practically spill into it. What the pictures don't show is that the nightclub is closed and the tennis court is over-grown with weeds; still, it's a pleasant place.

BUEA & MT CAMEROUN
There are two reasons to head for Buea, an hour from Douala – to enjoy the refreshingly cool climate at 1000 metres altitude or to climb Mt Cameroun. On the mountain,

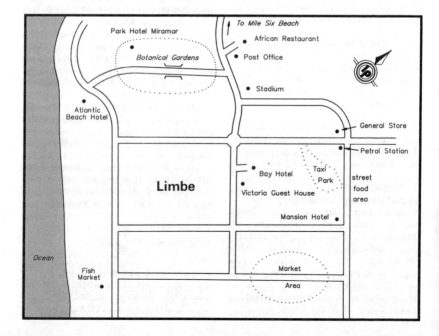

you'll pass through thick forests for the first third; after that it becomes sub-alpine meadows. Even if you don't climb, chances are you'll rave about the Mountain Hotel like everyone else. Far from luxurious, it has a rustic English charm even though it's run by French people. The severely teutonic German Governor's Palace is still part of the scenery.

The Germans knew what they were doing when they chose Buea as their capital. The scenery is spectacular and the climate delightful during the dry season, from late November through February, when there's sunshine. In March and April, it becomes cloudy, with a 50-50 chance of rain. Starting May, rain falls virtually every day, and Buea becomes a miserable, cold place. A climb at that time of the year wouldn't be pleasant. On the western slopes, it rains practically every day and the area records one of the world's highest rainfalls.

Mt Cameroun last erupted in 1982. At 4070 metres (13,352 feet), it is easily the highest mountain in Central and West Africa outside the Virunga mountains on the Zaïre-Rwanda-Uganda border. It is also one of the easiest to climb. The vertical ascent is approximately 3000 metres. In all it is a 27-km roundtrip.

Climbing Logistics

You need a permit to climb. The fee for a guide and a porter is about CFA 4500 and CFA 7000 per day, respectively. If you get to the second cabin, you will have to pay for two days even if you return the same day.

Some climbers avoid the fee by asking one of the local children at the market to guide them for the first hour or so; after that the trail is easy to follow as there is white paint on rocks all the way up. Others report that park officials aren't too strict about requiring guides. I wouldn't count on it though – their friends need the money. The Provincial Service for Tourism, at the entrance to Buea, issues the permits and will locate you an obligatory guide and an optional porter.

They're open weekdays 7.30 am to 2.30 pm and Saturday 7.30 am to 12.30 pm.

Those in great shape can start off from downtown at 5 am and be back by nightfall, around 6 pm, or earlier. Some people save an hour by riding to near the entrance, called Upper Farm. Don't plan on more than 30 minutes total in rest stops. If you're going to try doing it in one day, the chances are good that you won't get back by nightfall if you don't begin your descent by 1 pm.

Most people should count on taking 1 1/2 to two days for the climb and descent. Unless you stay overnight in one of the cabins and arrive at the top around 6 or 7 am, chances are you'll be enveloped in a cloud, with a visibility of a hundred feet. You'll pass three cabins on the way up, all unlocked. The first is in the forests at 1830 metres (about a 2 1/2-hour walk), the second at 2780 metres (another 2 1/2-hour walk), and the third at 3950 metres (another 1 1/2 hours). From there to the top is another good hour. Be sure you get to the top (Fako Point) and not Bottle Top, which is 29 metres lower (4041 metres).

Most climbers stay overnight at the middle cabin because the weather is so cold at the top one. The advantage of staying at the third cabin is that getting to the top at the crack of dawn is no problem and the chances of getting a good view are a thousand times better. The cabins are a far cry from those on Kilimanjaro; all you'll find is a hard wooden platform to sleep on.

It's much colder than you would expect up there. From the second cabin on, be prepared for below freezing temperatures. On the upper slopes, frost and snow are not uncommon. A light raincoat and a change of clothes are advisable, especially from February to October. Unless you are certain you can get to the top and back in one day, a sleeping bag is an absolute must.

Footwear is an important consideration. If you have weak ankles, or choose to climb in the rainy season (May to October), it would be a good idea to use hiking boots. The path is very steep, and there are numerous loose rocks just waiting to be slipped on. In the dry season you might decide that the safety factor is no longer such a major concern and go for the comfort of a good pair of running shoes.

There is water stored at all the cabins, but unless it is boiled or treated it's not drinkable.

Some climbers recommend bringing along rehydrating solution so as to replenish the sugar and mineral salts lost while sweating. The recipe is one litre of boiled water, 10 pinches of sugar, three pinches of salt and the juice of one lemon.

Mt Cameroun Race

Since the mid '70s, Guinness has sponsored an annual mad race (27 km) up and down the mountain. The winning time in 1987 was three hours and 46 minutes, the descent being made in about 70 minutes – truly amazing. It's so steep that the runners have to carry poles! And temperatures can vary from 25°C at the start of the race to 0°C at the summit. If you stay up the night before the race, you'll see the local people making sacrifices to appease the mountain spirits.

To enter the race, contact the manager of Guinness Cameroun in Douala (BP 1213, tel 422841/422906, telex 5327). The race takes place on the last Sunday in January. Usually about 250 runners enter. While Brits won a number of the races in the early '80s, Camerounians won in 1986 and 1987. If you're in Cameroun the last half of January, by all means go and watch, but don't expect to find a hotel room as thousands of spectators show up every year.

Places to Stay & Eat

For the price (CFA 1500 for a bed and CFA 600 for bedding), the *Presbyterian Mission* is highly recommended. It's a clean place run by a young German priest and his wife and

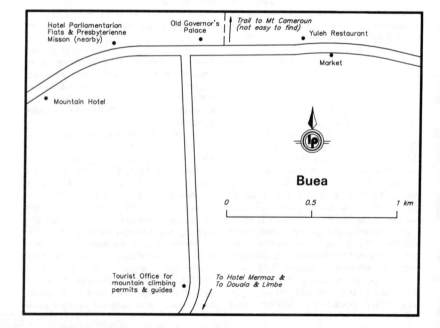

Hotel Parliamentarian Flats & Presbyterienne Misson (nearby)

Old Governor's Palace

Trail to Mt Cameroun (not easy to find)

Yuleh Restaurant

Market

Mountain Hotel

Buea

0   0.5   1 km

Tourist Office for mountain climbing permits & guides

To Hotel Mermoz & To Douala & Limbe

only 15 minutes by a path to the starting point of the climb, Upper Farm. *Parliamentarian Flats* (tel 324226), a hotel with 30 clean rooms and hot water for about CFA 6000 each, is nearby. It lacks charm but is preferred by Camerounians.

Almost all travellers with a few shekels to spare stay at the delightful, highly recommended *Mountain Hotel* (tel 312174/ 322251), which is like an old resort lodge. It is about 200 metres from Parliamentarian Flats. At about CFA 8500/11,000 for one of the 50 singles/doubles, you can't complain about the price. There's no air-con and with good reason – this place is mountain cool. The menu is CFA 4000, and there's even a chilly pool.

The eight-room *Hotel Mermoz* (tel 328228) is a more typical African hotel, with singles/doubles for CFA 4000/6000. You'd be better off trying the other places in town first. The rooms are slightly dirty, there's no water, and the noise can be a problem as this is also a nightclub. It's three km or so from the market and down the hill; the climate is noticeably warmer.

Meals at the Mermoz and the Parliamentarian Flats are not cheap – CFA 1200 at the former and CFA 2200 at the latter – but at *Yuleh Restaurant*, on your left about 150 metres before reaching Buea market, you'll find four African dishes for CFA 550 to CFA 750 each.

KRIBI

Kribi is Cameroun's best beach resort. The beaches here are white – in contrast to the black, sometimes rocky beaches at Limbe – and there aren't many tourists, especially during the long off-season. Avoid the heavy rain period, from June to mid-November. The best time is the dry season, from mid-November to February, but that's also when you'll find more tourists. The 203 km road from Douala is in good condition at that time of the year, and catching a bush taxi in Douala is no problem. The trip by taxi-brousse via Edéa takes about four hours.

Seven km south of Kribi at Grand Batanga you'll find the Chutes de la Lobé, one of a very small number of waterfalls in the world that empty into the sea. Sleeping on the beach is apparently no problem, and the locals are friendly. Even better beaches, however, lie between Kribi and Londji 26 km to the north. Londji is particularly lovely, with an immense bay, clean sand and palm trees.

Places to Stay

Since the *Grand Hôtel Palm Beach* closed in the mid-'80s, the only hotel on the beach has been the eight-room *Hôtel Kribi Plage* (tel 461123), closed in the rainy season. It has a family feeling, a good restaurant, and the CFA 8000 rooms with fans are quite decent. Reservations are absolutely essential. You can camp here as well.

In town, you'll find the 18-room *Hôtel de Kribi* (tel 461276), with air-con doubles for about CFA 11,000, a bar and a restaurant. *Auberge Annette*, however, has been remodelled and expanded, with 15 or so rooms, and may be as good as or better than Hotel Kribi. The 66-room *Strand Hôtel* (tel 461066) costs about CFA 6000 for a double. Others include the five-room *Hôtel de la Paix* and the *Auberge de Kribi*.

Outside Kribi, you can rent huts in villages, such as Cocotier Plage 15 km in the direction of Londji. In Londji, the 12-room *Hôtel du Golf de Guinness* has rooms without water for about CFA 2000.

BAFOUSSAM

Bafoussam is west from Yaoundé or Douala on a good road. It lacks the interest of Bamenda and Foumban. Some travellers use it as a base camp, especially since Foumban has so little accommodation. This is the country's major coffee and cocoa area.

Cameroun is not the largest producer of coffee in Central and West Africa (the Ivory Coast is), but the quality is tops in the area because the coffee here is grown at a higher altitude, allowing farmers to grow the higher priced arabica coffee, which thrives only in cooler climates (the cheaper robusta coffee is grown in the lowlands). You can buy some at Douala airport.

Bafoussam has about 125,000 inhabitants, mostly Bamiléké. They are noted for their wood carvings and vendors frequently line the road in front of the Hôtel le Président. An interesting way to see the surrounding hills would be to hook up with the Hash House Harriers and follow their rabbit-like jogging course on Saturdays from around 3 pm, but they don't run on a regular basis.

Several hours' walk directly north of Bafoussam is Lac de Baleng, a crater lake that is popular with foreigners and possibly free of bilharzia.

Twenty km south on the Yaoundé highway to Bandjoun is one of the most beautiful *cheferies* (chief's compounds) in Africa – it is even mentioned in tourist brochures. The huge huts of bamboo and straw are supported by tall carved pillars, like totem poles, and have elaborate, carved doorways and walls with geometrical designs. For nightclubs, the most popular is the new *Evasion*, a 10 to 15 minute walk from the market. The older *La Paillote*, on Rue du Marché several blocks from the market, is not bad either.

Places to Stay – bottom end

The *Protestant Mission*, 100 metres from the taxi park, reportedly no longer accepts travellers. If this is the case, then try the 15-room *Hôtel Fédéral* (tel 441309), two blocks from the gare routière. A single with breakfast costs about CFA 3250 to CFA 3500 (CFA 400 more for two). This is a quiet place with big beds, clean bathrooms and a restaurant that serves a three-course meal for CFA 1500.

Hôtel de la Mifi (not to be confused with Auberge de la Mifi), a 10 to 15 minute walk from the town centre, charges about CFA 4200 for an unadorned room without breakfast. The new *Hôtel le Kallao*, downtown several blocks off the main drag, has similar prices. Neither is better than the Fédéral; they don't have restaurants either.

If you want something better than the Fédéral, stay at the *Auberge de la Mifi*. Prices range from CFA 3750 to CFA 5000 for a decent room. The hotel, which is in the heart of town, has a restaurant with tablecloths! Half a block away, with rooms for CFA 6000 to CFA 7000, is *Hôtel le Continental* (tel 441458), a better place, perhaps, for a drink and a meal than for a room.

Places to Stay – top end

The new *Palace Garden Hôtel* (tel 441810, telex 7048), with rooms for CFA 12,500, is Bafoussam's finest and has a pool, a tennis court and a top restaurant, but is totally devoid of character. It's three km from the centre of town. Half a km further out you'll find the smaller *Hôtel Saré le Kamkop* (tel 441802), with rooms for CFA 7500 to CFA 9500, bungalows for CFA 11,500, and a restaurant and bar. Because of the pleasant surroundings, many expatriates prefer the Saré, but without wheels, you'll find the location a big drawback. If you don't reserve a bungalow, chances are they'll be taken.

Next in line is the big new *Hôtel de la Unité* (tel 441516) with rooms for about CFA 8000 to CFA 8750. It's on the main drag, a good 15-minute walk from the centre of town. The atmosphere rates a zero, but the rooms and lobby are quite decent and modern. The older 54-room *Hôtel le Président* (tel 441136), only a five-minute walk from the market, until recently was Bafoussam's top hotel, but with singles/doubles for about CFA 9500/11,000, now seems over priced.

FOUMBAN

An hour's drive north-east of Bafoussam, Foumban is over 1000 metres above sea level and is one of Cameroun's major tourist attractions – a great place for Camerounian art. If traditional African culture is your bag, you'd be crazy to miss the Royal Palace of the Bamoun tribe.

Royal Palace

Unlike the Bamiléké (around Bafoussam)

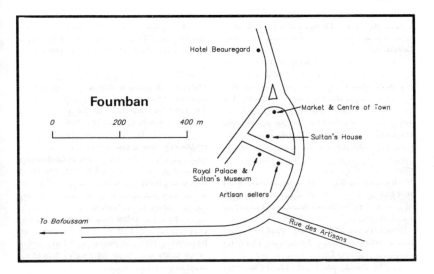

Foumban

0   200   400 m

Hotel Beauregard

Market & Centre of Town

Sultan's House

Royal Palace & Sultan's Museum

Artisan sellers

To Bafoussam

Rue des Artisans

who are grouped by allegiance to the chief in whose chiefdom they cultivate land, the Bamoun all show allegiance to a single chief, the sultan. In an area of the world where some countries, such as Gabon, have virtually no recorded history prior to the colonial era, it's exceptional that the Bamoun have an ongoing 'dynasty' – the present sultan, El Hadj Seidou Njimoluh Njoya, being the 18th king in a line dating back to 1394. The 17th sultan and the most famous, Njoya, envious of the German governor's palace in Buea, built his own.

Completed in 1917, this unique palace looks like a medieval chateau, with a vast hall of arms on the 1st floor. On the 2nd floor, the Sultan's Museum, open 8 am to 12 noon and 3 to 6 pm, contains a multitude of objects belonging to the previous sultans – colourful royal gowns, arms, musical instruments, war garments, statues, jewellery, books written by Njoya, dancing masks, etc.

Musée des Arts et des Traditions

This museum is open the same hours but closed Monday and Friday. It houses the extensive private collection of Mosé Yéyap and

is worth a visit. You'll see an important collection of pipes, clay statues, masks, gongs offered by the sultan to the nobles for their valiant war efforts, musical instruments and military armaments.

Rue des Artisans

Leading towards this second museum, the Rue des Artisans has a dozen or more artisan workshops of sculptors, basketmakers, weavers and embroiderers along the way. While many of the wooden carvings are new, some are old. You'll also see many examples of Bamiléké art, the style being extraordinarily free and expressive with a lack of finish to the surface. The smiling buffalo masks and amusing dance masks with large shell-like protrusions above the eyes are common examples. It is not difficult to spend a full day wandering around here.

Other Attractions

On Fridays the Sultan makes an appearance. It's only in his presence that the traditional Bamoun dance, Mbansié, is performed.

Market days are Wednesdays and Saturdays in Foumban and Sunday morning in

Foumbot, a small village known for its pottery. You'll pass through it on the road from Bafoussam.

The best time of all to be in Foumban is at the end of Ramadan – the celebration is one of the most elaborate anywhere in Africa. Horse races, processions and dances are all a part of the show. Seventy days later at Tabaski, the celebration is again elaborate and marked by a parade of marabouts (wise men and fortune tellers).

Places to Stay & Eat
Most travellers stay in Bafoussam rather than roughing it at *Hôtel Beauregard* (tel 482182). It's downtown near the market with 24 clean rooms for about CFA 4500 to CFA 5500 and two apartments for CFA 8500, none with air-con. You can eat there too. The *Mission Catholique* is friendly; donations (about CFA 100) are expected. You could check out the 10-room *Auberge du Foumban* (tel 441445), but prices are not likely to be any lower.

BAMENDA
Bamenda is popular with travellers primarily because of the mountain scenery and the altitude of well over 1000 metres, offering hiking, camping, or touring in the nearby mountains. Bamenda itself is an English-speaking city of about 60,000 inhabitants situated about 4½ hours' drive on asphalt road from either Douala or Yaoundé. An added plus of a trip to Bamenda is that you'll find lots of handicrafts. The baskets are outstanding and you'll also find beads, wood carvings and bronze statues.

The best store in the heart of town is Prescraft, open weekdays 8 am to midday and 2.30 to 5 pm, Saturdays 8 am to 1 pm. You'll find the same prices but a different selection at the cooperative, THCS Handicraft Shop, open 7.30 am to 5 pm every day except Sunday. It's several km from the centre of town on the road to the Skyline Hotel, about one-third the way up the escarpment and distinguished by its huge traditional-style gate. Prices are fixed at both

places. If you have wheels, take the 20-km trip west to Bali and the artisan centre there. You'll find a slightly different selection.

Hiking
Most of the hiking is done in the dry season, from late October until April. Unfortunately, the harmattan winds from the Sahara make the skies very hazy from November until the beginning of March when the first rains clear up the sky. You'll encounter only a few very basic hotels on the way; most people camp. If you want to pack food before you leave Bamenda, there are several supermarkets on the main drag, Commercial Ave, including Exim Vinson Supermarket.

The major hiking area is Ring Rd, a circular 367-km dirt road to the north-east of Bamenda. Until it's paved, don't attempt it in the rainy season as the roads become almost impassable. In the dry season you need at least two days to make the grand tour by car. Going anticlockwise on Ring Rd, look for the *chef's* palace in Bafut at Km 16; Kumbi River animal reserve at Km 60; Wum at Km 80 which has many bars and two cheap hotels (*Happy Day* and *Central*); Nkambé at Km 188; Kumbo at Km 258 (*Tourist Home* and *Merryland* hotels).

Places to Stay – bottom end
The *Presbyterian Mission* has dormitories and charges CFA 2000 a person. They also have lockers where you can leave your gear. It's on a hill on the outskirts of town, quite a way from the main church; ask for the 'church centre'.

If you'd prefer to be closer to the city centre, try *Hôtel Le Bien* (tel 361206), two km from the centre. This is a decent hotel with 25 singles/doubles for CFA 5500/6000 and a restaurant with a pleasant atmosphere. To save money, ask for one of their CFA 3300 rooms; they have three. The noisy *New City Hotel*, only a few blocks from the market, has singles/doubles for about CFA 3300/4400, clean private bathrooms, and a restaurant where CFA 1000 will buy you a full meal.

Other similarly priced hotels include the

Mezam National Hotel on Commercial St and the 10-room *Ringway Hotel* (tel 361162). The 16-room *Ideal Park Hotel* near the market charges a little more, about CFA 5000 a room, but the restaurant is good value at about CFA 1000 a meal. For local dancing places, try *Canne à Sucre*, *People's Palace* or *Monté Cristo*.

Places to Stay – top end

My two favourites are the *Skyline Hotel* (tel 361289, telex 5892, no credit cards) perched on a hill 1600 metres up overlooking Bamenda, and the *Safari Lodge* (reservations tel 333232 in Limbe) secluded in the mountains. It is designed as a weekend get-away spot for those suffering from the heat and humidity in Douala.

The Skyline, a 10-minute drive from downtown, has a long pool and air-con rooms with mini-bars for about CFA 16,500.

The Safari Lodge is near the airport, a 25-minute drive from Bamenda. The rooms, which cost about CFA 9000/11,000 with breakfast, and the restaurant are both quite satisfactory. Horseback riding is offered as well.

The best hotel in the centre of town is the *Ayaba Hotel* (tel 361321, telex 5387, AE cards), with singles/doubles for CFA 15,000/17,000 (no air-con). Modern and lacking in character but noted for its Sunday lunch, it has a pool, tennis court and the town's number one nightclub, *N'Jong Club*. A good notch down is the big new *Mondial Hotel* (tel 361832), a 10 to 15 minute walk from the heart of town. With singles for CFA 5500 to CFA 8000 and doubles for 7500 to CFA 9500, it's good value. The hotel is fairly tranquil, but the nightclub, *Mondial Club*, is said to be the second best in town.

NGAOUNDERE

Some 800 km north-east of Yaoundé by dirt road, Ngaoundéré is where you get off the train if you're headed north to Maroua and environs. There are no sights other than the Palais du Lamido, an immense 'Saré' best seen on weekends when the nobles come to pay their respects to the Lamido. At 1100 metres, the city has a relatively pleasant climate.

It wasn't until 1974 that the *Transcamerounais* arrived to Ngaoundéré (population 50,000). It now leaves twice a day for Yaoundé, at 7.20 am and at 7.20 pm. La Girafe, on the main drag not far from Cinéma le Nord, is a bar where 'everybody' goes for a drink. It is the beer stop for the 'Nairobi or Bust' expedition trucks and a good place to meet the locals.

Places to Stay – bottom end

A hotel near the centre of town with rock bottom prices and quality is *Relais le Chateau de l'Adamaoua*, with rooms for about CFA 3250. From Cinéma le Nord, go about 300 metres on the road leading towards the train station, then take a left for a block and ask. *Le Relais de Ngaoundéré* (tel 251138, telex 7650) is nearby, behind Cinéma le Nord. A much more respectable hotel, it has rooms for CFA 7000, hot water and good water pressure, and a central TV.

Places to Stay – top end

The best hotel in town is *Hotel Transcam* (tel 251041/251172, telex 7641, cards AE and D), with 40 singles/doubles for about CFA 13,500/14,500 and 10 bungalows for CFA 14,000. Two km from the centre of town, it has a nightclub, tennis, and TV/video in the rooms. The hotel has a 16-room annex, the *Hôtel de l'Adamaoua* (tel 251137), with doubles for about CFA 6500 without air-con.

The next best hotel is the new *Hôtel du Rail* (tel 251013) several km from the town centre. Singles/doubles without air-con are CFA 8500/9000, clean and popular.

Places to Eat

At or near the Cinéma le Nord, you'll find Lebanese shawarma sandwiches, and some African food stalls. Not far away are the *Dabaji Frères* supermarket, and a pastry shop, *Sabga*.

Of the hotels, the Relais le Chateau has

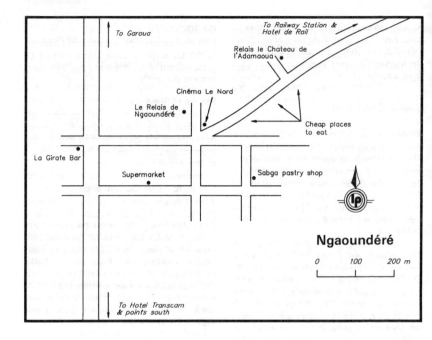

To Garoua

To Railway Station &
Hotel de Rail

Relais le Chateau de
l'Adamaoua

Cinéma Le Nord

Le Relais de
Ngaoundéré

Cheap places
to eat

La Girafe Bar

Supermarket

Sabga pastry shop

Ngaoundéré

0   100   200 m

To Hotel Transcam
& points south

cheap meals, and Le Relais de Ngaoundéré has an uninteresting restaurant with meals for CFA 1800 to CFA 2000. The set menu at the Hôtel Transcam is about CFA 3800, but there's an outdoor grill where you can get pizza for CFA 2000 or an entrecôte for CFA 2500.

AROUND NGAOUNDERE

Thirty km from Ngaoundéré, on the major road south to Meiganga, is *Le Ranch de Ngaoundaba*, a marvellous 30-room hotel on the side of a lake 1360 metres above sea level. Only open from November to May and popular with Jet Tours, it's almost like being on a ranch in the Western USA. You can swim (free of bilharzia), play tennis (clay courts), take a boat ride, fish, ride horses (in a ring), or hunt. The price is about CFA 12,000 per person including meals. To get there, charter a taxi, take a bush taxi going south, or rent a mobylette. No one rents

mobylettes for a business, so you'll have to ask around to stir up interest. It's reportedly not too difficult.

You could also ride to the Chutes du Tello, some beautiful, isolated waterfalls 50 km to the east of Ngaoundéré. They are more interesting than the nearby crater lakes, such as Lac Tison near town and Lac de Mbalang 22 km away, most of which are a kind of bilharzia soup.

THE BENOUE NATIONAL PARK

Midway between Ngaoundéré and Garoua is the country's second best game reserve, the Parc National de la Benoué, on both banks of the Benoué river and boasting large numbers of hippo, crocodile, buffalo and large antelope, as well as lion, monkey, giraffe, wart hog and brightly coloured birds that enjoy riding the backs of kob, a type of antelope.

The park is open from December to May,

the best viewing time being January to May, especially early in the morning and late in the afternoon. You'll have to pay an entrance fee of CFA 2500 and CFA 1500 for a guide (compulsory).

Places to Stay & Eat

You have three choices. The main one is the 20-room *Le Campement du Buffle Noir*, 40 km or so off the highway and near an impressive waterfall. Rooms in a boukarous (African hut) cost about CFA 8000. There is even a good restaurant where pâté de phacochère (wild boar) is the *pièce de résistance*. Reserve by calling the Service Provincial du Tourisme (tel 271020/271364) in Garoua.

If you want to get away from everybody, stay at the *Le Campement du Grand Capitaine* 110 km to the north. It has four boukarous with eight rooms, each for about CFA 5000, but no restaurant. Reservations can also be made at the Service Provincial du Tourisme. It may be worth the hassle because the view dominating the Benoué river is apparently spectacular. On the weekend, you may be joined by a hunting party. Much further to the east, there's still another place to stay, *Le Campement de Boubandjida*, with a restaurant and 16 rooms in eight boukarous at about CFA 8000 a room.

Hunting

The major hunting zones in Cameroun are around the savannah grassland national parks of the Benoué, Faro (to the far west of Benoué) and Waza. The season is 15 December to 1 June. How anyone could have the heart to kill a lion or elephant in today's Africa is beyond me, but it is permitted. Other trophies include kob, hippo, crocodile, Derby eland, and antelope. Only the rhino, giraffe and leopard are protected. The permit fee for large game is about CFA 85,000, good for six months. Killing an elephant or a giant eland will cost you CFA 150,000 extra, while for bargain slaughter the kobs are CFA 15,000.

GAROUA

Mid-way between Ngaoundéré and Maroua in the far north, Garoua offers nothing of great interest to see but it is a main junction town of the north.

Places to Stay

The catholic missionaries will probably tell you what they told me in Mokolo – that the government has asked them to stop giving rooms to non-missionaries. The missionaries at the *Mission Protestante*, one km from downtown, will ask you what organisation you're with and, depending on God knows what, may give you a bed for CFA 1500.

Auberge le Pacifique (tel 271503), a good two km from downtown on Rue de Sodecoton, has somewhat dirty rooms with fans for about CFA 5000, and has been known to extort much more when there are several people in the same room. *Chez Zabou*, next to the gare routière, has a number of rooms and might be cheaper. Another cheap place at the gare routière that may still exist is the unmarked *Chambre de Passage*; ask at the Restaurant de la Benoué.

The best hotel is *La Benoué Novotel* (tel 271204, telex 7625, cards AE, V and CB), which has rooms for CFA 16,845, pool, tennis, nightclub and Hertz. You can make reservations here for the campement at Waza park. *Le Relais St-Hubert* (tel 271321) is a block away. At CFA 6500 for a bungalow for two (CFA 7700 with air-con), it's good value.

Places to Eat

If you have wheels and are looking for a place to eat besides the hotels, try *Les Fali Bergeres* (tel 271177) 17 km away in Pitoa. Grilled chicken is the speciality and the outdoor atmosphere is agreeable.

MAROUA

Maroua (population 80,000), Cameroun's northern-most major city is popular with travellers, is the starting point for trips to Waza game park, Rumsiki and the Mokolo-Mora area. The city is fairly spread out but you should be able to find a bicycle for rent by asking around in the market, the city's centre and number one attraction.

Market

It's lively every day, especially Monday, the day of the Grand Marché. Ask a local jeweller to make you some jewellery, or look for one of the 'street-pharmacists' who will invariably have a magical herbal potion for whatever ails you.

Leather goods and African material are also hot items. If you buy indigo material, dip it in vinegar to keep it from running. You'll find the best selection of leather goods (cowhide, snake and crocodile) not at the market but across the Kaliao River on the southern side of town where the tanners work; just ask for the quartier des tanneurs. Otherwise you could pick up some perfume. Maroua might seem like a strange place for a perfume factory, but in the areas bordering the desert, perfume is a highly prized luxury item, especially among Muslim men.

Musée du Diamaré

This prominent red building at the market presents a disorganised jumble of treasures from the 10th century, including weapons, ritual regalia, agricultural implements, old pipes and bracelets.

Crafts

The Centre Artisanat next door gives a complete picture of local crafts, which are all reasonably priced. At the Cooperative de Tissage, next to Saré hotel, you'll find a modern house where people are sewing shirts, embroidered tablecloths, dresses, etc for sale at fixed prices.

Places to Stay – bottom end

At about CFA 3000 for one of the eight boukarous with fans, the tree-shaded *Relais Boussou* near the centre of town is great value. For the same price, you can also stay at the inconspicuous *Campement Haradé* (Ah-rah-DAY) downtown between the Petit Marché and the stadium, on the opposite side of the street. It may also still be possible to stay at the *Mission Baptiste* next to the SGBC bank; rooms used to go for CFA 100!

For a really decent hotel, try the *Relais Porte Mayo* (tel 291198), with 10 air-con boukarous for CFA 7900 each. This is the favourite drinking spot of the French *coopérants*. You'll also find African art dealers. Another possibility is the *Relais de Kaliao* (tel 291248), which has 10 boukarous with fairly decent beds and bathrooms, but the lighting is terrible, the atmosphere dead,

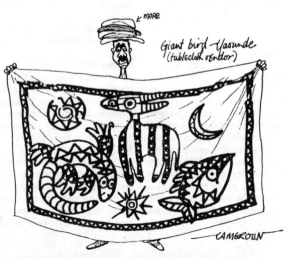

and it is located on the outskirts of town near the Novotel.

Places to Stay – top end

The two best hotels are the modern nondescript *Mizao Novotel* (tel 291300/4, telex 7639, cards AE, V, CB), a good km from downtown, and the *Motel Le Saré* (tel 291295/291194, cards AE), which is club-like with an African feel to it. The 60-room Novotel is newer and has more amenities (pool, tennis, nightclub, art vendors), but the Saré, which also has a pool, is special. Meeting the delightful French couple who run the Saré is enough reason to stay there, but they also have the best restaurant in town. Rooms at the Novotel are CFA 16,845; singles/doubles at the Saré are CFA 13,045/15,640.

Places to Eat

You can eat fairly decently for CFA 1000 to CFA 1500 at *Restaurant Kohi* about one km from the centre. Braised chicken goes for CFA 2500. For really cheap eats, try the *Restaurant Central* near the market, 100 metres in front of the Artisanat. There are about 30 dishes to choose from, most for CFA 400 to CFA 700. The plat du jour at the Relais Porte Mayo is CFA 3800.

Throughout the garden of the Saré the owners have placed lights inside huge African clay pots, which makes a nice backdrop as you dine at the best restaurant in town. The plat du jour will cost you CFA 4000.

Getting There & Away

To get to Waza park, you'll have to hitchhike or take a bush taxi towards Kousséri and get off half way. To get to Rumsiki, take a bush taxi or hitch to Mokolo and try your luck at hitching a ride from there. You'll find the gare routière just on the northern side of the big bridge crossing the Kaliao. Hitching works very well from Maroua to Mokolo. Take a cab to the police post at the entrance to town; the police officers there can be quite helpful finding you a free lift.

A taxi for the day should cost you about CFA 12,000 plus petrol. You can rent a car from Norcamtour (tel 291048, telex 7640, BP 134) at the Novotel or, cheaper, join one of their package tours of Waza and the Rumsiki-Mora area.

AROUND MAROUA
La Dent de Mindif

Serious rock climbers may be interested to learn that the most challenging climb in Central and West Africa is almost certainly *La Dent de Mindif* (Mindif's Tooth), about 35 km south of Maroua. The Japanese considered it to be such a challenge that they sent out a special team of climbers to make the ascent, all for the TV audience back home. They were successful.

Maga

On weekends during the dry season, many expatriates head for Maga, 80 km north-east on the Logone River. The attractions are the superb white sand beaches and the thousands of birds along the river. The *Campement de la Semry* in Maga has rooms for about CFA 7000. It has a pool, a tennis court and a restaurant.

RUMSIKI, MOKOLO & MORA

Bring your camera. This is one of the most fascinating areas in all of Cameroun and also one of the most photographed. You'll find photos of it in many of the tourist brochures. The attractions of the Mokolo-Mora area are the picturesque villages of the Matakam, the Mandara and the Podoko, perched on the side on rocky hills and resembling those of the Dogon in Mali. Each house looks like a tiny fortress.

Mokolo is most interesting on Wednesday, market day. If you're lucky, you might get to see a Matakam funeral, which is a celebration lasting several days with dancing, singing and millet beer drinking. Even the cadaver 'participates' by being exposed so that everyone can render homage.

The most well-travelled route is the 67-

km dirt road north from Mokolo to Mora, passing through Djingliya (Km 15, see the Centre Artisanal), Koza (Km 20, with a market on Sunday), Mora (the Sunday market is one of Cameroun's most colourful).

From Mora, you can drive or climb the five km route to Oudjilla, where all the tour buses invariably stop. A major attraction is the *chef* and his 50 wives; the latter put on a dance performance but, like everything else here, it'll cost you something. During the non-tourist season, the fees they ask are ridiculously high.

From Mora, you could continue north to Waza park, south-east to Maroua, or back to Mokolo via Meri. Otherwise you could go from Mokolo north-west to Mabas and Tourou (35 km) on the Nigerian border. At the Tourou market on Thursday, you'll see a curious sight – women wearing gourds decorated with geometrical designs as head pieces. Another alternative is Ziver, a heavily eroded area where you'll pass between lots of rocks and finally to a surprisingly green plateau. To get there, take the 11 km road to Nogoumaz and from there start walking towards Ziver. It is a three-hour roundtrip. Bring lots of water and a guide.

In Mokolo, you could try renting peoples' private mobylettes or, much cheaper, their bicycles. Hitchhiking is more feasible on market days and during the tourist season, December to May. None of the roads require four-wheel drive vehicles during the dry season.

The attraction of Rumsiki is the moon-like landscape including the nearby Rumsiki Peak, probably the most photographed site in Cameroun. You'll immediately be met by a host of boys who want to act as your guide. They'll take you to the cloth makers, blacksmith, the local bar, and finally to the *sorcier aux crabes* who will tell your fortune. He uses crabs in a clay pot to assist him in his divination. The more questions you ask, the more he will expect for his services at the end. At the Artisanat, open every day except during the long noon break, you'll find

gourds, harps and tools – nothing earth-shaking.

The area around Rumsiki is one of Cameroun's best hiking areas. The Pic de Rumsiki is a technical climb requiring ropes. What you'll see in addition to the unusual landscape are the villages of the Kapsiki. You'll need a guide, and they aren't cheap, costing up to CFA 10,000 for an all-day excursion.

The possibilities include a three-hour hiking excursion to Sina, the first Nigerian village; an all-day excursion to Mala and back via Sina; a long and tiring two-day excursion to Kill via Sina and Mala; and week-long excursions to Kapsiki villages such as Sir, Gouala and Lira. Be prepared for a lot of millet beer on the way and have some Nigerian money on you.

Places to Stay & Eat

Rumsiki The comfortable and well-maintained *Campement de Rumsiki* has a generator, bar and restaurant and charges CFA 7900 for one of its 26 bungalows, all without air-con or fan.

Mora The best place is the *Campement du Safari*, which has 12 air-con bungalows for about CFA 8000, 14 ordinary bungalows for about CFA 4500/6500, a pool and a restaurant with CFA 4000 meals. You can stay more cheaply at the rustic *Campement du Wandala*, with 21 bungalows for about CFA 4500 without air-con, and there's a meagre restaurant.

Mokolo You can no longer stay at the *Mission Catholique* outside town; the government recently forbade them to rent rooms to non-missionaries. So try the four-room *Bar l'Escale* on the main drag. The quoted price, CFA 5000, seems outrageous because the rooms are very spartan and don't even have windows. The real (African) rate might be less, so ask a Camerounian friend to enquire.

The newly renovated 24-room *Rucotel* (tel 295116) on the main road through town is pleasant and by far the nicest place to stay, with singles/doubles for CFA 9750/12,500. It has a nightclub which is open on Thursday and Saturday nights. The plat du jour goes for CFA 4000, and breakfast goes for CFA 900. For drinks with the locals, try *Chez Belingais Bar* near the CARE office, or *Ombre de Plaisir* a few blocks off the main road. For cheap eats, *Restaurant Central* at the market may be your only choice.

Getting There & Away
You can catch bush taxis from Maroua to Mokolo and Mora but no direct ones to Rumsiki. They leave from the gare routière in Maroua very early; 6.30 am isn't unusual. If you miss the first one, you can't be guaranteed of another. Bush taxi service between Mokolo and Rumsiki is erratic. The only day you can be sure there'll be one is Sunday, market day in Rumsiki. Check in Mokolo at both the autogare next to the market and the Grand Carrefour on the western side of town. The traffic on this road is light and tough for hitchhiking.

WAZA NATIONAL PARK
Waza is one of the finest game parks in Central Africa. It's not a park with beautiful views; all you'll see is flat scrubby terrain. Huge herds of elephants are the major attraction. There's also lion, giraffe, antelope, kob, hippo, baboon and various species of birds including ostrich.

Unlike most parks in Africa, the best time to see them is not in the wee hours of the morning or the late afternoon but in the hottest part of the day when they head for the water holes to cool off. For the same reason, the best viewing time is from March to May, the hottest part of the year – the sun literally rounds them up. Seeing 300 elephants at a single pond is not unusual. The more comfortable viewing time is from November to February.

The park is open from 15 November to 15 June and entrance costs CFA 2500. Obligatory guides cost CFA 2000 plus tip. A tour will take a minimum of three hours because the driving time to the major pond is

45 minutes. If you don't have a vehicle, ask vehicles as they pass the park entrance or, better, make friends with guests at the campement. For a guided tour, see Norcamtour at the Novotel in Maroua, or one of the travel agencies in Yaoundé and Douala.

Places to Stay & Eat
Sleeping in the park is forbidden, but you can stay in the village of Waza. Just ask the owner of the only bar-restaurant in the village; she'll find you a room.

If money is not a problem, stay at the pleasant *Le Campement de Waza* near the park entrance on the outskirts of the village of Waza. Air-con singles/doubles cost CFA 12,600/14,500 and bungalows with fans are CFA 11,500. You'll find a clean new pool, which non-guests can use for CFA 800, and a restaurant, which costs CFA 4350 for the plat du jour and CFA 1000 for a sandwich. Make a reservation through the Novotel in Maroua, Garoua or Douala.

Getting There & Away
Waza is 122 km north of Maroua on the paved road to Chad; the entrance is just off the highway. It's fairly simple to find a bush taxi headed for Kousséri early in the morning at the gare routière in Maroua . You can drive and return the same day from Maroua, or stay over night.

BERTOUA
About 345 km east of Yaoundé, Bertoua is rarely visited by tourists. If you'd like to see a little of the real African jungle and possibly Pygmies as well, Bertoua would be a good place to head for because it's the launching place for expeditions into the rainforests.

If you're interested in seeing Pygmies, you'll have to travel to either Yokadouma (about 250 km to the south-east) or Lomié (240 km to the south via Abong-Mbang). Both towns have cheap lodgings.

Places to Stay & Eat
Hôtel de l'Est (tel 241128) has a restaurant, and rooms for about CFA 5500. *Hôtel Relais*

Goldman and *Hôtel Restaurant 'BP'* may be cheaper. The *Mansa Novotel Bertoua* (tel 241333/241251, telex 8520) is the best hotel and has singles/doubles for about CFA 16,500/18,500, a pool and tennis courts. As at many inland hotels, ordering seafood is risky.

DSCHANG

The cool climate at 1400 metres is the main attraction of Dschang, 230 km north-east of Douala. Average temperatures are 16 to 21°C. April is the hottest month, when noon temperatures reach 31°C.

The town itself is rather boring. What attracts so many tourists in addition to the agreeable climate is the 50-room *Centre Climatique de Dschang* (tel 451056, telex 7016). Their facilities include tennis, a pool and horseback riding. Singles/doubles go for about CFA 11,500/14,000. For cheap African hotels, try *Hôtel Constellation*, *Ménoua Palace* and *Auberge de la Ménoua*.

GAROUA-BOULAI

This is the principal border town with the Central African Republic. If you get caught here overnight, you'll have two choices – the friendly *Mission Catholique*, which is next to the bus park and has rooms for CFA 4000, and the *Auberge Central*, with rooms for about CFA 2000.

KOUSSERI

In the far north just across the Chari River from N'Djamena, Kousséri is where travellers must stay overnight if they fail to make it to the bridge by 5.30 pm when the border closes.

Relais du Logone (tel 294157), overlooking the Logone River, is the best hotel in town and charges CFA 8460 for an air-con room and CFA 5865/6985 for a room with one/two beds and fan. It has the town's only restaurant, which is closed on Mondays. Half a km away towards town you'll find *Hôtel Kousséri Moderne* (tel 294091), which has modest rooms with two beds for CFA 5380, and a much nicer room with a single big bed, air-con and carpet for CFA 6480.

KUMBA

Some 140 km north of Douala, English-speaking Kumba is on the principal road connecting Douala and Nigeria. The market here is wild. You'll find goods from the world over (but no Camerounian artisan pieces), partly because many of them are shipped clandestinely from Nigeria where prices are frequently lower.

Places to Stay

The *Hôtel Star*, with six clean rooms, bar and restaurant, is highly recommended. It's a one-man show, but the owner will get you anything. You'll find it near the 10-room *Hôtel l'Authentique* (tel 354420) which, like the Star, has rooms for about CFA 6000. The *Même Pilot Hôtel* behind the bus station has a friendly staff and clean doubles for about CFA 4000. There is a good cheap restaurant next door. *Motor Lodging Hôtel* is near the truck park and is cheaper at about CFA 1500 a double.

MAMFE

Mamfé is the last major town in Cameroun you'll pass through if you're headed overland from Yaoundé or Douala to Nigeria (about 60 km to the west of Mamfé). The people here speak English. You won't find a bank at the Nigerian border, so look around for some Nigerian money. The maximum amount you can legally import is 50 nira.

Places to Stay

Expect to pay about CFA 3000 for a room with shower at the cheapest two hotels, the *Great Aim Hôtel* and the better *African City Lodging House*. *Inland Hôtel* and *Mamfé Hôtel* apparently cost about CFA 1000 more.

Central African Republic

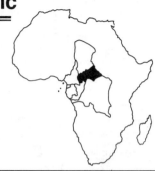

Hunting safaris are big business in the CAR. Ever since the French arrived more than 80 years ago, the chance to stalk and shoot large game has been the country's major attraction. The entire eastern half of the country is sparsely populated, and much of it is savannah, making it perfect for game.

Those with big bucks, such as France's ex-President Giscard d'Estaing apparently think nothing of paying US$10,000 for a two week safari and the opportunity to kill giant eland, lion, leopard and, until recently, elephant. Fortunately, there are those who are just as content to see the animals as to kill them.

Many visitors don't get even near the parks and game reserves because they are so remote. Their impression of the Central African Republic will be entirely different. The rainforests are what they are likely to remember.

The southern boundary with Zaïre is formed largely by the winding Oubangui River bordered by lush vegetation. This is the land of Pygmies, muddy roads, and river boats on their long journey to the Congo. And it's probably the butterfly capital of the world; collages made of butterfly wings are the most popular souvenirs of the CAR.

Bangui, the capital, sits on one side of the Oubangui, overlooking Zaïre on the other. Coming from Paris, you may not think much of Bangui, but if you've been travelling for several weeks on muddy roads northward through Zaïre or southward through war-struck Chad, it can seem like paradise.

HISTORY

History has not been kind to the Central African Republic. No country in Africa suffered more from slavery and colonial exploitation. The CAR also had the dubious honour of a modern day leader – Jean-Bédel Bokassa – who rivalled even Uganda's Amin with his atrocities.

Archaeological remains indicate a civilisation which existed before Egypt's heyday. The earliest inhabitants from among the present population, however, were Pygmies, who hunted and gathered in the forests. Over a thousand years ago people migrated west from Sudan and east from Cameroun into the area.

By 1600 the population attracted slave traders. Unlike West Africa, where most of the slave traders came along the coast, the Central African Republic suffered badly in two directions – from the coast as well as from the Arab empires in Chad and Sudan which needed slaves for themselves and for trade.

The Arabs' armed cavalries periodically swooped down on small settlements, depopulating whole villages at a time. Since no political structure unified the villages they were easy prey. Even in the late 19th century after slavery had been abolished in much of the world, the Arab empires in Chad continued raiding the area and many of the captives ended up at the slave markets in Cairo.

Colonial Period

In the late 19th century when Africa was carved up, France got most of Central Africa. Some time after colonisation, Chad and the area of the Central African Republic were split up, with the latter becoming Oubangui-Chari.

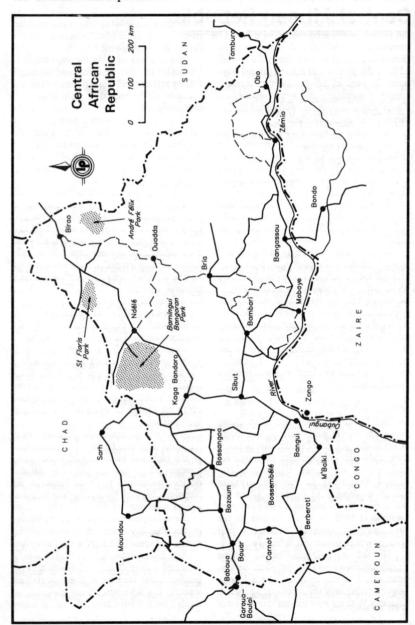

Without the expertise to exploit the area, the French government parcelled it into 17 concessions and handed them over to European companies in exchange for around 15% of the profits and a fixed annual payment. In need of labour, these companies simply conscripted the local population. Those who refused or deserted were killed or tortured and thousands died.

At the beginning of the 20th century the French public was outraged by reports of the inhuman conditions in the territory. Savorgnan de Brazza, the famous French explorer who made some of the first explorations in Central Africa, went on an inquisitory mission, but he died on the way back. The colonial administration thereafter made some vague efforts to curb the tyrannical excesses, but the brutality continued.

Despite famine, sleeping sickness, and severe epidemics of smallpox, the population resisted the French well into the 1920s. By 1930 coffee and cotton were on their way to becoming major crops. The forced labour provoked a series of unsuccessful rebellions during the 1930s. At the same time, Oubangui-Chari had become a favourite big-game hunting ground for French army officers and administrators. During WW II cotton production and diamond exports reached record levels.

Independence
In 1949 the charismatic leader Barthelemy Boganda, whose name adorns the major street in Bangui, founded the first political party calling for independence. He fought for independence for the next 10 years in the National Assembly in Paris alongside Houphouet-Boigny of the Ivory Coast. So when the country became a self-governing republic in 1958, he was a shoo-in for the presidency. An aeroplane accident a year later, however, put an end to his life.

His successor, David Dacko, became highly repressive and attempted no serious economic reforms; he acted like a French puppet, caring only about cultivating French interests. With the government at the point of

bankruptcy in 1965, the army's commander-in-chief, Jean-Bédel Bokassa, led a successful coup against his cousin.

Bokassa was cut from the same fabric as Idi Amin. In 1971 he celebrated Mother's Day by releasing all women from prison and executed all the men who were accused of murdering their mothers. The next year he decreed that thieves would have an ear cut off for the first two offences and a hand for the third. That seemed to have no effect, so he personally supervised a beating of imprisoned thieves; three dead and 43 maimed.

When burglars broke into his house he went to the prison and beat a number of randomly selected inmates to death, gouged out their eyes, and put their bodies on public display. On occasion, when foreign correspondents wrote stories the tyrant didn't like, he imprisoned them or personally assaulted them himself. On another occasion he had a hotel manager repatriated when a minister mistakenly complained of being served partially eaten cheese.

Bokassa could be crazy in other ways. At an independence day dinner party he gave a polished diamond to each of the wives of 13 ambassadors. When Qadafi visited him in 1976, Bokassa announced that he was adopting the Islamic faith and the name Salah Eddine Ammed. But after pocketing Qadafi's US$2 million gift and seeing Qadafi off to the airport, he again became Bokassa the Christian.

Two stories made world news. After amassing a fortune through his interference in the diamond business and squandering foreign aid on prestige projects, Bokassa decided he needed to be an Emperor like Napoleon, his idol. He hired a French firm to design a coronation robe with two million pearls and crystal beads for US$145,000, imported white horses from Belgium to pull his coach, and spent US$2 million on his crown.

On coronation day in 1977 several thousand guests attended, but not a single head of state. He entered Bokassa stadium wearing a golden wreath on his head, ascended the golden throne, placed the crown on his head and took an oath – à la Napoleon. The CAR became the CAE. The cost of this comic opera came to over US$20 million, and despite the derision that the event provoked in the international press, the French picked up most of the tab.

The second newsworthy story (which ultimately toppled Bokassa) was an order in early 1979 that all school children purchase special imperial uniforms made of cloth from his wife's factory.

Pupils took to the streets and were quickly joined by teachers, public employees and the unemployed. Riots resulted, which he could only put down by calling in Zaïrese troops, at a cost of 50 to 400 deaths. Several hundred teenagers were arrested and at least 100 of them were later taken from their cells and beaten or tortured to death, with Bokassa's active participation according to many reports.

The news hit the international press and Bokassa had become the new Idi Amin. France's Giscard d'Estaing, who reputedly accepted hundreds of diamonds as gifts from Bokassa when he was on hunting trips in the CAR, could take no more. He suspended military aid and began plotting a coup. When Bokassa went off to Libya looking for aid, the French seized the occasion to fly former president Dacko back to the Central African 'Empire' along with 700 French paratroopers to stage a coup.

Dacko wasn't too popular and stayed in power only until 1981 when the head of the army, General André Kolingba, took over. He remains president.

Meanwhile, the Ivory Coast had granted Bokassa refuge. But in 1983, even they threw him out when he bombarded Bangui with telegrams saying that he was returning. France reluctantly gave him a chateau outside Paris. One of his wives and 15 children joined him.

Three years later, fed up with living in a desolate chateau and believing Kolingba wouldn't dare kill him, Bokassa shocked the world by returning voluntarily from exile to be tried for treason, murder and cannibalism.

Even four French trial lawyers couldn't do the trick and in 1987 he was convicted on all counts and sentenced to death, but this was commuted to life imprisonment.

Today
Economically, things are pretty sad. The per capita GNP of US$180 is the second lowest in Central Africa. Only Chad's is lower. Diamond's keep the economy afloat. They account for about 25% of the country's foreign exchange earnings, and would account for much more if it were not for the enormous amount of smuggling – in the order of two-thirds of the total production. The diamond export tax encourages the smuggling; not only does the government lose revenue but it keeps production fairly static.

Coffee, cotton and timber are the other three major export earners, but none of them seem likely to take the economy out of the doldrums. Cotton prices are down and not likely to rise again until the early 1990s. The World Bank is investing in forestry, but production is down, probably due to the lack of reafforestation.

Politically, all is not quiet. When Kolingba came to power, he abolished the constitution and outlawed political activity, while promising a return to civilian rule by 1985, but this has not happened. Instead the government released 53 political prisoners.

Various opposition groups have formed in Paris. The government reportedly resents the French for providing this haven for its enemies, and now and then announces another coup plot involving a foreign power. Still, the French maintain a very strong presence, with a military base in Bangui and another in Bouar. The latter played an important role in the Chadian war.

PEOPLE
With a population of only about 2.7 million and a population density 1/20th that of France, the Central African Republic is one of the most thinly populated countries in Africa. The slave trade apparently had an

effect. Most of the people live in the western part of the country, while large areas in the east are virtually uninhabited.

The 80 or so ethnic groups in the CAR live together with little tribal rivalry, quite unlike most of Africa. One of the principal reasons is that there is a common language, Sango, which virtually everybody can speak, equally rare on the African continent.

The Banda are found more in the centre and the east, the Baya more in the west, and together they constitute roughly 60% of the population. The Mandja in the centre of the country follow them in importance.

Many of the people with whom you'll come into contact along the Oubangui (ou-BHAN-gee) River will be from the Oubangui tribe, whose members occupy many of the higher posts in the civil service.

In the northern areas, most of the Africans you'll see will probably be Sara, the same group that dominates southern Chad. They are somewhat taller and bigger than other Africans here.

The Pygmies were some of the original inhabitants of the area, however, they now number only a few thousand, mostly in the rainforests of the south-west. Their way of life is not only fascinating but considerably different from that of most Africans.

Pygmy clans are small with no hierarchy and no division of labour – no chiefs, for instance. Literally all the men have the same job, hunting, and therefore must have the same aptitudes. If a man can't hunt well, his wife may get up and leave. Also, a man must always pick a wife outside the clan and unlike many African cultures, monogamy is the rule, not because polygamy is frowned upon, but because hunting for more than one wife and children would be more than one man could bear.

Sharing is also the rule, but this is not difficult to comprehend since all they usually have is clothes, hunting instruments, cooking utensils and what they catch. Tribunals, prisons and most forms of coercion simply don't exist. Their only form of punishment is exclusion. In serious cases they may ban the culprit from the clan, but even that is usually temporary.

Pygmies are by no means unaffected by 'civilisation'. Today, many clans have become sedentary, establishing more or less permanent camps near Bantou villages and clearing land in return for manioc, bananas and manufactured items.

GEOGRAPHY

Landlocked in the middle of Africa, the Central African Republic is very poor despite its vast mineral resources and adequate rainfall. Bangui, with 470,000 inhabitants, is the only real city. Bambari and Berberati follow with about 45,000 people each.

The country is about the size of France and mostly rolling or flat plateau at 600 to 700 metres, falling to half that altitude near the Oubangui River. There is some variety, however. You'll find dense tropical rainforests in the south-west corner, and the vegetation gradually thins out northward, becoming dry scrub in the Sahelian north-east corner. The Bongo massif near the Sudan border rises to 1330 metres (Mt Toussoro), and the Yadé massif near the Cameroun border rises to 1420 metres (Mt Ngaoui).

There is very little land under cultivation (2%) because of the low population density, and the tsetse fly ensures that the number of cattle in the country is kept to a minimum.

Road conditions differ dramatically throughout the country. In the centre and west, excellent asphalt highways connect Bangui with Chad and Cameroun. In the east, all you'll find is dirt roads and during the rainy season they can become a mess. So not many visitors travel east of Bangui, except for those travelling overland to eastern Zaïre and those on safari.

All three national parks and seven of the eight hunting reserves are in the eastern half, primarily the north-east; many people on safari fly there rather than spend several days on dirt roads. In the south, those with time to kill might travel on the Oubangui River. It forms the southern boundary with Zaïre and connects Bangui with Bangassou to the east and Brazzaville (Congo) and Kinshasa (Zaïre) some 1200 km to the south-west.

CLIMATE

The country usually has enough rainfall to ensure adequate crops to feed its small population. The rainy season lasts eight months in the south (March to October) and four months in the north (June to September).

While temperatures can reach 40°C in the north between mid-February and mid-May, in most of the country, mugginess, not heat, is the main problem.

LANGUAGE

French is the official language. Sango is the national language and used considerably in government and on the radio. Originally a trading language along the Oubangui River, Sango is related to Lingala, one of Zaïre's principal languages. Some greetings in Sango are:

Good morning	m-BEE-bar-ah-moh
Good evening	m-BEE-bar-ah-moh
How are you?	TOHN-gah-NAH-nee-aye
Thank you	seen-GAY-lah MEEN-gee
Goodbye	bee-GUAY-ah-way

VISAS

Only nationals of France, Germany, Israel and Switzerland do not need visas. Tourist visas are usually easy to obtain because wherever there's no Central African Republic embassy, the French embassy usually has authority to issue them. Visa extensions cost CFA 2300 and are usually issued the same day; you must write a letter in French explaining why you want to stay longer.

Bangui is not a good place to get a visa to Sudan because the request must be sent to Khartoum, a process that takes two months or so. The same goes for visas to Gabon because the embassy may charge you CFA 6000 or so for the cable they send to Libreville, plus you must wait up to a week and pay an additional amount for the visa

itself. Visas to Zaïre, on the other hand, are issued while you wait and a single entry, one-month visa costs CFA 8000.

Exit visas are not required if you're leaving from the airport, but they may still be required if you're travelling to Zongo, the town in Zaïre across the river from Bangui. Check with the immigration office one block from the Place de la République on Rue Joseph Degrain in Bangui.

Diplomatic Missions Abroad

Abidjan, Algiers, Berne, Bonn, Brazzaville, Brussels, Cairo, Khartoum, Kinshasa, Lagos, Libreville, N'Djamena, Ottawa, Paris, Rabat, Rome, Tokyo, Washington, Yaoundé.

MONEY

US$1 = CFA 296
£1 = CFA 570

The unit of currency is the Central African CFA. There are apparently no banks outside Bangui. If you're in Bouar and need money, try the *Maison Murt*; they reportedly accept cash and travellers' cheques. In Bangui, try the BIAO bank because they change money quickly and charge no commission for travellers' cheques.

Many people crossing the river to Zongo (Zaïre) buy their Zaïres in Bangui because the black market rate in Bangui is often better than in Zaïre. The only problem is that the border officials apparently make a thorough search. (There is now a bank in Zongo, however.) You're prohibited from exporting more than CFA 75,000.

Banking hours are 6.45 to 11.30 am, Monday to Friday.

GENERAL INFORMATION
Health

A yellow fever vaccination is required, as is a cholera shot if you're travelling within six days from an infected area. Swimming is not safe anywhere because of bilharzia (schistosomiasis). AIDS is also a serious problem.

In 1986 an estimated 800 people died here of the disease, and over 4% of the adults in Bangui were believed to be infected. The rate of infection among prostitutes is particularly high. For drugs you can't do better than *Pharmacie Centrale* near the Place de la République in Bangui.

Security

Warning: thievery and muggings are serious problems in Bangui, especially around the market and along the river near the major hotels. Walking alone at night should be avoided. All of this is closely associated with one of the country's major social problems – alcoholism. If you start drinking with the locals, take into account that they'll be able to drink you under the table.

Business Hours

Business: Monday to Saturday, 7.30 to 12 noon and 2.30 to 5.00 pm. Government: Monday to Friday, 6.30 am to 1 pm, and Saturday 7.00 to 12 noon.

Public Holidays

1 January, 29 March, Easter Monday, 1 May, Ascension Thursday, Pentecost Monday, 13 August (Independence), 15 August, 1 September, 1 November, 1 December (National Day), 25 December.

The biggest holiday is National Day, which is celebrated with dancing, boat and horse races, theatre and wrestling. In the north, Muslims celebrate the End of Ramadan and Tabaski.

Photography

Ask at the tourist office on Ave Boganda to check if a photography permit is required.

Time, Post, Phone & Telex

When it's noon in Bangui, it's 11 am in London and 6 am in New York (7 am during daylight savings time). The mail service is reportedly very slow, so if possible, post your mail outside the country. The poste restante in Bangui is very efficient but charges CFA 125 per letter.

You cannot direct dial to Bangui. You can send a telex from the post office and the city's top two hotels.

GETTING THERE
Air

From Europe the only direct flights are on UTA and Air Afrique from Paris. Regular fares are sky high – about £950 for a 30-day excursion ticket from London. London's bucket shop prices, on the other hand, are quite reasonable, the cheapest being Aeroflot's flight via Moscow for about £420.

From New York you can take Air Afrique all the way to Bangui, changing in Abidjan, or Air France/UTA, changing in Paris. The return economy fare is US$2704 either way; the 45-day excursion fare is US$2078 (US$100 more in the high season).

Within Africa there are flights twice a week from Douala on Cameroun Airlines and Air Afrique, and once a week flights from Libreville on Air Gabon and from Kinshasa on Air Zaïre (unreliable).

Before Le Point Mulhouse went bankrupt you could get tickets (return portion valid up to one year) from Marseille to Bangui for between FF 3200 and FF 3800 (US$570 to US$680). There are rumours that they may reopen, or another company may offer a similar deal. In case Le Point does reopen, their office is in the centre of town near the Cameroun Airways office.

Car

From Yaoundé (Cameroun) to Bangui via Bouar, count on three days; the 700-km Bangui-Cameroun border stretch is asphalt all the way, but the 610-km portion in Cameroun is paved for only 70 km. From N'Djamena (Chad), most people take the route through Cameroun and Bouar because the road is paved for all but 270 km of the 1465-km distance.

The N'Djamena-Sarh-Bangui road is 205 km less, with 500 km of paved road in the Central African Republic, but the Chadian portion is so bad that most prefer the route through Cameroun.

Those travelling south to Zaïre should be prepared for the worst road conditions in Africa, with lots and lots of mud. To get to Brazzaville/Kinshasa, everybody puts their vehicles on the twice monthly riverboat. Count on paying CFA 45,000 for the vehicle and CFA 11,000 per person sleeping in it.

If you're headed for eastern Zaïre and cross over at Bangui, do it on a weekday because otherwise you'll have to stay in Zongo (thieves galore) until Monday to go through customs. The ferry (*bac*) costs CFA 6000 for a vehicle and three people. It operates weekdays 7 am to 4 pm and Saturday 7 am to 12 noon. Make inquiries at the port captain's office near the river.

The Zaïre border closes weekdays at 5 pm and Saturday at 4 pm. If the ferry breaks down, which is often the case, you can always get a canoe.

Most people bound for eastern Zaïre, however, cross at Bangassou, not at Bangui. The road from there to Kisangani, even though terrible and always muddy, is at least better than the road from Zongo to Kisangani.

On the 747-km road from Bangui to Bangassou, you'll encounter numerous wooden and metal bridges; anticipate several difficult stream crossings between Bambari and Kongbo. The road is best between December and March when there's little rain. (As you get closer to Kisangani, it rains all year long.) Be sure not to miss the spectacular falls three km east of Kembé, where you can camp. In Kembé you'll find a hotel and a campsite next to it; the latter costs CFA 600 a night.

In theory, there's petrol in Bambari and Bangassou, but inquire in Bangui on its availability. Bangassou, not Bangui, is where you go through exit formalities. If the ferry is operative, which isn't always the case, the two 12-volt batteries will probably need a charge from your battery, and the operator will probably want up to five litres of diesel fuel plus a tip. If you cross the river by pirogue, you can apparently run up a bill of CFA 10,000 or so.

Bush Taxi

Coming from Cameroun, you'll find cars at the border 159 km west of Bouar, and at Bouar itself. A bush taxi direct from the border to Bangui takes about 14 hours. Hitchhiking is also quite possible on this well travelled route, however, truckers frequently want as much as the car fare.

If you enter from southern Chad, finding bush taxis or minibuses will be more difficult because the road is not nearly as well travelled. The entrance points from Zaïre are across the river from Bangui and Bangassou. Buses leave from Bangassou to Bangui twice a week, typically on Wednesday and Friday.

Almost nobody goes overland to the Congo. If you do, take the bus from Bangui to Berbérate (Thursday or Saturday), then another bus to Nola. From there you should be able to pick up a motorised canoe headed downstream.

River Boat

Of the 150,000 visitors to the Central African Republic in 1982, more than 130,000 came by boat. Almost all of these were Africans and not tourists, but it illustrates the importance of *La Ville de Brazza* which ploughs the 1200 km between Brazzaville (Congo) and Bangui. This trip provides an excellent opportunity to meet Africans. You can also buy food in the villages along the way. The boat stops at eight; be sure your passport is stamped in Mongoumba (CAR) and Betou (Congo).

First class consists of a cabin with one double bed, bathroom and air-con. The price including all meals is about CFA 70,000. Tourist class consists of four beds to a room and the price per person without meals is about CFA 24,000. Second class is about CFA 12,000. The trip takes 10 days going downriver to Brazzaville, and 14 days returning. The price from Brazzaville is also slightly more expensive for that reason (about CFA 100,000 for 1st class, CFA 27,000 for tourist class, and CFA 13,500 for 2nd class). There may be student discounts, so ask.

Top: School children in a parade, CAR (BH)
Left: Tailor, CAR (KW)
Right: Old Pygmy man, CAR (BH)

Top: House painting, Ubangi-Chari Region, CAR (EE)
Bottom: Boali Waterfalls, CAR (BH)

There are two boats, which leave approximately twice a month, but the exact date of departure isn't fixed until about two weeks in advance. In Bangui see either ATC (L'Agence Transcongolaise des Communications) near the market, or L'Agence Centrafricaine des Communications Fluviales (BP 822, tel 610111). In Brazzaville, contact ATC (BP 74, tel 810441).

GETTING AROUND

Air
Inter-RCA has regular flights to the major inland towns, and Air Afrique (tel 614660) and Centravia (BP 125, tel 611122) charter small aircraft.

Bush Taxi
The Central African Republic has a good system of minibuses and bush taxis connecting Bangui with most of the major towns, including Bouar and Berbérate in the west, Bambari and Bangassou in the east, and Bossangoa and Kaga Bandoro in the centre.

Taxi
If you bargain well, taxis in Bangui should cost you about CFA 2500 per hour and CFA 19,000 per day plus gas. Hiring a cab by the day comes out a lot cheaper than renting a vehicle because if you plan to leave Bangui you need a chauffeur.

BANGUI
Bangui is in the heart of the tropics on the Oubangui River and bordering Zaïre. The rainfall here is heavier and the vegetation thicker than in the north. The city was founded by the French in 1889, and named after the rapids nearby. With the river on one side, hills covered with lush vegetation on the other, and broad avenues shaded by mango and flamboyants, the city has its charm.

Around the central market and along Ave Boganda you'll find most of the downtown activity. The centre of town is La Place de la République with a triumphal arch, a monument to Bokassa's coronation and empire.

For the African section of town, head five km out on Ave Boganda until it intersects with Ave Koudougou. This is 'Km 5', with the largest market, lots of bars, and dancing places. Decent cheap accommodation is nearby, but be careful in this area as a lot of muggings have been reported. If you're an adventurous eater, you'll love Bangui. You can find anything from cooked monkey, snake or wart hog to crocodile and antelope in some restaurants!

Information
Banks BIAO, Banque Centrafricaine d'Investissements, Union Bancaire en Afrique Centrale.

Embassies & Consulates Some of the major embassies include:

France
(tel 613000) BP 884
West Germany
(tel 610746) BP 901
Japan
(tel 610668) BP 1367
USA
(tel 610200) BP 924

The following countries also have embassies in Bangui: Cameroun, Chad, Congo, Egypt, Gabon, Ivory Coast, Nigeria, Senegal, Sudan, Zaïre.

There are three European consulates in Bangui:

Belgium
(tel 614041) c/o Mocaf, Ave du 1er Janvier, BP 806
Netherlands
(tel 614822) c/o Ponteco, Ave du 1er Janvier, BP 32
UK
c/o Diamond Distributors, Ave Boganda, open only 8 to 9 am.

Bookstores & Supermarkets The biggest bookstore is Papeterie Central next to the Minerva Hôtel. The bookstores at the Sofitel and Novotel sell postcards, books on the

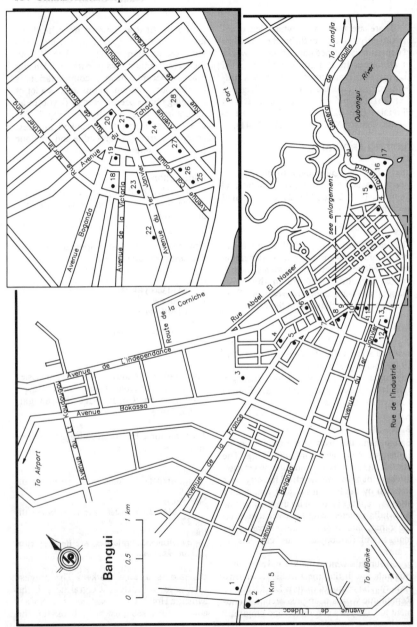

Bangui

1	Le Punch Coco
2	Bar 5/5
3	Stadium
4	National Hôtel
5	Le Sympathique Bar
6	Artisana
7	Le Mandarin Restaurant
8	Museum
9	SCORE Supermarket
10	La Pergola Restaurant
11	Equinox Club
12	Le Montana Restaurant & Nightclub
13	Pili Plli Restaurant
14	Bananas Snack Bar
15	French Embassy
16	Rock Hôtel
17	Sofitel
18	Peuch del Sol Nightclub & Oustaou Restaurant
19	L'Alinor Restaurant
20	Le Portugais Restaurant
21	Place de la République
22	US Embassy
23	Hôtel Minerva
24	Hôtel New Palace
25	Novotel
26	Tropicana Creperie
27	Le Bacchus Restaurant
28	Market

Central African Republic, and international newspapers and magazines.

Score is the major supermarket; it's on Ave Boganda about four blocks from the Place de la République.

Travel & Safari Agencies Bangui-Tourisme (tel 612500, BP 875, telegram 'Banguitour') Ave 1er Janvier; Agence Antas (tel 613688, BP 895). Ocatour (tel 614366, BP 655), the government agency, is near the centre of town on Ave de la Victoire. They run tours for groups of 15 or more. For safari guides, see Safeca one block from the Novotel, or ask at the Sofitel.

Boganda Museum

This museum is definitely worth a visit. The great variety of musical instruments is particularly interesting, as is the display of Pygmy utensils. There are some ancient artefacts as well. Paradoxically, even though the country is noted for its rainforests, wood carvings are fairly rare. The museum is one block from Ave Boganda behind Score. Hours: weekdays 8 am to 12 noon; Saturday 8 to 11.30 am.

Oubangui River

A canoe ride on the Oubangui River can be quite interesting. The Rock hotel area is where you'll find the boats.

Places to Stay – bottom end

Le Centre d'Accueil Touristique (tel 611256) costs CFA 650 for camping and CFA 2100/3100 for a singles/doubles. It's seven km from the centre of town (CFA 180 for a shared taxi) on the old road to M'Baiki, two km beyond Km 5.

Many overland travellers stay here because it's cheap and clean and has a nice ambience. The doubles have private showers. Take special precautions, however, as some of the rooms don't have locks and numerous travellers have reported being ripped off. There is a bar and a cheap restaurant on the premises (painfully slow service), and there are numerous African restaurants nearby.

The *Mission Catholique* allows travellers to camp for a small donation. The facilities include hot showers and a bar. They also have rooms, but they're not cheap. The *Centre Protestant de Jeunesse* also has cheap dormitory-style accommodation. It's a few km out along Avenue de l'Independence and you can catch bush taxis to the north and west out the front.

Places to Stay – middle

Hotels are outrageously expensive. The cheapest may be *Hôtel New Palace*, with singles/doubles for about CFA 11,500/13,500. The 13 rooms are spacious with air-con and private bath, and the bar downstairs is popular with Africans. It's in the heart of town at the Place de la République, a fairly noisy area.

Places to Stay – top end

The new *Sofitel* is the nicest hotel because of its setting on the banks of the Oubangui River. The terrace is a popular place for drinking and watching the hippos. The only drawback besides the high price is being two km from the centre of town. That's the major reason why some people prefer the *Novotel*, which is in the heart of the city. The very popular Rock Hôtel closed when the owner died and left the hotel to charity. Cheaper, and in the heart of town, is the *Minerva Hôtel*, a colonial-style hotel that is well maintained and has a popular bar. The similarly priced *National Hôtel* is the only hotel in this group that has an African atmosphere, but it's terribly managed and not recommended.

Sofitel Bangui (tel 613038), CFA 33,500/36,000 for singles/doubles, pool, all 60 rooms facing the river, TV/video, cards AE, D.
Novotel Bangui (tel 610279, telex 5297), CFA 27,500/29,000 for singles/doubles, pool, popular bar, TV/video, dwontown, cards AE, D.
Minerva Hôtel (tel 610233, telex 5240), CFA 14,000/16,500 for singles/doubles, 23 air-con rooms, bar, no restaurant, no credit cards.
National Hôtel (tel 612710), CFA 15,000 a room, terrace restaurant, crowded rooms, shared bathrooms, halls with red lights, several km from the centre of town, and telephone usually not working.

Places to Eat

Cheap Eats Finding a really cheap restaurant around Km 5 is no problem but finding one downtown is another matter. In the heart of town at the Place de la République there's an unnamed restaurant. Prices run from CFA 700 to CFA1400, eg the grilled fish is CFA 850.

Europe Assistance is perhaps more interesting and slightly cheaper. The restaurant is a shack which serves food you'll only find in Central Africa, such as monkey and porcupine stew. But there are only one or two dishes on any given day. It's about a one-km walk from the centre on Ave du 1er Janvier beyond the US Embassy and across from Le Montana.

The city has several snack bars, the most well-known being *Bananas Snack Bar* on Blvd de Gaulle which leads to the Rock and the Sofitel. Open every day until midnight, it is modern, popular, and serves, among other things, hamburgers and sandwiches for about CFA 1000 or half a chicken for CFA 2800.

Equinox nightclub, two blocks behind the US Embassy, has an adjoining snackbar that offers fare similar to Bananas and is open late.

The *Salon de Té de la Paix* is where you go in the morning for pastry and coffee and to watch people. They serve ice cream too. It's on Ave Boganda several blocks from the Place de la République.

African Don't miss *Maman Mado*, a well-known restaurant with a clean pleasant ambience serving exotic creatures like crocodile, antelope (*gazelle*), monkey (*singe*), wart hog (*phacochère*), plus more typical African dishes, brochettes and perch (*capitaine*). Most dishes are about CFA 2850. Open for lunch and dinner and closed Sunday, it's at the Artisan Centre, about two km from the heart of town.

A block off the Place de la République next to Le Portugais is *L'Oubangui Grill*, which serves grilled meats, fish and African food, typically for CFA 1800 a plate.

Le Pili Pili (closed Mondays) offers simple Central African cuisine with a few exotic dishes such as wart hog (CFA 2600). It's next to the river several long blocks beyond the US Embassy.

French The expensive *L'Oustaou*, open for dinner only and closed Monday, is one of Bangui's two finest restaurants, with a choice of inside or outside dining. The owner takes orders personally and oversees the service and food preparation. It's between Ave Boganda and Ave de la Victoire, three blocks from the Novotel and the Place de la-République.

Le Bacchus, around the corner from the Novotel, is equally good with high prices.

The mousses and terrines are homemade, and there's a special of the day that's moderately priced. It is only open for dinner and is closed on Sundays.

Le Montana, on Ave du 1er Janvier several long blocks beyond the US Embassy, is open every day except Friday. The food is good and the prices are moderate. The homemade terrines and fish dishes are outstanding and the atmosphere is very friendly.

The food at *La Pergola*, which is only open for dinner, is moderately expensive and doesn't get good reviews from the locals. The grilled meats and fish are generally said to be good, but the sauces tend to be somewhat pasty. To find it, start at the Place de la République, go four blocks out on Ave Boganda, then take a left. It is about 100 metres or so down the road.

Speciality Restaurants *La Pignatta*, open for dinner only and in the centre off Ave Boganda near Citec, offers pizza, some pasta dishes and steaks. The food is good, the atmosphere pleasant, and prices are moderate.

Lebanese food is the speciality at *Le Perroquet*, also open for dinner only and in the centre of town opposite the Cinéma Club. They have good brochettes and wine by the carafe, but the service can be a little on the slow side.

Le Portugais, a block off the Place de la République, is one eating establishment that has persisted while others have fallen by the wayside. It's the best place for those who want a decent inexpensive meal. They serve standard Portuguese fare as well as some North African and Spanish dishes such as couscous and paella.

Entertainment & Sports

Bars The Sofitel and the Rock have unbeatable locations on the bank of the river; have a drink on the terrace and look for hippos. The younger crowd likes Bananas. The bar at the Novotel downtown is also quite popular. The pub-like bar at the Minerva Hôtel is where you can meet local

expatriates. The terrace of the La Paix is more tranquil.

The big bar at the Hôtel New Palace at the Place de la République is typically crowded with Africans.

There are many African bars out around Km 5. The local brew, Mocaf, is popular with the patrons of these bars.

Nightclubs *Le Songo*, downtown facing the Renault dealership, is the newest nightclub and is expensive. *Le Scotch Club* at the Rock is equally expensive and plays music appealing to the European crowd. *Equinox*, one block behind the US Embassy is open every night. Most of the music played there is American. Drinks are CFA 1500.

Privé, at Le Montana restaurant on Ave du 1er Janvier is open air and fairly popular. It is closed on Fridays. *Blow Up* plays both African and American music. It is some three blocks from the Place de la République, next to Le Perroquet restaurant across from the Cinéma Club and just down from *Le Peuch del Sol*, another place with moderate prices. The music at Blow Up is mostly African and attracts both the African middle class and Europeans.

The adventurous should head for Km 5. Two of the most popular places are *Bar ABC* and, a block or two away, *Bar 5/5*. They frequently have live music and on occasion the country's most popular singer, Musiki, makes an appearance. Unlike those downtown which start late, the dancing here starts as early as 8 pm.

Cinemas Cinéma New Palace at the Place de la République has movies at 6 and 9 pm. There's no air-con. Cinéma Club three blocks away is another.

Sports There are pools at the top three hotels. For tennis try your luck at the local tennis club about four blocks from the Place de la République. There's also a nine-hole golf course with sand greens eight km from Bangui on the road to Damara.

Things to Buy

Markets The market downtown is very active, but the Marché Mamadou M'Baiki near Km 5 is even bigger.

Artisan Goods Head for the Artisanat (open every day until 6 pm with two hours for lunch) on Ave de l'Indépendance several km from the centre of town near the Pasteur Institute. Among other things, you'll find ivory, malachite, grass dolls, wooden carvings and masks.

Much of what is available comes from neighbouring countries, but the designs made with butterfly wings and the small rugs with a yellow background and angular patterns are from the Central African Republic.

If you're looking for high quality African art, the place to go is Perroni.

Music Finding records is quite difficult, and the quality of locally made cassettes is low. The best thing is to buy a good quality empty cassette and look for one of the small shops that will record your choice of their records. Musiki is the leading star. Canon Star, Super Commando Jazz and Makembé are also popular.

Getting There & Away

Air Inter-RCA has regular flights to the major inland towns.

Bush Taxi & Bus In Bangui you'll find bush taxis and minibuses headed in all directions from the gare routière – east to Bangassou via Bambari (Sunday and Tuesday, taking 3 days), north to Kaga Bandoro, north-west to Bossangoa (Sunday and Thursday, taking seven hours), north-west to the Cameroun border via Bouar (every day in small cars on good road, taking 14 hours), and west to Berbérate (Thursday and Saturday).

Even though most departures are around 9 am, you risk not getting a seat if you arrive later than 7 am. Those for Bouar start filling up as early as 6 am. The gare routière is located four km from the centre of town on Ave de l'Indépendance.

If you're heading for Cameroun and plan to catch the night train to Yaoundé, take the 240-km road north-west from the border (Garoua-Bouali) to N'Gaou-N'Dal (Cameroun) instead of going south to Bélabo as most people do. The early morning cars from Bouar to the border now do the trip in several hours, so you should be able to leave Bouar early morning and catch the train that night (about 9 pm).

The road from Bangui to Bouar is also good for hitchhiking, and can sometimes be done in one day. Whether you're hitchhiking to Cameroun or Chad, the best place to catch rides is PK 12, the police checkpoint on the outskirts of Bangui.

Getting Around

Airport Transport The airport departure tax is CFA 2000 for destinations in West and Central Africa, and CFA 3500 for destinations elsewhere. Bangui airport has a restaurant, bar and post office. A taxi into town (eight km) costs CFA 900 (CFA 1500 after 9 pm), but only the most persistent will get one for less than CFA 1500 at the airport. With luck, you may find a much cheaper shared taxi into town.

Taxi Cabs are plentiful during the day and do not have meters. Fares are CFA 90 for shared taxis (CFA 180 beyond Km 5) and CFA 700 for a taxi for yourself. After 9 pm the rates go up to CFA 125 and CFA 900 respectively. Taxis by the hour cost about CFA 2500 and bargaining is definitely required. By the day, expect to pay about CFA 19,000 plus petrol.

Car Rental Auto Location, downtown just off Ave Boganda about three blocks from the circular Place de la République, has cars for about CFA 18,000 a day, CFA 22,000 with driver. Also worth trying are Tsiros Location (tel 614446/612986) and Christelle Location (tel 613536).

AROUND BANGUI

There are two nearby trips that can be done as day trips if you have a vehicle. Those without their own transport should probably allow a full weekend.

Les Chutes de Boali

Boali waterfalls some 100 km north-west of Bangui are worth an excursion in the rainy season when the water is flowing well. You'll see little water during the dry season because the river has been diverted to a nearby hydro-electric plant. Don't be surprised if people try to charge you for picnic tables – up to CFA 2000! The falls are well signposted and about four km off the main road. There is a nearby hotel that charges around CFA 3500 per person.

Pygmy Territory

Another possibility is heading toward M'Baiki 107 km south-west of Bangui. This is a major coffee and timber-growing area and is the home of the Pygmies. While they average about 120 cm (4 feet) in height, some are much smaller. A few of their camps are located a little south of M'Baiki, but since they move about hunting in the rainforests, their settlements are rarely permanent and their worldly goods consist of nothing but the essentials.

The government tourist agency, Ocatour, may be able to answer some of your questions. They will also arrange tours for groups of 15 or more, which is not a bad way to gain a little insight into the Pygmy way of life.

NATIONAL PARKS & GAME RESERVES

The three game parks and eight game reserves harbour the 'big four' (elephant, lion, leopard and rhino) as well as giraffe, buffalo, roan antelope, topi, waterbuck, bushbuck, black rhino, monkey, baboon, cheetah, crocodile, wart hog, bee-eater, bushbaby and Lord Derby Eland. The number of animals that have been killed by poachers is staggering. In all of Africa, for example, the number of rhino has gone from approximately 60,000 in 1970 to 4000 in 1986. The slaughter in the Central African Republic is as bad as anywhere, the only difference being

that the wildlife was more abundant to begin with, so there are still some remaining.

The rhino, crocodile, leopard, elephant and giraffe populations have been particularly hard hit. The poachers are primarily gangs, many from neighbouring Chad and Sudan, but it's not unusual to hear of local businessmen and even public officials being involved.

The World Wildlife Fund (1250 24th St, NW, Washington, DC 20037) is helping to save the elephants, gorillas and other animals in the Dzanga-Ndoki, an area in the south-western corner near the Congo and Cameroun. This area is known to hold probably the last large concentration of elephants in the country, estimated at 3000, and it contains more primate species than any protected area in the world, including chimpanzees and some of the highest densities of lowland gorillas recorded in Africa.

Armed men seeking elephant meat and ivory regularly ride up the Sangha River from the Congo in motorised dugout canoes or come overland by foot from Cameroun. Trails of smoke can often be seen from a distance from the fires of successful hunters, who smoke the elephant meat before returning home with it.

Until 1986, anyone could walk into this expanse of wild land and shoot anything they wanted. Now it's illegal. The WWF is trying to get the government to declare the area a national park. With our help, maybe they will.

Photo Safari

Those interested in just seeing the animals usually go to one of the game parks. They're open December through May.

If you go on your own, don't expect to find petrol anywhere. For lodging, you'll find the *Hôtel-Campement de Mbossobo* in Ouanda-Djallé near André Félix with rooms or bungalows. There are also campements in La Gounda near St Floris, and in Koumbala.

Bamingui-Bangoran National Park

This park is by far the largest of the three. It's

north of Bangui on a 700-km road, half of which is paved.

St Floris & André Félix National Parks
These two parks are much smaller and more remote; most people fly there. Unlike the other two parks where the vegetation is mainly savannah, André Félix is mountainous.

BANGASSOU
This sleepy town of 35,000 is the major crossing point into Zaïre for travellers with their own vehicles. The *Tourist Hôtel* has rooms, but you can also camp there for a small fee or at the *Mission Protestante* for nothing. Wherever you camp, beware of thieves.

BOSSEMBELE
Bossembélé is a major crossroad to the north and north-west from Bangui. It has a fairly busy market, which sells mostly foodstuffs, but the town has little to offer the visitor. If you stay overnight there are a few cheap hotels and a couple of interesting bars, such as Bar-Dancing Wililoko. The main attractions of the area are the Bouali Chutes (see Around Bangui) and Lambi Chutes.

Lambi Chutes
Lambi Chutes are more spectacular than Bouali Chutes, rainy season or dry, but you need your own vehicle to get there. Going south to Bangui, after 20 km you reach a dirt road crossroad, which has a stop sign. Turn right and go 33 to 35 km and look for a marked side road on the left. If you come to a bridge over the river you have gone too far.

Getting There & Away
There are buses to Bassangoa (CFA 1800) and points north that leave from the roadside or you can catch them at the Petroca gas station from about 11 am to 1 pm. Buses to Bangui leave in the morning and they can drop you at the Boali Chutes turnoff (CFA 800).

BOUAR
This run-down town of 30,000 inhabitants is 160 km from the major Cameroun border crossing and pleasantly located on a plateau at an altitude of 950 metres. The country's largest military base is here; chances are you'll see French soldiers in the bars.

Les Mégalithes
One of the more interesting attractions of this area are the megaliths (*les mégalithes*), some of which are on the outskirts of town and weren't excavated until the mid-1960s. There are 70-odd groups of these curious, standing granite stones in varying arrangements in the Bouar area. Those of Beforo, Gam and Tia are to the north and east of Bouar. The megaliths, some of them weighing as much as three or four tons, appear to be evidence of an ancient culture that existed long before any of the present Africans arrived.

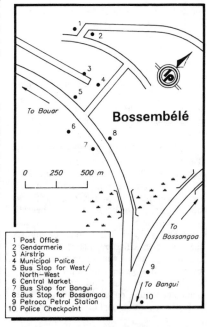

To Bouar

Bossembélé

To Bossangoa

To Bangui

1	Post Office
2	Gendarmerie
3	Airstrip
4	Municipal Police
5	Bus Stop for West/North—West
6	Central Market
7	Bus Stop for Bangui
8	Bus Stop for Bossangoa
9	Petroca Petrol Station
10	Police Checkpoint

0   250   500 m

Places to Stay

Hôtel Moura has clean rooms for about CFA 1700 a double. The *Foyer de la Jeunesse*, on the main drag, has dormitory rooms and clean bathrooms for about CFA 1200 a bed. *Hôtel des Relais* is another. The mission apparently does not accept travellers.

KAGA BANDORO

If you're headed overland from Bangui to the parks in the north-east, you may well end up spending the night at Kaga Bandoro, a village 337 km north of Bangui via Sibut. You can climb the Kaga, about three km from town, for good views of the surrounding area.

Places to Stay & Eat

You'll find a pension or two with very basic rooms for CFA 1000 and, in the main square, a Sudanese bloke who runs a restaurant which serves cheap food and tea. If you're lucky, you might get invited to stay at the workers' hostel of a local company.

In the evenings the market is lit up by oil lamps. You can get cheap munchies and sit and natter with the locals while sampling the delicious local booze, *hydromiel* (a sort of honey beer).

Chad

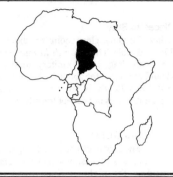

War is the major reason that Chad hasn't been seeing many travellers. It started in 1965 as a civil war, but by 1987, it was purely a Chadian-Libyan affair. The country's infrastructure is now in a shambles. Walk down the streets of N'Djamena and you'll see empty buildings riddled with machine-gun bullets and soldiers everywhere, many of them wounded. This war, plus falling cotton prices, has devastated the economy; Chad's annual per capita income of US$120 now ranks as lowest in the world.

Change is in the air. By early 1988 Chad had booted out the Libyans except from a relatively small area in the north. N'Djamena's charm is coming back. You can travel all over the south, to Lake Chad and overland to Niger. Travelling north-east of N'Djamena has become much less risky. It's no longer unusual to hear of travellers taking a truck to Abéché, for instance.

The far north, where well-equipped Libyan troops retreated in early 1987 following smashing victories by rifle-armed Chadian troops charging in Toyota pickup trucks, may one day again be open to travellers. It's the area of one of Chad's most interesting sites, Tibesti, the most mountainous area in the entire Sahara, with spectacular scenery, lunar-like craters, volcanic massifs, gorges and small desert lakes.

Even if Tibesti remains off-limits, N'Djamena, southern Chad and the Lake Chad area, particularly in conjunction with a side trip to Waza game park in northern Cameroun, are sufficiently interesting to make a short visit here quite worthwhile.

HISTORY

During the drought of 1984, you could walk across Lake Chad. About 2500 years ago, however, when Pericles was debating on the floor of the Greek Senate, Lake Chad was almost as large as present-day Greece and Yugoslavia combined. It even connected with the Nile. The area was much wetter, and wild animals were abundant. For this reason, some of the richest prehistoric archaeological sites in Africa are found within the territorial limits of Chad, especially in the far north around Tibesti, where hunters made rock engravings.

At about the time the lake began receding 2500 years ago, some of these hunters began raising cattle and establishing permanent settlements. A people collectively known as the Sao migrated from the Nile valley, settling around the lake. Legends depict them as giants capable of feats of superhuman strength and endurance. Their settlements eventually grew into walled cities of brick.

The Sao's forte was pottery; so if anyone tries to sell you some *ancien* pottery, at least you'll know how old it might be. Chances are, however, that it was made the day before. The Sao also developed the method by which all African bronze art is made today – the sophisticated 'lost wax' technique of metal casting.

The Arab Kingdoms

People east of Chad moved into the area, intermarrying with the Sao. In the 9th century, one of them established himself as king and founded the state of Kanem, which was to last for 1000 years. Chad was the intersection for two major African caravan routes, one north to the Mediterranean coast and the other east towards the regions of the lower

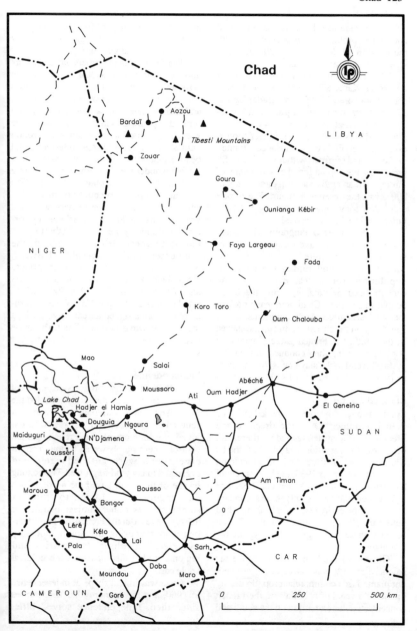

Nile. The trade in salt, copper, cotton, gold and slaves brought increasing contact with the Muslim world, and by 1200 AD Islam was the dominant religion.

The kingdom expanded, becoming known as Kanem-Bornu; its economy was solidly anchored in the slave trade. By the 17th century, it was an empire, with a sizeable army noted for its cavalry of men and armoured horses. The greatest king, Alooma, even had a small force of musketeers trained in Turkey and outfitted with iron helmets. So great was his reputation that the sultan of Turkey sent an ambassadorial party of about 200 across the desert to his court. The empire didn't last long, however, and by 1812 the Fulani had sacked the capital.

Two lesser Arab kingdoms flourished during this period. Like the Kanem-Bornu empire, they controlled the trans-Saharan caravan trails and raided the southern populations for slaves. Because of the decentralised political systems, the black people in southern Chad were easy prey to the well-organised Arab kingdoms which could rely on cavalries to round up the slaves. In the south, the French gained immediate popularity during their conquest of Chad by putting an end to the slave raids. In the north, resistance continued until 1930.

Colonial Period

Chad was one of the most neglected of all the French colonies. Only the dregs of the French colonial system ended up there, and because of high attrition, fully 42% of Chad's administrative districts had no French on their staff. As late as 1933, the largest school had only three grades. When Chad became independent there were only three secondary schools in the entire country. Northern Chad held virtually no interest for the French because there were no readily exploitable resources.

Cotton thrived in the much wetter southern area. It was native to the area but not planted as a commercial crop. So during the 60-odd years of colonialism, the French concentrated their attention on the south and on cotton, giving a French company (Cotonfran, later Cotontchad) a monopoly on purchasing and ginning.

The French made farmers pay a head tax and set cotton quotas for villages. The farmers had to plant more than a little because the prices paid were artificially low, and if they called this a 'colonial' crop and refused to plant, the village chiefs, whom the French appointed to ensure that the cotton quotas were met and taxes collected, could be as brutal as they damn well chose.

No wonder the southerners began hating the French as much as the northerners. The educated people who could organise opposition tended to be southerners who had grasped the meagre educational opportunities offered by the French. In this respect, the northerners clearly lost out to the southerners during the colonial period, inverting the relationship that existed prior to the arrival of the French. The northerners also lost during WW II, when Italy (which ruled Libya) and the pro-Nazi Vichy government of France signed a treaty giving Libya the Aouzou strip in northern Chad. This is the basis of Libya's present-day claim to that strip.

Independence

After WW II when 'progressive' political groups were formed, the southerners led the way. And when independence came, a southerner, François Tombalbaye, who enjoyed the support of the French, gained control. There simply weren't enough northerners who were both educated and organised to contend for power. The coming of age of the south jarred the north, which had become accustomed to think of southerners as either subject peoples or merely slaves. But the French had gone overboard in favouring the south, not only exacerbating ethnic animosities and regionalism but also upsetting the political apple cart.

Chad was in bad shape at independence in 1960, and the economy has deteriorated since then. Independence solved little, indeed, it set in motion a civil war that has turned into a war with Libya, with no end in sight.

The immediate advantages of independence went to the south. Administrators, civil servants and senior army officers all had to read and write, so the bulk of those recruited turned out to be southerners, who were better educated. It didn't take long for the northerners to view the new government dominated by southern civil servants as representing the interests of the southern Sara tribe which they felt behaved like conquerors.

Within two years President Tombalbaye declared all opposition political parties illegal and began killing off his political rivals. Revolts erupted, which he met with force and mass killings.

In 1966 FROLINAT, the guerrilla movement opposing the continued dominance of the southern elites, was formed in exile. There was a ground swell of support in the north for the rebels in the field, and the movement spread quickly. By 1968 the situation became very serious and the government was saved only by calling in French troops.

In 1971 Libya began supplying the guerrillas with arms. In the same year the government attempted a policy of national reconciliation by releasing some political prisoners and appointing Muslim ministers. But it didn't work. Qadafi took advantage of the situation by secretly offering to withdraw his support of FROLINAT in return for CFA 23,000 million in aid and Tombalbaye's recognition of Libya's right to occupy the northern border strip of Aouzou, half the size of Great Britain.

In desperation, Tombalbaye agreed but then he virtually went crazy. He got hooked on Haitian voodoo practices and went on a campaign of cultural revolution, requiring people to replace their Christian names with African ones, and forcing all civil servants and ranking military officers to undergo the *yondo* initiation rites of Tombalbaye's own tribe. The army summarily executed anyone refusing to undergo the ritual.

This was too much. The man who once boasted that he had survived more plots against his life than any other African leader finally saw his luck run out. He was assassinated in an army coup and replaced by another southerner, general Félix Malloum.

A year later in 1976 Qadafi was again sending arms and supplies to FROLINAT. But the Arab northerners were more loyal to the rebel leaders from their own areas than to FROLINAT, and as a result, the organisation was constantly plagued with internal dissent.

Three or four splinter groups formed, largely along tribal lines. Hissein Habré (ah-BRAY), now President of Chad, was the leader of one of these groups, members of the tiny Garone tribe in northern Chad around Faya-Largeau. In 1976, the FROLINAT leadership threw him out because of his opposition to Libya's occupation of the Aouzou strip. So he took his 500-man army and continued fighting on his own.

Libya responded by increasing its aid to the FROLINAT, which in turn inflicted some crushing defeats on the government army and marched within 250 km of N'Djamena (n-jah-MAY-nah). French troops came to the rescue once again. FROLINAT's defeat wrecked the chances of a conference on national unity held subsequently in Tripoli. The French seized the opportunity to sponsor a new political solution: a coalition government with Habré as President and Malloum remaining head of state.

A power struggle between Habré and Malloum was probably inevitable. Both Habré's and the government's armies were in N'Djamena. In early 1979 fighting broke out between the two. France declared itself neutral but in fact supporting Habré. Thousands of people in N'Djamena were killed and the city was badly damaged. A truce was arranged, and both Habré and Malloum were forced to resign.

But a year later fighting broke out again, this time between Habré's forces and those of the new president, Goukouni, a northern Toubou like Habré. A second more destructive 'Battle of N'Djamena' was waged, with many people fleeing the city, followed by two years of intermittent skirmishes. In June 1982 Habré's better trained and disciplined troops finally marched victorious into N'Djamena. Goukouni returned to the north to lead the rebel forces but Qadafi put him under house arrest in Libya when he attempted reconciliation with Habré in 1985.

Today

The war continues but it's no longer a civil war. Down to conscripting 12 and 13 year olds, the rebels changed sides in late 1986 and are now fighting the Libyans. In early 1987 Chad, with considerable military assistance from France and economic assistance from the USA, drove the Libyans back into the Tibesti mountains, their last stronghold. By early 1989 Libya held only the Aouzou strip. In N'Djamena the only evidence of a war was the presence of soldiers, some of them wounded. Whenever French troops are around the city livens up considerably, with the bars and night-clubs going at full steam and packed with soldiers.

Cotton is king in southern Chad, much like in the southern USA 100 years ago. Chad is the largest producer of cotton in Africa after Egypt and cotton accounts for about 70% of all export earnings. But when cotton prices fall Chadian farmers cannot just chuck it and plant something else. It takes years in Africa to introduce a new crop, and in the case of Chad transportation costs are about the highest in Africa, greatly limiting alternatives. So when world cotton prices took a nose dive in 1985 because of increased competition from Asia, with no expected price rise before 1990 or later, what did the World Bank recommend? Hang in there and continue planting. In the case of Cotontchad, this meant losing at least US$40 million a year for the next five years.

Chad's case can only make you laugh at the classical theory of world trade and comparative advantage, which says that everybody is better off when countries specialise in those goods which they can produce more cheaply than anybody else –

Chad has a comparative advantage in nothing. Everybody should pack their bags and leave. Farmers could, of course, just go back to the pre-colonial era of producing only subsistence crops and not even enter the world economy, but what would the government do for revenue? Meanwhile, the big question is whether the French will continue paying for the huge debts that Cotontchad is rolling up. It doesn't look like they have much choice.

On the brighter side, there is oil north of Lake Chad and a consortium led by Esso is exploring in the south. Relations between Chad and western nations couldn't be better. Foreign donors are pumping money into the country, and the USA is trying to ensure that there's enough food regardless of the harvests. And N'Djamena is coming back to life – new restaurants are opening up, the African bars are lively again, and buildings are being repaired and painted.

PEOPLE
Toubou

What you may hear is that Chad is divided between the Arabs in the north and black sedentary Africans in the south. This is an over-simplification. In the northern third of the country, the heart of the Sahara, the people are not really Arabic but indigenous Saharan people of the Tuareg-Berber type known as the Toubou, numbering about 150,000.

Toubou refer to themselves as Teda or Daza depending on whether they speak Tedaga or Dazaga, two dialects of a distinct Saharan language. Like the Arabs, they are Muslims (but only superficially). Unlike the Arabs, they do not consider themselves to be descendants of one mythical founder, rather, they consider themselves to be from a certain locality. Toubou, for example, means 'man from Tibesti'. They are all herders and nomads. Some are only semi-nomads, returning to their permanent villages during the rainy season from July to September. And they are very clannish, each clan with access to specific wells, pastures and oases. President Habré is from one of these clans.

Arabs

The Arabs live in the middle third of the country, the region of the former Kanem-Bornu kingdom. The northern limit is a wavering line between the 14th and 16th parallels north of which is too dry for millet even in the best of years. The southern limit is the 10th parallel, south of which the nomads don't wander. Arabs constitute about a third of Chad's population according to some counts and are mostly semi-nomads who range their herds over the Sahel, leaving the area above the 16th parallel to the Toubou. But not everybody here is Arabic; there are many sedentary farmers.

The broad classification 'Arab' disguises a lot of subgroups that could be classified as separate ethnic groups. One sizeable group is the Maba, centred around Abéché, who speak Bora Mabang. What's unique about the Maba is their pre-Islamic institution of age-grades, a device for handing power over to each successive generation as it reaches maturity. There are four such groups for each sex, cutting across kin and caste divisions. People born within a certain time period move together from one grade to another, bound together by strong bonds of friendship and obligations for mutual aid.

Sara

In the far south below the 10th parallel and including the area of Sarh, the population becomes more dense and almost entirely agricultural. Most are black Africans and non-Muslim. The largest group is the Sara, who account for about 30% of Chad's five million people. You may have seen pictures of Africans with artificially elongated lips. The Sara women used to do this, but it wasn't because they thought it was pretty. It was to make them unattractive to the slave raiders. Now the Sara occupy most of the civil service and higher military positions.

GEOGRAPHY

Chad is land-locked and almost twice as large as Texas, with a fourth of the popula-tion. The only major city is N'Djamena with about 400,000 inhabitants and about 300 metres above sea level; the southern towns of Sarh and Moundou follow with about 85,000 inhabitants each. Lake Chad is only two to three hours' drive west of N'Djamena and borders Niger, Nigeria and Cameroun.

When you're in N'Djamena and suffer-ing in 40°C temperature, it's hard to imagine that in the far northern tip of Chad in the heart of the desert there are real mountains, not just hills, and that temperatures frequently fall below minus 8°C. Two peaks rise well over 3000 metres, by far the highest points in the Sahara. This is the Tibesti region. When Lake Chad was at its largest several thousand years ago, these mountains formed the northern edge, and that's why the area is loaded with archaeological artefacts.

In the middle third of Chad, including N'Djamena and Lake Chad, you'll see a mixture of scrub and sand; this is the Sahel.

In the southern third the Chari and Logone Rivers, which originate in the Central African Republic, cut through the area as they flow northward to N'Djamena where they join before emptying into Lake Chad, which lacks an outlet. The local fishers are all busy between August and December because the Chari overflows its banks in the south, inundating huge areas of land. You could even jump in a boat at Sarh and go all the way to N'Djamena. But if you're there in May, don't be surprised if it has dried up around N'Djamena.

CLIMATE

Chad is hot, particularly March through May. Daytime temperatures of 45°C (115°F) and more are typical during this period. From December to mid-February, on the other hand, daytime temperatures are ideal and the evenings quite chilly, with temperatures lowering to 6°C or so.

In the south the rainy season is from June to September. The rainfall is much heavier than most travellers expect. In N'Djamena, on the other hand, the rainy season lasts only two months, from July to August. It takes very little rain, however, for the roads to become muddy and impassable.

LANGUAGE

French is the official language. The principal African languages are Sara (SAH-rah), spoken primarily in the south, and Turku, a form of pidgin Arabic frequently referred to as Chadian Arabic, spoken in N'Djamena and northern Chad. Greetings in Chadian Arabic:

Good morning	mah-lam-ah-LEK
Good evening	mah-sah-el-HAIR
How are you?	AH-fee-ah
Thank you	SHOE-kran
Goodbye	mah-sah-LAM

Greetings in Sara:

Good morning	lah-lay
Good evening	lah-lay
Thank you	dee-LAH-fee-ah
Goodbye	BAH-ee

VISAS

Only West German and French citizens do not need visas. They are usually good for 15 days and can be renewed without difficulty. You can obtain a Chadian visa in every country in West and Central Africa except The Gambia and São Tomé because all French embassies issue them except those in countries where there's a Chadian embassy. The waiting time at the French embassies is usually only 24 hours. It is also possible to get a Chadian visa in Kousséri (Cameroun) across the river from N'Djamena. Exit visas are no longer required.

If you're travelling to Cameroun, getting a Cameroun visa is no problem. They are issued near Kousséri, the only border point in Cameroun where this is possible. If you're travelling to Niger, you cannot get a Niger visa in N'Djamena or anywhere in Central Africa, but you can in Kano (Nigeria) at the Niger Consulate. In N'Djamena, the friendly Nigerian Embassy people issue visas to Nigeria for CFA 3637 in 24 hours, possibly the same day if you arrive by 9 am. The

French Embassy also takes only 24 hours in issuing visas to Burkina Faso, Gabon, Ivory Coast, Mauritania, Senegal and Togo.

Diplomatic Missions Abroad

Algiers, Bangui, Bonn, Brazzaville, Brussels, Cairo, Jeddah, Khartoum, Kinshasa, Lagos, Paris, Washington, Yaoundé.

MONEY

US$1 = CFA 296
  £1 = CFA 570

The unit of currency is the Central African CFA. If you come with West African CFA bills, do not expect people to accept them; the banks and hotels will, however.

Banking hours: Monday to Thursday 7.30 am to 2 pm; Friday 7.30 am to 12 noon; Saturday 8 am to 12 noon.

GENERAL INFORMATION
Health

A vaccination against yellow fever is mandatory as is one for cholera if you're travelling within six days from an infected area. For emergencies, there's Hôpital Central (emergency tel 3593) in N'Djamena. Two French doctors are Dr Guy Quilichine (tel 2227) and Mme Jean Marie (hospital tel 2340).

Security

Security is no longer a major problem except in the very far north where fighting continues and travelling is prohibited. In N'Djamena, you face the problem of running into armed soldiers at night who aren't sure what you're doing. They'll interrogate you, and if you don't have your passport on you, you run the risk of being detained all night. There are several streets around the Presidential Palace which you may not walk down, but they aren't blocked off. At night, if you make a mistake, the soldiers are likely to shoot first and ask questions later.

The risks of walking around at night in N'Djamena go up significantly after about

10 pm; most expatriates in town recommend not doing it. If you have a car or taxi, there's no problem going to a night-club. Just make sure you know where the prohibited streets are. And don't be surprised if you are stopped by soldiers and interrogated. Since the fortunes of war have turned in Chad's favour, however, the problems of walking around at night in N'Djamena will probably diminish significantly. So ask around.

Business Hours

Business: weekdays 8 am to 1 pm and 4 to 7 pm; Saturday 8 am to 1 pm. Government: Monday to Thursday and Saturday 7 am to 2 pm; Friday 7 to 12 am.

Public Holidays

1 January, Easter Monday, 1 May, 25 May, Ascension Day, Whit Monday, 7 June (Liberation Day), End of Ramadan (6 May 1989, 25 April 1990), Tabaski (14 July 1989, 3 July 1990), 11 August (Independence), 1 November, Mohammed's Birthday, 28 November, 25 December. Liberation Day is the major holiday, but it's nothing special.

Photography

You must get a permit, and the process takes anywhere from two days to a week depending on whether the people you're looking for are at their desks. The best time to catch them is 7 to 8 am. Go with two photographs and your passport to the Ministry of Interior, then the Director of the Sûreté, then the Treasurer to pay CFA 10,000, and then the Minister of Information for his signature. Even with a permit, never take a photograph of a soldier; it's very risky.

Time, Post, Phone & Telex

When it's noon in Chad, it's 11 am in London and 6 am in New York (7 am during daylight savings time). Postal service is reliable. International telephone connections are good, now that they're by satellite. To send a telex go to the N'Djamena post office.

GETTING THERE

Air

Twice a week, UTA and Air Afrique fly between Paris and Brazzaville, stopping at N'Djamena and Bangui (CAR) both ways – the only direct flights from Europe. Within Africa you can only get planes from Brazzaville, Bangui, Dakar, Niamey and Khartoum, all twice a week. Once a week there is an Air Afrique flight Dakar/Niamey/N'Djamena/Jeddah and a Sudan Airways flight Khartoum/N'Djamena/Kano/Lagos.

Car

To/from Cameroun Driving time from Maroua to N'Djamena is three to four hours; from Yaoundé, count on three days. A new bridge over the Chari River connects N'Djamena and Kousséri, but you can still take the ferry. The border there is open every day at 6 am and closes at 5.30 pm on the dot. Even an ambassador won't get across after then.

To/from Niger It's a cinch getting from Niger to N'Djamena via Kano and Maiduguri (Nigeria); the road is paved all the way. However, the adventurous may prefer the direct route through eastern Niger, from Zinder (Niger) to N'Djamena passing just north of Lake Chad; the trip takes about four days during the dry season. The road is paved from Zinder to the border (Nguigmi); finding petrol in Nguigmi is unusual. You're supposed to pick up a guide at the border, but some people have reported getting away without one. Giving a military guy a lift is one way to get rid of the guide, and your trip will be smooth sailing.

Continuing into Chad, you'll find the preferred route is now just north of Lake Chad via Bol, not via Mao. The road can become very muddy between July and September. At other times be prepared for lots of soft sand. Stop in Bol to get your passport stamped and don't be surprised if the gendarmes, sometimes a real pain, ask CFA 250 a person for 'supplementary hours'.

To/from CAR Most people travelling to/from the Central African Republic go via Ngaoundéré (Cameroun) because the road is in better condition and you get to see a little of northern Cameroun, a very interesting area.

If, instead, you go through Sarh in southern Chad, get your passport stamped in Guelengdeng en route. Anticipate a thorough baggage check at Maro, near the border. Between the border and Bangui (CAR), it's all asphalt road.

A third alternative, also via Sarh but 307 km longer, is to go south from N'Djamena into Cameroun to Maroua and Figuil, then east into Chad again to Sarh via Pala and Moundou. The advantage of this route is that you pass through northern Cameroun as well as southern Chad. The Maroua-Sarh portion of this route is the major road between southern Chad and Nigeria and carries much more traffic than the direct route through southern Chad.

To/from Sudan It's possible to enter Chad from Sudan, passing through Adré and Abéché. Anticipate long waiting periods if you're hitching and taking all your petrol if you're driving.

Bush Taxi

From both Cameroun and Nigeria you can get to the Chadian border post closest to N'Djamena by bush taxi. For instance, from Maroua (northern Cameroun), you can catch bush taxis to the border via Mora, a four-hour trip, and from there literally walk to N'Djamena. The border there closes at 5.30 pm sharp. From Maiduguri (north-eastern Nigeria), it's easy to get bush taxis to Mora or Maroua and from there to the Chadian border – an all-day trip. From southern Chad, Niger and Sudan, on the other hand, you'll have to hitch rides on trucks. Anticipate long waits.

If you're coming from the Central African Republic to Sarh, you may have to walk the 25 km from the border to the first town, Maro, because so few vehicles pass by. The police in this area are friendly but anticipate numerous thorough checks. At least one traveller had to translate letters and part of a Lonely Planet book to convince them he wasn't a mercenary! Between Sarh

Street Parade in N'Djamena, Chad (PM)

and N'Djamena, you're supposed to get your passport stamped in Guelengdeng.

GETTING AROUND
Travel Permit
You need an *Autorisation de Circuler*, sometimes referred to as a *laissez-passer*, to travel around the country, but check because the rules are constantly changing. The process is simple and can be done in a day if you're lucky, despite what you may hear to the contrary. Go to the Ministry of Tourism near the Hôtel Tchadienne and tell them your itinerary and licence number. If you're travelling by truck, just say, *'un camion particulier'*. The ministry will then give you a letter which you take to the Ministry of Interior where the minister himself signs it. The chances of finding him are much better between 7 and 8 am.

Few of those going to Lake Chad bother to get one, however, and many have travelled to Niger, Sarh and Abéché without one and encountered no problems – police rarely ask to see it. But who knows; you may be the unlucky one.

Air
Air Tchad is back in operation and flies to both Sarh and Abéché. In the harmattan season (December to March), don't be surprised if the pilot asks the passengers to help look for landmarks; on occasion the plane ends up in the wrong town! Every so often you hear of a plane barely missing camels on the runway in Abéché.

Truck
There are no bush taxis or buses in Chad, only trucks. The most frequent destinations from N'Djamena are Sarh and Abéché. One truck a day to Sarh is sometimes all there is; ask in the N'Djamena market.

Car
Travel in the south can be a big problem from June to October because of rain, lack of paved roads, and the widespread flooding.

The 562-km trip from N'Djamena to Sarh takes about two days; the road is full of potholes and in terrible condition. The N'Djamena-Moundou road is even worse.

N'DJAMENA
When Tombalbaye scrapped all the French names in 1973, Fort-Lamy became N'Djamena. In those days the city had a reputation for being one of the most pleasant in the Sahel; it is slowly making a comeback.

N'Djamena now boasts eight major restaurants, four supermarkets, three nightclubs, a thriving market, an interesting selection of artisan goods, a tennis club, a long pool at one of the hotels, and African bars galore, occasionally with live music. And when the French soldiers are in town, the place really livens up. What more do you want? 'Cheaper accommodation, fewer soldiers toting machine guns, and food that isn't quite so expensive,' you'll probably say. Well, no place is perfect.

The city is divided into two sections, the European quarter and the African quarter. The market is close to the dividing line. The modern section is spread out with wide streets lined with trees, plus it's where you'll find all the major restaurants, hotels and government buildings. It's also where all the fighting took place back in the late '70s; many buildings are still in a state of disrepair. The African section went largely unscathed; it's much larger, more crowded and livelier. Running from one end of the city to the other is the main drag, Avenue Charles de Gaulle, the only street exempted when they changed all the names.

Information
Banks BIAO, Banque des Etats de l'Afrique Centrale, Banque Nationale de Paris.

Embassies
France
    (tel 3793/3855) BP 431, near Hôtel du Chari.
West Germany
    (tel 3090/3102) BP 893.

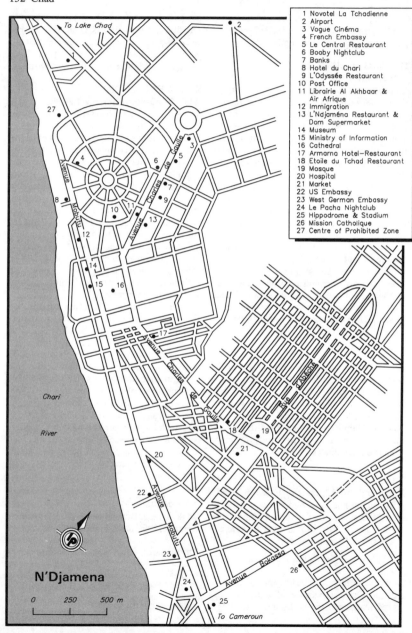

1 Novotel La Tchadienne
2 Airport
3 Vogue Cinéma
4 French Embassy
5 Le Central Restaurant
6 Booby Nightclub
7 Banks
8 Hotel du Chari
9 L'Odyssée Restaurant
10 Post Office
11 Librairie Al Akhbaar &
   Air Afrique
12 Immigration
13 L'Najaména Restaurant &
   Dom Supermarket
14 Museum
15 Ministry of Information
16 Cathedral
17 Armarna Hotel–Restaurant
18 Etoile du Tchad Restaurant
19 Mosque
20 Hospital
21 Market
22 US Embassy
23 West German Embassy
24 Le Pacha Nightclub
25 Hippodrome & Stadium
26 Mission Catholique
27 Centre of Prohibited Zone

To Lake Chad

Avenue Mobutu

Charles de Gaulle

Chari

River

Avenue Charles de Gaulle

Rue d'Abéché

Avenue Mobutu

Avenue Bokassa

N'Djamena

0   250   500 m

To Cameroun

USA
(tel 3269) BP 413, Ave Mobutu, near the river and not far from the market.

Other embassies include: CAR, Egypt, Nigeria, Sudan, Zaïre.

Bookshops & Supermarkets *Librairie Al Akhbaar*, in the centre of town next to Air Afrique, is the best place to find postcards and the only place to buy French and African magazines and newspapers, and sometimes the *International Herald Tribune*. It's open until 7 pm.

There are four supermarkets in the dead centre of town along Charles de Gaulle, all within three blocks of each other and all roughly equal in quality. *Alimentation Générale*, *Dom Supermarket* and *Alimentation du Centre* are three. Prices are very high – CFA 800 for a bottle of mineral water (unless you can find the 40% cheaper *Supermont* brand from Cameroun). For a beautician try *La Coquette* two blocks up from the Al Akhbaar bookshop.

National Museum
If there's a 'must see', it's the National Museum which reopened in 1986. Even though some 3000 objects were stolen when N'Djamena was partially sacked in the early '80s, the collection is still big enough to fill six rooms. It's near the river a block from the cathedral, and open 8 am to 12 noon except Sundays.

Places to Stay – bottom end
For those on the cheap, there are several possibilities. The *Mission Catholique* costs CFA 750 a night. It's a long block beyond the market going eastward away from the city centre, off Avenue Bokassa. The *Hôtel l'Hirondelle*, very near the central market and mosque, has rooms from about CFA 3500 to CFA 4500. You can camp on the lawn behind the *La Tchadienne* for CFA 1000 a person and use the outdoor shower by the pool and the toilets at the restaurant.

Places to Stay – top end
The best hotel by far is Novotel's *La Tchadienne* (tel 3311). Since Novotel took over in 1987 the hotel has been completely renovated. Overlooking the Chari River and a good km west of the centre of town, it has a popular poolside bar and disco. Rooms cost CFA 28,000 plus 17.5% tax.

Hôtel du Chari (tel 2013/3313), also on the banks of the Chari River has singles/doubles for around CFA 16,000/20,700 plus tax. The Chari has no pool or nightclub, the water operates only several hours each day and the rooms are slightly dusty with poor lighting. However, it has a wonderful view of the Chari River, the restaurant is quite good, and it's close to the centre of town, which is a real plus because cabs are hard to find.

A hotel that many travellers prefer to the Chari is *Amarna* (tel 2684), with singles/doubles for about CFA 17,000/22,000 including breakfast and laundry service. All rooms have air-con and water 24 hours a day; the double rooms have refrigerators. Since there are only five rooms, getting a room is a problem. It's part of the Amarna Restaurant on Charles de Gaulle, two blocks east of the cathedral.

Places to Eat
Le Central (tel 2218), in the heart of town on Charles de Gaulle near the Booby nightclub, is one of the two best restaurants in town. The vigorous Belgian who runs it offers continental cuisine, good service and dining inside (with air-con) or outside on the terrace. Most dishes are CFA 3700 to CFA 4700. It's closed on Wednesdays. Two blocks down the same street over Dom supermarket you'll find *Le N'Djamena* (tel 3922), run by a French couple and closed on Tuesdays. Prices and the quality of the food are similar, but portions are small. The menu is somewhat more interesting, however, and the atmosphere is more elegant.

Between these two restaurants you'll find *L'Odyssée*, or 'Chez Henri' (tel 2808), which is quite popular, serves good French food and is closed on Sundays. Dine inside with air-con or on the terrace. Most main courses are CFA 2600 to CFA 4000, and there's a good selection of pizzas for CFA 3000 to 4000 CFA.

The *Amarna* (tel 2684) serves French food in a pleasant indoor setting. Most main courses are CFA 2200 to 3200 CFA; the portions tend to be small. The capitaine (perch) and brochettes are especially good. Sandwiches and pizza are also served. You'll find it on Charles de Gaulle two blocks past the cathedral going towards the market. It's open every day.

The *Etoile du Tchad* (tel 3602) is further down, two blocks before the market, and open every day, evenings only. The reasonable prices (steak and fries for CFA 1400) and the rooftop setting make it a favourite of many. The brochettes and CFA 250 fruit drinks are highly recommended. Chicken, a few meat dishes and several vegetables are also offered.

Roses des Vents (tel 3602), several km west of the Tchadienne along the river and out of town, has tables near the river under the stars. Most dishes are CFA 2200 to CFA 3200. The food is quite decent, especially the brochettes, and the bar is the liveliest place in town when the French soldiers arrive. It's open every day, evenings only.

The *Tchadienne* has a decent terrace restaurant; the capitaine and veal cutlets (*escalope de veau*) are recommended. A four-course set menu is also offered. The *Chari* offers similar fare and a choice of inside or outside dining; the steak is recommended.

For pastry, there's the *Pâtisserie la N'Djamenoise* on Charles de Gaulle near the Air Afrique offices. Prices are very high, however. The cheapest places to eat are all around the market, where you'll find roast meat and milk shakes, and along Avenue Bokassa with all its bars.

Entertainment & Sports

Bars Chad has one of the best brews in all of Central and West Africa, Gala. Brewed in Moundou, you'll find it everywhere despite the country's atrocious roads. Not once in over twenty years of war has the brewery shut down for any significant time. It seems that the Chadians have their priorities in the right order. A big bottle goes for CFA 350 to CFA 500 in N'Djamena.

For African bars, head for Avenue Bokassa, which stretches from the river starting at the intersection near the US Embassy to one block east of the market. *Le Paradise* is one of the more popular ones. The most popular watering hole for travellers is the *Tchadienne* because it's on the river's edge and has a pool. In the centre of town, *L'Odyssée* is quite popular with local expatriates, including late Saturday mornings. At night-time, the bar at the *Rose des Vents*, two km west of the Tchadienne, is usually packed if the French soldiers are in town.

Nightclubs The city's principal dancing places, all good, are the *Booby Nightclub* on Charles de Gaulle in the centre of town, *Le Pacha* just east of the US Embassy on Avenue Mobutu running alongside the river, and the *Sao Club* at the Tchadienne. The Booby has a stiff cover charge of roughly CFA 3000 which includes a drink, while the Pacha's is only CFA 1000. The more adventurous should try one of the African nightclubs.

The African nightclubs are much cheaper, more interesting and not far from the market. *Le Relais Ambiance* is very lively and always has dancing, frequently to the tunes of a live Chadian musical group. There's no cover, and the beers are only CFA 500. If you walk eastward down Charles de Gaulle, about one km beyond the market you'll see a sign pointing off to your right; it's several blocks off the main drag. Thursday, Saturday and Sunday are the best days to go, particularly between 9 pm and midnight. The *Bar Amical*, which also has an excellent band, is on Avenue Bokassa near the market.

African Melody and L'International

Challal are two popular Chadian groups that play at these two places.

Cinemas Vog Cinéma has shows at 6.15 and 9 pm. It's near the centre of town at the far west end of Charles de Gaulle.

Sports The pool at the Tchadienne costs CFA 1000 for non-guests.

For tennis, there's the International Club (Base Kosei) several blocks beyond the Tchadienne along the river; you have to be invited by a member.

The Americans play softball on Saturdays at 4 pm on a field near the river about three km east of the US Embassy; visitors are welcome.

The horse races can also be fun – Saturday and Sunday afternoons starting around 3 or 4 pm at the hippodrome one km east of the US Embassy.

Things to Buy

Artisan Goods The Chadian wool rugs are beautiful but heavy. Other items available include leather sandals, gold, and boxes. These are all sold in the centre of town in front of the Librairie Al Akhbaar on Charles de Gaulle and outside the Tchadienne. You can find some of these items at the central market. There are also magnificent saris sold in five-metre segments in the CFA 5500 to CFA 13,000 range.

The Catholic Mission Gift Shop sells some unusual embroidery with patterns resembling the Tibesti rock drawings in northern Chad. The tablecloths and napkins are especially popular. The work is all done by a women's group. Officially the shop is only open on Mondays and Saturdays from 4 to 6 pm, however, the women work there every morning except Sunday, and they'll be glad to show you their wares. The Catholic mission is one big block east of the market off Avenue Bokassa.

Getting There & Away

Air There are twice weekly flights to/from Paris, Bangui and Brazzaville. Once a week Sudan Airways flies from Jeddah to Lagos via Khartoum, N'Djamena and Kano (Nigeria).

Bush Taxi Chad has no bush taxis or buses, so when you arrive at the border, you'll have to hitch. Even at Kousséri (Cameroun), only about 10 km from N'Djamena on the other side of the Chari River, you'll have to hitch or walk to N'Djamena. In Kousséri, you'll find bush taxis headed for Maroua and Maiduguri (Nigeria).

Trucks Ask around the N'Djamena market for trucks. Anticipate the trip to Sarh or Abéché taking two full days.

Getting Around

Airport Transport The airport departure tax is CFA 3500. There's a bank at the airport, but it's not always open. Taxis meet arriving planes, but since there are so few taxis in N'Djamena, finding one can be difficult. A taxi into town (three km) is CFA 500 (double at night).

Taxi Fares in N'Djamena are CFA 100 for a 'seat' in a shared cab and CFA 500 for a taxi to yourself. Taxis are very difficult to find; the hotels are the best places to look.

Car Rental Three local car rental agencies, all on Avenue Charles de Gaulle, include Société Soner (tel 3198, telex 5285), which has Peugeots and Volkswagons; Habiba, which has vehicles for CFA 20,000 a day; and Locauto (tel 2172). Afrique Services Auto near the Care garage has cars for CFA 14,000 a day.

LAKE CHAD & DOUGIA

Don't be fooled by the maps, most of which show Lake Chad as it was in the early 1960s – about the size of Belgium. Nowadays it gets to about half that size. In 1908 it dried up completely. The size of the lake varies considerably during the year, and the water level is at its highest from August to December. The average depth is about a metre and a half, which is why about 90% of the water flowing into it from the Chari River evaporates within a week or so.

The lake is full of papyrus and reed beds and floating islands of vegetation, also a few hippos and crocodiles. Most of the year you can see people fishing from their dugout canoes dotted across the lake.

Dougia, a small village 75 km west of N'Djamena that was once a single large farm, attracts expatriates on weekends between late November and mid-May when the hotel is open. The road is being improved.

To get to the lake, drive another 30 km or so beyond Dougia until you reach Hadide. A motorised boat from there costs about CFA 5000 plus the guide's fee, which can be up to another CFA 5000 depending on your generosity; petrol is not cheap in this area of the world. Ask for a guy named Ibrahim; he has a boat. Presumably, this can be done a lot cheaper with a non-motorised boat.

Hadjer el Hamis

If you're up for some climbing, there are several rock formations which jut out of the sand a few km from Hadjer el Hamis, about 20 km to the north-east of Hadide. One is 150 to 200 metres high and looks like an elephant. It's fairly simple to find a local who'll act as a guide. But take heed: one small section of the climb is so difficult and dangerous that if you slip and fall, it's adios amigos.

Places to Stay

The 15-room *Hôtel Dougia* has small rooms that are fairly clean and quite comfortable. The price for singles/doubles is about CFA 9000/11,000 plus meals. You can even try your luck with their windsurfer if there's any wind. Cotontchad technicians descend on the place on the weekends, so reserve in advance. Call the manager at the Hôtel Chari and ask for one of the newer, better bungalows. One even has air-con.

SARH

Sarh is a somewhat dull agricultural town with broad tree-shaded streets that belie its commercial importance. Up to two days by road from N'Djamena, it's the cotton centre of Chad and the most important transport junction in the country. It used to be the base for hunting trips until most of the animals were slaughtered. Quite a few Europeans live there, many of whom own property. Sarh means 'encampment', referring to the forced labour camps into which the Sara were brutally interned during construction of the railroad in the Congo.

Things to See

The museum near the Catholic mission may be interesting to some people, plus the artisans' workshop on the road to the airport has some of the best crafts in southern Chad.

Places to Stay & Eat

There are two hotels to choose from. The *Mission Catholique* will also take you in for about CFA 600 plus CFA 100 for a meal, but don't be surprised if the priest doesn't allow more than one night's stay. The *Baptist Mission* seven km from town also welcomes travellers. Next to the Rex cinema you'll find a place that serves milk shakes and yoghurt in pint glasses for CFA 250 – highly recommended. In the same area there are numerous places where roasted and other cheap food is sold.

ABECHE

Abéché was the capital of the powerful Ouadai kingdom, and when the French arrived it was Chad's largest urban centre with 28,000 inhabitants. By 1919 it was down to 6000 people because of major epidemics. Many travellers find it an interesting town – oriental in appearance with its mosques and minarets, narrow and winding cobbled streets, old markets (souks), nomadic traffic and rundown structures, including the sultan's palace. If you're interested in camel-hair blankets, this may still be a good place to buy them. Lodging is available here, and there is a restaurant.

Ouara a few km away may be worth

checking out. It has a huge six-metre thick wall surrounding the remains of a palace, mosque and sultan's tomb. Adré is 166 km east and on the border with Sudan; every now and then someone makes the trip overland to Sudan via this route.

Getting There & Away

The easiest way to get to Abéché is on the weekly Air Tchad flight from N'Djamena. The cheapest way is to follow the locals and hitch a ride on top of a tractor-trailor truck, a number of which leave each day in both directions. It'll be loaded to the gills with goods and have up to 100 people on top with their luggage. One traveller said: 'Arab headgear and lots of patience is recommended.'

You can also drive; chances are excellent the police will never ask to see your *Autorisation de Circuler*. The straight driving time from N'Djamena (750 km) in the dry season is roughly 18 hours. You'll find no petrol along the way, and from July to September, the route becomes exceedingly difficult. Expect to pay a fortune getting yourself dug out of the mud.

ZAKOUMA NATIONAL PARK

No game park in Africa has been more ravished by poachers than Zakouma, 200 km north-east of Sarh. It was once noted for its vast herds of elephant, buffalo, rhino, giraffe and many species of antelope; hunting in this area and around Sarh was Chad's prime tourist attraction. Since the early 1970s, poaching has gone on uncontrolled. Now there's little game to see, and the tourist camp is closed.

TIBESTI

The Tibesti mountains form the largest mountain range in the Sahara. Some of the volcanoes are still active, eg Mt Tousside (3315 metres), which still emits smoke. The therapeutic springs of Soboroum have geysers and hot sulphuric water. This is also one of the hottest areas in the desert, and 50°C temperatures are typical. Yet the Toubou, one of Africa's oldest tribes, have lived here for thousands of years. Always armed with knives and not very religious, they are constantly occupied with survival and, as a result, are probably the most suspicious, individualistic people in Africa. Without a Toubou guide, you might be risking your life.

Cave Paintings

What's most special about Tibesti are the cave paintings, some of the oldest in Africa. Many of the rock paintings and engravings date from 5000 to 2000 BC, depicting simple hunting scenes and providing evidence of the region's former tropical climate and abundance of water. Some of the principal sites are near Zouar and Bardai. In Ennedi there are also many paintings, most dating prior to 3000 BC. Until the Chadians boot out the Libyans, the area will remain off-limits.

The Congo

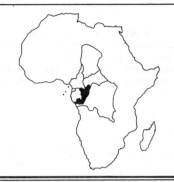

Everybody usually finds something to like about the Congo – safe, clean beaches, good ocean fishing, drinking beer with the locals, dancing to the music of some of Africa's most popular recording stars, or looking for carved wooden statues. Getting around is half the adventure. You can cruise down the Congo on a riverboat, travel by train to the coast, trek through the rainforests, or fly.

The Congo is like a small version of neighbouring Zaïre (the old Belgian Congo), only more relaxed with far fewer logistical obstacles. To get to the beach or go fishing, you can hop one of two daily aeroplanes from the capital city of Brazzaville to the port of Pointe-Noire, or take take a comfortable overnight train. If you want to enjoy the sights and nightlife of Brazzaville, you have less to worry about than in nextdoor Kinshasa where crime is the major topic of conversation.

Travelling in the interior, you'll find the road system in the central plateau area quite good in contrast to Zaïre's, which is probably the worst in Africa. And if you're an adventure lover, an overland trip from Brazzaville to Gabon or north-eastern Congo is as exciting as a trip from Kinshasa to eastern Zaïre, though not as time consuming.

HISTORY

The Congo was the first former French colony to go Marxist, in ideology if not in practice. Perhaps France was just being repaid for forcing onto the Congo one of the most infamous projects during the colonial era: the building of the Congo-Ocean railway, which resulted in the death of untold thousands of Africans.

Pygmies were the first to inhabit the area. Bantu groups, including the Téké and the Kongo, followed them and established powerful kingdoms. Some of these kingdoms were in the practice of capturing men from other areas. This played into the

hands of the Portuguese, who arrived here in the late 15th century. They offered these kingdoms European goods in exchange for slaves. As a result, a number of small independent kingdoms arose on the coast, each with the ability to milk the interior for slaves. When the Portuguese ships arrived, five or six times a year, they were merely handed the slaves. It was a simple operation for the Portuguese, but for the Congolese it created internal turmoil.

More slaves were taken from what are now the Congo, Zaïre and Angola than just about any other area of Africa – a staggering 13.5 million people over three centuries. When the slave trade ended in the late 19th century, the coastal kingdoms disappeared.

Colonial Period

Brazzaville is named after the famous French explorer, Savorgnan de Brazza. De Brazza made his first expedition here during 1875 to 1878, and crossed almost the entire country on foot. In 1880, during his second expedition, he hastily signed a treaty of friendship with Makoko, king of the Téké, to prevent Stanley from extending his territorial acquisitions beyond the Congo River. This agreement ceded certain land to France which included the site of what was to become Brazzaville. The area became known as the Middle Congo.

Having successfully combined their territories in West Africa in a federation called French West Africa, the French did the

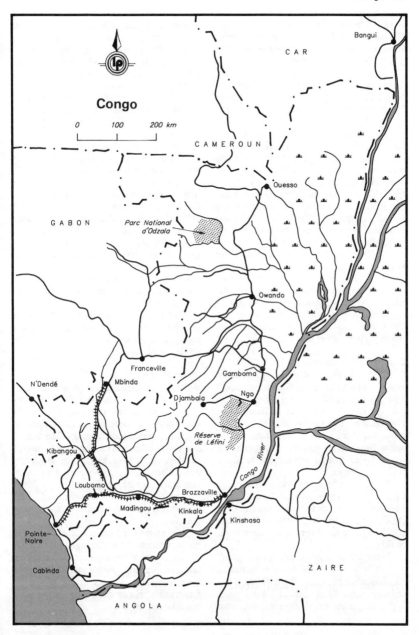

same in Central Africa. The Middle Congo, Gabon and the CAR-Chad became French Equatorial Africa in 1908. As the capital of this federation and a big new star on the African map, Brazzaville received half of the territory's civil servants and was the beneficiary of schools, a hospital, the Pasteur Institute for sleeping sickness research, and eventually a college.

De Brazza was instrumental in turning the entire area over to various private French companies, with the government collecting rent and typically 15% of the profits. The companies forced the Africans to work for them. They treated the Africans so brutally that stories of the atrocities surfaced in the French newspapers. The French public was outraged. The French government countered by sending de Brazza to investigate.

De Brazza died in 1905 during his return voyage, and little was done to curb the abuses. The companies continued to take Africans from their villages. Famine eventually resulted. In some areas, starvation wiped out two-thirds of the population between 1914 and 1924. Little wonder that the country's population today is so small.

Congo-Ocean Railway

In 1924 the French embarked on their most ambitious undertaking in French Equatorial Africa – the building of the Congo-Ocean Railway from Pointe-Noire to Brazzaville. The French badly needed this railroad because the Congo river was unnavigable below Brazzaville. Without an outlet to the sea the French Congo, as it came to be called, couldn't be exploited.

The French faced the same dilemma in Chad and the Central African Republic. The only outlet to the sea for these two areas was the Oubangui and Congo Rivers. But Brazzaville was as far down as the river boats could go.

What the colonials considered a 'great' project was a disaster for the Africans. Workers were cheap, so the builders of the railway resorted to forced labour on a frightening scale rather than use the most elementary technical processes which would have prevented an enormous loss of life.

The French went on man-hunts all over the Congo, the Central African Republic and southern Chad looking for Africans to work on the project. Thousands were dragged from their villages; many of them died or deserted. Finding and keeping labour was such a big problem that it took 14 years to complete the project.

During WW II Brazzaville took on even greater importance when de Gaulle selected it as the capital of Free France. His beautiful house there is a Brazzaville landmark. You may hear about the historical Brazzaville Conference of 1944 held to discuss French colonial problems. This was when de Gaulle declared that the time had come for the French African colonies to enjoy a certain degree of emancipation, including the abolition of forced labour, the election of African representatives to the French Constitutional Assembly and the formation of their own elected parliaments.

Thereafter, African political leadership developed and progressive political parties emerged, hand in hand with considerable strides in education.

Independence

Because the French had exploited the Congolese so brutally, particularly during the construction of the railroad, it is hardly surprising that these new leaders were attracted to communist ideology. The French saw this as a threat to their continued control, so they set about grooming moderate politicians to assume control at independence, which finally came in 1960. Fulbert Youlou became president and quickly established markedly pro-western policies.

The student and union leaders, however, had other ideas. When the unpopular Youlou drafted a scheme to merge opposition parties and make the trade unions toe the line, massive demonstrations took place in Brazzaville. He retaliated by imprisoning some labour leaders.

Thus began 'The Three Glorious Days' in mid-August, 1963, now the country's major holiday. The trade unionists declared a general strike, freed their arrested members, and forced Youlou to resign. The more radical elements seized power and appointed Massembat-Debat as president. Thereafter, they formed the National Revolutionary Movement (MNR) as the sole party, declaring itself Marxist-Leninist.

For an outsider, the period from 1963 to 1979 can seem a little confusing. It was a period of constant struggle between the army and the political party, with the militancy of the people and the trade unionists always a factor. Massembat-Debat held power for five years during which time the centre of power was in the MNR. The youth wing of the MNR developed a para-military force with enough power to threaten the army.

By 1968 they reached a stalemate, resolved by a political compromise replacing Massembat-Debat with a leftist army officer, Marien Nguouabi, and merging the party's civil defence group into the military. Proceeding to turn the country into a sort of African Albania, Nguouabi abolished the MNR and replaced it with the new Congolese Workers Party (PCT), which continued the Marxist rhetoric. Even the country's flag, red with a crossed hammer and hoe, resembled the Soviet's.

The French supported Nguouabi until he backed away from supporting the West's attempt to keep oil rich Cabinda out of Angolan hands. This led to his assassination and replacement by Yhombi-Opango who, they thought, would reassert the army's control over the party. He did, but when he went so far as to try destroying the PCT by annulling its congress, the trade unionists went to the streets in protest.

The PCT's central committee then met to prepare the congress and forced Yhombi to step down. By the time of the congress itself in 1979, the Congolese radio was accusing Yhombi of having embezzled over US$50 million, including some US$15 million donated by Algeria for a water project in the country's most impoverished area, the Bateke plateau. His purchase of a gold bed from abroad was one of the stories passing around. Colonel Denis Sassou-Nguesso took over the presidency and remains in power today.

Today

Since 1979 it has been the party, not the army, which calls the shots. Trade union militants are once again very influential, and demanding enactment of radical, anti-colonial measures. The French lost out. With Yhombi gone, they no longer had close ties with the government.

Previously the French oil companies considered it was in their interest to claim that the oil reserves were lower than forecast. But with the new radicalisation accompanying the rise of Sassou-Nguesso, they wanted to be the bearers of good news. The new director of the French oil company, Elf Congo, changed the company's tune, saying that their forecasts for petroleum production in certain fields were 100% higher than their previous estimates and that they would step up exploration. Production in crude oil thereafter rose significantly, from 1.2 million tonnes in 1979 to 6.3 million tonnes in 1985.

While the party spouts Marxist rhetoric, the country has clearly moved away from a pro-Soviet position to one of political neutrality. On the one hand, the government rolled out the red carpet to the French during Brazzaville's 100th anniversary celebrations and gave the Soviets second billing. Then the Congolese turned around and signed a treaty of friendship with the USSR, something few other African countries have done. This is a delicate balancing act, however, and could topple if the economy stagnates significantly.

Economically, pragmatism rules, not socialism. The president has gone on a campaign to encourage western investment and to return unprofitable state-run firms to the private sector, much to the applause of the west. The government even sends groups of Congolese on state department tours of the

USA and has invited American marketing professors to give management seminars in Brazzaville.

With per capita incomes of US$1300, Congo-Brazzaville (as the country is frequently called to avoid confusion with Zaïre) is a wealthy country by African standards – third in black Africa behind Gabon and South Africa. Still, food production is a major problem. The country cannot feed itself, and the problem only gets worse as people continue to move into Brazzaville and Pointe-Noire.

The revenue earned from all of the wood that the Congo exports from its extensive rain forests barely covers the country's food import bill. The government has simply given higher priority to improving transportation, building dams and paper mills, creating rubber plantations and forestry complexes. So don't be surprised by your restaurant bill – the cost of living is one of the highest in black Africa.

PEOPLE

The Congo has a population of two million; this compares with 100 million in Japan, which is roughly the same size. The major ethnic groups are the Kongo (45%) followed by the Sangha, the Téké and the Vili. The Kongo are also a major ethnic group in Zaïre and Angola, and were part of the Kongo kingdom centred in Angola which was flourishing when the Portuguese explorers arrived in the 15th century and reached its height a century later. You'll find the Kongo more around Brazzaville, the Vili more along the coast, the Sangha along the Oubangui and Sangha Rivers, and the Téké just to the north of Brazzaville.

Kongo and Téké are the two major art styles. Fetishes (*fétiches*) play an extraordinary role in both. In Kongo art, carved human figures are more realistic than in Téké art and are usually shown with the mouth open. If the figure is in a natural pose, it's probably an ancestral effigy, not a charm. Charms are more stiffly posed than the ancestral figures and are sometimes fairly large.

If you're buying a fetish, find out whether it embodies good spirits or evil spirits. Both depend for their power on magical substances inserted into cavities in the abdomen or head and are often covered with clay. Those that are the abode of malevolent spirits are embedded with nails or sharp iron pieces, which are driven into the figures to activate them in retaliation against persons who have committed a serious offence. Those that are the abode of benevolent spirits usually have more peaceful expressions and are activated by rubbing the nose or forehead while offering a prayer.

You may also see the Téké male charm figures (*buti*), which have rigid postures and are supposed to have a magical substance stuffed into their abdominal cavities. Their faces are usually lined and bearded, the feet bent, and the arms concealed by clay or some type of wrapping that secures the magical substance. They represent a specific ancestor and depending on the nature of the magical substance (*bonga*), they can counteract sorcery, cure diseases, ensure success in hunting, etc.

Without the magical substance, they are known as *tege* and are powerless. If yours is wrapped in clay, pack it carefully. Mine was broken in transport.

GEOGRAPHY

The country has three distinct zones. The northern area is very wet and covered with rain forests, which are virtually inaccessible for lack of roads. The central area, by contrast, is a succession of plateaux interrupted by valleys cut with deep gorges by rivers flowing toward the Congo River. Here too is what could be the Congo's bread basket, the 320 km-wide Niari Valley north-west of Brazzaville. It is largely savannah, making agricultural development easier. Roads in the plateaux are relatively good, and the altitude, varying between 500 and 800 metres, makes the climate more bearable.

The coastal plain is flat, drier and the coolest area in the country. Sizeable offshore petroleum reserves have helped make the port of Pointe-Noire the country's second largest city. Building roads through the thick vegetation is very costly so the road system is bad, especially between Pointe-Noire and Loubomo on the road to Brazzaville. Consequently the railroad plays a critical role, perhaps more so in the Congo than in any other country in Africa. It's also why three out of four Congolese reside near the 515-km stretch of track.

The Congo River, with the second highest water flow in the world, also plays a critical role. At Brazzaville, it forms a lakelike expanse, 33 km by 23 km, called Stanley Pool, separating Brazzaville and Kinshasa, then turns into rapids for most of the remaining journey to the sea. Steamers plough the river northward from Brazzaville, providing a critical link to the remote northern region.

CLIMATE

The Congo lies on the equator in the thick of the African rainforests. Excessive humidity, not heat, is the main concern. The best time to see the Congo is when when there's little or no rain, from June to September. Rains also sometimes let up slightly around Christmas or January. The worst times are November and February to April, when there are downpours virtually every day.

LANGUAGE

French is the official language. Lingala is the principal African language spoken in the north and around Brazzaville. Munukutuba, an offshoot of Kikongo, is the main African language in the south around Pointe-Noire. Some greetings in Lingala are:

Good morning	*BOAT-tay*
Good evening	*BOAT-tay*
How are you?	*san-gha-BOW-nay*
Thank you	*MAY-lay-zee*
Goodbye	*CAN-day MAH-lah-mou*

VISAS

Only West Germans and French citizens are not legally required to have visas, but even they are strongly advised to get one because there have been many instances where Ger-

mans and French without visas were refused entry. Written proof of exemption, even a notice on the wall at customs confirming such, won't help! An onward air ticket is required, but not all embassies, including the one in Gabon, demand to see it. Visas are usually valid for only two weeks (and are not renewable), but they are sometimes made valid for only five days depending on your nationality and where you apply. Luck also plays a role, although a shabby appearance won't help matters.

A visa is not required if you are merely transiting at Brazzaville to catch another flight and you have a ticket with a confirmed seat on the next flight to your destination. In that case, you will be allowed to leave the airport.

If you will be coming to Brazzaville via the ferry from Kinshasa, in addition to a Congolese visa you will need a *laissez-passer* from the Congolese Embassy in Kinshasa. They are usually processed in 24 to 48 hours. If you wait to get your visa in Kinshasa, you will be taking a risk. Relations between the Congo and Zaïre are strained, and every now and then they have a pissing match and close their borders for a week or a month. If this happens and you already have a visa, you at least stand a chance of getting in.

Exit visas are required for travellers staying in the Congo longer than 72 hours. On weekdays applications are received only between 7.30 and 10.30 am at the Service d'Immigration downtown 200 metres from the US Embassy. You can pick your passport up the same day between 3 and 5.30 pm. No photograph is required. On Saturday applications are received between 8 and 10 am and passports returned between 11 am and 12.30 pm.

Zaïre Visas & laissez-passer

Both a Zaïre visa and a laissez-passer are required to get from Brazzaville to Kinshasa. Laissez-passer cost CFA 1000 and are issued by the Zaïre Embassy in the heart of Brazzaville on Avenue de l'Indépendance two blocks from the post office. The embassy issues laissez-passer and visas in 24 and 48 hours, respectively.

Do not wait until you arrive in Brazzaville to get a Zaïre visa. What reportedly happens is that they issue you a visa and then refuse to issue you a laissez-passer on the grounds that a laissez-passer is issued only to people with visas obtained elsewhere. It sounds ridiculous, but don't take a chance. There are many other countries where you can obtain a Zaïre visa.

If you're travelling overland to Gabon, anticipate encountering numerous police posts along the route, especially between N'Dendé (Gabon) and Loubomo. They usually stamp your passport each time. The posts are not always obvious and if you miss one, expect a big hassle at the next police post on the way. Coming from or going to Gabon, don't fail to register with immigration at Loubomo.

Diplomatic Missions Abroad

Bangui, Bonn, Brussels, Conakry, Kinshasa, Libreville, Luanda, Paris, Rome, Washington, Yaoundé.

MONEY

US$1   =   CFA 296
£1   =   CFA 570

The unit of currency is the Central African CFA. Only the hotels will accept the West African CFA. You can exchange them with Air Afrique in downtown Brazzaville or at the airport; they usually do this as a matter of course. The M'Bamou Palace Hôtel will sometimes change CFA even if you're not a guest. This is a lot easier than going to the Banque Centrale (the only bank that can exchange West African CFA for Central African CFA).

You are not allowed to take out more than CFA 25,000, and the rule is strictly enforced. Anticipate a thorough search when leaving the country.

Banking hours are weekdays and Saturday, 6.30 to 11.30 am.

GENERAL INFORMATION
Health

Yellow fever and cholera vaccinations are required. The Congo is one of the 11 African countries worst hit by AIDS. Among prostitutes the disease is certainly rampant.

Brazzaville has two hospitals: Hôpital Général de Brazzaville (tel 812365/68) and Association Médicale des Français au Congo (hours: weekdays 8 am to 12 noon and 3 to 5 pm).

Two general practitioners in Brazzaville are Dr Grimaud Gerard (tel 812594) and Dr Zimmerman Jean-Marie (tel 812365/814536). Two of the best pharmacies in Brazzaville are Pharmacie de Garde (next to Hôtel le Tropical) and Bikoumou (nighttime: tel 810847).

In Pointe-Noire, the principal hospital is Hôpital A Sice (tel 942199). Dr Gerard Guenin (tel 941751) is on Avenue de Gaulle.

Security

Security is definitely a problem in Brazzaville, but nothing like it is in nextdoor Kinshasa. The downtown area is very dark at night. Normal precautions for a big city are required. Travelling upcountry presents no problems, but expect police checks every 30 km or so.

Business Hours

Business: weekdays 8 am to 12.30 pm and 3 to 6 pm; Saturday 8 am to 12.30 pm. Government: weekdays 7 am to 2 pm; Saturday 7 am to 12 pm.

Public Holidays

1 January, 18 March, 1 May, 31 July, 13-15 August (anniversary of the 1963 revolution, which coincides with independence), 1 November, 25 December, 31 December. The 'Three Glorious Days' holiday in mid-August is by far the biggest celebration.

Photography

A photo permit is required. Go to the Direction du Tourisme (tel 810953) in the Plateau section next to Asecna. As usual,

Top: Market in Malabo, Equatorial Guinea (HF)
Bottom: Loading produce for transport to Malabo, Equatorial Guinea (HF)

Top: Children, Equatorial Guinea (HF)
Bottom: Wide Avenue, Bata, Equatorial Guinea (HF)

photographs of the airport, and government and military installations are strictly forbidden.

Time, Post, Phone & Telex

When it's noon in the Congo, it's 11 am in London and 6 am in New York (7 am during daylight savings time). The post is fairly reliable, and making international calls is not a major problem. You can send a telex at the post office and at the Meridien and M'Bamou Palace hotels in Brazzaville.

GETTING THERE

Air

From Europe There are direct flights on various airlines from Brussels, Geneva, Paris and Rome. Taking Lina Congo is no problem; it's one of the top four or five African airlines. The cheapest route from London – about £420 roundtrip – is via Moscow on Aeroflot, but only if the ticket is purchased from a bucket shop.

From the USA A 45-day excursion ticket via Paris will cost you US$2078, but you can get much better deals from one of the budget agencies mentioned in the introductory Getting There chapter. You also have the option of flying to nextdoor Kinshasa and hopping the ferry to Brazzaville, however, you will have to wait at least a day in Kinshasa getting a laissez-passer from the Congo embassy.

Car

If you're headed to eastern Zaïre, you must cross over to Kinshasa and catch the river boat there. Almost everyone headed towards the Central African Republic takes the boat leaving from Brazzaville.

The preferred route from Libreville (Gabon) is via Mouila, N'Dendé (Gabon) and Loubomo, not via Franceville (Gabon). The distance is 1175 km, almost all on improved dirt road. While roads on the Gabon side are well maintained even during the rainy season, in the Congo the road can become impassable at times during the long rainy season (October to May), especially February through May. Four days' driving is typical, although it can be done in three days in the dry season if you push it. There is petrol in Loubomo, N'Dendé, Mouila and Lambaréné.

Bush Taxi

To/from Gabon If you're travelling to/from Gabon, almost everybody takes the train between Brazzaville and Loubomo. On the picturesque 100-km stretch between Loubomo and Kibangou, it's fairly easy to find both bush taxis and trucks. But between Kibangou and N'Dendé (185 km) in Gabon, you'll find only trucks. About twice a week there are beer trucks which run between the two (leaving N'Dendé Tuesday and Friday). Just be prepared for a very long beer stop and fiesta at each village on the way. Drinking is what life is all about in this area of Africa.

Kinshasa Ferry

Between Brazzaville and Kinshasa, there are ferries every hour on the hour in both directions starting at 8 am, the last one leaving at 5 pm, with no ferry at 1 pm. The trip itself takes only 20 minutes, but you should get there about 45 minutes in advance to allow sufficient time to clear customs.

There are two ferries. The Congolese one is newer and costs about CFA 2750 (CFA 1000 less for student card holders) one-way or roundtrip, whereas the Zaïrois ferry costs only about 200 Z (US$2). The Congolese ferry leaves Brazzaville at 8 am, Kinshasa at 9 am, etc. The Zaïrois ferry leaves Kinshasa at 8 am, Brazzaville at 9 am, etc.

River Boat

You can take a river boat to Bangui (CAR), Ouesso (north-eastern Congo), or Kisangani (eastern Zaïre). The boats move at a snail's pace, but if you have the time, you will find this an excellent way to see Africa and meet Africans. The boat to Kisangani leaves every Monday afternoon from Kinshasa. The boat to Bangui, one of which is *La Ville de Brazza*, leaves Brazzaville twice monthly and takes 14 days; the exact departure date is not determined until about two weeks prior to departure.

The cost per person is about CFA 100,000 for a 1st class cabin with a double bed, air-con, bathroom and all meals, CFA 26,000 for tourist class with four beds per cabin and no meals, and CFA 13,000 for 2nd class with no beds. If you ship a vehicle, expect to pay about CFA 47,500 for the vehicle plus at least CFA 13,000 per person even if everybody sleeps in it.

Contact ATC (L'Agence Transcongolaise des Communications, BP 74, tel 810441) in Brazzaville. It's about 300 metres in front of Hôtel Le Beach near the ferry for Kinshasa. In Bangui, contact ATC near the market, or l'Agence Centrafricaine des Communications Fluviales (BP 822, tel 610111).

GETTING AROUND
Air
Lina Congo (tel 813065) offers one to five flights a day from Brazzaville to Pointe-Noire (CFA 28,000 one-way), four a week to Ouesso, three a week to Loubomo, Nkayi and Owando, two a week to Impfondo, and one a week to Lékana, Souanké, Zanaga, Boundji and Kéllé.

Bush Taxi
There are bush taxi connections linking Brazzaville with Loubomo, Owando and Djambala but not with Pointe-Noire. On most other routes, you'll have to catch a truck. Between Brazzaville and Loubomo, almost all travellers catch one of the twice daily trains.

Car
Road conditions vary considerably in the Congo depending primarily on whether you're travelling in the plateau area (not too bad) or in the lowlands (terrible). The route connecting Brazzaville and Pointe-Noire, for example, is passable between Loubomo and Brazzaville but terrible between Loubomo and Pointe-Noire for this reason. The trip takes two days. It is advisable to bring an axe

because between Loubomo and Pointe-Noire, it is not unusual to find the road blocked by falling trees! Putting your vehicle on the train is expensive.

On the other hand, the roads north of Brazzaville in the plateau area are fairly decent as far as Djambala (382 km) and to Owando (532 km); about 275 km are paved. Beyond Owando the road becomes virtually impassable, which is why people take the river boat to Ouesso.

Car Rental
Eurocar, Hertz and Avis are all represented, as well as local companies. For the addresses of their offices, see the Brazzaville and Pointe-Noire Getting Around sections.

Train
There are two trains a day in each direction between Brazzaville and Pointe-Noire. From Brazza departures are daily at 6.15 am (old train) and 6.50 pm (express), arriving 9.20 pm and 6.30 am, respectively. From Pointe-Noire departures are daily at 6.25 am (old train) and 6.10 pm (express), arriving 9.30 pm and 6.10 am respectively. Don't be surprised if the old train arrives five or more hours late.

The express, on the other hand, typically runs about an hour late unless there is a major problem like a derailment, which is not unusual. It is very comfortable and one of the best in Central Africa. There are four berths to a cabin, and they are available every day in both directions. The bar-restaurant, however, is 2nd class quality and packed – all right for a drink, but you'd do better bringing your own food.

Prices on the express are about CFA 15,000 for a berth, CFA 12,000 for 1st class, and CFA 6300 for 2nd class. There are student reductions of 50% on the fares. Second class on the day train runs about 40% less than 2nd class on the night express, but the student reduction is less. Buy your tickets and reserve your seats in advance because when the gates open, there's a mad rush for seats and if you're behind, you may have to stand for much of the trip.

There is also a daily train from Loubomo to M'Binda (CFA 15,000/7500 for 1st/2nd class) at the Gabon border; from there you can hitch rides to Franceville (Gabon) 145 km away.

River Boat

La Ville de Ouesso and *La Ville de Mossaka* connect Brazzaville and Ouesso once a month during the dry season and twice monthly during the rainy season. There is no fixed schedule. The 1000-km trip takes 10 days up and six days back, stopping at about 20 villages along the way. The cost per person is about CFA 66,000 for 1st class, CFA 43,000 for 2nd class, and CFA 13,500 for 3rd class. Accommodation is similar to that on the boats to Bangui. Contact the river transport company, ATC, in Brazzaville for more information.

BRAZZAVILLE

Brazzaville provides quite a contrast to its twin city Kinshasa, which you can see just across the mighty Congo River. Whereas Kinshasa has three million people, skyscrapers and a multitude of restaurants and night spots, Brazzaville, with 500,000 people, looks like an innocent overgrown town nestled in greenery, with streets bordered by elegant mango and flamboyant trees which blossom in November, the city's real springtime.

Most foreigners prefer Brazzaville because it doesn't have quite the crime rate that has made Kinshasa so famous and given everybody there the jitters. To the residents of Kinshasa, Brazzaville is a breath of fresh air.

The river definitely enhances the city's atmosphere. There are a number of restaurants with good views of it, including several next to the big rapids on the outskirts of the city.

Of the eight sections of town, the four major ones are the Plateau, Poto-Poto, Bacongo and Moungali. The Plateau is where the administrative buildings were constructed when the French started building Brazzaville at the turn of the century; that's where you'll find the major shops, hotels and businesses. The two main streets are Avenue Eboué along the river and Avenue Lumumba one block up. Otherwise, forget street names; nobody knows them because every block or so they change.

Business activity is spread out in the various sections of town, each with its own market. The one in Poto-Poto is perhaps a little more colourful; the one on the Plateau is better for crafts. Streets get very dark at night and you won't see many people walking in the Plateau area after sundown. The Plateau is where you'll find most of the better restaurants and posh nightclubs. But if you're looking for African nightlife or a cheap hotel, head for Bacongo. It's a small version of Kinshasa's lively Cité area.

Information

Banks BEAC (Banque des Etats de l'Afrique Centrale), BCC (Banque Commerciale Congolaise), UCB (Union Congolaise des Banques), Banque Internationale du Congo.

Embassies Embassies are widely dispersed. Two principal ones downtown are the US embassy on Ave Amilcar Cabral a block from the M'Bamou Palace and the Zaïre embassy on Ave de l'Indépendance two blocks from the post office.

Belgium
  (tel 812963) BP 255 on Avenue Lumumba.
CAR
  (tel 814014) on Rue Alfassa facing Saint-François.
Gabon
  (tel 810590) on Avenue Fourneau.
France
  (tel 811423) BP 2089 downtown at the Place de la Poste.
West Germany
  (tel 812990) BP 2022.
USA
  (tel 812070) BP 1015 downtown on Avenue Amilcar-Cabral.

Zaïre
    (tel 812938) downtown on Avenue de l'Indépendance.

Other embassies include: Cameroun, Chad, Guinea, Italy, Nigeria. Many countries, such as the UK, use their embassies in Kinshasa as the official chanceries for the Congo. Consulates in the Congo are: Belgium (Pointe-Noire), Denmark, France (Pointe-Noire), West Germany (Pointe-Noire), Greece, Netherlands (tel 813426), Sweden, Switzerland (tel 812788), UK.

Bookstores & Supermarkets For guide books on the Congo, try ONLP around the corner from La Pizzeria. For coffee-table-style books, try Maison de la Presse (tel 810228) on Avenue Foch near the Marché du Plateau; it's open 8 am to midday and 4 pm to 7 pm. The M'Bamou Palace and the Meridien hotels also have small bookshops.

For maps of Brazzaville and the Congo, go to the L'Institute Géographique (tel 910780) in Bacongo beyond the Marché Total.

Presto and Score, both one block from the US Embassy, are the best supermarkets.

Travel Agencies Try Clav-Voyages & Tours-Congo (tel 814846/814946) at the Hôtel Cosmos, and Havas Congo Voyage (tel 811039) along the river road, Avenue Amilcar Cabral.

Rapids

The white-water rapids of the Congo river (*les cataractes du Congo*), 12 km from the centre of town considerably past Bacongo, are a 'must see'. They're huge – similar in size to those of the Colorado River in the Grand Canyon. The river is highest from February to May.

You can see the rapids while having a drink or eating at Les Rapides restaurant and contemplating the fact that 13% of the world's untapped hydro-electric energy is flowing in front of you. The rapids are much more impressive up close, so hire a pirogue to take you to the nearby sand bar.

Poto-Poto

The most colourful borough is Poto-Poto. Sunday afternoon is a good time to visit and if you're lucky, you might see some traditional dancing in the streets.

Basilique St Anne & Palais du Peuple

St Anne's Basilica, with a roof of bright green tiles from France, is the most prominent landmark. Built in 1949 and 85 metres long, this was the crowning achievement of the French architect Eyrelle, who built three other beautiful buildings in the city, including a house for Charles de Gaulle. An imposing example of the city's more modern architecture is the Palais du Peuple out near the airport.

Places to Stay – bottom end

Hôtel Exa has 19 clean rooms with double beds and showers for about CFA 3250 a room. Food and relatively cheap drinks are served in a tranquil setting. Getting a room apparently isn't usually a problem, which is almost too good to be true for Brazzaville. It's on the edge of the city on a dirt road in Quartier Massina of Makélékélé, eight km from the centre, next to the Kinsoundi textile mill.

Hôtel du Marché (tel 813835), several km from downtown in Bacongo just across from the Marché Total, has 14 small rooms with fans for about CFA 7500, also air-con rooms for about CFA 13,000. *Hôtel Grand K* (tel 812144) is 100 metres away and has 15 singles/doubles for about CFA 7500/9500 with fan. Rooms with air-con cost about CFA 10,700/14,000.

Le Petit-Logis (tel 811476) is popular with foreigners and is the best value for money among the bottom end. It has 41 spacious air-con rooms, carpeting and private baths but no hot water for CFA 8000 a room. It's 300 metres from the fancy M'Bamou Palace. *Le Ballon d'Or* (tel 814001), at the Rond Point de Moungali and two km from

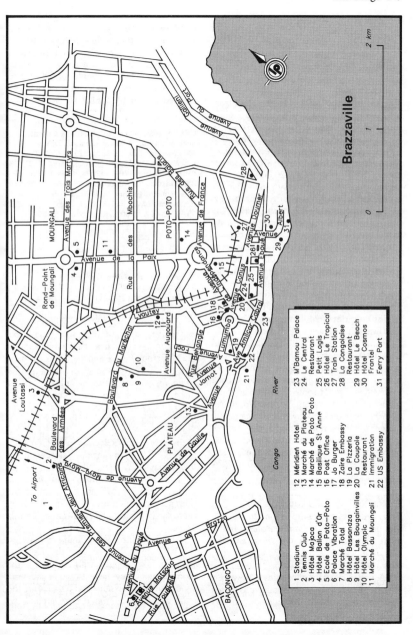

Brazzaville

1 Stadium
2 Tennis Club
3 Hôtel Majoca
4 Hôtel Ballon d'Or
5 Ecole de Poto-Poto
6 Palace Vibration
7 Marché Total
8 Hôtel Bassandza
9 Hôtel Les Bougainvilles
10 Hôtel Olympic
11 Marché du Moungali

12 Méridien Hôtel
13 Marché du Plateau
14 Marché de Poto Poto
15 Basilique St Anne
16 Post Office
17 Jo Burger
18 Zaïre Embassy
19 La Pizzeria
20 La Coupole Restaurant
21 Immigration
22 US Embassy

23 M'Bamou Palace
24 Le Central Restaurant
25 Petit Logis
26 Hôtel Le Tropical
27 Train Station
28 La Congolaise Restaurant
29 Hôtel Le Beach
30 Hôtel Cosmos
31 Frantel

32 Ferry Port

the town centre, has nine rooms with fans for CFA 8000 and with air-con for CFA 11,000. *M'Foa*, on Avenue du 28 Août 1940, is another, with rooms for about CFA 8500.

Places to Stay – middle

One km from the heart of town across from the Pullman Cosmos you'll find the slightly rundown *Le Beach* (tel 812958, telex 5277), which has 15 large rooms for CFA 18,000 to CFA 21,000. The well maintained, nine-room *Hôtel Ma Jo Ca* (tel 818337) charges about CFA 17,500 to CFA 20,000 for a very decent room and is definitely good value. It's on the outskirts of town fairly near the airport and recommended if you're just staying overnight. There's no restaurant but breakfast is served.

Hôtel Bassandza has 10 newly renovated singles/doubles for CFA 16,500/17,500 plus a terrace restaurant. It's off a main road between the airport and the centre of town. One block away you'll find *Les Bougainvilles* (tel 814463), with rooms for about CFA 17,000. It has a quiet ambience and a terrace restaurant that serves French food.

Hôtel le Tropical (tel 810364), at about CFA 14,000 a room, is the best hotel in its price range and in the centre of town three blocks from the M'Bamou Palace, on the same street. The 21 rooms are clean and spacious with hot water. *Ntsona Hôtel* (tel 810971) is one block away with identically priced rooms but not as good. If they're full, try *Hôtel Jumbo* about five blocks away, between the M'Bamou Palace and Jo Burger; the rate there is about CFA 13,000 to CFA 15,000 a room.

Places to Stay – top end

Brazzaville is not lacking in four-star hotels. The palacial PLM *M'Bamou Palace*, in the heart of town next to the river, and the *Méridien*, a good km from the town centre, have the best reputations.

A better deal for the money, however, may be the slightly less expensive *Cosmos Pullman*, a good km from downtown and overlooking the river. *Residence Marina*, with 24 posh rooms, has the distinction of being the most expensive hotel in Central and West Africa. Downtown near the Banque Centrale, it caters to people looking for an intimate atmosphere with extras, such as a Mercedes available for hire.

M'Bamou Palace (tel 812012/812157, telex 5329), CFA 30,000/32,000 for singles/doubles, tennis, small pool, nightclub, TV/video, cards AE, D, V.
Méridien (tel 810910, telex 5233), CFA 28,000 a room, tennis, short pool, nightclub, cards AE, D, CB.
Cosmos Pullman (tel 812098, telex 5342), CFA 25,000 a room (CFA 3000 more for a 'superior room'), pool, tennis, nightclub, cards AE, D, CB.
Residence Marina (tel 814954, telex 5250), CFA 35,000 to CFA 45,000 a room, pool.

Places to Eat

Cheap Eats *La Congolaise* is the place to head for if you want a decent meal for the lowest price possible, typically CFA 2200 for a huge meal. Open every day until 10 pm, it's about five blocks from the train station in the direction of the brewery.

Jo Burger is like a MacDonalds but more expensive; at night they have Lebanese shawarama sandwiches. It's two blocks from the M'Bamou Palace and one block from the post office. Across the street you'll find *La Coupole*, which offers primarily grilled dishes, such as braised chicken, for CFA 3200 to CFA 4200, plus a pleasant terrace setting. Open for dinner only, it's closed on Sundays. *Le Rivage*, a block away from both of these, has a few selection in the CFA 1300 to CFA 3200 price range but so few clients that its days may be numbered.

Le Central, one block from both La Coupole and the M'Bamou Palace, is the most popular watering hole downtown. They serve sandwiches for CFA 800 and full meals as well.

Snack-Bar La Liberté, halfway between the M'Bamou Palace and the Cosmos Pullman, is so popular with Africans in the morning that they have to serve cafeteria style. Coffee, croissants and pastries are the main attractions. *Baba Presto*, around the corner from La Pizzeria, is a more expensive pastry shop.

Tiffany's Snack Bar, one block from the post office in the direction of the river, serves simple fare, including sandwiches for CFA 800.

Chez Charton (Vietnamese) and *Les Caimans* are other cheap restaurants you might inquire about. For dirt cheap African food downtown, there are numerous stalls 100 metres across from the M'Bamou Palace.

Italian *La Pizzeria* (tel 811183), downtown one block from the US Embassy and closed on Sundays, is very popular and recommended. There's a huge menu, with pizza for CFA 3400 and spaghetti for CFA 2900, among other dishes. The setting, both inside and on the terrace, is one of the nicest in town.

Also recommended is *Chez Gigi* (tel 814867), an air-con restaurant that serves very good French and Italian cuisine. Closed on Tuesdays, it is two blocks from the train station on the same street, in the direction of the post office. Next door and closed on Mondays you'll find *Le Capricorne*, also with air-con and offering pizza for CFA 3200, plus other Italian selections for CFA 3200 to CFA 4300.

Chinese *Le Pekin* (tel 814705), a block from the M'Bamou Palace, is popular and recommended. Open every day, it has an extensive Chinese menu and an attractive oriental atmosphere. Most main courses are in the CFA 3200 to CFA 4300 range.

La Table de Juko (tel 810444) between the M'Bamou Palace and the Cosmos Pullman, is a little unusual in that it offers three types of cuisine (Asian, French and African). It has an attractive setting, and the service is quite good. It is closed on Mondays.

Lebanese *L'Arc-en-Ciel* (tel 814062), nine storeys up in the heart of town next to Jo Burger, offers good Lebanese cuisine and a panoramic view. Prices are moderate to high. It is closed on Sundays.

French *Le Bambou* (tel 813290), four km from the centre of town near Cimetière de Ngouaka, is reportedly one of the best restaurants. Entrecôte is the speciality. It is open every day except Tuesday.

Chez Colette, four blocks beyond the train station, is popular with the French, especially for Sunday lunch. Don't let the unpretentious terrace setting fool you. The menu is excellent with prices to match; no main course is less than CFA 4000.

Le Soleil (tel 814572), a block from the M'Bamou Palace, is a good French bistro with a limited selection. Most main courses are in the CFA 2700 to CFA 3700 range. It's open every day, and you can dine outside or inside with air-con. *Les Ambassadeurs*, 100 metres from the US Embassy, is much more expensive.

Entertainment & Sports

Bars Getting the local brew is difficult in the Plateau area. They all want to sell you a small can of foreign beer for CFA 800. *Le Central* is one of the few that does and charges CFA 500 for a big bottle. It is the most popular watering hole downtown, while the bar at the *Petit Logis* two blocks away caters to those looking for a more derelict ambience. It closes around 10 pm. The fancy bar at the *M'Bamou Palace* is usually dead.

Around the Marché Total in Bacongo and around the Rond Point in Moungali, are several popular African bars.

Nightclubs There are four major nightclubs in the Plateau area: *Le Scotch* at the Hôtel le Beach, *Le Kébé-Kébé* at the M'Bamou Palace, *Le Ram Dam* at the Méridien, and *Le Saturne* at the Cosmos Pullman. All have covers of about CFA 3500 and, for the most part, are closed on Mondays. Many local expatriates prefer these because they don't feel the other sections of town are safe at night.

Le Banatha (tel 814582), open every day

and facing the general hospital in Quartier des Ambassadeurs, has a nightclub and a restaurant serving both African and French food.

Far more interesting are the nightclubs in the African section of town. For live music your best bet is probably *Palace Libération*. It's open-air and one good block from the Marché Total on a side street, Rue Mère Marie, with a CFA 1000 cover on weekends. *Le Pacha* is next to the Marché Total and one of Brazzaville's best known. Dancing partners are not hard to find. There's a CFA 2500 cover (CFA 3000 on Saturday). *Chez Bibi* is similar and in the same area.

The common people's dancing joint is *La Barrière*, about six blocks from the Marché Total. People drink outside and in the street, but dance inside. *Milex* is also well-known but further out on the outer fringes of Bacongo and next to the river. You can also go 12 km to the rapids and dance at *Les Rapides*.

Two drinking and dancing places in the Moungali area are *La Source Mary Luiz* near Rond Point Moungali and one block behind Hôtel Ballon d'Or, and *Elysée Bar* 100 metres from the Rond Point.

Cinemas Le Vog (tel 812885), one block from the post office, shows most of the latest movies. Shows are at 6.30 and 9 pm.

Sports The top three hotels all have pools and tennis courts. For CFA 1000 to CFA 1500, people not staying at the hotels can use them. The best place for tennis, however, is *Le Tennis Club de Brazzaville* not far from the airport and next to the Stade de la Révolution. They have 10 well maintained clay courts. You can become a temporary member for about CFA 27,000 for two weeks, or about CFA 38,000 for a month.

Golfers can try out the nine-hole golf club 12 km west of town near the World Health Organisation. The location overlooking the river is ideal, with lush green fairways, sand greens, and clubs for rent. For information, ask at the M'Bamou Palace or at the Méridien.

Things to Buy

Artisan goods Each of the four major sections of town has its own market. Marché Total in Bacongo is the most active because it's also a transportation hub, but the Marché du Plateau is better for African souvenirs including wooden carvings, fetishes (not always on display), drums, straw products, ivory, malachite and paintings.

One of Brazzaville's major places of interest is the Ecole de Peinture de Poto-Poto, a well-known art school and one of the few places in Central and West Africa where you can pick up oil paintings by Africans. Most of them are fairly abstract and in the CFA 10,000 to CFA 50,000 price range. It's slightly hidden next to the Rond Point Moungali on Avenue de la Paix several km from downtown, and open weekdays and Saturdays 7 am to 6 pm.

Music One of the best music stores is Pierre Moutouari's on Avenue Matsone in Bacongo several blocks from Marché Total. Popular Congolese singers include Pierre Moutouari (Somsa band), Locko Massengo (Rumbayas International band), Youlou Mabiala (Kamikaze band), Pamelo Mounk'a (Les Grands As band) and Jacques Loubelo.

Getting There & Away

Air Lina Congo (tel 813065) has one to five flights a day to Pointe-Noire and less frequent flights to Ouesso, Loubomo, Nkayi, Owando, Impfondo, Souanké, Kéllé, Lékana, Makoua, Zanaga and Boundji.

Bush Taxi You're only likely to take a bush taxi from Brazzaville if you're headed north toward Djambala or Owando. Almost everybody travelling between Brazzaville and Pointe-Noire takes the train. Bush taxis leave from the Terminus Mikalou about 6 km from the centre of Brazzaville on the road headed north. Get there early, around 6 am. The fare is about CFA 2200 to Ngo and CFA 6500 to Owando.

Train There are two trains daily between

Brazzaville and Pointe-Noire via Loubomo. For specifics, see the initial Getting Around section.

Getting Around

Airport Transport At Brazzaville airport, there's no departure tax. You'll find a bar, Eurocar and Hertz, but no bank or restaurant. If you have West African CFA, Air Afrique will exchange it for Central African CFA. Departure procedures are very slow, so come early. A taxi to the airport (five km) should be CFA 1000, but expect to pay CFA 1500 coming from the airport (CFA 2000 after 8 pm). Bargaining is required. As an alternative there is an urban bus service which passes by the front of the airport.

Bus Buses ply Brazzaville's principal streets until 9 pm.

Taxi Fares are CFA 100 for a shared taxi and, if you take a taxi to yourself it is CFA 500 to CFA 700 for a 'course'. Meters are not used. Rates increase by CFA 300 at 8 pm. You can get a taxi by the hour for CFA 2500 and a taxi for the day for CFA 15,000 to CFA 20,000 plus petrol, but you'll have to bargain. They are plentiful, but not always easy to find at night. Green and white is the colour.

Car Rental At Brazzaville airport, you'll find Eurocar (Le Mai SA, tel 812148, telex 8263), Hertz (tel 810910), Chancelle (tel 813202) and Leader. In town, you'll find Eurocar across from the M'Bamou Palace hotel, Hertz at the Meridien (tel 810910), Avis (tel 811581/813643, telex 5366) in care of the M'Bamou Palace, and Auto-Location (tel 811611).

POINTE-NOIRE

The petroleum industry is what draws most people to this port city of 200,000 people. For others, the main attractions are the beautiful, safe beaches and the excellent fishing. The beach is on the edge of town behind the train station, which is an architectural jewel. There are windsurfers for rent on the beaches, and the lagoons along the coast abound in swordfish, barracuda, tarpon, tuna and skate.

The city is divided between the modern section near the water and the African section to the east called the Cité. Avenue du Général de Gaulle is the main drag in the modern section, stretching from the train station through the centre of town. The Rond Point Lumumba is the centre of the Cité; you'll find the picturesque Marché de Tié-Tié there as well.

Nowhere are things really cheap because the oil boom, or what's left of it, has jacked up prices. The Transcongo car race ends in Pointe-Noire. If you're here around the first week in April, the city is likely to be rather festive, preparing for the onslaught of vehicles.

Information

Consulates Belgium (tel 941192); France (tel 940962); Germany (tel 942003).

Bookstores Librairie Paillet on Avenue Général de Gaulle is the city's best.

Travel Agency Manucongo (tel 942629, telex 8915) is next to the Novotel.

Places to Stay – bottom end

None of the hotels are cheap; the least expensive are in the Cité. What's unusual is that the rates seem to be somewhat negotiable – especially if you're staying more than a night or two. It might help to make an African friend and have him go enquire about the rates. The people are accustomed to seeing foreigners with big bucks, not those on a limited budget.

Hôtel Kingoy (tel 941846) charges about CFA 9000 a room for a night, some with air-con. You might negotiate a lower price if you take a room with a fan. *Hôtel Mapila* is similar and has rooms for about CFA 9000 with fan, CFA 13,000 with air-con. *Mantala Auberge* has rooms for CFA 8000 with fan and exterior bath.

On the main drag (Général de Gaulle) in the main section of town near the beaches,

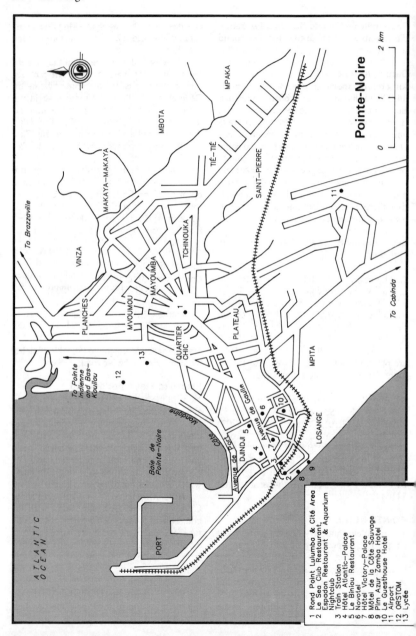

Pointe-Noire

0   1   2 km

1 Rond Point Lulumba & Cité6 Area
2 Le Sea Club Restaurant,
   Espadon Restaurant & Aquarium
3 Nightclub
4 Train Station
5 Hôtel Atlantic–Palace
6 Le Biniou Restaurant
7 Novotel
8 Hôtel Victory–Palace
9 Môtel de la Côte Sauvage
10 Pim Azur Zamba Hotel
11 Le Guesthouse Hotel
12 ORSTOM
13 Lycée

you'll find *Salt Motel* (the sign says 'SAT'). The rooms are big with balconies but old, in a noisy area, and overpriced at about CFA 16,000 a room; maybe you can bargain with them. The *FLM* (tel 941196) has decent singles/doubles for CFA about 14,000/15,000 and an excellent nightclub, but it's about six km from the centre of town.

Le Guesthouse (tel 940564) charges about CFA 18,000 a room. The rooms are fine and the hotel is only a few blocks from the centre of town. For the same price a room, the *Beausejour* (tel 940944) is definitely over-priced. For the money, about CFA 15,000/18,000 for singles/doubles, the *Victory-Palace* (tel 940704, telex 8267, cards AE, D, V) is the best hotel in town and in the centre of town on Avenue Général de Gaulle. The rooms have TVs, refrigerators and carpeting.

Places to Stay – top end

The *Novotel* downtown on Général de Gaulle is quite popular, but it's a 15-minute walk to the beach, which is why a lot of people prefer the equally nice *PLM Azur Zamba*. A 15-minute walk from downtown, it's directly on the beach and has one of the best restaurants in town.

The best value for money, however, is *Motel de la Côte Sauvage*, which is on the beach nearby and has virtually all of the amenities of the PLM Azur Zamba. Accordingly, it's difficult to recommend the similarly priced *Atlantic-Palace*, an older hotel in the centre of town with a pool and nightclub but with about as much appeal as an outdoor toilet on a rainy night. It is a little over a km from the beach.

M'Bou-M' Vounvou Novotel (tel 941200, telex 8240), CFA 28,500/31,000 for singles/doubles, pool, tennis, car rental, cards AE, D, V, CB.

PLM Azur Zamba (tel 940272, telex 8297), CFA 23,000 to CFA 26,000/CFA 23,500 to CFA 26,500 for singles/doubles, beach, pool, tennis, cards AE, D.

Motel de la Côte Sauvage (tel 942626, telex 8355), about CFA 21,500 a room, beach, pool, mini refrigerators, TV/video, cards AE, D.

Hôtel Atlantic-Palace (tel 941712, telex 8287), about CFA 19,500 a room, cards AE, D.

Places to Eat

For inexpensive food, *La Rotonde* bar across from the Atlantic-Palace serves sandwiches. Otherwise, about the only place to get cheap food is in the Cité area.

Among the hotels, the *PLM Azur Zamba* has the reputation for serving the best food. Another recommended restaurant is *Le Sea Club* (tel 941211), an open-air restaurant next to the ocean with good seafood. It is closed on Sundays. Next door you'll find *Espadon*, which is more elegant and also closed on Sundays. The *Pizzeria* near the Novotel gets good reviews from the local expatriates.

For French food, two of the best are *Le Biniou* (tel 942227), across from the Novotel on Avenue Général de Gaulle (closed Sundays), and *Chez Paulette* (tel 941688) (open every day), with a four-course menu for CFA 7000 plus a la carte selections, including some seafood.

Le Mékong, on Général de Gaulle across from the Migitel, serves pretty decent Chinese food. *Le Chaudron* adjoining the Migitel serves both Vietnamese and Congolese food.

Entertainment & Sports

Bars *La Rotonde*, in the centre of town is a very active bar. There are many more bars in the Cité; *Parafifi* is one of the better known ones.

Nightclubs Pointe-Noire has more than its fair share of *boîtes*. In the centre of town, the best by reputation are *Jhimisy*, *L'Aristophane* and *Mikado*. The only one that might have live music is *Le 421*, also in the centre of town. They all have CFA 2000 cover charges, and most are closed on Mondays. *Kayes*, at the FLM, is pretty lively and open from Thursday through to Sunday, but you'll need wheels to get there. The *Aquarium* on the beach near the Sea Club restaurant is another.

In the Cité, the two that the locals seem to prefer are *Caméléon* (the sign reads 'Night Spot') and *Total-Bar*.

Sports You can play tennis at the Novotel for CFA 1500 to CFA 2000 per 45-minute session. The best pool for doing laps is at the Atlantic-Palace. Windsurfers and small sailboats are available for rent at the Cercle Naval for CFA 1500 an hour and CFA 10,000 per half day, respectively. It's north on Avenue du Port, several km from the centre of town, and open weekdays 3 to 7 pm and all day weekends.

For fishing, call 942705 or inquire at the PLM Azur Zamba for charter boats. February through April is the season for tarpon, November through April for barracuda and carp, and May through September for sea bream, tuna and other fish.

If you just want to lie on the beach, you'll find a more secluded beach at Pointe-Indienne 15 km north of the city.

Things to Buy
Mabounga Daniel's Galeries des Arts Décoratifs sells some high quality leather wall hangings and batiks, among other things. Ask at the Novotel for directions.

Getting There & Away
Because of the terrible road conditions between Loubomo and Pointe-Noire, almost everyone arrives in Pointe-Noire by train or plane from Brazzaville. For specifics, see the initial Getting Around section at the start of this chapter. Ask in the Cité for bush taxis to nearby towns.

Getting Around
Car Rental In addition to taking taxis, you can rent a car from Hertz (tel 941712, telex 8236) at the Hôtel Atlantic-Palace, Eurocar (tel 940359, telex 8263), and Panda Location (tel 941776).

CHUTES DE LOUFOULAKARI
If you have wheels, take a drive to the impressive Loufoulakari Falls 80 km west of Brazzaville, about half-way between Brazzaville and Boko on the dirt road running alongside the river. The trip takes about an hour and a half, but the road is almost impassable at times from February to May. *L'Auberge de Loufoulakari* overlooking the falls has rooms and serves Congolese food.

DJAMBALA
About 380 km north of Brazzaville via Ngo and the Reserve de Léfini, Djambala is in the centre of the Congo's plateau area and can be reached in one day by private vehicle. Two-thirds of the trip is on paved road; the remainder is on good all-weather dirt road. Lina Congo also flies there. Hotels include *Hôtel de Djambala* and the nine-room *Auberges des Jeunes* on the road to Camp Matsouaniste.

KINKALA & MATOUMBOU
These two towns, both on the railroad line, are only an hour's drive west of Brazzaville on paved road towards Pointe-Noire. Kinkala's best hotel is the three-storey *Hôtel de Makoumbou* (tel 852053) with 15 rooms; the *Hôtel de Kinkala* is another. In nearby Matoumbou, there's the *Hôtel de Matoumbou* (tel 852057) with 12 air-con rooms and a restaurant.

LOUBOMO
About 400 km due west of Brazzaville on the railroad line to Pointe-Noire, Loubomo is the country's third largest city and is at the edge of the plateau area, with thick rainforests separating it and Pointe-Noire. The road between the two cities is horrendous. Loubomo is where you get off the train if you're headed overland to Gabon. Don't forget to get your passport stamped here.

Places to Stay & Eat
If you're looking for the cheapest accommodation possible, first check out *Le Buffet de la Gare*, which is at the train station in the centre of town and has five rooms for CFA 5500 and a restaurant, and then *Hôtel Niari* and *Mistral 'KB'*.

If you're looking for the best hotel in town, check out the *Grand Hôtel* (tel 910102/3) and the *Bayonne* (tel 910227), both in the centre of town. The Grand has 39 rooms, some with air-con, unlevel floors, sagging mattresses, and is reportedly decorated in the worst African art done by a French lady whose portrait is hanging in the hotel. The Bayonne has 24 air-con rooms with a bar and a restaurant.

OWANDO

Some 532 km north of Brazzaville, Owando marks the end of the plateau area and the beginning of the great rainforests. The easiest way to get here is on a Lina Congo flight. By road, the trip takes about two days, half of it on paved road. *Hôtel Oyo, Hôtel Lékouyou, Hôtel Itoua, Hôtel du Marché,* and *Hôtel du Parti* are ones to enquire about.

Equatorial Guinea

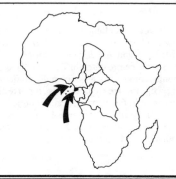

Tarzan would have loved Equatorial Guinea, and so will you if you're the type who likes to get off the beaten track. Yet on arrival in Malabo, the capital city on Bioko Island, or Bata on the mainland, you may wonder why you came. Poverty is rampant, and the economy is so stagnant that the only thing to cheer up the locals is the nearest bar.

The country areas are an entirely different world. Equatorial Guinea is very much a land of jungles, with cloud covered volcanoes providing a backdrop to almost every view. The vegetation is so thick at times that paths can simply disappear beneath your feet. Without surfaced roads, the only way to move about in some parts would be to swing from the vines.

There are areas throughout the country where almost nobody lives – perfect if you're looking for isolated beaches with scenic surroundings. Equatorial Guinea is unlikely to disappoint the adventurous traveller – especially if you speak Spanish and like socialising with the locals.

HISTORY

Equatorial Guinea is a small country that gets little press except when there's a major scandal. The first such scandal was back in the late 1920s when working conditions on the cocoa plantations were so slavery-like that the League of Nations had to send a special mission to study the situation.

The second scandal wasn't so much a single event as a decade (the 1970s) during which the country was saddled with a ruler of the same calibre as Idi Amin or Jean-Bédel Bokassa – Macias Nguema (n-GUAY-mah) – Africa's Citoyen Robespierre.

Contact with Europe dates from 1470 with the Portuguese discovery of the tiny island of Annobon near the island of Bioko. During the 19th century, Britain used Bioko (until recently called Fernando Pó) as a

maritime base. In the second half of the century, the Spanish returned and established cocoa plantations.

The mainland, Rio Muni, is much larger in area and population, though largely ignored by the European powers until 1900 when it was united with Bioko as a single colony under Spanish rule. Much of it remained unexplored for another quarter century. Most of the Spanish lived on Bioko, which is why Malabo (MAH-lah-boh), not Bata on the mainland, is the capital today.

Cocoa is the raison d'être of Bioko. About 90% of the cocoa produced in the country is grown on the island's fertile volcanic soil. For several decades until the 1920s, Bioko was the largest producer of cocoa in the world. While Africans cultivated many small plots, the Spanish landlords, many living in Spain, owned big plantations and controlled most acreage and production.

Since the local labour pool was small, labourers had to be brought from elsewhere in Africa, primarily from Liberia, Nigeria and Ghana. Returning Ghanians started planting cocoa on their own, and Ghana soon became the world's leading producer.

Labourers from Liberia worked under slave-like conditions, recruited apparently under false pretences and receiving no pay until they returned to Liberia. The matter came to the attention of the League of Nations in the late 1920s, and an international scandal resulted.

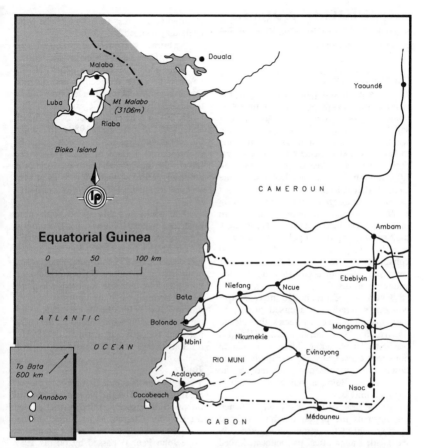

Independence

Spain had done little to develop the country, preferring to leave things in the hands of the few large landowners. After WW II, the Spanish government took a much more active role, subsidising cocoa and coffee exports to encourage production, building roads to open up the hinterland of Rio Muni, and improving the educational system. Nevertheless, the Africans were treated as legal minors until 1959 when they were finally granted full citizenship.

By then, however, it was too late. A nationalist movement, led by the Fang tribe in Rio Muni, was already well underway. Pressure mounted, and by 1968, Spain was forced to grant independence. A Fang nationalist, Macias Nguema, won the election and relations with Spain went from bad to worse.

Nguema ordered all but one Spanish flag to be pulled down and encouraged his supporters to intimidate the 7000 Spaniards still living in the country. Anti-white incidents in Mbini were followed by an exodus of Spanish residents and a near collapse of the economy. Nguema even ordered that boats be destroyed, thus closing off the country from the outside world.

The Reign of Terror

This was just the beginning of an 11-year reign of terror rarely publicised in the international press, making Nguema, the self-styled 'Unique Miracle', possibly the worst modern-day dictator in Africa. In terms of brutality and devastation to a country's economy, he takes the cake, surpassing even Idi Amin in Uganda and Bokassa in the Central African Republic.

Using an alleged coup attempt in early 1969 as an excuse, Nguema had his foreign minister and ambassador to the UN executed, the first of a long line of political rivals who were killed or tortured to death for alleged conspiracies. Every few months, another supposed 'plot' surfaced, resulting in more and more deaths.

Even the Church did not escape Nguema's wrath. He accused priests of participating in the conspiracies, then closed down their schools and expelled the Spanish teachers. Thereafter, children were taught only political slogans. He eventually closed down the churches and expelled all the missionaries. Being a journalist became a capital crime.

At the peak of his lunacy, an estimated one-third of the population had fled the country, and of those remaining over 10% were jailed as political prisoners in forced labour camps. Rumour has it that he celebrated one Christmas holiday by bringing out a group of prisoners and having them executed in the stadium while a band played sweet tunes.

About 50,000 people are thought to have been killed during the 11 years. Altogether, the country lost fully half its population, and almost every politician prominent at the time of independence was dead or in prison. The listing of the country's cabinet of ministers in *Africa South of the Sahara 1975* is accompanied with the statement: 'It has been reported in the press that some of the Ministers may be dead.'

Nguema virtually destroyed the economy. Cocoa and coffee production fell by 80%, and most farmers either left the country or were reduced to subsistence farming. Per capita incomes fell from one of the highest in Africa at independence in 1968 (US$320) to a level of those in the Sahel, about US$175 in the early 1980s. To combat the labour shortage on the cocoa farms, he re-introduced a form of slavery – forced labour like the Spanish had used during the colonial period – justifying it as a step towards socialism. Yet production continued to fall.

You could probably spend your entire time in Equatorial Guinea just listening to Nguema stories. Fortunately, it's all over – unlike Amin who escaped, Nguema got his just desserts in 1979 following a successful coup led by Theodore Obiang Nguema, a nephew, who became angered when his brother became one of the numerous random victims. Just before being executed in his native village, Nguema burned up the entire national treasury, an estimated US$105 million. Theodore is still President.

Today

When the new Nguema first came to power, the future looked bright. He released most of the political prisoners, lifted restrictions on the Catholic Church, and resumed official relations with Spain and other countries. Pope John Paul II passed by on his 1982 African tour, and Guineans voted to approve a new constitution, one of the most liberal in Africa. However, the economy continued to stagnate, and the political situation remained uncertain.

By 1987 Nguema had faced three unsuccessful coup attempts. As in many African countries, coups here don't require a huge force. The one in 1986 involved only 30 civilians and military officers. These were all low-key, virtually in-house coup attempts. The people remain as tranquil as ever and the country looks like Sleepy Hollow.

If you look at the economic indicators, the economy shows no signs of improvement, with cocoa and coffee exports almost as low as ever. During the first half of the 1980s, large fiscal and balance-of-payments deficits, low foreign exchange reserves, a depressed level of economic activity, and inflationary pressures plagued the country. The second half of the '80s hasn't been much better.

With the expulsion of the Spanish landlords in 1970, labourers abandoned most of the cocoa plantations and production dropped drastically. Workers on contract, mostly Nigerians, left during the 1970s. By 1986, cocoa production was still only about one-eighth of its pre-independence levels. The new government appealed to the former Spanish landowners to return, but few have taken up the invitation because of the government's reputation for corruption and high-handedness, as well as the country's uncertain future and scarce labour pool.

A few cocoa plantations are reportedly being converted to banana plantations and others are now being replanted with foreign technical assistance, primarily from Spain. But progress has been painfully slow. Many of the old cocoa plantations are still abandoned. As long as prices remain low, there is little the country can do.

Coffee suffered the same fate as cocoa during the 1970s. Grown primarily by the Fang in northern Rio Muni near the Camerounian border, it is now the third major export crop, having fallen behind lumber. The quality, never very high, deteriorated after independence and hasn't improved. Production has rebounded somewhat but remains below pre-independence levels. Its chances for revival are even less than for cocoa.

The news has not all been bad, however. With the replacement of the worthless non-convertible *ekuélé* by the CFA franc in 1985, the country had a valuable hard currency. Now, if you compare the markets to 1984 when the cupboards were all bare, you'd see a huge difference. Many stores have reopened and the markets are jammed with both local and imported foods, clothing, medicines, etc. The streets look and sound more like those of a living African country than a museum piece. All of this seems to have rubbed off on the people. They seem nicer, noticeably at the airports where hassles have largely stopped.

The country entered into its first stand-by arrangement with the IMF, agreeing in principle to implement tax reforms to encourage production, liberalise domestic prices, and limit the deficit. But that collapsed in May 1986 as did plans to build a Novotel in Bata (now being revived).

The EEC is helping out in the road building sector, and the World Bank, France and Spain are prepared to invest millions of dollars in the cocoa sector if prices seem likely to rise and the government can get its act together. The donors will also have to get their acts together because much money has been wasted on badly planned and executed development programs.

Whether the present regime with all this assistance can lift the country out of its present economic quagmire remains to be seen, but many economic factors, such as the world market for cocoa and coffee, are simply beyond its control. Exporting food crops to its prosperous neighbours, Gabon and Nigeria, may be the only answer.

PEOPLE

The Fang dominate the mainland, representing about 80% of the people there. Before Macias Nguema's time, there were also 30,000 to 40,000 Nigerian migrant workers on Bioko who constituted a majority of the population. The Nigerians were all repatriated in 1976 and few have returned.

The original inhabitants of Bioko, the Bubi, number about 15,000, but they are now outnumbered on the island by the Fang, some 20,000 of whom were brought over by force from Rio Muni during the 1970s to work on the cocoa plantations. Others flocked to the island to join the civil and military services. As for Europeans, before independence there were about 7,000, mostly Spaniards. During the 1970s, they dropped to about 200 or so and only a few have returned.

Travellers searching for black magic may be in for a real treat in Rio Muni. The Fang have held on to their traditions. Sorcerers, for example, play a particularly strong role in community life.

One of the more fascinating celebrations is the *abira*, a classical ceremony which helps cleanse the community of evil spirits. Then there is the *balélé*, an incredibly intense and vibrant dance; a certain passion and sexuality embraces the dancers, causing them to go into all sorts of violent contortions. This dance is executed by the *onxila*, a well-known dance group wearing costumes of grass skirts, metal and grass bracelets for the arms and legs, leopard and monkey skin belts, topped off with feather head-dresses which are shaken wildly.

Along the coast of Rio Muni you are more likely to see the *ibanga*, an extremely suggestive but less frenetic dance than the *balélé*. If at night you see dancers who are all covered with a white powder, that's probably it. On Bioko, the Bubi also dance a form of the *balélé*, particularly on holidays and at Christmas time. So be on the lookout for these dances; they are likely to provide the best memories of your trip.

GEOGRAPHY

The country is made up of two provinces: cloud-covered Bioko Island (and a number of other tiny islands) 40 km off the coast of Cameroun, and Rio Muni, the much larger mainland section wedged between Cameroun and Gabon. The total population is about 400,000, split about three to one between Rio Muni and Bioko.

Bioko, formerly call Fernando Pó, is a mountainous, jungle island, with three extinct volcanoes covering most of the island and cocoa trees seemingly everywhere but in the south, where pure jungle takes over. The land is very fertile, so farmers are constantly chopping away at the vines to keep the jungle

from engulfing the plantations. Black sand beaches surround most of the island. The road system is good by African standards, with surfaced roads circling the island.

Rio Muni is far less interesting geographically, being thickly forested and rather flat along the coast and turning into plateau as you move eastward. Because most of the cocoa is grown on Bioko, the island is more important economically than the mainland. But Bata, the largest town in Rio Muni, has more people than Malabo – some 40,000 inhabitants. Only a quarter of the population lives in urban areas, the rest being farmers. Virtually everyone is very poor, with average incomes hovering around US$200 per annum.

CLIMATE

Like neighbouring Gabon and southern Cameroun, Equatorial Guinea is a rainy area. On Bioko Island, the rainy season begins in March and ends in mid-November, and is heavy from June to October, especially July and August. Rainfall on the mainland is somewhat lighter.

LANGUAGE

Equatorial Guinea is the only country in Africa where the official language is Spanish. Fang is the major African language. Some greetings in Fang follow:

Good morning	*m-BOH-low*
Good evening	*m-BOH-low*
How are you?	*yoh-non-vuoy?*
Thank you	*AK-kee-bah*
Goodbye	*mou-kah*

VISAS

Visas are required of everyone and are obtainable in only one or two days in neighbouring Cameroun (Douala and Yaoundé) and Gabon (Libreville) as well as at the embassies in the following list. Except in Madrid, they may demand to see an onward airline ticket. Visas are usually good for only 15 days, and getting an extension is next to impossible. Exit visas are no longer required.

In Malabo, you can get visas to neighbouring Gabon and Cameroun, among other countries (see the Embassies section under Malabo). Apparently the Gabon and Cameroun embassies do not require onward airline tickets in order to issue visas.

Diplomatic Missions Abroad

Addis Ababa, Douala, Lagos, Las Palmas, Libreville, Madrid, New York, Paris, Rabat, Yaoundé.

MONEY

US$1 = CFA 296
£1 = CFA 570

The unit of currency is now the CFA, so there is no longer a black market. Since the banks are frequently without cash, it's advisable to bring all the CFA you'll need with you.

Banking hours: weekdays 8 am to 12.30 pm; Saturdays 8 am to 12 noon.

GENERAL INFORMATION
Health

Both cholera and yellow fever vaccinations are required. One guy who didn't have his cholera vaccination had to pay CFA 2000 in exchange for a stamp in his health certificate – but he didn't get a shot. For a good doctor, ask US or French embassy officials. Dr Khalil (AP 930, tel 2901) does lab analyses.

Security

You have little to worry about despite the high alcohol consumption and poor state of the economy – the lack of visitors has apparently discouraged pickpockets. Violent crime is virtually non-existent.

Business Hours

Business: weekdays 8 am to 1 pm and 4 to 7 pm; Saturday 9 am to 2 pm. Government: weekdays 9 am to 3 pm; Saturday 9 am to 2 pm.

Public Holidays

1 January, 5 March (Independence Day), Good Friday, 1 May, 25 May, Corpus Christi, 5 June, 7 July, 3 August, 13 August, 12 October, 1 November, 8 December, 25 December.

Photography

A permit is required, and never issued! If you try to take pictures in town, the police will stop you and your camera could be confiscated. They'll think you're a spy.

Time, Post, Phone & Telex

When it's midday in Equatorial Guinea, it's 11 am in London and 6 am in New York (7 am during daylight savings time). The mail system is reportedly very unreliable in terms of incoming mail, but mailing letters out is no problem. If you must take a chance and have mail sent there, use the Spanish phrase *Lista de Correos* for *Poste Restante*.

Calling outside the country is very difficult and best forgotten. For telexes, your only hope is the post office.

GETTING THERE
Air

From Europe and North Africa, there are two direct flights a week to Malabo – on Iberia from Madrid and on Air Maroc from Casablanca. You could also fly to Douala (Cameroun) and connect with one of the four weekly flights to Malabo. There are direct flights to Douala from Brussels, Frankfurt, London, Marseilles, Paris and Rome. Two other possibilities are flying to Libreville (Gabon) and connect with one of the three weekly flights to Malabo, or to Lagos (Nigeria) and connect with one of the two weekly flights to Malabo.

From the USA your fastest and cheapest routes to Malabo are also via Madrid and Casablanca. Once a week Iberia and Air Maroc fly out of New York connecting with their respective flights from Madrid and Casablanca. If you fly to Douala, you'll have to spend at least a night there. In addition to flights on various airlines to Douala via Europe, both Nigeria Airways and Air Afrique offer two weekly flights to Douala, changing in Lagos (Nigeria Airways) and Dakar or Abidjan (Air Afrique).

Flying to Bata is more of a problem. Ecuato Guineana de Aviación has six flights a week from Malabo and two flights a week from Libreville. There are no direct flights from Douala to Bata, but on Monday and Thursday the Cameroun Airlines flight from Douala to Malabo arrives half an hour before Ecuato Guineana de Aviación takes off for Bata.

Car

Driving to Rio Muni from Cameroun, you should count on a half day from either Yaoundé or Douala to Ebébiyin (300 km), almost all on paved road, and a day from there to Bata (353 km), all on dirt road.

It is also possible to go south from Ebébiyin to Mongomo and pick up the mainland's only asphalt road, Mongomo to Ncue (120 km). You won't save any time, however, because the southern route via Mongomo is longer. It is certainly no coincidence that the best road on the mainland goes to Macias' home town.

You cannot drive from Bata to Libreville because the only way to cross the border at Acalayong/Cocobeach is by dugout canoe (but ask anyway, in case there's a new car-carrying barge). So you'll have to backtrack to Ebébiyin, where you can connect with the dirt road in northern Gabon leading to Libreville.

You could take your vehicle on the ferry to Bioko, but you'd have to be nuts to go through the hassle. The road system on the island is pretty good, however, with asphalt roads circling the island.

Bush Taxi

Travelling to Rio Muni, you have the alternative of taking bush taxis from Cameroun or Gabon. If you're short of money, you may not have to take bush taxis at all because hitchhiking is easy. There are so few foreign travellers that drivers apparently like picking them up just for the novelty. If you do take bush taxis, count on two days from Yaoundé

(Cameroun) to Bata via Ebébiyin (at the Cameroun-Gabon border in the north-east corner of the country).

Libreville to Bata usually takes two days, but can be done in one long day if you start early and connections are perfect. Bata to Libreville, however, requires one and a half days even if you have a good run. Broken down into segments and not including waiting time, Bata to Acalayong via Mbini takes seven or eight hours, and crossing the inlet to Cocobeach (Gabon) in a motorised canoe takes about two hours, depending on the tides. Thereafter, it's another two hours to Libreville.

Ferry

There's an overnight ferry, the *Trader*, to Malabo from Douala and Bata, leaving once a week from both cities (Tuesday night from Bata and Thursday night from Douala, or vice versa). From Malabo the *Trader* leaves every Monday and Wednesday night – Monday for Bata and Wednesday for Douala, or vice versa. Be warned, however, that schedules are subject to change.

There are four classes, with prices varying from about CFA 13,000 to CFA 20,000 to/from Bata, and CFA 17,000 to CFA 20,000 to/from Douala. Berths are included except in the lowest class. The ferry leaves all three cities around 6 pm and takes about 12 hours either way. Tickets are sold only on the day of departure. In Malabo, the offices are at the old port near the centre of town.

GETTING AROUND
Air

The only flights within the country are between Malabo and Bata on Ecuato Guineana de Aviación, every day except Sunday.

Bush Taxi

On Bioko there are good bush taxi connections between Malabo and the island's two other major towns, Luba and Riaba; count on an hour at most to either one. The taxi/minibus park in Malabo is one block from the market. Vehicles leave regularly during the day. You can also hire them by the hour or day.

On the mainland bush taxis plough the coastal road, Bata-Mbini-Acalayong. You'll also find taxis headed north-east from Bata to Ebébiyin – dirt road all the way. Elsewhere, the only choice may be a truck, or nothing.

Forget about car rentals – they don't exist.

Ferry
Once a week the *Trader* goes back and forth between Bata and Malabo. For the itinerary and prices, see the Ferry section on page 164.

Bioko Island

MALABO
With a grand total of four restaurants, three hotels, numerous dilapidated buildings, little food in stock and a bar on every corner – or at least a street vendor who'll sell you a shot of liquor, cigarettes or gum – Malabo is a long way from being a tourist attraction. This wasn't always the case. Until the 1960s the Spanish colonial buildings were well maintained and there were apparently some fine restaurants and hotels.

The potential for tourism remains, however. With the ocean waves on one side and cloud-capped Pico Malabo on the other, the island's location is appealing even though there are no good beaches nearby. Most travellers to Africa never see the real tropics; Bioko is in the heart.

With a population of only about 25,000 people, the entire town, called Santa Isabel during Spanish times, can be covered on foot. Inner-city taxis are almost non-existent. You'll probably see a number of Spanish and French men, many of them technical advisors. There are a number of Russians, North Koreans and Chinese as well, but God knows where they are. Checking out the stores and chewing the fat with the locals at the bars is about all there is to do until the evening, when restaurants, bars and nightclubs wake up.

Information
Banks There are two banks: Banco de Guinea Ecuatorial and Banco de Credito y Desarrollo. The latter is for all intents and purposes closed, and the former is frequently without cash.

Embassies Cameroun, France, Gabon, Nigeria, Spain, USA (AP 597, tel 2607/2467).

Bookstores & Supermarkets Libreria MBA Ndemezoo, downtown on Avenida de la Libertad near the intersection of Calle de Rey Boncoro and around the corner from the Cameroun Embassy, is a tiny bookstore of sorts, with several postcards, stationery, and several recordings of local musicians.

Next door is Mini Mercado El Cedro, one of the better places for imported food. It's indeed 'mini', but you can get bottled water (CFA 500) among other things. Supermercado Africa near the Spanish housing complex, 'las caracolas', also caters to expatriates and has imported food items at high prices. Food is also sold in several other new stores, near Ayuntamiento (city hall) on Calle de Nigeria and on the same block as El Cedro.

For local produce try the Mercado Central, next to the stadium on Calle de Patricio Lumumba. Unusual for African markets, there's lots of liquor for sale. It's also the cheapest place to stuff your belly.

Travel Agencies There are none. For reservations and reconfirmations on Cameroun Airlines, go to the Camerounian Embassy downtown on Calle de Rey Boncoro near Avenida de la Libertad; they open around 9 am.

Centro Cultural Hispano-Guineano
Besides the old colonial buildings, you might check out the new Spanish cultural centre at

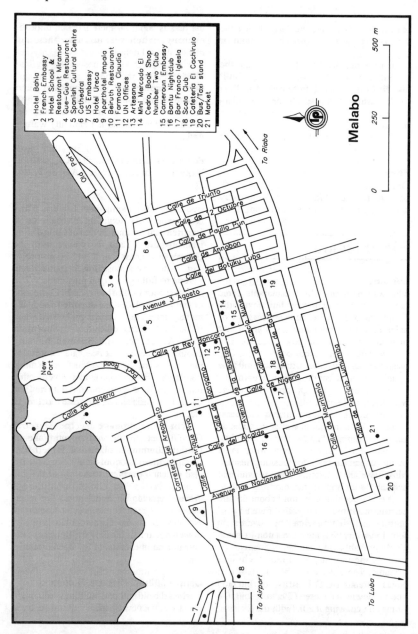

Malabo

1 Hotel Bahía
2 French Embassy
3 Hotel School &
   Restaurant Miramar
4 Gue-Gue Restaurant
5 Spanish Cultural Centre
6 Cathedral
7 US Embassy
8 Hotel Ureca
9 Aparthotel Impala
10 Beiruth Restaurant
11 Farmacia Claudia
12 UN Offices
13 Artesana
14 Mini Mercado El
   Cedro, Book Shop
   Number Two Club
15 Cameroun Embassy
16 Bantu Nightclub
17 Bar Franco Iglesia
18 Scala Club
19 Cafeteria El Cachirulo
20 Bus/Taxi stand
21 Market

To Riaba

0   250   500 m

Calle de Triunfo
Calle de 2 Octubre
Calle de Paulio Pun
Calle de Annobon
Calle del Botuku Luba
Avenue 3 Agosto
Calle de Rey Boncoro
Calle de Acacio Mane
Avenue de Bo
Calle de la Libertad
Calle de Nigeria
Calle de Mangamo
Calle de Enrique Nvo
Calle del Alcalde
Carretera del Areopueto
Avenue las Naciones Unidas
Calle de Patricio Lumumba
Calle de Mauritania

New Port
Port Road
Calle de Algeria

To Airport
To Luba

the end of Avenida 3 de Agosto near the harbour, a striking Spanish-style building downtown above the new port. You may find something interesting going on.

Cathedral

Several blocks away on Calle de Paulio Pun, above the old port, you'll find the cathedral. It's gothic with stained-glass rose windows, high ceilings, and an ornate sermon platform – no great loss if you don't get around to it. Sunday mass is at 8 and 10.30 am and 7 pm. The rest of the time you can spend bar hopping.

Those into architecture may find the dilapidated three-storey court building, several blocks from the cathedral on the same street, rather interesting.

Places to Stay – bottom end

The choices are limited. *Hotel Bahia* (tel 3321) has clean singles/doubles with fans for CFA 7000/11,000 and a pleasant patio overlooking the ocean, where Frederick Forsythe sat and wrote *The Dogs of War*. (The city of Clarence in the book is actually Malabo.) At the end of Calle de Argelia above the new port, it's a hundred metres or so beyond the French Embassy, a short walk from the Spanish cultural centre and a five to 10-minute walk from the city's heart. There's no hot water, restaurant, air-con or electricity during the day, and the lobby and patio (along with the people there) seem to be in varying stages of decay.

Hotel Flores near the post office is as cheap as you'll find. Singles/doubles are CFA 5000/7000. Running water is available only about an hour in the morning and an hour in the evening, and don't count on any electricity. Or make a friend – travellers are such a novelty, chances are that if you fraternise with the natives, you'll be offered a bed.

Places to Stay – top end

Coming from the airport, you'll pass two hotels on your right. The first, on the outskirts of town, is the *Hotel Ureca* (tel 3319), which charges about CFA 7500 to CFA 9500

for singles and CFA 9500 to CFA 13,000 for doubles; only a few have air-con. There's no restaurant or hot water, and electricity and water are cut off during most of the daytime. Nevertheless, the rooms are clean and decent, and there's good lighting and a balcony plus a tennis court in playable condition. It's a 10-minute walk to the nearest restaurant and a 15-minute walk to downtown.

Several long blocks further into town you'll pass near the *Aparthotel Impala* (tel 2492) at the end of Calle de Enrique Nvo. It's the best Malabo has to offer, with apartments for about CFA 13,000. Many expatriates live here, so getting a room isn't easy. You'll find the rooms clean with air-con, hot water, electricity 24 hours a day, a balcony, dining table and sink. There's no restaurant, but Beiruth Restaurant is only a block away.

Places to Eat

The town only has four major restaurants. *Beiruth* (tel 3330), a block from the Impala on the same street, Enrique Nvo, and a ten-minute walk from the Ureca, offers four main courses, one of which is Lebanese. This place is popular because the manager is friendly, the food decent and the service quick, and you have your choice of inside or outside dining. A meal will run you CFA 2500 to CFA 4500. It's open every day from 7 am to 11 pm.

The food and service are equally good at *Gue-Gue* (tel 2331) but not the setting. You'll find it downtown on the Carretera del Aeropuerto across from the Spanish cultural centre, near the new port and open every day 7 am to 11 pm. The choices are different, prices slightly lower, and the bar is a popular watering hole for the expatriate community.

On the same street several blocks away, in the direction of the old port and cathedral, you'll find the *Escuela de la Hosteleria 'Miramar'*, a restaurant school with the most pleasant position on a cliff with a good view of the harbour, usually accompanied by a breeze. The three-course fixed menu for about CFA 4200 includes drink, though the choice is very limited. Hours for ordering are 1 to 2.30 pm and 7.45 to 9.30 pm. It's closed Saturday evening and all day Sunday, as well as for the Christmas break (approximately one week before Christmas through the first week in February).

For a light meal or drinks, there's *Cafeteria El Cachirulo*, in the centre of town near the corner of Bata and 3 de Agosto, a very popular place with expatriates and the better-off locals. They serve sandwiches (many choices for about CFA 650), ice cream, beer and the best coffee in town, but they're often short of many items.

Entertainment & Sports
Bars For daytime relaxation in pleasant surroundings, try one of the quaint bars in front of the Ayuntamiento (city hall) on Nigeria. For tranquillity and great views at sunset, you can't beat the patio at the Hotel Bahia. Expatriates also head for *Cachirulo* and *Gue-Gue*, but if you want to mingle with the locals, there are scores of other bars to choose from. Many of them now serve food as well. One of the more popular ones is *Bar Franco Iglesia* at the corner of Nigeria and Acecio Mune, a half block from Scala 1 Club.

Nightclubs *Bantu* (or *Don Fausta's*) has aircon and is the number one dancing spot in town, popular with expatriates and locals alike and good even by big city standards. Don't expect much action before midnight. You'll find Africans to dance with and drinks for only CFA 1000. It's downtown on Alcalde near Libertad, three blocks from Beiruth Restaurant. *Scala 1 Club* is only a notch down and worth a try if you get tired of Bantu. It's two blocks away at the intersection of Bata and Nigeria, two blocks from Cachirulo on the same street.

Club Joey, a favourite of the natives, is several km from the centre of town on the south-eastern side of town leading towards Riaba. *Number Two Club* downtown on Avenida de la Libertad, near 3 de Agosto and next to Mini Mercado El Cedro, and *Discoteca La Nina*, nearby at Acecio Mune and

Rey Boncoro, are two others worth trying perhaps.

Cinemas Cine Jardin is your only choice. It shows Kung Fu film after King Fu film. It's on Calle de Mongomo, one block behind the Spanish cultural centre. Show time is 7.30 pm.

Sports For tennis, there's a decent court at the Hotel Ureca. The best courts in town, however, are at the US Embassy and the German Technical Assistance Organization (GTZ). For swimmers, there are no accessible pools, nor are there any good beaches except near Luba, an hour's drive from Malabo. And don't expect much sun from June through October. (Rio Muni has better beaches; they also get more sun.)

Hikers may want to try 3106 metre Pico Malabo, also known as El Pico. You could simply walk up the 30-km road to the top; any other route would be extremely difficult because of the thick jungle. The problem is getting permission because the government's radio transmission antenna is on top. Both the Foreign Ministry and the radio station people have the authority to grant permission, but without connections, you are unlikely to get it. The starting point is about 15 km outside Malabo on the hard surfaced road to Riaba. Look for a dirt road off to your right and a manned gate house next to it.

Things to Buy
Artisan Goods The country produces very little in the way of artisan goods. The only outlets are both downtown: a hole in the wall place on Avenida de la Libertad just to the left of Mini Mercado, and Artesana Guineana half a block away on Calle de Rey Boncoro. Your chances of finding anything interesting are poor.

Music For Guinean music, your best bet is Herbo Music, downtown on Avenida 3 de Agosto, 50 metres from Cachirulo. Have them make you a cassette from the various records they have for such purpose. Local stars include Maele, Baltasar Nsue and guitarist Toto Guillaume.

Getting There & Away
Air Ecuato Guineana de Aviación offers six flights a week to/from Bata and two flights a week to/from Libreville, while Cameroun Airlines offers four flights a week to/from Douala. You can also fly twice weekly to/from Lagos on Nigeria Airlines.

Ferry Once a week, the *Trader* ploughs between Douala and Malabo and between Bata and Malabo, see the Getting There section at the start of this chapter.

Getting Around
Airport Transport The departure tax at Malabo airport is CFA 1000. You'll find a bank and a bar-restaurant there. Before arriving, make sure your shots are up to date; like many islands in the world, enforcement is strict. Have an extra photograph; they'll ask for it. The luggage search is no longer particularly time consuming.

Taxis from the airport into Malabo (seven km) are about CFA 3000, and bargaining is definitely required. They are unmarked, so don't think there aren't any. Since there aren't any buses, the only way to reduce the cost is to try sharing a cab.

Taxi Finding a taxi downtown is like looking for a shooting star. If you get one at the airport, make arrangements then and there for future pick-ups. Otherwise, you may never see one again. Bush taxis going to Luba and elsewhere are stationed one block from the market. Connections are good. Chartering taxis is relatively expensive; by the hour count on paying not less than CFA 4000 plus petrol.

LUBA
For the best beaches on the island of Bioko or a view of the interior, head toward Luba, an hour's drive south-west of Malabo. At the base of the volcanoes and bordering the ocean, Luba has a backdrop similar to Malabo's, except the town is much smaller and the surroundings are more impressionistic. With only a thousand inhabitants or so, it's perhaps easier to meet people. While most of the beaches around the island have black sand, the isolated beaches near Luba have white sand. If you have the time, head east towards Riaba; the road passes over cultivated plateau and the Moka Valley with its crater lake.

Places to Stay & Eat
Hotel Jones, the only hotel in town and right in the centre, is where most travellers stay who can afford CFA 7000/11,000 for singles/doubles. It's run by a grouchy old German who speaks German, French, English and Spanish and gives the place character if nothing else. There's a bar that looks something like a hunting lodge, a patio for drinks, a TV, and edible food – not bad for such a small village.

About seven km before Luba in the direction of Malabo there's a lovely white, sandy beach and a friendly fishing village where some travellers have passed a few days. You can camp on the beach, but register with the police; otherwise you might cause trouble for the fishermen. If the police catch you without a permit, they'll fine the fishermen and refuse to let you pay the fine!

Getting There & Away
To get to Luba and Riaba, take a public taxi at the taxi-bus park one block from the main market in Malabo, charter a taxi by the hour, or hitchhike. The hard-surfaced road is narrow and would be completely engulfed by grasses and vines were it not for the road crews. This is not a trip for those with weak hearts – your driver will probably race blindly around the corners at life threatening speeds as mine did.

Rio Muni

BATA

Capital of the mainland, Bata lacks Malabo's picturesque volcanic setting. The streets are wide and clean by African standards, and to some people the town has its charm. There's little of interest to see. Rio Muni has the best beaches in the country, however, and some of the most beautiful are near Bata. You'll find several isolated ones along the coast south of Bata. One lined with coconut trees is only several km from downtown in the direction of the airport.

Places to Stay – bottom end

Hotel Rondo behind the telecommunications building is clean, serves meals and costs CFA 3000 to CFA 5000. Smaller and friendlier than the top end Pan-Africa, it's recommended even though the location isn't as choice. For about CFA 3500 or so, you can reportedly stay at either *Hotel Finisterre* or, dirtier, *Hotel Central*. For cheaper places still, look for a *casa de huéspedes* around the market.

Places to Stay – top end

Bata's best hotel is nothing special – the big *Hotel Pan-Africa*, with decent rooms for about CFA 7500 to CFA 10,500 and an attractive location facing the sea. Ask for a room on the beach side; the view is superb. *Hotel Continental*, in the city centre and apparently a good notch down, is slightly cheaper.

Entertainment

Bar Miramar on the beach in the direction of the port, about three km from Hotel Pan-Africa, is worth visiting at sunset for beer and *grafis* (small crayfish) when in season. At night, try the *Black & White* disco – a good place to meet both the locals and expatriates, as well as to dance with the locals.

Getting There & Away

Air There are flights every day except Sunday to/from Malabo and two flights a week to/from Libreville, plus every Monday and Thursday the Douala-Malabo flight on Cameroun Airlines arrives, hopefully, just in time (half an hour) to make the Malabo-Bata flight on Ecuato Guineana de Aviación.

Car Unless there's now a car-carrying barge connecting Cocobeach and Acalayong, the only way to drive from Bata to Libreville is backtracking via Ebébiyin.

Bush Taxi Libreville-Bata takes about one and a half days via Cocobeach, where you must take a motorised canoe across the lagoon. Yaoundé-Bata takes about two days via Ebébiyin.

Ferry Once a week, you can take the *Trader* to/from Malabo.

Getting Around

Taxi Taxis in Bata are extremely scarce, but bush taxis headed for Mbini and Ebébiyin are easy to find.

EBEBIYIN

Ebébiyin is noteworthy only because it's in the far north-east corner of Rio Muni, where many travellers stay before or after crossing the Cameroun border. The only hotel is *Hotel Mbengono*, with fairly clean rooms for CFA 2000. There's no running water, but you can take a bucket bath in the back. The only restaurant in town gets frozen seafood from Cameroun – not bad actually.

Gabon

Gabon gets mixed reviews. Some complain it's too expensive. Others say the traditional African culture disappeared with the discovery of oil. If you're seeking the 'real' Africa, however, Gabon is as real as anywhere else. Peace Corps volunteers tend to enjoy it, because socialising is what life is all about here.

Although much of the country is poverty-stricken, Gabon is the wealthiest country in Black Africa (US$3650 per capita) because of oil and minerals. Consequently, the average Gabonese, unlike many Africans, can afford to buy you a beer and many of them will. For those who have been travelling through Muslim dominated West Africa where Coca Cola is king, not beer, Gabon can be a refreshing change. If you don't like the local beer (Regab), palm wine, or the local corn and manioc squeezings (*mengrokom*), just try to grin and bear it.

But there's more to Gabon than socialising. Albert Schweitzer put Gabon on the map when he founded his hospital here in 1913. You can see it, then venture into the heart of the African jungle by taking a canoe trip down the Ogooué River.

If you like your creature comforts, sports, and western entertainment, Libreville and Port-Gentil have them all – posh hotels, seafood restaurants, shopping centres, nightclubs, bowling alleys, tennis clubs, squash courts, sailing, golf, horse riding – you name it. For fishing Gabon is a paradise. A fishing trip along the spectacularly beautiful estuaries south of Port-Gentil is an adventure you'll never forget. Or just lie on the superb beaches – right in Libreville.

HISTORY

Two things in particular stand out about Gabon's history: less is known about Gabon prior to the colonial period than any other country in Africa and, second, no country in Africa, perhaps the entire world, has gone through such a dramatic transformation in the 20th century – from mud huts in the rainforests to mini-skyscrapers. Before the 20th century, only one settlement, Libreville, warranted being called a town.

Early History

Of the present inhabitants, the Pygmies were the first to arrive in the area. The first Bantu people began migrating into Gabon around 1100. Thereafter, other Bantu tribes moved into the area, but the strongest migration was of the last group, the Fang, who came southward from Cameroun starting in the 18th century. The environment, mostly rainforest, wasn't conducive to the growth of towns, much less empires like those that arose elsewhere in Central and West Africa.

In 1472 the Portuguese arrived, but they virtually ignored Gabon, concentrating their attention instead on the nearby island of São Tomé. Dutch, French and British ships began arriving sometime thereafter in search of ivory and slaves. The coastal tribes became middlemen and raided settlements in the interior for slaves.

Eventually the coastal tribes no longer produced anything – the slaves did all their work. By ruining fraternal relations between villages, concentrating power in the chiefs of the coastal tribes, and upsetting the balance of power between the coastal and interior tribes, the slave trade destroyed the social fabric.

Colonial Period

By the middle of the 19th century, the slave trade had come to an end. The French signed treaties with various coastal chiefs, thereby assuming the status of protector. In 1849, they captured a slave ship, releasing the passengers at the mouth of the Komo River. The slaves named their settlement Libreville (Free Town).

In the late 19th century, various French explorers, including the renowned Savorgnan de Brazza, travelled up the Ogooué River looking for the headwaters of the Congo River; hostilities from the natives forced some of them to turn back. When the European powers carved up Africa, France snatched Gabon. Libreville became the capital of the French Congo, but a few years later it was transferred to Brazzaville. Thereafter, in 1910, Gabon became one of the four territories of French Equatorial Africa.

Exploitation of Gabon was left to French private companies which forced the Africans to work for them. Like Africans elsewhere in French Equatorial Africa, the Gabonese revolted against this new form of slavery, but each revolt was eventually put down.

Nowhere in Africa did the French do less

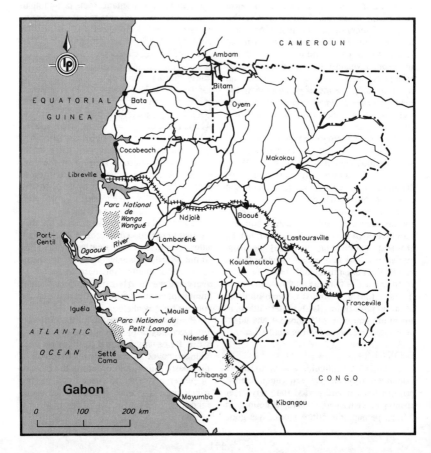

in terms of development – they built few roads and left agriculture basically untouched. The only economic activity of interest was forestry along a narrow coastal strip. As late as independence in 1960, 75% of the country's exports consisted of timber, particularly the semi-hard *okoumé*, a giant forest tree that the Gabonese use for making canoes and foreigners use for making plywood.

Independence
The mayor of Libreville, Leon M'Ba, whose name adorns a major street in Libreville, formed the first political party in the mid-1950s and was elected Gabon's first president following independence in 1960. He was a popular man, in part because he used to end his speeches by tossing coins to the crowd.

The new government started off with two strong political parties in existence. A coalition government was formed and the leader of the opposition, Jean Hilaire Aubamé, became Foreign Minister. This lasted until 1964 when the military staged a successful coup. The next day French paratroopers intervened to reinstall M'Ba, saying they were acting pursuant to a bilateral defence agreement with Gabon.

By the time M'Ba died two years later, Gabon had become a de facto one-party state. His diminutive 31-year-old deputy, Albert-Bernard Bongo (he is $1^1/2$ metres or five feet tall), took over and has remained president ever since. Later converting to Islam, he is now El Hadj Omar Bongo.

Manganese (around Moanda) and uranium (around Mounana) exploitation began almost immediately after independence and started the 'Gabonese Miracle'. Oil production began its spectacular growth in 1967. By the end of the decade, the GDP had doubled in real terms.

In the '70s manganese and uranium production levelled out, but the four-fold increase in oil prices in 1973 and the doubling of output sent Gabon into nirvana. Oil prices peaked in 1977, the year Gabon

spent a staggering US$1 billion hosting the most extravagant summit in the history of the Organization of African Unity (OAU). David Lamb describes the event in *The Africans*:

Presidents roared through Libreville, the somnolent capital on the Atlantic coast, in Mercedes-Benzes and Cadillacs with sirens wailing, each jammed into the back seat between his bodyguards. (Bongo, like President Mobutu Sese Seko of Zaïre, used Moroccan bodyguards, not wishing to trust his safety to local soldiers; Idi Amin used Palestinians.) The Gabonese honor guard, wearing red velvet capes and holding gold swords, lined the entrance to the conference hall....There was no laundry service in Libreville that week because the city's women had been recruited to perform traditional dances in honor of the arriving presidents. Nor were there any working prostitutes because Bongo had swept the streets clean with the warning to the nation's ladies of the night: 'Open your hearts during the summit, but not your bodies'....Some journalists arrived at their assigned hotels and found buildings still under construction; the hotel had no employees, doors, water or electricity, and the guests' $50-a-night 'rooms' were nothing more than open space in uncarpeted corridors, to be shared with bags of cement.

Thereafter, oil prices went tumbling and Gabon's ambitious US$32 billion development plan (with the exception of the *Transgabonais* railway) was shelved.

Today
Bongo remains firmly in power. The Moroccan troops and French mercenaries continue acting as palace guards. Every so often he reshuffles the cabinet so as to distribute the lucrative posts to the small number of political faithful who make up the country's political elite.

Everywhere in downtown Libreville you will see the same picture, mounted in a glass cabinet and lit at night, of Bongo in a debonair pose and a pin-striped suit with scenes of bustling commercial activity below.

Despite some 400 French airborne troops, all is not calm. An opposition party called Morena is actively fighting for a two-party system, but is outlawed and operates out of Paris. Every now and then members are arrested and, as occurred in 1982, given stiff prison sentences for distributing leaflets or other such horrendous activities.

Between 1985 and 1987, oil revenues dropped 66%. For the first time ever, unemployment has become a problem. The gutsy Bongo cut government spending drastically. As a result, Gabon is weathering the storm fairly well.

Bongo is now making preparations for the day when the country runs out of petroleum, estimated to occur in the mid-1990s unless there's another major strike. His strategy is to rely on the country's vast mineral deposits. The third major export earner, manganese, is suffering from low world prices, but it will last until around the mid-2100s at the present rate of exploitation. Production should go up now that the *Trans-gabonais* railroad to Franceville is completed.

Bongo would like help in financing the third phase of the *Transgabonais* to Belinga in the north-east so that the country can mine the rich iron ore deposits there, but low world prices for iron ore have made the expensive project uninteresting to investors. Meanwhile, the country's second major export earner, timber plywood, shows no signs of letting up.

With over half the population involved in the agricultural sector, many people are simply not prospering from the country's wealth and progress. Certainly the workers in the cities have relatively high incomes by African standards, but considering that the cost of living is among the highest on the continent, the somewhat inflated salaries are rather deceptive. In reality most of the benefits are reaped by the political elite and a small middle class. It's no accident that despite its tiny population, Gabon is the world's 20th largest consumer of French champagne.

PEOPLE

No one is sure exactly how many people live in Gabon. One major publication on Africa said the 1985 estimate was 700,000; another said 1.2 million. The government tends to overestimate the number to make the country appear less wealthy per capita. Regardless, Gabon is an anomaly in Africa – almost everybody has work. Indeed, the government is studying ways to increase the fertility of Gabonese women.

Africans from all corners of the continent have come here looking for work, most of them ending up with jobs in the mining centres, the ports and the construction industry, with the Gabonese preferring prestigious posts in the government and services sector. Because of this job stratification, the labour movement is weak, and the government keeps it under close control. Some 50,000 French people are here as well – more than when Gabon was a French colony!

Among the Gabonese, the Fang (primarily in the north and north-east) are the dominant ethnic group (30%), followed by the Eshira (20%) and the M'Beti (15%) in the south-east. Between half and three-quarters of the people are Christian – the highest percentage of Christians in continental Central and West Africa. El Hadj Omar Bongo is of the one percent that is Muslim, but his relations with the Arab world are strained.

While Gabon's relative wealth and contact with the west have made life easier for its citizens, they are worse off than other Africans in terms of preserving their cultural identity. All the young men want to leave the villages for Libreville. What they find is an undistinguished modern city run by foreigners.

A hundred years ago the Fang were producing some of the most beautiful wood carvings in Africa. Their masks were almost oriental in quality, with elongated, heart-shaped faces that are reminiscent of Modigliani. Today they don't even bother making cheap imitations. Now, the only place you can see these masks is in museums. When looking at a museum piece, note the skin and the fleshy parts of the body of these statues – they have no decorative enhancement. By their exceptional attention to these parts, the artists seem to have been expressing a certain sensuous humanism.

What's ironic is that the Fang were among the fiercest tribes in Africa (reputedly practising cannibalism although that has never been proven). During the 19th century they were the pre-eminent ivory-hunters, exchanging ivory for European goods, especially guns. Mary Kingsley, an Englishwoman travelling in these parts in 1894, wrote:

To be short of money in a Fang village is extremely bad, because these Fangs, when a trader has no more goods to sell them, are liable to start trade all over again by killing him and taking back their ivory and rubber and keeping it until another trader comes along.

GEOGRAPHY
Gabon is the size of Great Britain. The area covered by rainforest is 74%, among the highest in Africa and only 1% of the land is cultivated. (Gabon imports over 50% of its food.) Inland, you'll find a series of plateaux with a number of peaks of about 1000-metre; the major plateaux are the Crystal mountains in the north, and the Moabi uplands and Chaillu massif in the south.

Cutting the country almost in half is the Ogooué River, passing through Franceville and Lambaréné on its way to the sea. Port-Gentil, the centre of operations for Gabon's on-shore and off-shore oil rigs, is on an island at the mouth of the Ogooué and cut off from the rest of the country except by air and ferry. The river is navigable between Port-Gentil and Ndjolé; big boats and barges plough up and down carrying passengers and cargo.

The estuaries all along the coast are perhaps the most beautiful areas but they are also so inaccessible that few travellers see them. The four major ones south of Port-Gentil are Fernan Vaz, Iguéla, N'Dogo and M'Banio. Unfortunately the cost of flying can be rather prohibitive. Only the last of the estuaries, near the Congo border, is connected to the mainland by an all-weather road.

The capital city of Libreville is at the mouth of an estuary in the north. A 12-km ferry ride across that estuary will take you to Pointe-Denis, the best of all the beaches near Libreville.

An asphalt road leads inland from Libreville for 161 km, but all the roads are dirt except around Franceville and Ndjolé. Why are there so few paved roads when Gabon is so rich? It's not just because the cost of building roads through the impenetrable tropical forest is enormous. Bongo simply had other priorities – primarily the *Transgabonais* railway to Franceville, the centre of Gabon's rich manganese and uranium deposits.

CLIMATE
The weather is warm, with typical midday temperatures around 30°C. Excessive mugginess is the main problem. The best time to

Kuta Mask

Kwélé Mask

visit is during the dry season, from June through to September. During the rest of the year the rainfall is rather heavy. In the main rainy season (January to May) the rain sets in between 4 and 6 pm almost every day. It usually stops by 6 am the next morning, and by 8 am all the clouds have generally evaporated and the sun becomes unbearable by midday.

LANGUAGE

French is the official language. The principal African language is Fang; about half the people speak it. Eshira is spoken by about a quarter of the population. Some greetings in Fang are:

Good morning	m-BOH-tay
Good evening	m-BOH-tay
How are you?	yoh-non-vuoy
Thank you	AH-kee-bah
Goodbye	mou-kah

The local word for people of European descent is *otangani*. Travellers with light skin will hear the word whenever children are around, just as *mzungu* is heard all over East Africa.

VISAS

Nationals of France and Germany do not need visas. If your passport has a South African entry stamp, you'll be denied entry. In the days of the oil boom, getting a visa was very difficult, mainly because there weren't enough hotel rooms. Those days have passed, at least if you get your visa in Europe or in the States. The Gabonese Embassies in London and Washington, for example, now issue visas in several days (instead of a month) and have dropped two long-standing requirements: proof of a roundtrip airline ticket (or a letter from a bank proving sufficient funds to leave the country) and a confirmed hotel reservation (or a *certificat d'hébergement* from a Gabonese citizen certifying that you'll be provided with lodging).

If at all possible, get a visa outside Africa because Gabonese embassies in many African countries still insist upon sending a

cable to Libreville, and they may not get a response for a week or more. Some may still be asking to see a roundtrip ticket. In Yaoundé (Cameroun), the embassy has been known to require travellers to pay the cost of the telex – CFA 6000 – and the visa, in addition to a wait of two to five days to get a response. In Malabo (Equatorial Guinea), on the other hand, the Gabonese embassy has been known to issue visas in 24 hours.

In past years travellers have reported getting visas in Douala (Cameroun), Lagos (Nigeria) and Lomé (Togo) with no hassles. At the embassy in Kinshasa you need a letter from your embassy. You may also find visas easier to get in Chad where the French Embassy issues them.

Police at Libreville airport almost never give travellers problems, but at the borders they sometimes do. Officials in Bitam, for example, told a French traveller heading south from Cameroun that the two pre-

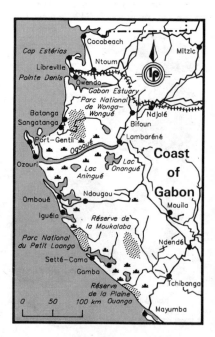

Top: Grass bridge near Franceville, Gabon (BM)
Left: Braiding a child's hair, Gabon (BM)
Right: Weaver, Gabon (BM)

Top: Typical road scene in Zaïre (EE)
Bottom: Tea plantations near Goma, Eastern Zaïre (EE)

viously mentioned requirements still applied and turned her away when she was unable to produce a confirmed hotel reservation or lodging certificate. It is quite possible that they were just looking for a bribe, but it is wise to be extremely careful about bribing the law in Gabon. People have been known to get into serious trouble for trying (naturally the trouble only comes after moneys have been parted with). The moral is never to travel without all your papers on you.

If you're travelling overland to the Congo, be sure to get an exit stamp at Ndendé, 40 km from the border. If you're headed for Kinshasa, don't wait until arriving in the Congo to get your Zaïre visa because the Zaïre Embassy in Brazzaville issues *laissez-passer* to take the ferry from Brazzaville to Kinshasa only to those with Zaïre visas obtained outside the Congo.

For visas to Equatorial Guinea, the embassy in Libreville gives same-day service. The embassy for São Tomé in Libreville takes up to three days.

Diplomatic Missions Abroad
There are Gabonese diplomatic missions in the following cities:

Abidjan, Algiers, Bangui, Bonn, Brazzaville, Brussels, Cairo, Dakar, Geneva, Kinshasa, Lagos, Lomé, London, Madrid, Malabo, Nouakchott, Ottawa, Paris, Rabat, Rome, São Tomé, Tokyo, Washington, Yaoundé.

MONEY

US$1 = CFA 296
£1 = CFA 570

The unit of currency is the Central African CFA. Citibank has a branch in Libreville one km inland from the Dialogue hotel, and one in Port-Gentil two blocks back of Score. It and Barclays are the best banks for changing money. The limit on exporting CFA is CFA 200,000.

Interior banks are far and few between, and won't always change money that isn't tied to the French franc. If you're likely to spend any extended period travelling outside Libreville and Port-Gentil, it would be wise to stock up on CFA.

Banking hours: weekdays 7.30 to 11.30 am and 3 to 4.30 pm; closed Saturday and Sunday.

GENERAL INFORMATION
Health
A cholera vaccination is required. A yellow fever vaccination is required if you have been in an infected area within six days prior to your arrival in Gabon or if you'll be spending more than two weeks in the country. Sexually transmitted diseases in Gabon are as bad as or worse than anywhere else in Africa; an estimated 30% of the women are infected with one disease or another. Despite the lack of statistics on AIDS ('SIDA' in French) it is undoubtedly becoming a major problem, especially among prostitutes.

There are three hospitals/clinics in Libreville; the Peace Corps uses Fondation Jeanne Ebori (tel 732771; 24 hours service). Two doctors who speak English are Dr Balestie and Dr Fiton at the Cabinet de Groupe (tel 720923/722650) several blocks up the hill from UTA. Two of the best pharmacies in Libreville are Grande Pharmacie des Forestiers (tel 722352) at the Galerie M'Bolo, and Pharmacie de Glass (tel 721195) near the Sheraton.

Security
The low unemployment rate in Gabon has made Libreville and Port-Gentil a lot safer than might otherwise be expected of growing cities with lots of money floating around. This may be changing now that the oil boom has died down. Regardless, normal security precautions are definitely required.

Business Hours
Business and government: weekdays 8 am to 12 noon and 3 to 6 pm; Saturday 8 am to 1 pm.

Public Holidays

1 January, 12 March, Easter Monday, 1 May, End of Ramadan (6 May 1989, 28 April 1990), Pentecost Monday, Tabaski (14 July 1989, 3 July 1990), 16-18 August (Independence), 1 November, 25 December. Independence is by far the biggest celebration. The festivities are more evident in the towns and villages than in Libreville itself.

Photography

A photo permit is not required. However, be very careful what you photograph in Gabon. Even if the building or subject matter doesn't seem sensitive, the police may think it is, so if you don't want to risk having your camera confiscated, ask first.

Phone & Telex

When it's noon in Gabon, it's 11 am in London and 6 am in New York (7 am during daylight savings time). International telephone connections are good. Telex facilities are available at the main post office and the top five or six hotels in Libreville.

Almost all of the public telephones in Libreville require a special telephone card, which can be bought for about CFA 4000 from the telephone headquarters in the centre of town near Air Afrique. However, there's a coin operated public telephone in Libreville on Boulevard de l'Indépendance one block north of the main post office.

FOOD & DRUGS
Restaurants

Finding real Gabonese food, especially in Libreville, is sometimes difficult because many of the cheaper restaurants throughout Gabon are actually Senegalese, occasionally Togolese or Ivorian. In Camerounian or Congolese restaurants, you're more likely to sample true 'Gabonese style' food, often including some type of bush meat, such as antelope and wild boar (*sanglier*).

Itanga

Itangas are an unusual local fruit definitely worth trying at least once. When in season, they're everywhere. About 10 centimetres long, egg shaped and violet-coloured when ripe, they're prepared by steeping them in hot water for several minutes, then eaten with salt and hot pepper. The green meat around the nut has a consistency similar to yam, but a taste all of its own.

Kola Nuts

You'll find kola nuts, the 'African No-Doze', in every market and many small shops. They're terribly bitter, but tolerable when washed down with beer. Most important, they'll keep you up when dancing all night. Splitting one with someone else or receiving a piece as a gift is a sign of friendship and respect.

Iboga

Africans sometimes chew or smoke *iboga* (ee-BOH-gah), a hallucinogenic plant that is used in some adolescent initiation ceremonies. It's a small plant with white flowers and golden yellow fruit that grows wild everywhere but perhaps more so in the south-east where the Mitsogho cultivate it around their homes. They scrape off the bark and chew it, sometimes smoking it in a pipe.

If you chew a little of this nasty tasting bark, it'll give you a buzz like kola nuts or coffee, keeping you awake. Apparently some people make themselves throw up so that they can eat more to keep the all-night buzz going. Some say the Pygmies were the first users, aiding them to beat the drums (*tam-tams*) all day long. But if you take a lot...wow!

GETTING THERE
Air

There are direct flights from Brussels, Paris, Rome, Madrid and Geneva on Sabena, UTA, Air Afrique, Swissair and Air Gabon. Many frequent fliers consider Air Gabon to be one of the three or four best African airlines serving Central and West Africa, so don't hesitate taking it. There are good connections with West African cities as well. From East

Africa, you will probably have to change flights at Douala, Brazzaville or Kinshasa.

Car

Despite the country's wealth, Gabon has fewer km of paved roads than just about any country in Africa of comparable size – less than 400 km in the countryside. However, the dirt roads are fairly well maintained, and during the rainy season, the rains usually occur at night. So even though the roads can get muddy and slippery when it rains, the roads in Gabon are actually not as bad as you might expect. All the same, driving times are certainly longer in the rainy season. It would be a good idea to come prepared for all eventualities by carrying a strong rope or a cable. Extra petrol supplies are more or less essential.

The following driving times are for the dry season (June through September):

Yaoundé-Libreville via Oyem (940 km) – two long days
Libreville-Brazzaville (1245 km) – three to four days
Libreville-Lambaréné (232 km) – three to four hours
Libreville-Franceville (762 km)– two days

The Libreville-Lambaréné road is paved for two-thirds of the distance. You cannot drive from Libreville to Port-Gentil.

The major road to the Congo is via Lambaréné, Mouila and Ndendé. During the dry season, you can make it from Libreville to the Congolese border in one long day. You cannot drive along the coast from Libreville to Equatorial Guinea because there are no car-carrying barges at Cocobeach, only canoes. (But do ask – as this could change). For now the only route to Equatorial Guinea is via Oyem.

Bush Taxi

If you're headed for the Congo, the major route is via Mouila and Ndendé. Do not expect to see much traffic south of Ndendé. There's reportedly a truck from Ndendé to Kibangou (Congo) every Tuesday and Friday; anticipate quite a few beer stops along the way.

You can also get to the Congo via Franceville. The big advantage is that all but about 150 km of the trip is by train. After taking the *Transgabonais* to Franceville, take a series of bush taxis south-west to Moanda, Bacoumba and Mbinda (Congo), then board the Mbinda-Loubomo train, and at Loubomo transfer trains and proceed to Brazzaville or Pointe-Noire.

From Yaoundé, the trip takes one or two days to Oyem. There, you'll find taxis direct to Libreville; they charge about CFA 14,500 and take about 15 hours.

The Libreville-Bata (Equatorial Guinea) route is via the border town of Cocobeach. You'll find motorised dugout canoes to take you across the inlet to Acalayong; the cost is about CFA 3800. If you are quoted a lower price, be suspicious – the boat owner will probably take you downriver where you'll have to pay a CFA 2000 exit tax.

GETTING AROUND
Air

Air Gabon has regular flights from Libreville to all the major interior towns, including at least three a day to Port-Gentil. For coastal regions Air Inter Gabon (Port-Gentil tel 753317/20 and telex 8204; Libreville tel 731028) offers regular flights. All their flights leave from Port-Gentil.

To charter a plane, contact Air Affairs Gabon (Libreville tel 732513/732010, telex 5360); Héli-Afric (Libreville tel 731028, Port-Gentil tel 753317/20); or Air Service at the Libreville airport.

Bush Taxi

Bush taxis are expensive in Gabon. It costs CFA 8000 from Libreville to Lambaréné, and over twice that for the Libreville to Franceville route. They are also more dangerous in Gabon than elsewhere – the drivers are maniacs and are liable to get drunk if given half a chance. If your driver does get drunk, your best bet would be to catch the next car.

In Libreville, the bush taxi gare is one

long block from the Marché du Mt-Bouët. They go in all directions, but the number of people travelling is relatively small, so don't expect much choice of vehicles. Go early; the chances of your catching one after 10 am are slim. If you're headed for Franceville, Moanda or Lastoursville the train is cheaper and faster. For other destinations, you can sometimes cut costs significantly by taking trucks. The place to catch them in Libreville is on the outskirts of town at PK 5.

Train

The *Transgabonais* to Franceville was inaugurated in December 1986. Be appreciative – it cost over US$4 billion and took 12 years to complete. Count on paying about CFA 33,200 for 1st class, which is not much less than the cost of flying, and CFA 22,100 for 2nd class. First class has air-con and a dining car but no sleeping car. In 2nd class it's pot luck – there are some decent new cars but also 'cattle cars'.

The trip takes less than 11 hours, with departures in both directions every day except Tuesdays and Thursdays. Owendo, 6 km south of Libreville, is the starting point. Trains usually leave on time, so don't be late. Trains leave Owendo at 8 pm except Saturdays (9 am), and Franceville at 12.30 pm except Mondays and Fridays (7.30 pm). To be sure, consult the *L'Union* newspaper or call the station (tel 723539).

Most stations are way out of town and taxis charge outrageous prices. Unfortunately there is often no alternative.

Boat

There are three ferries per week (taking 12 hours) connecting Libreville with Port-Gentil. There is also a river boat to Port-Gentil once a week down the Ogooué River from Lambaréné (or Ndjolé). This is an 18-hour trip. For details of both, see the Port-Gentil Getting There & Away section.

If you just want to take the small barge between Ndjolé and Lambaréné, the trip only takes about seven hours and costs about CFA 3500. There are boats almost every day. You can stock up on food and drinks at stores near the docks in both Lambaréné and Ndjolé. Have your camera ready – this is a very scenic trip.

Car Rental

Avis, Hertz and Eurocar are all represented, as well as local companies. For the addresses of their offices, see the Libreville and Port-Gentil Getting Around sections.

LIBREVILLE

Finding the 'real Africa' in Libreville takes a little searching. At first glimpse, it looks like a diminutive Miami Beach – 300,000 people with big beach hotels, office buildings, wide highways, fancy shopping centres, and taxis everywhere. You won't find any beggars, and there are good beaches right in town – a rarity for major African cities.

Those who insist on having their creature comforts shouldn't find too much to complain about. You can go bowling, take in a first-run film, eat a thick juicy hamburger or a fancy sundae, and go dancing all at the same place. Otherwise you could take in one of the city's numerous fancy restaurants or posh nightclubs.

Those searching for the real African experience may be about to turn the page, but wait! First impressions can be deceptive, and indeed in the case of Libreville this is the case. There is more to Libreville than meets the eye. The city does have its fair share of lively African bars and perseverance will inevitably lead you to one of the city's few cheap restaurants.

The people can be very friendly; perhaps you'll end up in an African home as I have done. Peace Corps volunteers certainly enjoy themselves here; so don't write off Libreville without a try. Just be careful if you decide to drink with Gabonese. When it comes to drinking beer or palm wine, what you may view as an extraordinary day of boozing is likely to be routine for them.

Boulevard de l'Indépendance runs along the water. The heart of the city is between the Presidential Palace and the Novotel

Rapotochombo, both on this street, plus the area three or four blocks inland. Three of the livelier African sections, all near the centre, are Nombakélé, the area around Marché Mt-Bouët, and Akebéville nearby. Quartier Louis, which you enter on Boulevard Joseph Deemin just beyond the Dowé Novotel, is a major restaurant area.

Information

Banks Citibank, Barclays, BIAO, Banque Nationale de Paris, Banque du Gabon et du Luxembourg, Banque de Paris et des Pays-Bas.

Embassies Some of the major embassies are the following:

Belgium
(tel 732992)
Congo
(tel 732906) BP 269
Equatorial Guinea
(tel 732583) in Likouala Moussaka near the stadium
France
(tel 763021) Blvd de l'Indépendance, BP 2125
West Germany
(tel 760188) BP 299
Japan
(tel 732297) BP 2259
São Tomé
(tel 721466) BP489
UK
(tel 722985) BP 476
USA
(tel 762003/4, telex 5250) Blvd de l'Indépendance, BP 400
Zaïre
(tel 720256) BP 2257

Other embassies include: Algeria, Cameroun, Canada, CAR, Egypt, Italy, Ivory Coast, Mauritania, Morocco, Nigeria, Senegal, Spain, Sweden, Togo. In addition there is a Netherlands consulate.

Bookshops & Supermarkets The best bookshop is *Sogalivre*, one block from the Paris-Gabon supermarket. There are also bookshops at the major hotels.

The best supermarkets are *Paris-Gabon*

in the heart of town at the corner of Rue la Fond and Rue Schoelcher, and *Rénovation* across from Hôtel Rapontchombo.

Travel Agencies Eurafric Voyages (tel 723707, telex 5458) downtown on Rue la Fond near Paris-Gabon is the best. They arrange excursions, including Lambaréné (seven people minimum) for CFA 20,000 a person. If you are interested in spending a day sailing (two people minimum) they can arrange it for about CFA 24,000 per person.

Musée des Arts et Traditions

This museum, downtown on the ocean road one block from the Rapontchombo, is worth a short visit. There are only two rooms of wooden carvings, masks, musical instruments, and a temple, but the animated guide makes the tour worthwhile. Hours are weekdays from 8 am to 12 noon and 3 to 6 pm; Saturday from 8 am to 1 pm.

Marché du Mt-Bouët

Closed on Monday, this vibrant market a km from the centre, a few blocks north of the stadium, is worth checking out, but it suffers in comparison with West African markets.

L'Eglise St-Michel

St-Michel church, in N'Kembo about a km further inland from Mt-Bouët, is interesting because of the unusual wooden columns carved by a blind Gabonese craftsman. There are 31 columns in all, each with a biblical scene carved in an imaginative and vigorous style. It is worth making the effort to go on a Sunday morning, as the mass is sung in a local language accompanied by drums.

Palais Présidentiel

The president's mansion, downtown on the ocean road and the broad Cours Pasteur, several blocks north of the post office, was built in the 1970s at a cost of US$800 million and is a Libreville landmark. The marble is from Italy (even though Gabon produces its own), and the Greek columns are unique in this area of the world, another example of Bongo's strong attachment to western culture. No photographs are allowed.

You cannot see inside the palace, but reportedly among the contents are an elevated throne-like marble chair, a long marble-topped desk with push button controls to make walls recede and doors open, a banquet hall for 3000 persons, a bathtub big enough to swim several strokes in, two theatres, and a nightclub.

Places to Stay – bottom end

Libreville is very expensive. Try the *Maison Catholique*. They have modern double rooms for about CFA 4500 and serve meals for CFA 2750 a day, or CFA 600 for breakfast. To get there, go to the cathedral near the Dowé Novotel and follow the road inland for about two km; then ask.

Another possibility is the *Mission School* near the gare routière; they have been known to offer accommodation to travellers during the school holidays (July to September). *Maison Liebermann*, across the street, may be closed. If not, you should be able to get a bed for about CFA 2200.

Among the cheaper hotels, *Hôtel Mont Bouët* (tel 722008) is definitely one of the best – well managed, firm beds, renovated rooms, clean private baths, about CFA 8800 a room with fan and CFA 12,500 with air-con. In short, in Libreville you can't do better for the money. It's near the centre of town between the Komo Cinéma and Marché du Mt-Bouët.

If Mont Bouët is full, try *Hôtel Ozouaki* (tel 741600) on the same street as the Hôtel Mt Bouët, about 1 1/2 km further out on a winding road, beyond the Marché Mt-Bouët. The rooms are about CFA 11,000, with hot water, shared bathrooms and sagging mattresses. (There are two Ozouaki; this is the better one.)

La Corbeille (tel 723957), a few blocks from both the stadium and Marché du Mt-Bouët, has big rooms with air-con for about CFA 13,500. Be warned that the room keys are all the same.

Places to Stay – middle

Hôtel Tropicana (tel 731531/2, telex 5558, no cards), with singles/doubles for about CFA 17,000/21,500, is the best hotel in its price range and hence frequently full. It has an excellent beach but no pool, clean and functional rooms, and a good restaurant with moderate prices – and is only one km from the airport (10 km from downtown).

Hôtel Louis (tel 732569/97), in the Louis area three km from the city centre, has rooms for about CFA 16,500. A small hotel with 18 rooms, the Louis has decent rooms, TV, carpet and a good restaurant in a good restaurant area, Quartier Louis.

If a small, French-run bed & breakfast hotel sounds inviting, try *Hôtel Glass* (tel 760312), one block inland from the Sheraton and about one km from the city centre. Rooms go for about CFA 16,500.

Places to Stay – top end

The newest hotel is the de luxe *Re-N'Dama Sheraton* on the water about a km from the centre of town. The *Dialogue* and the *Ikoumé Palace Inter-Continental* are equally good but four and five km from the centre. The Dialogue has the advantage of being on a good usable beach, while the Inter-Continental is one block inland. The deluxe, newly renovated *Rapontchombo Novotel* is ideally situated in the centre of town, but unfortunately, the beach in front cannot be used. This is also true of the *Dowé Novotel*, which is only 1 1/2 km from the centre. It is a particularly uninspiring hotel.

The new *Mont de Crystal* (49 rooms) is also bang in the centre of town. If you're looking for a good beach hotel with slightly more reasonable rates, your best bet is the *Hôtel Gamba* out near the airport, about 11 km from the centre. Because it's such good value for money, it is popular and usually full, so you will definitely have to make a reservation.

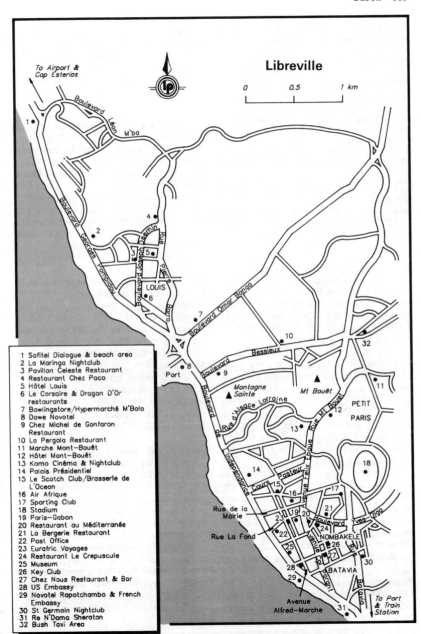

Libreville

0   0.5   1 km

1 Sofitel Dialogue & beach area
2 La Maringa Nightclub
3 Pavillon Celeste Restaurant
4 Restaurant Chez Paco
5 Hôtel Louis
6 Le Corsaire & Dragon D'Or
   restaurants
7 Bowlingstore/Hypermarché M'Bolo
8 Dowe Novotel
9 Chez Michel de Gonfaron
   Restaurant
10 La Pergola Restaurant
11 Marche Mont—Bouët
12 Hôtel Mont—Bouët
13 Komo Cinéma & Nightclub
14 Palais Présidentiel
15 Le Scotch Club/Brasserie de
   L'Ocean
16 Air Afrique
17 Sporting Club
18 Stadium
19 Paris—Gabon
20 Restaurant au Méditerranée
21 La Bergerie Restaurant
22 Post Office
23 Eurafric Voyages
24 Restaurant Le Crepuscule
25 Museum
26 Key Club
27 Chez Nous Restaurant & Bar
28 US Embassy
29 Novotel Rapotchambo & French
   Embassy
30 St Germain Nightclub
31 Re N'Dama Sheraton
32 Bush Taxi Area

Re-N'Dama Sheraton (tel 723915, telex 5432), CFA 31,500 a room, pool, tennis, casino, ocean front, cards AE, D, V, CB.

Okoumé Palace Inter-Continental (tel 732033, telex 5271), CFA 28,000 to CFA 34,600, pool, tennis, squash, nightclub, cards AE, D, V, CB.

Dialogue (tel 732055, telex 5355), CFA 31,100 a room, pool, tennis, casino, ocean front, cards AE, D, V, CB.

Rapontchombo Novotel (tel 764742, telex 5350), CFA 27,200/31,100 for singles/doubles, pool, casino, ocean front, cards AE, D, V, CB.

Mont de Crystal (tel 731531, telex 5558), CFA 27,200/31,100 for singles/doubles, pool, cards AE, D, V, CB.

Dowé Novotel (tel 764750, telex 5451), CFA 24,600/28,500 for singles/doubles, pool, cards AE, D, V, CB.

Hôtel Gamba (tel 732736/732267, telex 5375), CFA 23,600/27,500 for singles/doubles, pool, tennis, windsurfers, excellent beach, cards AE, D.

Places to Eat

Cheap Eats *Les Cedres* (tel 730830) is in Quartier Louis across the street from the Dragon d'Or Chinese restaurant, a 10-minute walk north of the Dowé Novotel. It is closed Mondays. They serve decent Lebanese fare in the CFA 1200 to CFA 3000 price range.

Le Bon Coin is also in Quartier Louis, about one km up the hill from Les Cedres, and is famous for its reasonable prices. A meal with a quarter carafe of wine will run you about CFA 2000. There are six or seven choices, including shrimp, grilled chicken and steak. The service takes five minutes, and the restaurant is popular with both Africans and foreigners. They also have rooms for CFA 11,000 a night.

Chez Paco is right across the street. The selection here is bigger and prices are slightly higher. *Maritime des Iles* is 50 metres down the street and almost identical to Chez Paco. *Chez Papa Union*, which is nearby, is a Peace Corps favourite. *La Case Bantu* is yet another in the same area.

You'll find the very cheapest restaurants, however, around Marché du Mt-Bouët. *La Boucherie* is typical; steak and peas go for CFA 1000. Finding real Gabonese food is difficult. *L'Estuary*, for example, serves Senegalese food for CFA 800 to CFA 1500. They also have good yoghurt here.

In Quartier Nombakélé there are also numerous good restaurants. Try *Mama Martine's*; she serves good Camerounian food for CFA 700 a plate.

Hamburgers & Fast Food *Bowlingstore*, a few blocks inland from the Dowé Novotel on Boulevard Triomphal, has the best hamburgers in town. As a further claim to fame they also serve crepes, pizza, full meals and terrific ice cream, but it's not cheap, eg sundaes cost CFA 2300. You'll find a cinema and bowling alley too. *Pelisson*, downtown on Avenue Colenol Parant, is one of Libreville's oldest 'institutions'. Drinks, ice cream and pastries are the main attraction.

You can get a fairly decent hamburger and go skating at the *Sporting Club* owned by Madame Bongo. It is downtown near the stadium on what the locals call Rue Akebéville. For cheaper fare, you can't beat *Gabon Fast Food* next to Hôtel Mt Bouët, several blocks from the Komo Cinéma. Hamburgers are CFA 650; steak and fries cost about CFA 1900. It's closed on Mondays.

If all you're looking for is braised chicken or fish, head for *Mini-Restaurant* downtown in Nombakélé next to La Bergerie restaurant and a block from the Commissariat Central.

Seafood *Le Pescadou* (tel 740733) is one of Libreville's top seafood restaurants. It is in the heart of the city on the street behind the US Embassy. The prices are moderate to expensive, and it's open every day.

The very cozy *La Bergerie* (tel 763093) is also recommended, although it is somewhat on the expensive side. It is on one of the main drags in Quartier Nombakélé near the Commissariat Central. There is a good selection of French food, but a number of fish dishes are available. They also have pizza and pasta. Sunday is their rest day. *L'Ancre de Bacchus* (tel 721300) specialises in seafood and is quite good. Unfortunately like so many others it is expensive. It is on the ocean road between the Dowé Novotel and the Dialogue, about three km from the city centre. Nearby on the same road is *Coconuts* (tel 732969), which serves good seafood and meat dishes plus exotic drinks. It's moderate to expensive and is closed on Mondays.

If you're looking for a restaurant with a fancy setting, try *Le Corsaire* (tel 732221), an expensive French restaurant where fish is the speciality. It's about a 10-minute walk from the Dowé Novotel on the main drag leading into Quartier Louis. It is closed on Sundays.

French Three of Libreville's top restaurants, popular for many years but all expensive, are *Brasserie de l'Ocean* (tel 721500) downtown across from the French Embassy, *Le Crepuscule* (open every day, tel 722593) downtown behind Bata shoes, and *La Pergola* (closed on Mondays, tel 722351) 50 metres off Boulevard Bessieux between the Dowé Novotel and Cinéma Komo.

For more moderately priced French food, try *Chez Michel de Gonfaron* (tel 762476) on Boulevard Bessieux 200 metres from the Dowé Novotel. It's a longtime local favourite, but the setting is about as ordinary as they come.

For cheaper French food try *Chez Nous*, two blocks behind the US Embassy, or *Le Libreville* three blocks further inland in Quartier Nombakélé. Both are closed on Sundays.

Italian *Le Pizzaiolo* (tel 723689) offers pizza and Italian specialities in a pleasant setting and is recommended for the moderate prices. Open every day, it's downtown in Quartier Nombakélé, two blocks behind Chez Nous and a block from Le Libreville.

The moderately priced *Restaurant au Méditerranée* has live music every night. There are various types of pizza, spaghetti, meat and fish dishes on the menu. It's in the city centre two blocks from Air Afrique on the same street and is open for dinner only.

Asian Most of the good Asian restaurants are in Quartier Louis, just beyond the Dowé Novotel heading out of town. The two best Vietnamese restaurants, both moderately priced with delightful settings, are *La Tonkinoise* (tel 732431), which is closed on Sundays, and *Vietnam*, which is closed on Wednesday. They are somewhat closer to the water in Quartier Louis on the same road as the Hôtel Louis (about a 15-minute walk from the Dowé Novotel).

Le Pavillon Celeste (tel 730013) has very good Chinese food with an elegant setting. Closed for Sunday lunch, it's one km from the Dowé Novotel and about two blocks beyond Le Corsaire on the main road leading into Quartier Louis.

For much cheaper Chinese food in an ordinary setting, try *Le Dragon d'Or*, a 10-minute walk from the Dowé Novotel in the direction of the airport. It is closed on Mondays.

Entertainment & Sports

Bars The bars in Libreville that attract foreigners are nothing to write home about. Two that are fairly popular are *Chez Nous* in the centre of town two blocks behind the US Embassy, and *Bar Les Copains* on the ocean road, two blocks before the Sheraton if you're coming from the centre of town.

On the other hand, African bars, particularly those in Akebéville and Nombakélé, are as lively as you'll find in Africa. One of the Peace Corps favourites is *M'Passa* in Nombakélé, not far from the Peace Corps office. Their nickname for the bar, 'Attack Bar', suggests going alone may be unwise. *Trois Coins* and *Pas Mal* are others in the same general area.

Quartier Akebé Poteau behind the Togolese Embassy also has several good African bars (taxi drivers know the embassy).

Nightclubs Unless otherwise stated, expect to pay about CFA 3500 for a beer at the top nightclubs. In the Komo Cinema area, there are four dancing places. *Sun 7*, one block from the Komo (closed on Mondays), is popular with the younger set (below age 30). *Le New Komo*, at the Komo Cinema and run by a French couple, is a pretty fancy place, and the crowd is mainly expatriate.

Fizz & Jazz and *Le Topkapi* (closed on Sundays) are only one or two blocks away from Le New Komo. The popular *Le Scotch Club*, across from the French consulate, is open every night. It only about five blocks further toward the centre of town.

Le Night Fever, near the stadium on what the locals call Rue Akebéville, is particularly fancy with a large dance floor. It's closed on Mondays.

As for African nightclubs, the only place that has mixed African and expatriate clientele is *Maringa*, on the ocean road about one km beyond the Dowé Novotel. They have a particularly good mixture of African and western music and a spacious dancing floor.

Foreigners are a rare sight in the remaining night clubs. One of the most popular is *St Germain* in Nombakélé on Rue Batavia. The CFA 2000 cover includes a drink. Only a few blocks away is *Key Club* which is open every night. *Balafon* is another in the same general area but in the direction of the stadium, only about a block from Night Fever on Rue Akebéville.

In Akebéville, you might ask about *Royale Bantou*, *Le Moulin Rouge* and *La Tour d'Argent* – good places for African music in past years.

Cinemas The fabulously modern *Bowlingstore*, several blocks inland from the Dowé Novotel, has two studios and shows first-run movies. They change nightly, so consult *L'Union* newspaper. Most shows are around 6.30 and 9 pm and cost CFA 1800. You can eat and bowl there as well.

Le Komo, downtown several blocks from Air Afrique in the direction of Marché Mt-Bouët, is a decent cinema but can't quite match Bowlingstore. There's an adjoining nightclub.

Sports For tennis, there are courts at the Sheraton, Dialogue, Gamba and the Inter-Continental. If you aren't a guest, you can still play. The Inter-Continental charges CFA 1500 during the day and CFA 2000 at night.

For squash, there are two air-con courts at the Inter-Continental; the cost is only CFA 1000.

The best beaches in town are between the Dialogue and the airport, which includes hotels Gamba and the Tropicana. The top seven hotels all have pools. The olympic pool at the Complexe Omnisports is open every afternoon; the fee is CFA 500.

For windsurfers, try the Hôtel Gamba; those at the Dialogue are all privately owned.

The Golf Club de l'Estuaire on the road to Owendo has an 18-hole golf course with sand greens.

Things to Buy

Hypermarché de M'Bolo Don't miss Hypermarché M'Bolo next to Bowlingstore – for Africa, it's a marvel. You'll find a little bit of everything, from bookstores and gift shops to travel agencies and banks.

Artisan Goods You'll find Senegalese and Hausa traders downtown along Avenue Colenol Parant near Pelisson and behind the post office. Hard bargaining is required because starting prices are highly inflated. Most of the wooden carvings and ivory are not from Gabon, however, the soapstone carvings are Gabonese. You can find an even better selection of the soapstone (and baskets) near the airport at the *Village Artisanal*, M'Bigou, where they are carved. The only problem is that soapstone is fragile and doesn't ship well.

Music At Bowlingstore and around Marché de Mont-Bouët, you can find recordings of modern Gabonese music. The three biggest stars, all men, are Akendéngue, Hilarion Nguema and Makaya Madingo.

Two of the most popular women vocalists are Ma Philo Batassouagha and the president's wife, Madame Bongo, a member of the group Kunabeli de Masuku. In 1985 Bongo made it illegal to record cassettes from records. According to the gossip, he did this to increase sales of his wife's records. Those making a living selling records and cassettes took revenge by surreptitiously taking all of her records off the rack.

Apparently Madame Bongo recently left her husband for a musician. It seems that they took a healthy portion of the national treasury with them.

Getting There & Away
Air From Europe, there are direct flights from Brussels, Paris, Geneva, Rome and Madrid. There are also good connections with West African coastal capitals.

Bush Taxi Taxis de brousse from Yaoundé (Cameroun) to Libreville take at least three days. You can continue travelling southward by bush taxi from Libreville to Lambaréné, Ndendé and the Congo border, after which you may have no choice other than trucks in the direction of Loubomo (Congo). In Libreville, you can pick up bush taxis at the gare routière, among other places.

Getting Around
Airport Transport There is no airport departure tax. The airport, recently expanded, has a bank, restaurant, Eurocar, Avis and Hertz. A taxi from the airport into town (12 km) is only CFA 1000, double that after 9 pm. In practice, however, you'll be lucky if you manage to bargain a taxi driver down to even CFA 2000. Downtown, on the other hand, getting the CFA 1000 rate to the airport frequently requires little bargaining unless you're departing from a major hotel.

Bus There are city buses but you won't see many. Buses leave every 15 minutes or so from the gare routière to the train station and port at Owendo. The fare is CFA 150.

Taxi Fares are CFA 100 for a shared taxi (double for fairly long trips). Fares for a taxi to yourself are CFA 500 for a 'demi course' (up to about six km) and CFA 1000 for a 'course' (up to about 12 km, including to Libreville airport). In some instances, the driver may insist you pay the 'demi course' fare even though there are other passengers in the cab. Rates double at 9 pm. Taxis are plentiful.

Taxi drivers rarely know the names of streets, so you'll have to give directions such as: 'It's in Quartier Louis, several blocks beyond the Dowé Novotel.'

Car Rental You'll find Avis (tel 732833, telex 5360) at the Rapontchombo, Hertz (tel 732011, telex 5271) at the Okoumé Palace and Eurocar (tel 766659, telex 5458) at Oka Voyages on Rue des Chaques Postaux. Autos Gabon (tel 752742) is the local rental company.

AROUND LIBREVILLE
Pointe-Denis
If you're looking for beaches that are less crowded than those in Libreville, you might hop on a boat to Pointe-Denis, about 12 km away on the other side of the estuary. You can camp overnight, stay at the *Résidence Pointe-Denis* for about CFA 15,500/18,000 for singles/doubles, or return the same day.

Getting There & Away The ferry leaves at the port next to the Dowé Novotel. To reserve a place on the ferry or a room at the Résidence Pointe-Denis, call Hôtel Dialogue. The cost of the ferry is CFA 3500 roundtrip. Departure hours are as follows: Saturday 9.30 am, 2.30 and 5.15 pm, Sunday 8.30, 9.30 and 10.30 am, and weekdays (except Thursdays) 9.30 am. Return hours: Saturday 4.30 pm, Sunday 4, 5 and 6 pm, and weekdays (except Thursdays) 4.30 pm.

Cap Esterias
Another possibility is heading 32 km north of Libreville to Cap Esterias. You'll find good beaches here, although they are a little rocky in places and can be fairly crowded on Sunday.

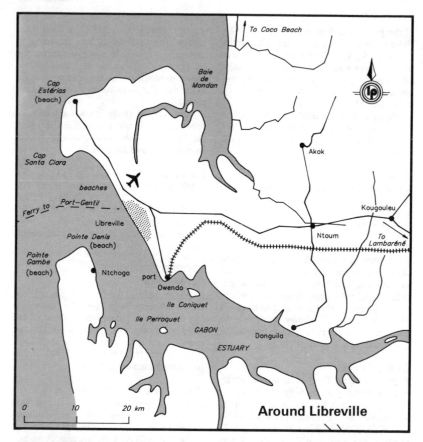

Around Libreville

Legend/labels on map:
To Coco Beach
Baie de Mondan
Cap Estérias (beach)
Akok
Cap Santa Clara
Kougouleu
beaches
Ferry to Port-Gentil
Libreville
Ntoum
To Lambaréné
Pointe Denis (beach)
Pointe Gambe (beach)
Ntchogo
port
Owendo
Ile Coniquet
Ile Perroquet
GABON
Donguila
ESTUARY
0   10   20 km

Places to Stay & Eat *L'Auberge du Cap*, on the beach, is run by a friendly French fellow and has five decent, rustic rooms (for about CFA 7000 to 8000) and a pleasant restaurant (not very cheap). There's no telephone, but getting a room any day but Sunday is usually not a problem.

Le Relais de Cap Esterias (tel 720884) is fancier and next to the ocean, with singles/doubles for about CFA 15,500/18,500 and a Sunday lunch buffet for CFA 7500. The cheapest place to eat is at *La Valise* next to the Auberge; there are about six main dishes, each for about CFA 2750.

Getting There & Away A taxi one-way to Cap Esterias will cost about CFA 6000. Hitchhiking should be fairly easy on weekends; the place to catch rides is a little beyond the airport.

PORT-GENTIL

At the mouth of the Ogooué River 140 km south-west of Libreville, Port-Gentil is an oil town on an island (Ile de Mandji) flooded with expatriates. The northern point of the island is Cap Lopez, where you'll find the Novotel and the best beach. For a city of 100,000 inhabitants, Port-Gentil has more restaurants, nightclubs and shops than many African cities five times the size; it even has a casino and a decent hospital. The African sections full of night clubs can be almost as lively and interesting as those in Libreville.

The main drag with stores galore is Avenue Savorgnan de Brazza, which runs north-south through the modern section, one block from the water. Running parallel to it along the water is Boulevard du Gouverneur de Chavannes, where you'll find the Meridien and the city's most famous landmark, the Café du Wharf. Another major road is the wide Autoroute leading towards the airport. The popular African quartiers (Mosquée, Chic, Balise, Grand Village and Aviation) begin six blocks or so inland.

Information

Banks Citibank (tel 752935/6) is two blocks behind the Score supermarket. Trading hours are weekdays 8 to 11 am and 2.30 to 4.30 pm.

Consulates There are US and French consulates and a Chamber of Commerce (BP 403, tel 753820/2).

Travel Agencies The best travel agency is Eurafrique Voyages (tel 753833, telex 8234); SNCDV (tel 752475) is another.

Places to Stay – bottom end

Le Provençal (tel 753388), in the centre of town three blocks behind the Café du Wharf, is your best buy. It's a French-run hotel with ten rooms for about CFA 10,500/12,000 for singles/doubles. It also has one of the best restaurants in town. *Le Printemps*, with rooms for about CFA 11,000, is not as good. It's one km from the centre of town above a Lebanese restaurant on the autoroute.

The next cheapest hotel is *Le Ranch* (tel 752528), with singles/doubles for about CFA 14,300/16,500. The atmosphere is very pleasant and it's relatively close (1½ km) to the beach. The only drawback is that it's usually full on weekends and a good four km or so from the centre of town.

Hôtel Abone (tel 753157), downtown across from the squash club (Club Balboa) has rooms for about CFA 18,000 to CFA 20,000. If you want a hotel with decent rooms in a downtown location, this small hotel may be your only choice. *Hôtel Atari* (tel 753121), downtown one block from Le Provençal, was recently renovated and may be better.

Places to Stay – top end

The deluxe *Meridien* has the advantage of being downtown on Boulevard Chavannes overlooking the water; the only problem is that you can't use the beach. The big advantage of the equally nice *Novotel* is that it's the only hotel with a usable beach, but it's about five km north from the centre of town.

If you're looking for a hotel with character and an air of exclusivity, then try *L'Auberge du Forestier*, a few blocks north of the Provençal. There is no pool or tennis court, but it looks like a Swiss chalet and probably has the finest restaurant in town.

Many people in the oil industry stay at the *Hôtel Abela-Hibiscus* because the rooms, service and restaurant are all quite decent and the prices are 40% less than the others. The only problem is that it's on the autoroute between the port and downtown, and you have to take a taxi to go anywhere.

Novotel Port-Gentil, CFA 27,100/31,100 for singles/doubles, pool, use of tennis club next door, Avis, tel 750242, telex 8326, cards AE, D, V.
Meridien Relais Mandji, CFA 27,700/31,100 for singles/doubles, pool, Hertz, tel 752103/5, telex 8234, cards AE, D, V.
L'Auberge du Forestier, CFA 29,800 to CFA 31,900 a room, 10 rooms, tel 752980, telex 8304, AE only.
Hôtel Abela-Hibiscus, CFA 16,600/19,600 for singles/doubles, good working tables, restaurant with CFA 4500 three-course specials, tel 753922/752948, telex 8271, cards AE, D, V.

Places to Eat

Cheap Eats *Le Printemps*, one km from the town centre on the major north-south road leading towards the Novotel and the airport,

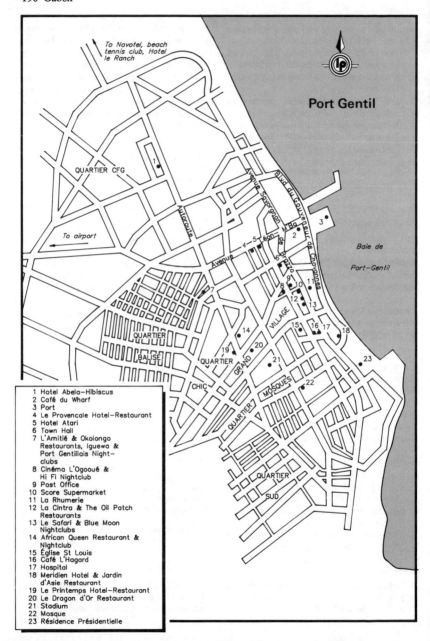

Port Gentil

Baie de Port-Gentil

1 Hotel Abela–Hibiscus
2 Café du Wharf
3 Port
4 Le Provencale Hotel–Restaurant
5 Hotel Atari
6 Town Hall
7 L'Amitié & Okoiongo
  Restaurants, Iguewa &
  Port Gentillais Night-
  clubs
8 Cinéma L'Ogooué &
  Hi Fi Nightclub
9 Post Office
10 Score Supermarket
11 La Rhumerie
12 La Cintra & The Oil Patch
  Restaurants
13 Le Safari & Blue Moon
  Nightclubs
14 African Queen Restaurant &
  Nightclub
15 Église St Louis
16 Café L'Hagard
17 Hospital
18 Meridien Hotel & Jardin
  d'Asie Restaurant
19 Le Printemps Hotel–Restaurant
20 Le Dragon d'Or Restaurant
21 Stadium
22 Mosque
23 Résidence Présidentielle

serves fairly inexpensive Lebanese fare. *La Braise*, one long block from Club Balboa, is where you'll find braised chicken and fish. It's open every evening. For cheaper fare, there's *L'Amitié* and *Okolongo* next to the African nightclubs Iguéwa and Port Gentillais, about one km from the centre of town just off the Autoroute. Full meals cost about CFA 750 to CFA 1500.

French *L'Auberge du Forestier* (expensive and closed Sunday) has the reputation for being one of the two best in town.

Le Provençal is open-air and offers a special plat du jour. *African Queen* (tel 752246), on the Autoroute one km from the centre of town (closed on Sundays), is also quite good but is a little expensive. *Le Café du Wharf* has fairly decent meals as well; the plat du jour is CFA 4500. If you're really hungry, try *Café de l'Hagard*, which offers a full four-course meal for the same price. It's next to the hospital, one block from Avenue Savorgnan de Brazza.

Asian *Le Dragon d'Or* serves Chinese food. It is about one km from the centre of town, just off the Autoroute, near Le Printemps. *Jardin d'Asie*, next to the Meridien, is another.

Pizza & Hamburgers *Le Cintra*, on the main drag downtown between the Score supermarket and Air Gabon, has pizza selections for CFA 1800 to CFA 3000, as well as meat and fish dishes in the same price range. They also have good draft beer. *Le Retro*, two blocks behind Score (open every day), also serves pizza, crêpes and ice cream, but is not as popular as Le Cintra.

The Oil Patch, on the main drag near Le Cintra, is very popular and serves hamburgers for CFA 2500 to CFA 3500 among other things, including sandwiches from CFA 1000. *La Rhumerie*, across from Score, serves fancy ice cream concoctions plus sandwiches and crêpes. It's closed on Sundays, but otherwise it's open until 11.30 pm every day.

Entertainment & Sports

Bar The most famous bar in town, a meeting place for everyone and virtually a landmark after being open for so many years, is the old *Café du Wharf* downtown across from the port.

Nightclubs The four that cater to foreigners are *Blue Moon* and *Le Safari*, both near Score, plus *HiFi* at the Cinéma L'Ogooué and *African Queen* on the Autoroute, about one km from downtown. The cover charge for each of these places is about CFA 4500; this includes one drink. Much more interesting are the African nightclubs, such as *Iguéwa* and, next door, *Port Gentillais*, both open Thursday to Sunday and just off the Autoroute, about two blocks from the African Queen. You'll also find a lot of Africans at *Igiri Samba* and the *Baobab*, one block from the African Queen. Most of these places have a CFA 2500 cover charge, which includes one drink.

Cinema The Cinéma l'Ogooué, one block behind Score supermarket, shows all the latest flicks. The hours are 6.30, 8.30 and 11 pm, with a different film at each hour. Casino Kewazingo is downtown on the main drag near Score.

Sports There are tennis courts at the Club Sogara next to the Novotel. The nearest beach is at the Novotel as well.

If you're interested in squash you can play downtown at the Club Balboa (tel 753668) for CFA 3000 a game or CFA 20,000 a month. You can also use the sauna and hot tub there for CFA 3500.

Sailors should head for the Sogara sailing club; you might find people needing extra crew, especially on Sundays when the regattas are held.

Getting There & Away

Air Air Gabon has at least three flights a day to/from Libreville. Air Inter-Gabon (tel 753317/20, telex 8204) offers regular service from Port-Gentil to the southern coastal villages, such as Sette Cama, Iguéla and Mayumba, and also rents vehicles. To charter aircraft, contact Héli-Afric (tel 753317/20).

Ferry There's a ferry that leaves Libreville every Monday, Wednesday and Friday for Port-Gentil, and departs Port-Gentil the following day. The trip takes some 12 hours and the fare is about CFA 13,000. The departure hours change according to the tide. For information, call the port (Port-Gentil tel 752366; Libreville tel 723928).

River Boat To add a little interest to your trip, you could float down the Ogooué River to Port-Gentil. The Ogooué is navigable by barge for 315 km up to Ndjolé where the first rapids begin.

From Ndjolé there's a small barge to Lambaréné, and from there you can take a bigger boat to Port-Gentil. The big boat leaves Port-Gentil on Monday mornings and arrives the following morning at Lambaréné, where you get off or connect with the small barge that takes you on to Ndjolé. The small barge leaves Ndjolé Wednesday morning and connects with the big barge which leaves Lambaréné Thursday morning for Port-Gentil.

The trip between Port-Gentil and Lambaréné takes about 18 hours and stops at villages along the way; the cost is about CFA 11,000 1st class and CFA 8000 2nd class. The big boat is very rustic, with no beds or restaurant, although you can buy drinks. In Point-Noire, buy your ticket from Delmas-Vieljeux at the far southern end of Avenue Savorgnan de Brazza. Bring your own food.

You can take a similar overnight barge from Port-Gentil southward to the lagoon of Fernan Vaz, stopping at Omboué, Ste-Anne and Ndougou. The barge leaves on Tuesdays and Saturdays; ask at Café du Wharf for details.

Getting Around

Taxis Taxis are fairly plentiful during the day and cost the same as in Libreville.

Car Rental There are numerous car rental agencies, including Hertz (tel 752231) at the airport and the Meridien, Avis (tel 750242) at the Novotel, Eurocar (tel 750380) at the airport. The two local companies, Gabolocar (tel 753582) and Loca Service (tel 752844), are also at the airport.

LAMBARENE

Albert Schweitzer put this town on the map, and his hospital is still the major draw card. Lambaréné is some 300 km up the Ogooué River from Port-Gentil, with about 30,000 inhabitants, now Gabon's third largest city. Schweitzer and his wife came here in 1913 and built the first hospital about three km upstream from the present one, which dates from 1926. He died at the latter in 1965; you can see his grave. The idea was to build a hospital that would attract as many people as possible by providing the most familiar surroundings. So the patients were fed by their families, who camped out at the hospital.

With the new annex built in 1981, the hospital looks more like it was prefabricated in Switzerland – nothing but the most up-to-date equipment. At a time when everybody else in Africa seems to be turning away from modern hospitals and copying the Chinese barefoot doctor approach, this once innovative hospital now seems strangely out of step.

Schweitzer was obviously a gutsy guy, certainly deserving of the many accolades that he received. But he was no saint. John Gunther visited Schweitzer here and wrote about him in *Inside Africa*; he had problems reconciling Schweitzer's lofty greatness with the tyrannical and bigoted qualities he apparently possessed. In his writings, Schweitzer would display warm empathy for Africa on one page and on the next write that Africans are unreliable, and that they steal and lie. In one passage he describes a woman bravely facing an operation, and on the next page complains: 'It is really no easy matter to be a surgeon for savages.'

The original hospital stands alongside the new one; part of it has been converted into a museum. The museum hours are 9 am to midday and 2.30 to 5 pm, except on Sunday when it's open from 11.30 am to 5 pm. You can buy postcards and T-shirts, and there's a gift shop with local crafts made largely by people from the leper colony. The hospital is not in Lambaréné itself, which is on an island, but on your left just before crossing the bridge.

In Lambaréné you can get a canoe (*pirogue*) near the Sofitel for CFA 500. Walking from the centre of town will take you an hour. A taxi (not easy to find) will cost CFA 1000.

Around Town

What's interesting besides the hospital is a pirogue ride to the lakes. The vegetation is lush, and you may see pelicans, hippos and crocodiles along the way. The big lakes (Ezanga, Evaro and Onangué) are 30 to 40 km down river; a trip to the lakes by motorised pirogue takes 5½ to 7½ hours roundtrip. The Sofitel Lambaréné arranges trips; the cost is about CFA 10,000 to CFA 12,000 a person (minimum six persons) depending on how long you stay. Or you could take a half-day trip to the nearby lakes

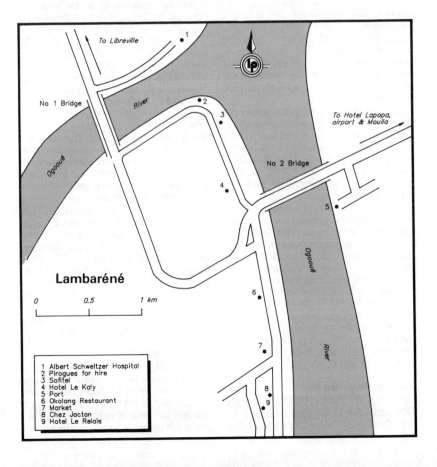

To Libreville

No 1 Bridge

River

Ogooué

To Hotel Lapopa, airport & Mouila

No 2 Bridge

Ogooué

River

Lambaréné

0   0.5   1 km

1 Albert Schweitzer Hospital
2 Pirogues for hire
3 Sofitel
4 Hotel Le Kaly
5 Port
6 Okolong Restaurant
7 Market
8 Chez Jactan
9 Hotel Le Relais

for about CFA 5000 (minimum four persons). Of course if you can arrange the trip yourself it is bound to be cheaper.

The Sofitel also arranges all-day fishing trips; the price, including fishing equipment and lunch, is about CFA 65,000 for up to four people and about CFA 90,000 for five or six people. A half-day fishing trip for up to four people costs CFA 22,000. If you are in a group of at least four, try negotiating on your own. You may be able to get a lower price. The pirogue owners are on the river bank near the Sofitel.

Places to Stay – bottom end

The hospital no longer puts up travellers. Among the cheap African hotels, the major one is *Hôtel Lapopa*, with about 15 basic rooms for about CFA 3500 and CFA 6000 (with fan). It's across the No 2 bridge on the road leading to the airport, a 15-minute walk from the centre of town.

Chez Jactan (tel 781039), formerly the Angleterre, is an old house with a super location along the river. There's no sign and it's not well known. If you can see Le Relais 100 metres up the hill, you're there. The rooms go for about CFA 2750 and 5500; the more expensive ones are upstairs with mosquito nets but no fan.

The two *Missions Catholiques* north from downtown provide the cleanest accommodation. The sisters are reportedly very pleasant and receptive. A bed in a dormitory room will cost you about CFA 2200; private rooms are CFA 500 more. You might also try *Hôtel Le Kaly*, an obscure little hotel behind the church. It has a restaurant which serves *toutes grillades*.

If your only concern is price, inquire whether the *Collective Rurale de Lambaréné* and a small *case de pasage* near the market still exist. They reportedly have accommodation for about CFA 1500.

Places to Stay – top end

Sofitel Ogooué Palace (tel 781114, telex 8501, cards AE, D) has singles/doubles for CFA 27,000/31,000. You'll find a pool (CFA 1000 for non-guests) and tennis courts with lights. The location on the outskirts of town near the river is not ideal. There is no view of the river or the hospital on the other side, and a 15-minute walk into town. In the centre of town you'll find the run-down *Le Relais* (tel 781033), with rooms for about CFA 13,600 and CFA16,000.

You can also stay 30 km south-west of Lambaréné on the edge of Lake Evaro. This would be a good choice if you're looking for tranquillity, good fishing, rainforests, or the chance perhaps to see a few animals, especially during the dry season from June through to September and from mid-December through to the end of January.

Hôtel du Lac Evaro (or *Le Relais d' Evaro*) (Libreville tel 732729, Lambaréné tel 781075) costs about CFA 17,500 a room, or CFA 52,000 for a weekend special for two. This is also the lunch stop for pirogue trips organised by the Sofitel.

Places to Eat

You'll find some cheap kebab stalls across the river around the docks. Cheap restaurants are hard to find – it's very much a matter of asking around. One restaurant well worth looking for is a Senegalese restaurant that is at the far end of the market.

Restaurant-Bar Okolongo (tel 781188), in the centre of town near the river, is French owned. The Okolongo is the only decent restaurant besides the Sofitel's. It has three-course meals for CFA 5000 to CFA 6000, quick service, air-con, tablecloths, and background music. If you like exotic food, you won't find a better restaurant in Central Africa. Try the boa constrictor in mushroom sauce, wild boar (*sanglier*) with fine herbs, as well as more typical French fare.

Getting There & Away

There are flights on Monday and Saturday from Libreville to Lambaréné and return. Don't expect to find a taxi at the airport, which is several km from the centre. You'll probably have to walk or hitch a ride, unless you're staying at the Sofitel, in which case a bus will meet you. The Sofitel also has a bus (*navette*) that leaves from the Sofitel Dialogue in Libreville on Thursdays and returns on Wednesdays. A third alternative is to take a bush taxi. A fourth alternative is to go to Port-Gentil and take the Monday river boat up the Ogooué River to Lambaréné; for details, see the Port-Gentil Getting There & Away section.

For a motorised pirogue from Lambaréné to Lake Evaro just ask the French owner of the Okolongo. His price is about CFA 45,000 roundtrip.

FRANCEVILLE

The last stop on the Transgabonais railroad and on a plateau over 400 metres high, Franceville is a major town in large part because President Bongo, a Batéké, was born nearby to the east. Why else would you find an international airport and an Inter-Continental hotel in a town of 25,000 inhabitants? It's also important because the manganese and uranium mines are not far away.

The city is spread out with one main section resting on the edge of the mountain and the other sections dribbling down the sides. While many streets are paved, some sections have slumped off into the ravines, never to be seen again. Walking is nearly impossible, but fortunately white and blue taxis are everywhere. Chances are you may see Peace Corps volunteers driving around in beat-up old Land Cruisers with the flag on the door. Travellers are rare so chances are they will welcome you wholeheartedly; buying a round or two of beer helps.

The major tourist attraction is Poubara Falls south of Franceville, at Mvengué, 20 km from Franceville. There's a foot bridge there made of vines which you can walk across. To get there, hitchhike, hire a taxi or rent a car from Avis (tel 677172) or Translima, both at the airport.

Places to Stay

For a cheap hotel try around the Marché Poto-Poto.

The top four hotels all have pools. The best is the big new *Leconi Palace Inter-Continental*, with singles/doubles for 29,000/34,000, pool, tennis. It is several km out of town. Call the Inter-Continental in Libreville for reservations.

Le Poubara (tel 677370), between the

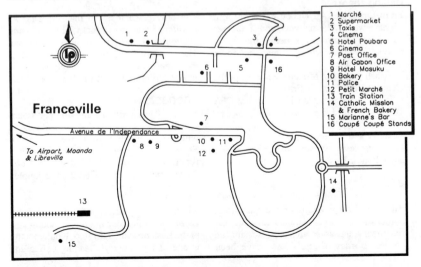

Franceville

To Airport, Moanda & Libreville

Avenue de l'Independance

1 Marché
2 Supermarket
3 Taxis
4 Cinema
5 Hotel Poubara
6 Cinema
7 Post Office
8 Air Gabon Office
9 Hotel Masuku
10 Bakery
11 Police
12 Petit Marché
13 Train Station
14 Catholic Mission
    & French Bakery
15 Marianne's Bar
16 Coupé Coupé Stands

market and the business district, offers tennis and a nightclub. The restaurant is reputedly very good. *Hôtel du Plateau* (tel 677029) is near the market and has a nightclub. *Le Masuku* (tel 677351) is near the business district and has a tennis court. All are comparable in quality (three stars) and price, (about CFA 16,000/18,500 for singles/doubles).

Places to Eat

Around Marché Poto-Poto, you'll find some cheap restaurants. For fairly decent grilled chicken, try 'Action Man', a Nigerian who sells food outside. Avoid his beef at all costs (the same applies to the other outdoor meat vendors). You'll also find good inexpensive food at the Petite Marché in the business district across from the bakery. One place that has been recommended is a blue Congolese restaurant with a veranda. It is near the middle of the market. A favourite is their salted fish and nkoumu (a leafy vegetable) in peanut sauce with manioc.

The only restaurants serving decent continental cuisine are at the four major hotels.

Getting There & Away

From Libreville, Air Gabon has about four flights a week. Alternatively, you could take bush taxis (two days) or better, the *Transgabonais* (see the Getting Around section for the schedule).

Bush taxis for Moanda leave from the Quartier Poto-Poto in Franceville. They're reliable, fast and reasonably priced at CFA 1000. Also, daily vans run between Franceville and Koulamoutou, stopping at Moanda and Lastoursville along the way. From Franceville you can go north to Akiéni and Okondja by taxi.

BITAM

A very active town with a large market, Bitam is 36 km south of the Cameroun border in the heart of Fang country. It is the first town you pass through after crossing the border. Border officials here have been

known to give travellers a hard time; they may be looking for drinking money.

If you're headed for Cameroun, you may need to get an exit visa stamped in your passport here, so check. If you're headed south the taxis between Bitam and Oyem tend to be reliable, but be warned that those to/from Libreville are frequently in atrocious condition.

Surprisingly, you'll find an area (*quartier*) of Hausa traders from northern Nigeria. You'll find them around the market and the Place de l'Indépendance.

Places to Stay

Hotels include the five-room *Rachelle* with bar and electricity, the 14-room *Hôtel du Peuple* and the 25-room *Hôtel des Voyageurs*. Also check out the *Mission Catholique*.

BOOUE

On a beautiful site along the Ogooué River, 415 km east of Libreville, Booué is about the half-way point on the Transgabonais to Franceville and in the centre of a principal logging zone.

Places to Stay

The only place to sleep may be *Chez l'-Habitant* or, if you're lucky, at the *Mission Catholique* on the northern outskirts of town. The 20-room *Les Cascades de l'Ogooué* is in a magnificent setting overlooking the rapids. Unfortunately it's rather expensive.

COCOBEACH

Some 120 km north of Libreville via Ntoum (on the road to Lambaréné), Cocobeach is where you catch a motorised canoe to Equatorial Guinea. The *Rest House* has rooms for about CFA 1750, while *Hôtel Restaurant* costs about CFA 2200 a double.

KOULAMOUTOU

About three-quarters of the way from Libreville to Franceville, 55 km south-west of the Lastoursville train stop, Koulamoutou is one of the country's leading coffee and cocoa areas. The town is spread out alond the banks of a river that runs through the middle of town. You might look around for one of the cubist-like *mvoudi* or *bodi* masks characteristic of the area, or climb 800-metre Mont Kondzo nearby. There are some caves (*grottes*) on the way up, but you'll miss them without a guide.

Places to Stay

You can try to get a bed at the *Mission Catholique* on top of the hill, *colline Mayi*, or with the American Protestant missionaries. Otherwise there's always the expensive *Relais Mulebi Bouenguidi* (tel 655169), which is a part of the nation-wide Novotel chain (telex 5349, Libreville).

LASTOURSVILLE

While the *Transgabonais* was being constructed, Lastoursville, called 'Lozo' by the locals, was a boom town; now it's less so. However, this small town is still a fun stop

on the *Transgabonais*. It has the reputation of being a truckstop, as many truck drivers spend the night here before continuing on to Franceville. The train station is way out of town on the other side of the river.

The town itself is fairly compact with a main strip of shops just up from, and running parallel to, the river. There are lots of good small bars; just follow the music to find one.

For excursions, enquire about the *grottes* (caves) outside of town, three km from the gendarmerie. You'll need a guide to find them and a torch to see the stalactites and stalagmites. You could also take a pirogue ride on the Ogooué, however, finding one could be difficult as they are disappearing fast these days. Another place worth visiting from here might be the Boundji waterfalls.

Places to Stay

You'll find a relatively cheap African hotel just east of the intersection of the main road and the road to the new hospital. You might

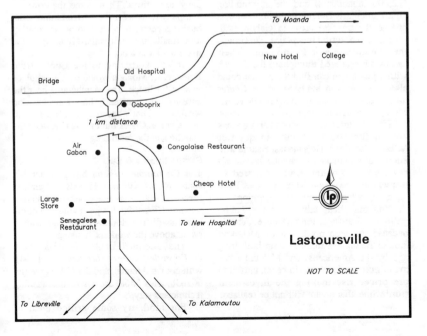

Lastoursville

also enquire at the *Mission Catholique* on the way out of town towards Libreville. For directions to the new, expensive hotel, ask at the train station. It's on the road to Moanda, near the college overlooking the town.

Places to Eat

There is a good Senegalese restaurant with safe food and a limited menu near the centre of town, about one km south of the Gaboprix supermarket. At a second restaurant run by a Congolese woman, there's a good chance of getting some bush meat. To find it, go east one block on the road that leads towards the new hospital then take a left on the small road that curls back to the main drag. The restaurant is about half way down on the right. Forget about street meat here; it's the worst in Gabon.

MAKOKOU

Some 610 km east of Libreville, Makokou (12,000 inhabitants) and the surrounding area, particularly Bélinga to the north-east, is one of the prettiest areas in Gabon, with jungles and beautiful mountains. This is also the country's major Pygmy area. Their camps are scattered throughout the forests; with a guide you can find them. You could also hire a pirogue and head for *Les Chutes de Loa-Loa* 10 km away on the Ivindo River. Mongouli waterfalls are much further away.

If you're interested in wood carvings, ask around for Thomas Issoko in quartier M'Bolo Bas-Fond. He's the last Bakota who knows how to make the famous *masque du reliquaire*, a wooden statue covered in leather used as a shrine to the ancestors. Even his children have no interest in learning!

You may hear talk about the Transgabonais being extended here. That's because the area north-east of Makokou around Bélinga (a mining camp built long ago by the Americans) and Mékambo has major iron ore deposits. However, until iron ore prices rise making the investment worthwhile, that dream will not be realised.

Places to Stay & Eat

Some travellers have been lucky and found a bed at the *Catholic Mission*. There's also a *Mission Protestante*. Alternatives include *Les Merveilles de l'Ivindo*, with bungalows in a garden next to the river, the newer *Ivindo-Palace* (tel 3069) and the Relais Mulebi, *Relais de l'Ivindo* (tel 3069).

For African food, try the popular *Relais de la Corniche* on Boulevard Bongo, the main drag. For dancing, there's the *Mbala* on the Alar Mitang road.

MOANDA

Manganese, and lots of it, is the raison d'être of Moanda, 60 km west of Franceville by paved road. This 'suburb of Paris' is a modern city, smaller and more compact than Franceville, with one of the largest French populations in the country and all of the amenities that go with them, except good roads. The mine is on top of the hill. Below it are the pleasant 'suburb' homes of the company executives. Then come the rows of company houses for the African miners, the business centre of town with a new market and, finally, the unorganised housing of the masses – all in a big valley.

If you're driving to the Congo from Franceville, Moanda would be a good place to stop for lunch. The marché area near the gare routière can really hop, especially on weekends. That's because there's plenty of money here. Check out the bars between the marché and the main drag.

Places to Stay & Eat

The *Catholique Mission* has pleasant but sparse rooms with double beds and air-con for CFA 5000. Some have talked the Father down to CFA 4000. It's just to the side of the business district; look for the huge church rising above the workers' housing.

The 75-room *Relais Mulebi* (tel 661038), the *Foyer des Cadres de la Comilog* (tel 334), with pool and tennis, and the *L'Auberge* (tel 661038, telex 5568) are where most visiting technicians stay.

For food, try some grilled meat or

chicken just behind the market; both are plentiful, fresh and delicious. Moanda has the best coupé-coupé meat in the country. You can pick out your own piece of meat and eat it fresh from the grill. There are also some good Senegalese restaurants in the area.

MOUILA

Mouila is the major town between Lambaréné and the Congo border. On Sundays, you're likely to find a number of people picnicking, bathing (despite bilharzia!) and fishing at Lac Bleu five km away. There's a road, but taking a two-hour pirogue ride from the downtown docks (*débarcadère*) to the lake would be far more interesting.

Places to Stay & Eat

The *Mess Militaire*, open to travellers, has seven rooms with air-con and a bar-restaurant. You might try your luck with the American and Catholic missions. There's also a *Relais Mulebi* (tel 861096) and the 20-room *Hôtel de Lac Bleu* (tel 861096) along the Ngounié River, with a restaurant and a disco. Two other nightclubs are *O Imogu* and *O Wetsiga*.

N'DENDE

N'Dendé is notable to travellers headed south to the Congo as it is the last town before the border. Don't forget to get your exit visa here. Those with wheels could visit the park to the south of N'Dendé, but ask first in town as you may need permission or a key. As for lodging, all you're likely to find in town is a room behind the general store for about CFA 600.

NDJOLE

Ndjolé is 235 km east of Libreville on a fairly good road. It's a quiet, old town where the *Transgabonais* meets the the Ogooué River. Once a week (usually Wednesday) there is a small barge from Ndjolé to Lambaréné some 130 km to the south-west. The train station is out of the town.

Places to Stay & Eat

There is a small market with a lot of bars just up from the banks of the river. Behind the market is a *Chambre de Passage* – a clean hotel with rooms for CFA 7000 to CFA 8000. You'll also find the 17-room *L'Escale* with a bar-restaurant, the 22-room *Missanga* (tel 793007), and *Hôtel de la Barrière*, which charges about CFA 4000 for a double.

OYEM

Some 400 km north-east of Libreville on the road to Cameroun, Oyem is in the centre of Fang and cocoa country. As in Bitam 75 km to the north, there are numerous Muslim Hausa traders and even a small pink mosque to cater for them.

If you feel like some real exercise you could try climbing Mont Nkoum 32 km away; coming from Bitam, you'll recognise it by the giant metal cross which was planted on top by some protestant ministers.

Places to Stay & Eat

In Oyem, *La Cabosse* (tel 986088), which costs about CFA 8200 a double, has only seven rooms but operates both a restaurant and a nightclub, the *Nthe*. The local Novotel is the *M'Vet Palace* (tel 986226).

TCHIBANGA

A prosperous town 612 km to the south of Libreville in savanna surrounded by forests, Tchibanga is the major starting point for safaris to the Réserve de Moukalaba to the north-west and to the Réserve de Ndendé to the east. Excursions can be arranged at the Relais Mulebi, *Relais de la Nyanga* (tel 8006). There's also the 35-room *Hôtel Dissiégoussou*, which has air-con and a restaurant.

WILDLIFE

Gabon has three national parks: Parc National de Wonga-Wongué east of Port-Gentil, Parc National de l'Okanda in the centre of the country, and Parc National du Petit Loango about 300 km south of Libreville.

None of these are accessible by road, but

some of the reserves are, such as the Réserve de la Lopé adjoining Okanda park and the Réserve de Ndendé in the far south bordering the Congo. Lopé reserve, for example, borders the railroad – five hours on the train from Libreville/Owendo to Lopé, two stops before Booué. You may be able to stay in a rustic campement. A good number of buffalo, elephants and various types of antelopes are in the reserve. Unfortunately, the rainy season is time to see most of the animals.

FISHING

Two areas renowned for fishing are Iguéla and Sette Cama. They are isolated spots bordering two large estuaries (*lagunes*) on the coast, 150 km and 250 km, respectively, south of Port-Gentil. Tarpon is the speciality; they are furious fighters and can weigh up to 70 kg. December through February is the season. Perch, barracuda, ray, bass and sailfish are also plentiful.

There are lodging facilities at both: the *Centre Saint-Aubert* (BP 1851, Libreville) at Iguéla and the *Centre Touristique de Sette Cama* (BP 240, Port-Gentil). The reserve at Iguéla has about 600 protected elephants.

During dry spells you can sometimes get to Iguéla by road from the mainland but not to Sette Cama. Most travellers take the Saturday flight on Air Inter Gabon out of Port-Gentil; it stops at both.

São Tomé & Principe

A veritable paradise on earth awaits the visitor to these remote islands. With cloud-capped volcanoes, jungle greenery, plus crystal-clear waters not yet discovered by the skin diving crowd, São Tomé e Principe would undoubtedly be on almost every travellers' list of places to see if getting there were not so difficult.

It used to be that you had to lie through your teeth and go through all sorts of shenanigans to get a tourist visa. Fortunately this has changed recently.

If you get a charge out of being the only tourist in a country, exploring unknown places, snorkelling in the clearest waters on the western coast of Africa, or camping on remote beaches practically unknown to the outside world, and you've got the wherewithal to get there, by all means go.

HISTORY

Having first spotted São Tomé in 1469, the Portuguese began settling the place 16 years later and quickly started amassing slaves, with the result that almost overnight São Tomé became the largest sugar-producing country in Africa. The sugar boom was short-lived, however, when the slaves staged a successful revolt in 1530 and the plantation owners fled to less troublesome Brazil. However, because São Tomé served as the major staging post for the slave trade between the Congo and the US, slaves remained critical to the economy.

In the 18th and 19th centuries, the Portuguese established large cocoa and coffee plantations (*rocas*), which likewise depended on slavery. While slavery was officially abolished by 1875, it was replaced by a system of forced contract labour. Revelations of the slavery-like nature of this system resulted in an international boycott of São Tomé cocoa in the years before WW I. Nonetheless, the system continued and resulted in a massive influx of labourers from Cape Verde, Angola and Mozambique, bringing considerable ethnic and cultural diversity to the islands.

Independence

Labour problems were endemic but always put down brutally by the Portuguese, the worst example being a labour strike in 1953 when Portuguese troops gunned down over a thousand plantation workers. Working conditions improved thereafter, but the spirit of nationalism was already ignited and by 1960, São Tomé had its first modern nationalist party. The 1974 coup in Lisbon that brought Salazar's downfall prompted demonstrations and strikes on the plantations and a mutiny by black troops, causing Portugal to grant independence a year later.

By then, however, almost all of the 4000 Portuguese settlers and plantation administrators had fled the country, leaving less than a hundred whites behind. This, coupled with the departure of most of the Cape Verdean workers, left the country with virtually no skilled workers and the economy in a shambles. It also forced Manuel Pinto da Costa, the country's first president and initially a moderate, to move to the left and nationalise most of the abandoned plantations before the year was out.

A rightist opposition party exiled in Gabon began making preparations for a coup attempt. In 1978, with an invasion appearing imminent, the Cubans and Angolans, among others, sent troops to assist. The invasion

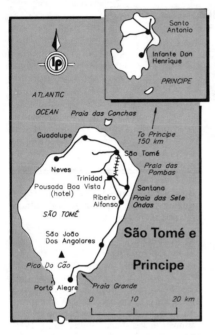

ments. Virtually all the vegetable oil, flour, rice, dried milk, sugar and flour is donated. Foreign aid is also behind the locally grown fresh vegetables – tomatoes, cabbage, radish, lettuce and eggplant – most of which comes from a demonstration farm in Mesquita financed by France's US$5 million aid program. This all seems pretty bleak until you realise that before independence 90% of the island's food had to be imported because of the lop-sided dependence on cocoa.

Foreign aid accounts for over 40% of the country's GNP (the only African countries with higher percentages are the Cormoros and Cape Verde) and touches every sector of society. The French are rebuilding telephone, water and electrical systems and renovating the airport; the West Germans are renovating the port; and the Swedes have supplied a mass transit system – nine Scania buses. Portuguese, Swedes, Italians, Cubans, Koreans and Chinese help in the hospitals. The Portuguese operate the only functioning library and movie theatre as well as the national television, which broadcasts two nights a week. The French-run trade school has the island's only functioning printing press, which may soon be used to print the nation's rarely published newspaper, *Revolução*.

The governments top priority is revitalising the cocoa and coffee plantations for generating foreign exchange. The African Development Bank, the World Bank and others are helping to rehabilitate some of the cocoa estates, which still account for 90% of São Tomé's export earnings. But in the late 1980s production remained at only one third that of the pre-independence level of 10,000 tonnes per year. The state, which now owns 90% of the land, may be in over its head. A five-person committee operates each nationalised cocoa plantation, and the government provides all materials, sets wages and controls the marketing of all agricultural produce. Change is in the air, however. The country recently adopted a policy of putting the 15 largest plantations in private hands.

As for secondary priorities, crop diver-

didn't occurred and since then, with the help of Cuban military advisors and Angolan troops, da Costa has consolidated his power considerably.

Today

With a per capita income of about US$295, roughly 50% higher than that in the Sahel, São Tomé is badly off, though not at the bottom of the economic barrel in West and Central Africa.

In one respect São Tomé is at the bottom. Its life expectancy at birth is 39 years, the lowest in Africa and possibly the world.

In the markets you'll see women tending wooden stalls but with little to offer other than manioc, breadfruit, rice, fish and, occasionally, tomatoes and pineapples. While this scene may be picturesque, it is really an African facade masking extensive foreign aid. The country imports half its food and most of this is donated by foreign govern-

sification is one, but progress has been slow. Oil prospecting was discontinued in 1974, and there are no indications that it will be resumed. Fishing and tourism, which are potentially lucrative, remain untapped sources of foreign exchange. One of the ministers recently stated that they wanted to build a casino, sporting facilities and a 175-room tourist hotel – a sign of some movement towards the west.

Economically São Tomé is heavily dependent on Angola. This, not antagonism towards the west, accounts for the country's close ties with the communist bloc. If São Tomé were to become less dependent on Angola, its foreign politics would probably change. For now, you'll see Russian, Cuban, East German and North Korean advisors everywhere.

PEOPLE

There are five native groups amongst the islands' 108,000 inhabitants. The most powerful are the *filhos da terra*, the mixed-blooded descendants of imported slaves and Europeans (mostly Portuguese) who settled on the islands in the 16th and 17th centuries.

Intermarriage has been common, but the influx of contract workers until 1950 tended to re-Africanise them. The *Angolares* are descendants of former castaway slaves from Angola who reputedly survived a shipwreck in 1540; they are now primarily fishermen. Then there are the *forros*, descendants of slaves freed when slavery was abolished in 1875. Finally, there are the *servicios* (migrant labourers) and the *tongas*, their children born on the island.

The language, architecture, crafts and artistic expression are all Creole. There are more than 50 folkloric groups on the two islands which perform during the 28 principal festivals during the year between May and January. If you're lucky, you may get to see the *tchitoli*, a unique theatrical performance dating back to the time of Charlemagne which was introduced long ago by sailors from Madeira. Combining music, mime and dance of that era, it has been 'Africanised'

over the years, especially in the music as well as the dance performed by the Angolares.

GEOGRAPHY

The archipelago of São Tomé e Principe is the second smallest country in Africa (the Seychelles is the smallest). It is also the most difficult to get to, being 320 km off the coast of Gabon with few connections to the continent. About 108,000 people inhabit the islands; a quarter of them live in the capital city, São Tomé.

Only two km north of the equator, the island of São Tomé is primarily dense mountain jungle, capped by Pico de São Tomé (2024 metres) which is surrounded by a dozen other inactive volcanic cones all over 1000 metres high. The eastern slopes and coastal flatlands are covered by huge cocoa estates, formerly owned by Portuguese companies, along with a number of small farms. Towards the north, the terrain gets drier, with rolling hills and baobab trees. The island of Principe, some 160 km to the north-east, is much smaller and flatter. The principal town is São Antonia.

CLIMATE

Rain, not heat, is the major concern. June to September is the heavy rainy season, but you'll find high humidity and some rainfall all year round. No matter when you go, take an umbrella.

LANGUAGE

Portuguese is the official language. Most people speak a creole language called *forro*.

VISAS

Everyone is required to have an entry visa. As late as 1987 tourist visas were still not being issued, but since the opening of the new tourist hotel, the country has opened up considerably. The easiest place to get one is Libreville, Gabon. The people at the embassy there are friendly and issue tourist visas in 24 hours for CFA 7500. Exit permits are no longer required. Prior to the new policy, people on official business had to show proof of an invitation, usually in the form of a letter from the government. Chances are this policy hasn't changed.

Visas are valid anywhere from two weeks to two months and are obtainable only in Lisbon, New York, Libreville (Gabon) and Luanda (Angola). Except in Luanda where getting a visa is reportedly very difficult, visas are usually obtainable in one to three days.

Diplomatic Missions Abroad

Libreville (tel 721466, three day service), Lisbon, Luanda, New York (São Tomé e Principe Mission to the UN, 801 2nd Avenue, Room 1504, NY, NY 10017, tel 212-6974211).

MONEY

US$1 = Db 73
£1 = Db 170

The unit of currency is the Dobra (Db). It is wildly over-valued, so travelling is quite expensive unless you deal on the black market, which is active but particularly risky here. The rate is 40% to 50% higher than the official rate. Hard currency and travellers' cheques can be exchanged only at the Banco National de São Tomé e Principe. In 1986 the two major hotels began accepting AE credit cards.

Banking hours: weekdays 7.30 to 11.30 am; closed on Saturdays and Sundays.

GENERAL INFORMATION
Health

A yellow fever vaccination is mandatory if you're coming from an infected area or will be staying more than two weeks; also a cholera shot if you're coming from an infected area within six months.

Security

No African capital is safer than São Tomé.

Business Hours

Business: weekdays 8 am to 12 noon and 3 to 6 pm; Saturday 8 am to 12 noon.

Public Holidays

1 January, 3 February, 1 May, 12 July (Independence Day), 6 September, 30 September, 21 December, 25 to 26 December.

Photography

There is no permit system, but use great caution – the government is apparently paranoid about imperialist infiltration. So ask before you photograph anything, otherwise people may think you're a spy.

Time & Phone

When it's noon in São Tomé, it's noon in London and 7 am in New York (8 am during daylight savings time). Local telephone and telegraph service is not too bad, but international connections are poor.

GETTING THERE
Air

From Europe, you could take one of the twice-weekly flights from Lisbon on *TAP Air Portugal*. You can also fly to São Tomé from Libreville (Gabon). The Angolan airlines *TAAG* flies to São Tomé twice a week from Luanda with connections to Lisbon and Sal Island (Cape Verde). Once a month *Aeroflot* stops over on its Moscow/Cairo/Cotonou/São Tomé run.

From Libreville (Gabon), getting to São Tomé used to be a major hassle. No longer. In 1986 a new airline, *Equatorial International Airlines*, rehabilitated the sole aeroplane of the defunct *LASPT* airlines and now has three flights weekly. If they purchase a second plane as planned, they'll extend service to Douala (Cameroun). They are represented in Libreville by British Caledonian airlines. The one-way cost from Libreville is US$115 (hard currency only) with no return flight restrictions. US$220 (hard currency only).

You can also charter a plane in Libreville from *Air Affaires Gabon* (Libreville tel

732513/732010; telex 5360) or *Air Service*, which are charter companies at the Libreville airport. The smallest plane is a five-seater and costs approximately US$1500 one-way or round-trip (if you're returning the same day).

Ferry

A new French-built, flat-bottomed ferry reportedly connects São Tomé with Libreville and Douala. The one-way cost is CFA 25,000 from Libreville and CFA 35,000 from Douala. São Tomé-Principe costs Db 1205 and getting government permission is no longer a problem. Transcolmar in São Tomé (between the centre and the fort) has the scoop. Turimar, another shipping company, is responsible for larger vessels going to Luanda, Bissau, Portugal, etc. Their office is next to the Banco Nacional in São Tomé.

GETTING AROUND

Air

Equatorial International flies to Principe three times a week for US$50 return. At São Tomé airport, there's no departure tax. You won't find a bank there, and you cannot rely on finding a taxi either. Hitching a ride into town usually isn't very difficult, however.

Bus & Taxi

On São Tomé, the bus system is good; you can take one to just about anywhere on the island. Hitching is also easy. Taxis, on the other hand, are virtually non-existent. If you ever find a taxi, make sure you arrange for future pick-ups. While over half of the 287 km of roads around the island are paved, they're deteriorating fast. For a map of the island see the one on the wall inside the Hotel Miramar. It's the only one you'll find.

São Tomé

Sleepy and spotlessly clean are words frequently used to describe São Tomé, the capital city of some 25,000 inhabitants and the only town of any importance on the island. Largely unaffected by modern influences, with buildings of varying colours and wooden balconies, and a large avenue bordered with fire-coloured *flamboyants* extending toward a 16th century baroque cathedral and a 19th century Portuguese fort, it is reminiscent of a small Portuguese town.

Taxis are scarce. Visiting technical advisors have to rely exclusively on the sponsoring ministries for transportation. Others on official business have to deal with the foreign ministry, the Ministério dos Negócios Estrangeiros.

Information

Banks Banco Nacional de São Tomé e Principe, Banco Nacional Ultramarino.

Embassies Gabon, Portugal.

Cathedral & Fort São Sebastião

For sightseeing, you could take a look at the baroque cathedral dating back to the 16th century and then take a walk down the wide avenues bordered towards Fort São Sebastião, overlooking the ocean. The latter is now the National Museum and contains a collection of 19th and early 20th century furniture from homes of the wealthy Portuguese families who once ruled the island. Also included in the collection are Portuguese and Spanish religious art, old canons and statues of the nation's founders.

La Casa de Repouso

About 15 km from São Tomé and a km up the mountain is La Casa de Repouso, where you can get a panoramic view of both the interior mountains and the coast. Nearby in the tropical jungle is a waterfall called *São Nicolau*.

Beaches

São Tomé is famous for its white, sandy beaches and clear waters. Some of the most beautiful beaches and clearest waters are at the northern end of São Tomé at Praia das Conchas. You'll need a vehicle to get there.

The best beaches near town are a few km south of São Tomé at Praia das Pombas, which is a great place to start exploring the beaches. Two other beaches further to the south are Praia das Sete Ondas, just north of Ribiero Afonso, and Praia Grande, about 40 km from São Tomé below São João dos Angolares. At most of these beaches, you'll find virtually no undertow and not a tourist in sight. Dugout canoes, crystal-clear water, and an occasional dolphin complete the picture.

Places to Stay

For a cheap hotel, if you don't mind irregular electricity and water, try *Pensão Carvalho* or *Pensão Turismo*, both downtown, with rooms for about Db 1000 to Db 1500. Paying with US dollars is no problem; they usually prefer it.

Hotel Me-Zochi in Trinidade, eight km from São Tomé, is better. Despite the poor water supply, it's not a bad place for the price. The restaurant has a fixed menu and serves food from 12.30 to 2 pm and 7.30 to 8.30 pm.

The brand new *Hotel Miramar* on the outskirts of town overlooking the bay is the country's first tourist-class hotel. A very pleasant but over-priced hotel, it has about 60 singles/doubles for US$70/80, a tennis court, videos, hot water and the best restaurant in town. You must pay in US dollars or AE credit cards except at its sidewalk cafe, the place to be seen.

The restored *Pousada Boa Vista* has rooms for half the price (Db 1400 to Db 2000) and now accepts AE credit cards. It's a good notch down and much smaller with only 20 rooms or so. Most of the visiting technicians used to stay there until the Miramar opened. Not all the rooms have hot water. The restaurant has a fixed menu for about Db 300. Hours for ordering: 12.30 to 2 pm and 7.30 to 8.30 pm. It's 15 km southwest of town past Trinidade, on a mountain at 1000 metres elevation, hence it's cooler with a scenic view. You'll have to hitch a ride to get into town.

If you are travelling in the countryside outside São Tomé it is difficult to find accommodation.

Places to Eat

You'll find at least three places to get decent food besides the hotels. *Celestino's* is nothing great but one of the two best in town. It has a fixed menu for about Db 300, and you must reserve at least two hours in advance. *Club Nautico* downtown overlooking the ocean has a fixed menu for about the same price. It is also the best place to go for a drink and snacks but the pool hasn't been working for years. *Omstep* in the centre of town is cheaper than the others. Go early as they sometimes run out of food and beer.

Nightclubs

Very late in the evening, very late, you could try the most active nightclub in town, *Batalan*. It's indoors with air-con, plays a variety of music and has a Db 100 cover charge. Smoking is prohibited! There's a remote chance you might see Conjunto Africa Negra, the best-known local music group.

Things to Buy

Almost everyone stops by the 'special shop', Loja Franca, where you can find most essentials and some non-essentials. It takes hard currency only. They carry some of the locally made shirts which, however, are quite expensive and nothing special. Forget about looking for handicrafts – there's very little.

Principe

Smaller than São Tomé, Principe is a beautiful, flatter island with many birds, particularly parrots.

Other than the crews of Russian trawlers which frequently visit the tuna processing plant, you'll probably be the only foreigner on the island. One correspondent spent the afternoon lying on the beach drinking vodka with a Russian trawler crew to celebrate the fact that they'd found a foreigner there – the first time, apparently, in 18 visits!

Places to Stay & Eat

For a bed, try *Pensão Palhota* in São Antonia, which charges Db 2400 for a double.

There is also a *Residencia Oficial* where you can stay for Db 500 per night. It's quite smelly as it's near a tuna processing factory.

Meals at the Residencia cost about Db 60, and will inevitably consist of fish.

Getting There & Away

You can get there from São Tomé on a Transcolmar ferry for Db 1205 one-way or on an Equatorial Airlines flight for US$50 return. From São Antonio you can take taxis or small boats around the island and to the beaches.

Zaïre

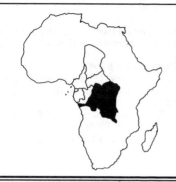

The former Belgian Congo is to Africa what the jungles of Brazil are to South America. Many would think you are out of your mind to travel overland. Going from one end of the country to the other can take a month. The road system is probably Africa's worst. For part of the journey, you can travel by train or river boat.

Indeed, a trip on the Zaïre River is the *sine qua non* of an adventure in Zaïre – absolutely not to be missed. You'll pass through some of the thickest rainforests in Africa. Fortunately, the famous Primus beer seems to make its way into every nook and cranny of the country. Travelling overland is not for everyone by a long shot. Those that do won't have any trouble coming up with stories for their grandchildren. Others simply fly.

The far eastern region, with Virunga park, Lake Kivu and the snow-capped Ruwenzori mountains, is considered by many to be the most spectacular area in all of Central and West Africa. You can even climb active volcanoes. In the far south, there's Lubumbashi, which has lush tropical surroundings and a relatively cool climate.

Kinshasa is just the opposite – huge and muggy with a high crime rate. Still, the former 'Leopoldville' has its admirers. For starters, it's the music capital of Africa. Zaïre must surely produce more recording stars than any other country in Africa. No self-respecting traveller would fail to take in one of the Zaïrois bands in the lively Cité area. Other people are more attracted to the fine restaurants. For the rugged, however, Kinshasa is like Kathmandu – a starting point for a fantastic adventure into the hinterland.

HISTORY

As in all the thick rainforest areas of Central Africa, the first inhabitants were nomadic hunters and gatherers, some of them Pygmies. Primitive communism was the order of the day. Men and women were equally responsible for finding food, and the few means of subsistence were shared by everyone. Those near the rivers found a life of fishing and farming less hostile and confining than in the forests.

Communities eventually arose along the rivers. The villagers relied on the Pygmies to supply meat and labour; the Pygmies relied on the villagers for iron implements, salt and some food. The villagers began acquiring possessions and improving their existence while the Pygmies did not. Eventually, village clans developed, with the wealthier ones dominating the source of labour.

Empires

The development of village clans created a social base for a major new phenomenon – the growth of empires in the savanna areas. Between the 13th century and the arrival of the Belgians in the late 19th century, numerous kingdoms arose. The first, the Kongo empire, extended over vast territories, each headed by a chief in charge of collecting taxes in goods, cloth or slaves (primarily criminals and prisoners of war).

When the Portuguese arrived in 1482, they converted the king to Christianity and for a brief period good relations existed. Soon, the Portuguese were demanding slaves. In the 16th century alone, they shipped some 60,000 slaves out of the Kongo empire. By the 17th century, the demand for slaves was more than the Kongo could

Top: Lega women, Zaïre (EE)
Left: Karasimbi Volcano near Nyiragongo, Eastern Zaïre (EE)
Right: Moss covered vegetation on the way up Mt Ruwenzori, Eastern Zaïre (EE)

Top: Steamer on the Zaïre River (EE)
Bottom: Enia fishing canoe, Boyoma Falls, Zaïre (EE)

provide. So the Portuguese initiated their own raiding parties. Eventually, their interests collided and war erupted in 1660. Outmatched, the Kongo lost. Their heyday was over.

By the 18th century, the two most powerful kingdoms were in the southern copper belt: the Luba in northern Katanga and the Landa further south. Kings had hundreds of wives and concubines, and court officials abounded. In 1906, a German explorer, Leo Frobenius, found magnificent towns with the principal streets lined on both sides for km on end with rows of palm trees, charmingly decorated houses, velvet and silk materials everywhere, and every man carrying intricate inlaid knives or other sumptuous weapons of iron or copper.

In the mid-19th century, Arabs from the island of Zanzibar in East Africa invaded eastern Zaïre and established equally magnificent towns and thriving plantations. Their fine houses had all the luxuries of urban life along the coast of East Africa – beds, furniture, coffee tables, elaborate doorways and European luxuries such as candles, sugar, matches, silver, glass goblets and decanters. Common soldiers slept on silk and satin mattresses, in carved beds with silk mosquito curtains! The most powerful Arab slave trader of the day, Tippu Tip, had some 50,000 guns at his command.

Colonial Period

European governments showed no interest in exploring the Congo. It took an American newspaper reporter, Stanley, to spark their interest. After Stanley's historic journey to Africa in the early 1870s to find Livingston (he did at Lake Tanganyika), he made an equally historic voyage down the Congo river in 1874 – the first European to do so. Smallpox, starvation, crocodiles and battles with local tribes killed over half his men. Stanley proved that above the rapids on the lower Congo, there were thousands of km of navigable waters.

The British weren't interested. King Léopold II of Belgium was. Léopold envisioned a way to capture the trade of the entire lower Congo basin – build a railroad around the rapids and launch steamers up country. So he hired Stanley to establish road and river communications from the river's mouth to Stanleyville (now Kisangani). The French saw Stanley as a threat, so in 1880 they sent Simon de Brazza to claim neighbouring Congo-Brazzaville (now the Congo). The European scramble for Africa was on; King Léopold had provided the spark.

The 'Congo Free State' was neither free nor a colony. It was Léopold's own private estate. Following the example of railroad development in North and South America, he granted land and mineral rights to companies that would build railroads. For an area almost twice the size of Luxemburg, one company built the line from Matadi on the sea to Léopoldville (now Kinshasa); others built those in the south. Léopold himself managed one of the operations.

A booming demand for rubber, following the development of rubber tyres, saved him from going broke. The only problem was that the operations needed labour. Slavery was the solution. Europe eventually caught wind of Léopold's ghastly atrocities and an international scandal developed. Outraged and embarrassed, the Belgian government forced their king to cede the Congo to Belgium in 1908. In acquiring a colony, Belgium also acquired Léopold's huge debt from lavish spending on his palaces and other public buildings in Belgium. The debt at one time absorbed nearly 20% of the country's revenue.

Belgium did almost nothing to develop the Congo. Private companies moved in and began extracting copper, diamonds and other minerals from the rich fields in Shaba and elsewhere. Educating the masses was too much of a bother. Instead, the government left it to Catholic missionaries, agreeing only to subsidise primary schools. At independence the Belgian Congo had a grand total of half a dozen African university graduates. Belgium did, however, build

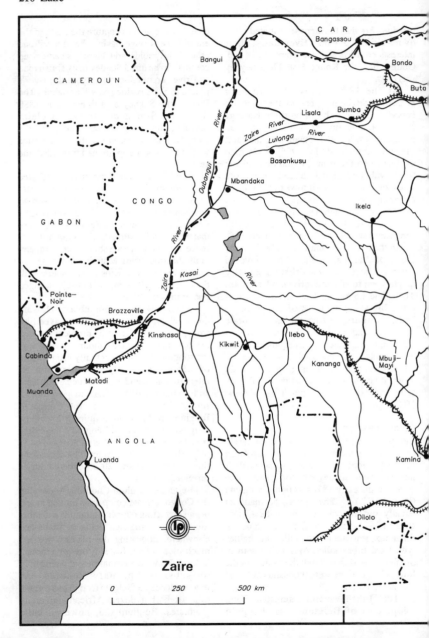

Zaïre

0   250   500 km

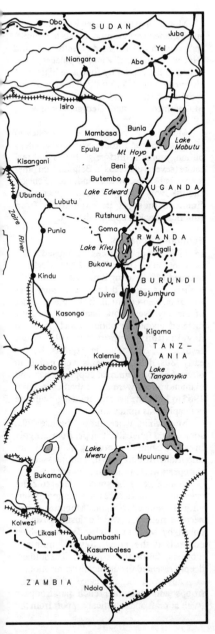

almost 50,000 km of roads and began the largest construction project in colonial Africa – Inga dam on the lower Congo, with a capacity to supply half the electricity produced at the time in all of western Europe!

Independence & Civil War

Politically, Belgium did absolutely nothing to prepare the Congo for independence. Political parties in West Africa began in 1915. In the Belgian Congo, they weren't allowed before 1955. For years the Belgians had simplified their rule by playing one African tribe off against another. For this reason and because the colony was so large, the political parties became almost entirely tribally oriented. In 1958 France made neighbouring Congo-Brazzaville self-governing and this became the event that ignited politics in the Belgian Congo.

A year later Belgium had to send troops to quell rioting in 'Léo'. Disturbances continued and more troops were required. Almost overnight, Belgium, never having seriously considered granting independence, made a 180° turn. Shocked African politicians were told they had six months to prepare for elections and independence.

Only two of the parties had any real loyalty to the idea of all-Congolese unity. One of them, headed by Patrice Lumumba, won the election. Lumumba became prime minister and his major rival, Kasavubu, became president. Six days later, the army mutinied. Five days thereafter, with backing from the Belgian-owned mining company, Moise Tshombe, the governor of Katanga province (now called Shaba) announced the secession of his province. With Katanga went the government's major source of revenue. Civil war was inevitable.

Lumumba pleaded for help from the UN and the UN began the most critical operation in its history. When the UN didn't do exactly what he wanted, Lumumba asked Russia for troops as well. This was the straw that broke the camel's back. Soon thereafter, Lumumba was overthrown by an alliance of the army, led by Joseph Mobutu (moh-BOU-tou), and regional politicians, headed by Kasavubu. They expelled the Russians and handed Lumumba over to Tshombe in Elizabethville (Lubumbashi), where he was murdered.

Civil war continued. With the aid of UN troops, the central government finally gained control of Katanga in 1963. But Russia, France and other countries refused to contribute any longer to the UN operation. Bankrupt, the UN withdrew. To keep Katanga from seceding again, Kasavubu had no choice but to accept Tshombe into the government.

Meanwhile, pro-Marxist troops took control of major parts of the east. The US took note. Under Mobutu, the army went there to regain control and with the aid of American and Belgian paratroopers and about 1200 foreign mercenaries, they succeeded.

Mobutu

Within a year Mobutu, supported by the west, staged a bloodless coup. Luck was with him – copper prices started to skyrocket. A former journalist and a member of the Ngbande tribe, Mobutu consolidated his power by returning power to the local chiefs, buying off his enemies, and turning his friends into millionaires. Corruption became a way of life, permeating the entire government bureaucracy.

His famous 'authenticity' campaign began in the early '70s. The Congo became Zaïre, Léopoldville became Kinshasa, Elizabethville became Lubumbashi, and Stanleyville became Kisangani. He then ordered all Zaïrois to replace their Christian names with African ones. Mobutu Joseph Desiré became Mobutu Sese Seko (his full name – Mobutu Sese Seko Koko Ngbendu wa za Banga – means 'the all powerful warrior who, because of his endurance and inflexible will to win, will go from conquest to conquest leaving fire in his wake'). Then he forbade bureaucrats to wear western attire, expropriated US$500 million in foreign enterprises, and threw out the important Asian business community.

Mobutu's extravagances were numerous and included various monuments to himself, stadiums, the World Trade Centre, the ultra modern Voice of Zaïre and 11 palaces, some linked to the capital by four-lane highways. He even spent US$15 million to sponsor the world championship fight between Muhammed Ali and George Foreman in 1974.

Mostly, however, he used the money to amass a personal fortune estimated at US$3 billion, primarily in foreign banks and real estate (several chateaus in Belgium and other homes in France, Switzerland, Italy, Senegal and the Ivory Coast). Record copper prices financed most of it; huge loans from American banks supplied the rest.

Economic Collapse

In 1975, copper prices collapsed. The honeymoon was over. By 1977, the GNP had tumbled 14%, leaving Zaïre with the world's highest per capita debt. The country was bankrupt. Neo-colonialism became the order of the day. New York banks and the IMF dictated economic policy which involved devaluations, import controls, wage restrictions, reductions in payrolls. By the early '80s, debt repayments were eating up 60% of export earnings; copper, cobalt and diamond prices were lower than ever. From 1965 to 1984, the average annual growth rate per capita was minus 1.6%!

Meanwhile, twice during the late '70s, some 5000 guerrilla troops from Angola invaded Shaba, capturing Kolwezi, an important mining town, and massacring European workers and missionaries.

In the face of the greatest threat to Zaïre since the Katanga secession, Zaïrois troops virtually refused to fight. 'Mobutisme' had become merely a way to justify absolute power by Mobutu's Ngbande tribe, which controlled the army. Several hundred thousand Zaïrois fled to Angola. The soldiers deeply resented the ethnic discrimination.

Only with the assistance of Moroccan troops and Belgian-French paratroopers (with aircraft and logistical support from the

US) did they recapture the area. Eventually, Mobutu and the Angolan rebel leaders came to an agreement – Mobutu wouldn't assist anti-guerrilla forces in Angola in return for their ceasing to invade Shaba.

Today

The economy is in a real mess. Every year, the government must reschedule its debt with the IMF. Rescheduling alone is predicted to add over US$1 billion to the debt by 1991. The country imports a shocking 50% of its food requirements; you'll find stores stocked with South African products, from toilet bowl cleaners to cocktail snacks (immediately prior to independence, the country was self-sufficient in food).

Mobutu has had to eat humble pie on numerous occasions, by devaluing the currency, dissolving the state minerals marketing company, courting patronising Belgian industrialists and, upon World Bank insistence, replacing the leadership of Gécamines, the all-important mining company.

Some progress is being made, but with per capita incomes having plummeted to below US$200, the country has a long way to go. A majority of government workers earn the equivalent of US$30 to US$40 a month, or roughly the price of two sacks of cassava, the amount to feed a family of four for a month.

How do people make ends meet? Teachers charge their students; police at road-blocks collect *matabiches* (bribes) from motorists; doctors and nurses expect tips. Anyone walking down the streets of Kinshasa wearing a watch or jewellery is likely to be robbed on the spot. If you send out international mail, postal workers are liable to remove and resell the stamps.

Mobutu's political problems are almost as severe. Mutiny within the army is a constant threat. To keep on top of his enemies, he maintains several competing intelligence agencies. No less than six countries – the USA, Belgium, France, China, West Germany and Israel – are

propping up the regime with military assistance.

The human rights picture is dismal. Amnesty International claimed that 100 political prisoners, criminals and suspects had been killed in Zaïre's prisons in 1982 and 1983.

Sanford Ungar, in *Africa: The People and Politics of an Emerging Country*, reports that just after returning from a triumphant state visit in Washington with Reagan, Mobutu found out that a US congressional delegation was meeting with 10 former members of parliament who had been jailed for advocating the establishment of a second political party. Furious, he sent police to attack and beat his audacious opponents as they left the hotel where they'd been meeting. US officials had to stand by and watch.

However, Mobutu has been in power longer than just about any African president (Houphouët Boigny of the Ivory Coast has been in power five years longer). As long as Zaïre continues paying back the New York banks and keeps up its virulent attacks against Libya's Qadafi, support from the west seems assured.

PEOPLE

Zaïre has about 33 million people, with some 3.5 million in Kinshasa, 800,000 in Lubumbashi, 700,000 in Kananga, and 500,000 in both Kisangani and Mbuji-Mayi. Most of the remaining population is rural, primarily in the central and southern parts of the country.

Ethnically, Zaïre is extremely varied. The most numerous people are the Kongo who live in the Kinshasa area, the people of Kwangu-Kwilu, the Mongo who live in the great forests, the Luba in the south, the Bwaka and the Zande. Huge sections of the northern rainforests – Pygmy territory – are practically deserted. As long as the forests remain, the population there simply cannot increase.

One of the special things about Zaïre is the rich variety of art. There are more major styles here than anywhere on the continent – Kongo, Mbun, Mbala, Kwésé, Yaka and Pende in the west, Luba and Songe in the south, Lega, Bembe, Mbole, Mangbetu and Azande in the north, and Kuba, Lele, Wongo, Lulua and Salampasu in the centre. It's all a little bewildering.

The art of the Luba is probably the most well-known. All over black Africa you'll find examples of their ornate, roundish masks with large bulging eyes and protruding nose and mouth. They are worn typically in a masked dance to celebrate the arrival of an important visitor or the death of a village dignitary.

The art of the Kuba also stands out. If you see a mask with geometric patterns and decorated with cowry shells, beads and raffia cloth, chances are it's Kuba. Some masks can be rather crude looking and made from straw; others are very elaborate and ornate. Kuba art also takes the form of charms, wooden cups, game boards, spoons, tobacco pipes, combs, three-legged stools, miniature hair ornaments, vessels and cosmetic boxes with geometric decorations.

Luba Mask

GEOGRAPHY

Zaïre is imposing. Just look at the Africa-wide statistics: it is the third largest country (after Sudan and Algeria), with the third largest population (after Nigeria and Egypt), the third highest mountain (Mt Ruwenzori at 5119 metres), rainforests as extensive as those in the rest of Central Africa combined, and the second longest river, the Zaïre, which is second only to the Amazon in water volume.

The country's mineral resources are also impressive. Sixty percent of the world's cobalt, 90% of the world's small industrial diamonds, and a significant portion of the world's copper all come from southern Zaïre.

Exploiting these resources is a gargantuan task. As large as the US east of the Mississippi, Zaïre has about 1750 km of paved highways in the countryside, which is less than a road from New York to Miami. The road system is so bad that virtually all overland travellers cross in the north-east corner, by-passing Kinshasa. There are trains from Kinshasa to Matadi and from Lubumbashi (Shaba) in the south-east to Ilebo, Kindu and Kalemie, but travelling from Kinshasa to Lubumbashi by road and rail still takes several weeks.

While most of southern Zaïre is tropical grassland, with rolling hills around Lubumbashi, the northern half of Zaïre is mostly flat lowland covered with rainforest. There, the roads become incredibly muddy. Most travellers headed east from Kinshasa go via the Zaïre River (called the Congo River in the Congo), which curves through the country on a path that is even longer than the Mississippi. As with the Niger River, however, a long series of rapids near the coast make it impossible for ocean-going ships to enter. Only from Kinshasa inland will you see Mississippi-style riverboats ploughing the Zaïre.

Zaïre's most beautiful area, the eastern border with Rwanda and Uganda, is also its most inaccessible. The attractions here are Lake Kivu, the gorilla sanctuary near the lakeside town of Bukavu, and Virunga

National Park north of the lake, which includes the snowcapped Ruwenzori (ROU-when-ZOR-ee) mountain range and active volcanoes.

CLIMATE

About a third of Zaïre, including Kisangani, lies north of the equator, where it rains year-round, though less from December to February. In the rest of Zaïre, including Kinshasa, Lake Kivu and the Shaba area, there's a dry spell, with overcast days, from June to September. The heavy rain period is February to May. Despite its equatorial location, Zaïre is not one of Africa's hotter countries. Humidity, not high temperatures, is the killer.

LANGUAGE

French is the official language. Of the 200-odd local languages and dialects, the major one is Lingala, spoken primarily in Kinshasa and along the rivers. You'll hear more Kikongo west of Kinshasa, Swahili in the east and north-east, and Tshiluba in the south and central area. Some expressions in Lingala are:

Good morning	m-BOH-tay
Good evening	m-BOH-tay
How are you?	san-goh-BOH-nee
Thank you	MAY-lay-zee
Goodbye	CAN-day, MAH-lah-mou

VISAS

Visas are required by all. Visas are valid for one to three months, depending on how long you request, and the longer you stay, the more they cost. Some embassies require that you have an onward airline ticket, a letter of introduction from your embassy, a vaccination certificate, US$500 in cash or travellers' cheques (US$250 if staying less than 15 days). In Bangui (CAR), Zaïre visas are issued while you wait and cost CFA 5000 for a one-month single-entry visa and CFA 9000 for multiple entry. In both Dar es Salaam (Tanzania) and Nairobi, they are issued in 24 hours; four photos, a vaccination certificate and a letter of introduction are required. You can get a visa in all neighbouring countries, but if there's a Zaïrois embassy in your country of residence, get one there.

Some embassies refuse to issue visas to travellers who could have obtained one at home. This randomly applied rule hinges often on residency, not on nationality. Embassies of Zaïre in Africa don't require Britons working in Africa to return to the UK to get a visa for example. On the other hand, Canadians cannot get a visa in Washington even if they reside in the USA. In Africa, some travellers have gotten around the problem by fabricating stories about how they reside in countries without a Zaïrois embassy. Regardless, they invariably insist that you present them with a request/letter of introduction from your nearest embassy.

If there's any chance you may enter Zaïre twice, get a double-entry visa because obtaining an extension in Zaïre is time-consuming. In Kinshasa, the process takes four or five days and requires a letter from your embassy. The service de Immigration will ask for two photos, a vaccination card, a medical certificate of health (to show you don't have any transmittable diseases) and a letter from your embassy. The certificate of 'good health' can be obtained from any small polyclinic without undergoing any test or examinations. As for the letter of introduction, if you wrote the letter yourself, many embassies will just stamp it. The British Embassy charges £5 for this and, reportedly, much more if they write the letter themselves. You can also get visa extensions in most of the major cities.

If you'll be travelling overland to/from Uvira or neighbouring Burundi, don't panic if you only have a single entry visa. It's true that the most frequently travelled road (via Bukavu on Lake Kivu) is like a snake, passing in and out of Zaïre and Rwanda, but as you leave Zaïre for the first time, the Zaïrois border guards aren't supposed to stamp your passport – they don't consider you to be leaving because 25 km down the road you'll be winding back into Zaïre again.

If officials at the second border point are hurting for money, they may hassle you and either demand a *cadeau* (gift) or make you buy another visa there. This is unlikely to happen if you're travelling by bus, but it might if you're hitching or travelling by private vehicle. Even if it does, the cost won't be any more than what you would have paid for the more expensive double-entry visa! As for the short Rwandan leg of the journey, you can get a transit visa at the border.

If you will be travelling to/from Brazzaville (Congo) via the ferry at Kinshasa, you'll need a *laissez-passer* to cross the river in addition to a visa, but reportedly this is no longer required – better double-check, however. They are issued in Brazzaville by the Zaïre Embassy and in Kinshasa by the Service d'Immigration de Zaïre at the corner of Ave Tombeur and Ave du Plateau. The process takes 24 hours in Brazzaville and 24 to 48 hours in Kinshasa.

You'll be taking a risk if you wait until arriving in Brazzaville to get a Zaïre visa. They will issue you a visa (in 48 hours) and then refuse to issue you a laissez-passer on the grounds that a laissez-passer is issued only to people with visas obtained elsewhere. It sounds ridiculous, but don't take a chance. You risk having to dish out a small fortune to fly the 10 km between the two cities!

In Kinshasa, you can get visas to all neighbouring countries. Most embassies require a letter of introduction from your embassy. Those for the Congo cost about US$13 and are issued in two days. Those for Gabon (Zone de Kitambo) cost three times as much but are issued while you wait. You can also get visas to Burundi in Bukavu (184 Ave du Président Mobutu) and to Zambia in Lubumbashi. Rwandan visas, however, are no longer issued in Goma or Bukavu. If you have no Rwandan visa, you may be able to get a *permit provisoir*, good for seven days, at the border for US$50! Or ask at the Belgian Embassy in Bukavu or Goma; they have been able to help some travellers.

Diplomatic Missions Abroad Abidjan, Accra, Addis Ababa, Algiers, Athens, Bangui, Berlin, Berne, Bonn, Brasilia, Brazzaville, Brussels, Bujumbura, Cairo, Conakry, Cotonou, Dakar, Dar es Salaam, Geneva, The Hague, Harare, Kampala, Kigali, Lagos, Libreville, Lisbon, Lomé, London, Luanda, Lusaka, Luxemburg, Madrid, Monrovia, Nairobi, Nouakchott, New Delhi, N'Djamena, New York, Ottawa, Paris, Rabat, Rome, Stockholm, Tokyo, Tunis, Vienna, Washington, Yaoundé. Consulate: Kigoma (a visa takes two weeks there!).

MONEY

US$1 = 200 Z
£1 = 350 Z

The unit of currency is the zaïre (Z). Inflation is high. Real prices, however, are fairly constant because the zaïre is a floating currency, which is why prices herein are given in US dollars. For the same reason, the black market rate is virtually the same as the official rate, although it improves the further you move from Kinshasa. The principal advantage of changing money in small shops or on the street is the huge savings in time – a few minutes compared to an hour or more at the banks. Don't let them load you up with 5 and 10 Z notes, otherwise you'll need a wheelbarrow to cart them away.

Currency declaration forms were abolished in 1986 but not everyone seems to realise this, especially around Kisangani. Some immigration officers, for instance, still demand to see them. So some travellers recommended asking the border patrol or airport officials for a currency form; chances are they'll say the forms are no longer required but then give you one anyway. Without a form, you are fair game for the inland police. Being hassled by them is common because no one can make ends meet on a meagre government salary. Everyone wants a *cadeau*. Still, many travellers pass through Zaïre without any problems.

Cashing travellers' cheques can be a

major problem is Zaïre. Commission ranges from 1% to 20% and many banks outside Kinshasa won't accept them. Outside Kinshasa, the best bank for changing travellers' cheques is the Banque Commerciale Zaïroise. Their commission is very low and their service is faster.

Banking hours: weekdays 8.30 to 11 am for changing money; closed weekends. Banks: Barclay's, Citibank, Banque Commerciale Zaïroise, Banque de Kinshasa, Banque de Zaïre, Union des Banques Zaïroises (avoid).

GENERAL INFORMATION
Health

A vaccination against yellow fever is required. Zaïre is one of the African countries worst hit by the AIDS (*SIDA* in French) epidemic, so avoid prostitutes. Malaria is also particularly bad here. Almost every Peace Corps volunteer seems to have had at least one bout, and in eastern Zaïre the problem is worse because there's a chloroquine-resistant variety.

The quality of the hospitals is poor. In case of an emergency, try Centre Medical de Kinshasa (tel 23156/7) or Clinique de Ngaliema (tel 30315/7) on Ave des Cliniques. In Kinshasa, you'll find several pharmacies along Blvd du 30 Juin as well as Interpharma at the Intercontinental hotel.

Security

Security is a major problem in Kinshasa. In terms of danger, other Central African cities are peanuts compared to Kinshasa, and only Lagos in Nigeria can rival it in West Africa. The problem is theft and assault, not murder. There's an average of about one reported assault/theft a day on foreigners. Groups with knives and guns have attacked travellers in broad daylight, so even walking around Kinshasa during the daytime poses some risk. The downtown area around the Memling Hôtel is particularly bad. Avoid wearing jewellery and watches, and don't carry so much money that your pockets are bulging.

If possible, avoid arriving at Kinshasa airport during the night. Just driving from there to the city centre is risky and you may be stopped along the way by bandits. And carry a passport with you at night, otherwise the police are likely to hit you with a fine if they stop you.

Security is also a major problem in Zongo (across the river from Bangui). It has been called the 'biggest den of bandits in Africa'. Don't spend the night there. One group on an overland truck that camped there was raided by a group of about 40 locals who pinched everything in sight and left some nasty injuries. The incidents of theft between Zongo and Bumba is also extremely high, so travel in a group. If you're driving, pick up other foreign travellers.

Business Hours

Business: weekdays 8 am to 12.30 pm and 2.30 to 5 pm, Saturday 8 am to 12 noon. Government: weekdays 8 am to 12.30 pm and 1 to 4 pm, Saturday 8 am to 1 pm.

Public Holidays

1 January, 4 January, 1 May, 20 May, 24 June (Zaïre Day), 30 June (Independence), 1 August, 14 October, 27 October, 17 November, 24 November (Anniversary of the New Regime), 25 December.

Photography

A photo permit is required. The Office National du Tourisme (TOURZAIRE) issues them as well as some border posts. You'll find TOURZAIRE at Kinshasa airport, downtown Kinshasa, Bukavu, Goma, Moanda and Bunia. The cost is negligible. Taking photos of government buildings, airports, bridges, dams, ports (ie anything of military importance) and personnel is forbidden. Avoid taking snapshots where police might see you; the chances are good they will think of some rule you've violated. Police have nabbed travellers for taking snapshots of such scenes as markets, so be careful.

Time, Post, Phone & Telex

When it's noon in Kinshasa, it's 11 am in London and 7 am in New York (8 am during daylight savings time). Eastern Zaïre and the southern Shaba area are one hour ahead of Kinshasa time. The post restante in Kinshasa is fairly reliable. International telephone connections are good and, for Africa, relatively cheap. You can call from the post office on Blvd du 30 Juin in Kinshasa until late at night; the rate per minute to the UK is the equivalent of about US$2 a minute. Calls to the US cost about 20% more. There are telex facilities at the post office as well as at the Intercontinental hotel.

GETTING THERE

Air

From Europe, there are direct flights to Kinshasa from Brussels, Frankfurt, Geneva, Lisbon, London, Paris and Zurich. You could also fly to Brazzaville (Congo) and take the ferry across to Kinshasa, but you'd have to get a laissez-passer in Brazzaville, which takes 24 hours.

There are no direct flights from New York. You could fly via Abidjan (Ivory Coast) on Air Afrique, via Lagos (Nigeria) on Nigeria Airways or, better, via Europe.

Car

Few people go through the incredible hassle of getting to Zaïre by vehicle. However, to get from Central or West Africa to East Africa, there's almost no way to avoid Zaïre. The most frequently travelled route is via the Central African Republic and the north-east corner of Zaïre – from Bangui (CAR) to Bukavu (2503 km) via Bangassou (CAR), Kisangani, Komanda, Butembo and Goma. Since the principle route is quite a challenge in itself, the alternate routes – Bangui to Kisangani via Lisala, and Kisangani to Bukavu via Kindu – are not recommended. The chances of finding petrol between Kisangani and Goma (1136 km) are poor, so you'll need jerry cans.

You'll pass through three rainfall zones: the north around Bangui where there's a dry spell from November to February, the equator zone around Kisangani where it rains all year, and the area south of the equator where there's a heavy rain season from February to May. Most of the route is north of the equator, so from December to February is a slightly better time to be travelling. When it rains, the muddy roads are as bad as you'll find anywhere in Africa. Getting stuck is guaranteed. The worst stretches are from Bangassou to Buta and from Kisangani to Goma. It's not unusual to hear of people taking two days to make it just from Bangassou to Bondo, a 200-km stretch.

From Bukavu, you can head east to Kenya via Rwanda and Uganda, south to Lubumbashi and Zambia via the Lake Tanganyika steamer, or south-east to Burundi and Tanzania (via the newly paved Cyangugu-Bujumbura road or the older route via Uvira).

Getting to Kinshasa by car is no easy feat. You could drive south from Cameroun, passing through Gabon and the Congo, and take the ferry over from Brazzaville. The road is not paved for the most part but it is passable all year; the straight driving time is one week, a day or two more during the heavy rain season, from February to May. Alternatively, you could take the Bangui-Brazzaville or Kinshasa-Kisangani ferry/river boats. Driving between these points is impossible.

Freighter

A few wealthy souls come to Zaïre by way of freighter. From Antwerp, you can go with Compagnie Maritime Zaïroise or Compagnie Maritime Belge, both of which offer bi-weekly service to Matadi, Zaïre, stopping in Dakar and Abidjan. Compagnie Maritime Belge, for instance, charges about US$2000 to US$2500 for a 17-day, one-way trip. In downtown Kinshasa, see CMZ (tel 24602) or AMIZA (tel 24602/3) at the intersection of Aviateurs and l'Equateur, two blocks from the US Embassy.

GETTING AROUND

Air

Air Zaïre (tel 76222 – 24 hour information) has a bad reputation, but service has improved since 1986 when UTA started managing it. Moreover, they offer a 40% discount to those under 26 with student ID, although many offices require that you also produce a letter from your university stating that you are in Africa for studying purposes, ie research. Regardless, it takes a lot of talking. Air Zaïre has frequent flights to all of the major interior cities (as well as service to other African countries). Kinshasa/Goma, for example, costs about US$130 one-way.

There are several reliable airlines offering regular passenger service that are not listed in the airline schedule books. The most well-known is Scibe-Airlift (tel 22276/23562, telex 21057) on Ave des Inflammables in Kinshasa, which offers a 50% discount to students with student cards but is less reliable (frequent and long delays) than Air Zaïre.

Zairean Airlines (tel 23533, telex 21525) on Blvd du 30 Juin in Kinshasa, ACS (Air Charter Service) (tel 28502/27891) and Katale are others. For correct information, you'll have to go to their head offices and not agencies. ACS, for example, has flights from Kinshasa to Lubumbashi on Tuesday and Saturday around 8.30 am and return flights on Wednesday morning and Saturday afternoon. It also has two flights a week to Bukavu.

One traveller reported getting a free lift on one of Scibe-Airlift's cargo planes, but it took a few days of talking and a lot of smiles.

There are also regional airlines which fly only between towns in a given region. VAC (Virguna Air Charters), for example, has daily flights between Goma and Bukavu as well as weekly flights from Goma to Beni, Kindu and Kalemie. Swala and Broussair are two others that fly between Goma and Bukavu. In addition, Air Rwanda offers roundtrip flights from Kigali to Goma on Saturdays. To charter a plane, contact Scibe-Airlift or Zaïrean Airlines.

Car

Few people travelling overland in Zaïre risk taking their own vehicles; the roads are simply terrible. Forget it unless you have a four-wheel drive vehicle or road bike.

Driving from Kinshasa to Lubumbashi is feasible, but few people attempt it because the trip takes two weeks and the roads are bad, the worst section being from Idiofa to Mweka. Getting stuck after a rainfall is almost guaranteed. You'll only find petrol in Kikwit, Ilebo (black market), Kananga, Mbuji-Mayi, Kamina and Kolwezi, so bring about four jerry cans. There's a ferry at Ilebo.

Most frequently, those who decide to take a vehicle through Zaïre are those on their way to Kenya and East Africa; they almost invariably take the route from Bangui (CAR) to Lake Kivu via Kisangani. This is an extremely tough route and usually very muddy, but the trip is done all the time by local truckers and by well-equipped and well-manned overland trucks from London to Nairobi. The best (and driest) time for doing this stretch is December-February and June-September. See the Overland Bangui-Lake Kivu section following.

Car Rental

In Kinshasa, Eurocar, Avis and several local companies all rent vehicles. Avis is also represented in Lubumbashi.

Overland by Taxi, Train, Bus, Truck

Kinshasa-east/west If you're headed west towards the coast to Matadi (362 km), take the SNCZ train. In Kinshasa, the train station is on Blvd du 30 Juin about three blocks from the SOZACOM skyscraper. The train takes about eight hours, leaving Kinshasa every Monday, Wednesday and Friday at 7.15 am, and from Matadi on alternate days at the same hour. A deluxe cabin with a meal costs about US$12; 2nd class costs about US$4.

If you're headed east all the way to Lake Kivu (2867 km), count on the trip overland via Kananga taking four to five weeks, which is why almost everyone flies or takes the boat from Kinshasa to Kisangani (roughly two weeks) and trucks/buses from there to Lake Kivu (another week).

Kinshasa-Lubumbashi Travelling south-east from Kinshasa all the way to Lubumbashi (2916 km) takes 10 to 14 days. It's an exhausting trip but logistically simple (unless you're driving) compared to, say, the Bangui-Bukavu trip through north-eastern Zaïre.

The trick is getting to Ilebo (932 km), because once you're there, you can take a twice-weekly train to Lubumbashi. The quickest way is by vehicle. Trucks direct to Ilebo leave every day and take two days. Or, better, take a luxury bus to Kikwit. They leave Kinshasa from the SOTRAZ depot near the post office every morning and afternoon; the road is paved all the way. From there you'll find trucks heading for towns in the direction of Ilebo which is 405 km away.

The most painless way to get to Ilebo is by the ONATRA river boats – the *Mudimbi* and the *Gungu* – which leave weekly in either direction taking six days up river and four days back. They're comparable to ONATRA's steamers to Kisangani, which have three cabin classes. A final possibility is by barge. They plough very slowly up and down this stretch of river; getting a ride is reportedly not too difficult.

From Ilebo, the *ordinaire* train departs on Tuesdays and the *rapide*, which has a dining car, on Saturdays. From Lubumbashi, they leave on Saturdays and Thursdays, respectively. But verify this at the train station or ONATRA; schedules change frequently in Africa. Students with a school ID get a 50% discount. Both trains take about four days and are in atrocious condition – among the worst in Africa. Even budget travellers recommend going 1st class if you're travelling the entire distance (about US$20 on the ordinaire); 2nd class is bad news and 3rd class is an absolute nightmare. Nick North's description of this 'mobile slum' says it all:

The term 'first class' is something of a misnomer to say the least. The train could more accurately be described as a mobile slum. There was no water or electricity and none of the windows had glass in them. Our first class compartment had no door and the table over the sink had disappeared. Everything was thickly coated with the grime of many years. The seats had huge holes in them from which the foam stuffing had been torn, the back of one seat (which would have formed the middle bunk) had been completely destroyed, leaving only the wooden frame. The top bunks were relatively intact, though at night you could hear rats running up and down what used to be the ventilation shafts along the roof.

Add to this such delights as a woman eating peanuts while watching her child go to the toilet on a cloth on her lap, and then seeing her simply fold the cloth up and put it to one side, and you get an idea of the quality of the journey. A man with a brush did come along occasionally and sweep up the peanut shells, sugar cane pulp, fruit peelings, children's urine, etc.

Notwithstanding all this, the journey itself was slightly disappointing, though some of the views during the latter part of the trip were excellent. There was quite a lot of food available up until the last day, but most of this food was fruit and therefore most likely seasonal – we were pleased we had taken extra supplies from Lubumbashi. We left at 1 pm on Saturday and arrived in Ilebo at 6 pm on Wednesday.

Lubumbashi-Lake Kivu On the south-north, Lubumbashi-Bukavu route, most travellers take either the Lubumbashi-Kindu train and trucks from Kindu to Bukavu (580 km to the east on Lake Kivu), or the Lubumbashi-Kalemie train to Lake Tanganyika and a ferry north to Uvira/Kalundu (120 km south of Bukavu). You can catch the trains and ferries only once a week, however. In Kindu, the train departs southward on Friday or Saturday and takes three or four days, sometimes longer. If you have school ID, ask for the 50% student discount. Drunks are sometimes a problem, so as the Paul Simon song says, make a friend – he'll be your bodyguard.

The Zaïrois ferry from Kalemie has several classes. First class is a two-bed cabin with shower; 3rd class is the deck. The schedule is fixed in principle but highly erratic in practice. How long the ferry stays at a port depends on how much cargo there is to load and unload. Moreover, it frequently breaks down. When I was there in mid-1986, only the north-south Tanzanian ferry connecting Bujumbura and Mpulungu (Zambia) was operating. Chances are the ferry won't arrive before it's scheduled to; just don't be surprised if it leaves a lot later, even days later. For what it's worth, the schedule is as follows:

Arrive		Depart
Kalemie	---	4 pm Sun
Kigoma	7 am Mon	2 pm Mon
Kalundu	7 am Tues	9 am Tues
Bujumbura	10 am Wed	12 pm Tues
Kalundu	1 pm Tues	4 pm Tues
Kigoma	7 am Wed	4 pm Wed
Kalemie	7 am Thurs	---

Bangui-Lake Kivu Bangui (CAR) south-east to Bukavu (2503 km), cutting across the north-east corner of Zaïre, is the major route connecting Central and East Africa. Those who can withstand the bumps, breakdowns and long waiting times on this arduous trip will be rewarded by the opportunity of seeing some of the most spectacular scenery in Africa, including Virunga National Park and the snow-capped Ruwenzori mountains. Take a week off and climb them; you'll never forget it!

Most of the route is north of the equator, the driest part of the year being from December to February. Even then, it rains and most stretches of roads are muddy. About half-way through Virunga National Park you'll cross the equator, south of which the rains fall heaviest from February to May. Not counting major stops along the way, the trip on the major route takes roughly 10 to 14 days – three weeks or more if it's raining heavily.

The most well-travelled road is Bangui/Bangassou/Buta/Kisangani, then Komanda/Butembo/Goma/Bukavu. There are three major variations: Bangui to Kisangani via Zongo and Lisala instead of Bangassou (CAR); Buta to Komanda via Isiro instead of Kisangani; and Kisangani to

Bukavu via Kindu instead of Komanda and Goma.

Getting from Bangui to Bangassou is no problem; buses do the trip in two days. There, you'll find a ferry. If it's not working, take a pirogue (canoe). The Bangassou-Buta road is terrible and worse than the Buta-Kisangani stretch. Both are well-travelled, so finding a ride shouldn't be too difficult. In Buta and Kisangani, you must report to immigration. They may want a *matabiche* (bribe).

Kisangani is a hub for travellers coming from all directions. So getting the latest travel information should be easy from here on. Trucks are about all you'll find between Kisangani and Goma except in Beni (taxis morning and afternoon to Butembo) and Butembo (early morning buses to Goma on Mondays and Thursdays). In Kisangani, you'll find trucks about six km from the centre in Kibibi; look around the market for a ride. The Goma-Bukavu road is excellent all year round. Buses do the trip in five or six hours. The Goma-Bukavu ferry takes about the same time.

Bangui-Lake Kivu – alternative routes The great advantage of taking the first alternative route via Zongo, Bumba and Kisangani is the possibility of catching the Kinshasa-Kisangani river boat, which is surely one of the great highlights of any trip to Zaïre. You'll encounter rain year-round on this route except around Bangui, where there's a dry spell from November to February. There's a ferry from Bangui to Zongo every day except Sunday until around 4 pm; the Zaïre immigration offices are closed, however, on Saturday afternoons and Sundays.

You'll find a bank in Zongo as well as in Gemena and Bumba. Getting from Zongo to Lisala by a series of trucks can easily take three days. From Lisala or Bumba you can catch the river boat. It passes three times a month in either direction, leaving Kinshasa on Monday afternoons and arriving in Lisala and Bumba seven or eight days later. From there, it's another three days to Kisangani. The ferry people can tell you exactly the location of the steamer on its journey.

If you can't wait for the boat, you'll have to catch a truck to Buta and another on to Kisangani or take one of the many barges that tugs pull up and down the river between Bumba and Kisangani. It may take a few beers to convince the barge captain to take you along. You'll have more breathing room than on the river boats, but the barges are very slow and take a week or more to Kisangani.

Taking the second alternative route, via Buta, Isiro and Komanda, means you'll miss Kisangani, an interesting city. It's also less travelled, so you should expect much greater difficulty in finding trucks.

The third alternative route, via Kisangani, Kindu and Bukavu, is even more challenging. From February to May, you are likely to encounter impassable sections. Just getting to Kindu takes a week, sometimes two, because the traffic between Lubutu (connected by an asphalt road to Kisangani) and Kindu is almost non-existent. Here's what one traveller, John Kelly, had to say about it:

From Kisangani we headed to Bukavu via Lubutu. It was mid-March, a distance of 1200 km and it took us 10 days putting in at least 10 hours every day. Any further into the wet season and we would have been stuck in Zaïre for some time.

It rates as the most desperate piece of road I've ever encountered. It should not be attempted by people not willing or equipped to dig themselves out of bogs above their wheel-arches up to five or six times a day. There are log bridges that will need rebuilding and a well directed prayer before you can cross. A good winch would be your single most valuable possession, and even in the dry season if you need parts or service on your vehicle, it's going to take several weeks to get to either and back. We spent five days in the middle without seeing another vehicle. Even when perfectly dry it would be a bloody horrible road because it is cut up so much. It was quite an achievement to get through it and is amongst my most vivid memories of Africa.

As for the towns along the way, Punia has very little of anything and is worth avoiding, especially since the Securité Nationale people are going to want

to see you if you stay overnight and probably accuse you of being mercenaries.

Kindu is pretty reliable for petrol; get it at the depot downstream beside the river. But if the train hasn't been in for a while, you'll have to buy it off blokes in the street with 44 gallon drums for about US$1 per litre instead of US 40c. There is a big Indian population here; these are the fellows to change money with and get information about the roads. Get as many different opinions on the road ahead in as many different places as you can. They'll all be different. The trick is to decide which ones are nearest the truth. We had to make several detours because of broken bridges.

Kamituga can be heaven if you're on this road and it's in the condition it was for us. It's a mining town and signifies the last of the really bad road. It has a very reliable petrol supply. To find this go to 'The Club', the executive watering hole for the mining company. If nothing else you can get a terrific meal here of lamb chops and real vegetables with soup and dessert for US$2. There's cold beer and if you meet one of the ex-pats, they'll probably offer to put you up in the company's guesthouse and line up petrol and a mechanic if you need one, as well as shout you drinks all night.

Because of broken bridges, only those on motorcycles should attempt the more direct Punia-Bukavu road. Incredibly, vehicles have made it but time-wise it's longer. Instead of travelling by road, you could take the Kisangani-Ubundu train and the three-class, Ubundu-Kindu steamer, which takes four to six days. You're likely to end up waiting days for one or the other to depart, however. If there were one time to break down and buy an airline ticket, this would have to be it.

Bangui-Kinshasa You could take the twice monthly riverboat from Bangui to Brazzaville. See the Central African Republic chapter.

Lake Kivu-East Africa If you're at Lake Kivu and headed to East Africa, you'll find it easy to cross the border at Bukavu or Goma (before 6 pm) and catch minibuses to Kigali (Rwanda) via asphalt roads – a half-day trip. If you're headed to Burundi, you'll have to take a bus or bush taxi from Bukavu south to Uvira on a road full of pot-holes. A bus leaves

Bukavu every day between 7 and 7.30 am; another leaves in the afternoon. Taxis leave when they fill up. From Uvira, take a short taxi ride to the Burundi border, then on to Bujumbura by bus, altogether a five to seven hour trip from Bukavu, depending on connections. Money changers abound at the border.

Kinshasa-Kisangani Steamer

One of the great African adventures is taking the steam boat up the famous Zaïre (ex-Congo) River from Kinshasa to Kisangani or vice versa – a 1734-km trip. You'll pass by numerous villages and through some of the thickest rainforests in Africa. This trip is not for everyone by a long shot. It's hot and muggy and far from tranquil. Over a thousand people will be floating along with you, most of them on the three or more barges tied to the steamer's bow.

The place is a floating zoo with chickens cackling, pigs squealing, goats tied up anywhere and everywhere, live crocodiles, loads of dead monkeys and other wild animals piled on the deck along the way, waiting to be put under ice. You'll find the smell of smoked fish everywhere, people sprawled all over the deck, radios blasting away, people joking, babies crying and Primus beer flowing all during the trip (making it a good occasion to make some Zaïrois friends).

Each boat has three classes of cabins. First-class is two bunk beds, a cabinet, toilet and shower. Each steamer also has one or two 1st-class deluxe cabins which are about 60% more expensive and have air-con; meals are served in the air-con dining room or your room.

Second class consists simply of three or four bunk beds. For a shower, you'll have to share a crude one on the barge roof. Unless your group occupies an entire room, you won't be able to lock your cabin (thieves abound). And expect your cabin mates to stuff all manner of things inside. Second-class passengers can eat in the 1st-class dining room (US$2 a meal) and drink at the bar but only beer is available.

Third class is the incredibly crowded deck; finding space to sleep isn't easy. Make sure your ticket has a cabin number written on it; otherwise, you may find all the cabins full.

Fares per person (paid in zaïres) are approximately as follows: US$170 for 1st-class deluxe, US$115 for 1st class, US$45 for 2nd class, and US$32 for 3rd class. Fares from Bumba to Kisangani are about one-quarter these amounts. ONATRA reportedly offers student fares, so enquire. First class includes three western-style meals; 2nd and 3rd class include one filling meal a day, typically rice, beans and meat (frequently monkey).

You can buy food all along the way (sardines, fresh bread, rice and occasionally fresh fruit) as well as eat in the 1st-class dining room for about US$2.50 a meal. The water is not treated, so bring bottled water or purification tablets.

The length of the trip varies with the height of the river. The average journey time is 11 to 12 days to Kisangani and seven days for the return (six days when the river is high). The steamer leaves Kinshasa three times a month on Monday at 5 pm, and Kisangani three times a month on Friday or Saturday. Going upriver, you should be at Mbandaka by day four, Bumba by Wednesday, and Kisangani by Saturday. Don't be surprised if the boat is several days late. A broken motor is not an uncommon event. One traveller reported three children dying on the way, the steamer stopping for their funerals.

There are three steamers which plough this course. The best is the *Colonel Kokolo*, followed by the *Colonel Tshatshi* and the *Colonel Ebeya*. But double-check this. Every now and then, one is overhauled. The boat stops at Bolobo, Mbandaka, Lisala, Bumba and Basoko. If you're limited for time, you could take the steamer from Kinshasa to, say, Mbandaka and fly back.

For information and reservations in

Kinshasa, go to the harbour or the Division des Tarifs on the 2nd floor of ONATRA (tel 24761/-4 ext 1136), across from the city's major landmark – the SOZACOM skyscraper. They don't accept reservations by phone or telex, but they do accept them from travel agents. You have to be on the boat hours before departure. If not, forget your cabin. They sell more tickets than there are beds.

You could also take a cargo boat. The best places to ask are AVC and Nocafex, companies next to each other on the harbour beach. If there's a boat leaving, you can get on one by being friendly and buying a few beers for the captain. You'll need an official government authorisation, but the captain can and probably will get this for you.

Western Zaïre

KINSHASA

Kinshasa is a vibrant city that evokes a variety of opinions. On the one hand, it's huge (3½ million people), muggy and dangerous. On the other hand, the nightlife is as lively as, or livelier than, anywhere else in Africa, and its restaurants compare favourably with those in Abidjan and Dakar. Also, the city's lay-out is more attractive than that of many African cities.

No city in Africa has a street so dominating and impressive as the Blvd du 30 Juin, the Champs-Elysées of Africa. It's eight lanes wide and runs almost the full length of the city. On it you'll find many of Kinshasa's major stores and offices, the main post office, and the city's number one landmark – the 22-storey SOZACOM building (the mineral marketing company). About five km from the centre along the river, you'll come to Gombé. It's a chic residential area where you'll find the Hôtel Intercontinental, far and away the city's best hotel, and the Peace Corps (4383 Ave des Bourgmestres), a good place to pick up information about travelling upcountry.

The pulse of the city, however, is the Cité (see-TAY), the main artery being Ave Kasa-Vubu, which runs perpendicular to the Blvd du 30 Juin, starting at the post office. When you arrive at Le Rond Point Victoire, four km down Kasa-Vubu, you'll be in the heart – the Zone de Matongé (mah-tone-JHAY). This is the vibrant African quarter where you'll find cheap hotels, lively bars, African food and the Zaïrois musical groups on which the country stakes its reputation.

Almost any night of the week you can walk into the Vis-à-Vis nightclub around midnight and hear OK Jazz, one of Zaïre's most famous groups. If you get tired of 'Congo' music, go and listen to the Bobongo Stars, a rock band that plays on Friday nights. No other city in Africa has as much live entertainment as Kinshasa.

Information

Tourist Office The national tourist agency, TOURZAIRE (tel 25858), has offices at the airport and downtown at Résidence de la Rwindi on Blvd du 30 Juin. They issue photo permits.

Banks Zaïrois banks are notoriously slow, so Barclays downtown at 191 Ave l'Equateur is probably the best bank for changing money. Banks: Barclays (tel 22356), Citibank, Banque de Paris et des Pays Bas, BCZ (Banque Commerciale Zaïroise), UZB (Union Zaïroise de Banques). You can also change money in Kinshasa at the airport or at the Intercontinental and Memling hotels, even if you're not a guest.

Embassies Some of the principal embassies are:

Angola
    (tel 32415) 4413-29 Blvd du 30 Juin
Belgium
    (tel 25525, telex 21114) Building Cinquanten, Place du 27-Octobre, BP 899
Burundi
    (tel 31588) 4687 Ave de la Gombé
Canada
    (tel 22706, telex 21403) Edifice Shell, Blvd du 30 Juin, BP 8341

CAR
    (tel 30417) 11 Ave Pumbu
Congo
    (tel 30220) 179 Blvd du 30 Juin
France
    (tel 22669, telex 21674) Ave République du Tchad, BP 3093
Gabon
    (tel 68343, telex 21455) Ave 24 Novembre, BP 9592
West
    Germany (tel 26933, telex 21110) 201 Lumpungu, BP 8400
Japan
    (tel 22118) Ave Mbuji-Mayi, BP 3668
Kenya
    (tel 30117) 5002 Ave Ouganda
Netherlands
    (tel 30638, telex 21126) 11 Ave Zongo-Ntolo, BP 10299
Rwanda
    (tel 30327) 50 Ave de la Justice
UK
    (tel 23483/4/5) Ave de l'Equateur, BP 8049
USA
    (tel 25881/2/3, telex 21625) Ave des Aviateurs, BP 697
Zambia
    (tel 23038) 54 Ave de Ecole

Other embassies include: Algeria, Austria, Benin, Brazil, Cameroun, Chad, Egypt, Ethiopia, Guinea, Italy, India, Ivory Coast, Liberia, Mauritania, Morocco, Nigeria, Portugal, Spain, Sweden, Switzerland, Tanzania, Togo, Uganda.

Bookshops Kinshasa's bookstores are nothing to write home about. Two of the better ones are L'Echoppe, near SOZACOM at the modern Galeries Présidentielles shopping complex on Blvd du 30 Juin, and La Détente at 3 Ave Mbuji-Mayi, just off Ave de la Justice in Gombé. Magazines and newspapers in English usually arrive at the Intercontinental's bookshop on Tuesday afternoon.

Supermarkets Two of the most popular supermarkets are Express Alimentation on Blvd du 30 Juin, a block from Hôtel Memling, and Super Yaya two blocks away at the intersection of l'Equateur and Aviateurs. Both carry inexpensive L'Eau Vive mineral water.

Travel Agencies Two of the best travel agencies are Amiza (tel 24602/3, telex 21019), two blocks from the US Embassy at the corner of Aviateurs and Equateur, and Zaïre Travel Service (tel 23232/88) at 11 Blvd du 30 Juin near Hôtel Memling. Two others are ZC Voyages (tel 23418/26784, telex 21586) downtown at Lukusa and Bandundu Avenues, and Zaïre Safari (tel 24889/25828) on Blvd du 30 Juin. All of them arrange trips to eastern Zaïre, including Virunga park, Lake Kivu, Bukavu and the gorilla sanctuary in Kahuzi-Biega park. Expect to pay about US$1000 a person for a nine-day trip – more if there are only a few of you.

Cité
Kinshasa is a city to experience, not 'see'. If you spend all your time in the Cité area, fraternising with the locals, you will be experiencing far more than looking at Kinshasa's sights. Many nightclubs become lively starting around 9 pm. The bars liven up a few hours before.

Marché Central
As in most cities, the Marché Central is fascinating; vendors sell everything from rice and fish to locusts and snakes. You'll find it about six blocks behind Hôtel Memling in the direction of the Cité. Go before 2 pm, when it starts closing down.

Academie des Beaux-Arts
If you're in the Hôtel Intercontinental area, stop by l'Academie des Beaux-Arts on Ave 24 Novembre a few km away. Started by the Jesuits in 1953, it's a fine arts academy where on Sundays from 10 am to noon, you can buy student pieces. Next door the the city's museum.

Cité de l'OUA
Five km further west along the river you'll come to the Mont-Ngaliema quarter and the

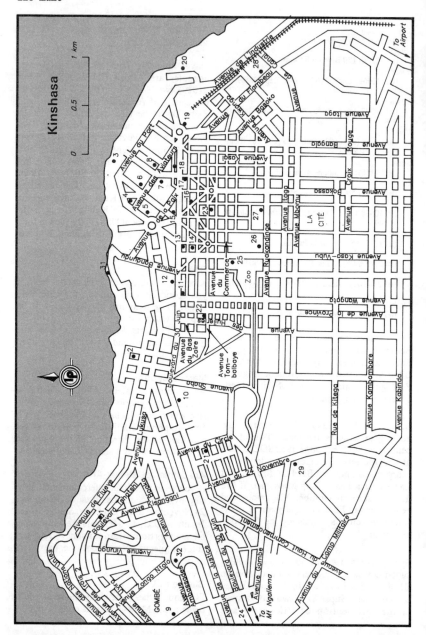

Kinshasa

1	Chez Tao Restaurant
2	Centre d'Accueil Protestante
3	Brazzaville Ferry
4	Le Plein Vent Restaurant
5	Mona Lisa Restaurant
6	AMIZA Travel Agency
7	Café de la Presse
8	US Embassy
9	Intercontinental
10	Le Mandarin Restaurant
11	Cozy Restaurant
12	Bus Terminal
13	Post Office
14	Jambo Jambo Nightclub
15	Kin's Inn & Big Steak
16	Hôtel Memling
17	La Gaffe Restaurant
18	SOZACOM skyscraper & New Bistro
19	Train Station
20	River Boat Port
21	Peace Corps
22	L'Etrier Restaurant
23	Immigration
24	Golf Course
25	Restaurant du Zoo
26	Parc de la Revolution
27	Marché Central
28	Guest House Hotel
29	Beaux Arts Centre
30	Stade du 24 Novembre
31	ONATRE Ferries Booking Office
32	Place de la Victoire

Cité de l'OUA, the site of the 1967 Organization of African Unity conference. You'll get a feeling for how extravagantly African governments spend on these affairs – elegant houses for each head of state, a huge conference hall, restaurant and swimming pool. And the conferences only last four days! The presidential palace is here as well. The best place to observe the rapids and have a picnic is near Mimosas Island.

Chutes de Zongo

You can travel to these major rapids some 70 km downriver from Kinshasa. Zaïre Safaris on Blvd du 30 Juin next to the Sabena building charges US$60 and up, depending on the size of the group. Or, much cheaper, take a taxi to the *rapides* downriver on the outskirts of town just beyond the president's residence.

Places to Stay – bottom end

One of the best places for the money is the *Centre d'Accueil Protestante* (tel 22852). For a clean room with dirty communal bathrooms, they charge about US$5 a bed, slightly less if you say you're Protestant. Beware – unwary travellers occasionally get ripped off. It's in a quiet residential area on Ave Kalemie, several blocks off Blvd du 30 Juin near the Casier Judicial, a 15-minute walk towards the river from the post office. If you arrive after 3 pm, the manager may have left.

Most of the cheap hotels are in the Cité, particularly around the Rond Point Victoire, an area that's anything but tranquil. Many of them are reluctant to give you a room because they're used as brothels which brings them more money. Still, they're decent and a tip may help get you a room. At 28 Ave du Stade du 20 Mai, a street leading from the Rond Point towards the stadium, you'll find *Hôtel Yaki*, which has a friendly management and charges about US$4 a room.

The well-known *Hôtel Matongé* (tel 68066) is nearby on the same street and a stone's throw from the Rond Point. It's in a different league and quieter than many. They charge from about US$6 to US$15 for five categories of rooms; the more expensive ones have air-con. Even if it's full, which is usually the case, the popular terrace is a good place for a drink. As in many hotels throughout Zaïre, they won't allow two men to stay in the same room.

Hôtel le Creche is two blocks away on the opposite side of the Rond Point. They charge about US$7 to US$10 for five categories of rooms, all with air-con. It's as popular as the Matongé and the noisiest hotel around because of the band on the top-floor terrace, which literally fills the entire Rond Point with music at night on weekends.

For a hotel with dirt cheap prices, about US$2 a night, try *Hôtel Kita Kita* on Ave Croix Rouge, which runs into Kasa-Vubu eight blocks behind the central market, roughly half way between Blvd de 30 Juin and the Rond Point. Another one in the same price range is *Hôtel Sanda*, just to the left of Kasa-Vubu as you're walking towards the Matongé area from downtown. *Hôtel Mini Kapi*, at 88 Rue Sundi, is yet another.

Places to Stay – middle

For a medium priced hotel, try the eight-room *Hôtel Estoril* downtown on Ave du Flambeau on the eastern side of Blvd du 30 Juin. It's near the train station, a short walk from the heart of town, and charges US$25 to US$30 for a decent room. Thieves have ambushed travellers walking in broad daylight in this and other areas of Kinshasa, so be watchful. It's better than the *Guest-House* (tel 30295/23490), which has a good restaurant and charges about US$5/10 for singles/doubles. It is further out on the same street and not within walking distance of downtown, but easily reached by taxi.

One of the better hotels in Kinshasa in the US$10 a night category is *Afrique Hôtel* (tel 31911). The beds, bathrooms and lighting are all poor, but the rooms are clean, the air-con works, the management is friendly, and there's a pleasant area outdoors for drinks. It's seven km from the city centre, but getting a taxi is a cinch because it's on the western extension of Blvd du 30 Juin (Ave Colonel Mpia), several km beyond the Intercontinental.

Places to Stay – top end

The 500-room *Intercontinental* has no serious competitors. It has everything from squash and tennis courts to a bank, travel agency and pharmacy. The drawbacks are the high room prices, which don't include tennis and squash, and the suburban location, about five km from the centre. In the centre, the newly renovated *Memling*, run by Sabena, is clearly the best, plus the 325 rooms are large and less expensive and there are always taxis outside.

For a beautiful, tranquil setting, try the *Okapi* about 10 km from downtown – a US$6 taxi ride. It's the most reasonably priced of the three major hotels, and has two tennis courts and an olympic-size pool. Taxis are usually stationed there during the day and early evening.

Intercontinental (tel 27284/27355, telex 21212), US$115 to US$145 for singles and US$125 to US$160 for doubles, pool, tennis, squash, casino, bank, travel agent, Avis, pharmacy, shops, cards AE, Visa, D, MC.

Hôtel Memling (tel 23261/5, telex 21654), about US$60 to US$80 for rooms, pool, gym, casino, disco, video room, panoramic restaurant, cards AE.

Hôtel Okapi (tel 80020/81444), about US$45/55 for singles/doubles, pool, tennis, cards AE, D, CB.

Places to Eat

Cheap Eats Finding cheap food in the Cité area is no problem, especially around Le Rond Point Victoire. A bowl of beans and rice will cost you less than US$0.50. Finding a cheap restaurant downtown is something else. For inexpensive sandwiches and cheap local beer, try *La Gaffe* on Blvd du 30 Juin near SOZACOM. *Kilimanjaro*, a popular pastry shop with ice cream and sandwiches, is a block away near the US Embassy. It's open Monday to Saturday until 6.30 pm. Around the Memling are three other pastry shops with dine-in facilities, such as *Patisserie Moseka*.

For a decent meal in the US$3 to US$6 range, you can't beat *Café de la Presse* across from the US Embassy and *Mona Lisa* (tel 23193) three blocks away at 58 Ave du Port, about a block from Air Zaïre. Both serve full meals as well as sandwiches. Of the two, the Mona Lisa is clearly better, but it's also a little more expensive.

African *Moambe* – a spicy sauce with peanuts, palm oil, meat (typically chicken) and served with rice – is the national dish. Grilled *capitaine* (perch) is another favourite. Ordinary African food, such as *fufu* (a mashed potatoes-like glob of yams and manioc), *maboké* (a local fish), brochettes and all kinds of greens are sold on the streets in the Cité.

One of the best African restaurants is *Inzia* (tel 30435), also known as Chez Mama

Ekila. It's at 6 Ave Cadeza in Gombé. You can order exotic dishes such as *porc-épic* (porcupine), *phacochère* (wart hog), *gazelle* antelope) and *singe* (monkey) as well as ordinary fresh water fish, such as *capitaine*. They also serve more common Zaïrois dishes such as *fufu* (mashed manioc or yams), Zaïrois rice and a local specialty called *loso*.

You can also get good Zaïrois food and continental dishes at the *Restaurant du Zoo* (tel 23395), an old favourite from colonial days. Closed Monday, it's reasonably priced and near downtown at the corner of Ave Kasa-Vubu and Commerce, four blocks off Blvd du 30 Juin.

French Three of the finest and most expensive French restaurants (open for dinner only) are *Le Caf Conc* (tel 26132) at 13 Ave de la Nation, *L'Etrier* (tel 22583) in Gombé at the corner of Ave des Huileries and Ebeya, and *La Devinière* (tel 81571) in Binza 10 km from downtown. The Caf Conc, which is closed Monday, specialises in shell fish and, like L'Etrier, offers piano music. La Devinière has the nicest setting of any restaurant with a magnificent view from the villa's terrace. It's closed on Sundays.

Another superb French restaurant is *Le Relais* (tel 26574) in the heart of town on Blvd du 30 Juin, one block from the Memling. Open for lunch and dinner (except Sunday lunch), it also offers piano music on Monday, Wednesday, Friday and Saturday. *La Pergola* (tel 23313, also a block from the Memling at 16 Rue Bas-Zaïre, offers good French food as well as Zaïrois specialities. The dining area is outside under a thatched roof.

For somewhat more moderately priced French meals, try *Kin's Inn* (tel 25211) next to Le Relais. Open every day except Sunday from noon to midnight, it has a big menu, good music and a popular bar. *Big Steak*, next door and closed Monday, is equally popular, as is the modern *New Bistro* (tel 23763), which is down the street at the SOZACOM building and has a short menu but good French food. It is closed on Sundays.

Swiss About the only place in Central Africa that specialises in Swiss fondue is *Le Plein Vent* (tel 25318), which is three blocks off Blvd du 30 Juin on Ave du Port running along the river. It's on the top floor of the Flamboyant building, a block from Super Yaya supermarket; the view of the river is superb. Open for dinner from Tuesday to Sunday, they offer seven cheese and meat fondues for about US$10.

Chinese The best Chinese restaurant is unquestionably *Le Mandarin* (tel 22068) on the 7th floor of the INSS building on Blvd du 30 Juin. The menu is extensive and if you like, you can eat outside. You won't regret this one.

Indian For Indian food, your only choice is *Cozy* (tel 23540) on Blvd du 30 Juin in a shopping centre in Gombé. Considering the very reasonable prices, you aren't likely to complain about the food, which is good but nothing special. It's closed on Mondays.

Entertainment & Sports

Bars Along Blvd du 30 Juin near the Memling you'll find *Kin's Inn*, which has a terrific pub-like bar, and *Big Steak* next door, with a terrace that is perfect for people-watching. For cheap beers, try *La Gaffe* on the same street, a block before the SOZACOM skyscraper. It has a street-side patio and is a block from *New Bistro*, a modern restaurant next to SOZACOM with a bar that's about as popular with expatriates as Kin's Inn.

All around the Rond Point Victoire, there are innumerable African bars (*ngandas*). Two good places to start are *Club le Palmare* and a second *Big Steak* nearby. From Wednesday to Saturday, musicians play on Big Steak's terrace overlooking the Rond Point.

Nightclubs Nightspots with Zaïrois musicians are all in the Cité. A good place to start is *Hôtel la Creche*, facing the Rond Point Victoire. It has a Zaïrois band playing on its roof-top terrace from Thursday to Saturday starting fairly early in the evening, and there's no cover charge.

One of the most well-known places is *Vis-à-Vis* next door to Hôtel la Creche, where Viva la Musica and the ever-popular OK Jazz, which performed for the first time in 1956, play from Friday to Sunday starting around midnight. Other groups play during the rest of the week. Nearby on Rue Gambela, you'll find *Chez Kara*, which has an orchestra seven days a week, and *Un-Deux-Trois*, the centre for the Zaïrois Musical Union and a popular outdoor dancing place. Two other popular ones are *Faubourg* and *Veve Centre*.

M'Bilia Bel sings at *Type Ka*, at the corner of Ave de la Funa and Blvd Central, while at the large *La Maison Blanche*, a good km from the Rond Point at the intersection of Ave de l'Université and Bongolo, a famous group invariably performs on the weekends.

For dancing to recorded Zaïrois music, the common people head for places such as *Daito Dancing Club*, on Ave du Stade du 20 Mai about 300 metres from the Rond Point Victoire, and *Karmel* a block away. Both are usually packed.

Expatriates tend to prefer the flashy discos with western music in 'their' area. Three of the most popular are *VIP* (closed Sunday), several blocks behind the Palladium movie theatre on Blvd du 30 Juin, *Jambo-Jambo* (closed Sunday), not far away behind the main post office, and *Play Boy Club* (open every day), at Hôtel Singa on Ave du Flambeau. Jambo usually has a band; the others don't.

On Friday nights around midnight, the under-30 crowd all head to *Bobongo* (closed from Sunday to Wednesday), also on Ave du

Flambeau several km from the city centre. That's the only time you can hear the *Bobongo Stars*, a very popular African band that plays western music. The cover is about US$5 on Friday and US$2.50 on Thursday and Saturday, when there's recorded music. *Big Boy*, another strobe-lit disco, is only two blocks away.

Cinemas The cinemas all have one showing nightly starting at 8.30 pm. The best is Palladium (tel 23290) on Blvd du 30 Juin near the post office. In the Cité, there's Venus at the Rond Point Victoire.

Sports The major private sporting club is the Amicale Sportive de Kinshasa (tel 59467) in Joli-Parc, about 10 km from downtown beyond the Intercontinental. If you're a good tennis player, they might let you play. The Intercontinental and, further out of town, the Okapi both have courts; the Intercontinental charges about US$6 an hour for the use of its tennis and squash courts. For US$5 more, you can play with the club pro. For US$5, non-guests can use the Intercontinental's pool, but only from 10 am to 12 noon on weekends. Serious swimmers may prefer the Hôtel Okapi's olympic-size pool.

The *Cercle de Kinshasa* (tel 31731) has an 18-hole golf course with sand greens and rough fairways. Non-members can play during specified hours. It's on Blvd du 30 Juin near the Intercontinental.

Americans play softball on Saturday and Sunday afternoons; see the marines at the US Embassy.

Things To Buy

Artisan Goods L'Académie des Beaux-Arts on Ave du 24 November only opens its two display rooms on Sunday from 10 am to noon. Student pieces for sale, many of which are influenced by European art, include oil paintings, modern works of sculpture, ceramics and wood carvings. Nearby, at the intersection of Ave Kisangani and Boka, is the Centre Culturel Boboto (tel 30001), which offers a similar selection and is open

from 9am to noon every day and 4.30 to 6 pm from Monday to Thursday. You'll find cheaper, inferior oil paintings downtown at the Petit Marché behind Hôtel Régina, which is several blocks from the train station on Blvd du 30 Juin.

Malachite You don't have to buy ivory to come home with jewellery that's truly African. The beautiful dark green malachite from southern Zaïre is sold all over Africa and it's less expensive and less morally reprehensible than ivory. Downtown across from the train station at the end of Blvd du 30 Juin is the Marché de l'Ivoire, one of the cheapest places to buy malachite necklaces and other jewellery, as well as Zaïrois masks.

Nearby, across from the US Embassy, Procure St Anne has a shop where you can buy malachite, as well as wood sculpture, carved chests, stationery and Zaïrois dolls. The church's shop is open weekdays from 10 am to midday and 3.30 to 5 pm and Saturday from 10 am to midday. For the finest, most beautifully carved malachite in town, head for L'Artiste Shabien on Ave de l'Equateur, three blocks from the US Embassy. Prices are high and fixed.

Music Zaïre's 'Congo' music is at the top of all the Central and West African 'pop' charts. The Latin influence is obvious; you may at first think you're listening to rumba music. Over the past two decades, Congo music has exercised a profound influence over the musical development of the rest of black Africa. Today, every bar in Central and West Africa seems to be playing it. For records, if you don't find anything in the Galeries Présidentielles, try Sedec on Ave Isiro, and Sansui on Ave de la Paix.

Two of the leading stars are Tabu Ley and Franco, while Kanda Bongo is one of Zaïre's wizards of soukous. Others are Samaguana, OK Jazz, Langa Langa, Bella Bella, M'Bongo, Papa Wemba, and female vocalists Pongo Love, M'Bilia Bel and Tshala Muana. The Zaïrois honour their musicians by giving them titles. Tabu Ley is

Seigneur Rochereau, Franco Luambo is Maître Franco, and the deceased Kasanda was called Docteur Nico.

Franco, along with Hilarion Nguema of Gabon, has taken on the cause of AIDS. One of his songs that hit number one on the African hit parade warns, 'you, brothers and sisters, carriers of the virus, don't contaminate the others', and calls on students 'not to let themselves be attracted by any unknown person', alluding to the widespread use of prostitutes by students in the large cities.

Getting There & Away
Air Air Zaïre flies to all major inland cities. Scibe-Airlift, Zaïrian Airlines and Air Charter Service offer more limited service; they are less reliable than Air Zaïre.

From Congo-Brazzaville – the ferry
Between Kinshasa and Brazzaville, there are ferries every hour on the hour in both directions starting at 8 am, the last one leaving at 5 pm, with no ferry at 1 pm. The trip takes only 20 minutes, but you should get there about 45 minutes in advance to allow sufficient time to clear customs. There are two ferries. The Congolese one is newer and costs about CFA 2750 (CFA 1000 less for student card holders) one-way or roundtrip, whereas the Zaïrois ferry costs the equivalent of about US$2. The Zaïrois ferry leaves Kinshasa at 8 am, Brazzaville at 9 am, etc. The Congolese ferry leaves Brazzaville at 8 am, Kinshasa at 9 am, etc. Without a *laissez passer*, you won't be allowed on.

From the CAR – the steamer There's a riverboat from Bangui to Brazzaville twice a month. See the Central African Republic chapter.

From Rwanda/Burundi – overland There are good road connections from Rwanda and Burundi to Goma and Bukavu, both on Lake Kivu. The most popular overland route from Lake Kivu to Kinshasa is by truck and bus to Butembo and Kisangani, and by river boat from there to Kinshasa. You cannot travel overland from Kisangani to Kinshasa except by heading south all the way to Kananga.

From Zambia – overland The most popular overland route from Zambia to Kinshasa is by bus, bush taxi or train to Lubumbashi, by train from there to Ilebo (four days), by truck from there to Kikwit, and by bus from there to Kinshasa. Once a week, you can also take a river boat from Ilebo to Kinshasa.

Getting Around
Airport Transport At Kinshasa's N'Djili airport, there's a departure tax of US$10. You'll find a bank, Avis, Hertz and a restaurant. The cheapest way to get downtown (25 km) is by public bus. Number 16 passes by on the main highway in front of the airport every half hour. Downtown, you can catch this bus on Ave Kasa-Vubu next to the post office. A taxi should cost no more than the equivalent of US$15 regardless of the exchange rate unless you arrive at night when the rates go up. From the city centre to the airport, you can get cabs for half this rate on the street but not at the hotels.

Bus SOTRAZ buses are cheap and ply all the main routes, particularly Blvd du 30 Juin and Ave Kasa-Vubu. The SOTRAZ station is downtown near the post office. You'll find buses headed for Matadi and, twice daily, for Kikwit.

Taxi Taxis do not have meters. A seat in a shared cab costs the equivalent of about US$0.30. A 'charter' (taxi to yourself) costs a minimum of US$2, more if the ride is more than about four km. Expect to pay about US$5 to US$6 per hour and US$40 plus petrol by the day. At night, rates go up and taxis are difficult to find except at the Intercontinental in the Corniche and in the centre next to the Memling hotel, where they're stationed all night.

Car Rental You'll find Eurocar (tel 25966, telex 21530) in the Mayombe building on Blvd du 30 Juin, Hertz (tel 23322, telex 21191) at 11 Ave des Aviateurs, and Avis (tel 28005/23260) at the Intercontinental and Memling hotels. Amiza (tel 24602), a tourist agency, also rents cars.

LE LAC DE MA VALLEE
To see some of the countryside, hire a cab for the day in Kinshasa and head south-west along the road to Matadi. Some 30 km along the road you'll come to signs pointing to Le Lac de Ma Vallée, a small lake with scenic surroundings, a restaurant and waterfalls two km away where you can swim.

Travelling another 95 km south-west on the road to Matadi will bring you to Les Jardins Botaniques de Kisantu, a botanical garden with plants from all over the world and a restaurant.

MBANZA-NGUNGU
Some 30 km beyond the jardins botanique, the road to Matadi passes through Mbanza-Ngungu (population 100,000). This was a resort area for the Belgians in colonial times because of its temperate climate. You could take the train or bus there.

The *Cosmopolite* is the city's best hotel and quite pleasant. Ask the kids to show you the prehistoric *grottes* (caves) five km away.

MATADI
Matadi, 352 km south-west of Kinshasa, is Zaïre's major port. Outside of Matadi, you can see the village of Palabala with a great view of the river, the *cavernes* (large caves) inhabited by fishermen, and Vivi, the first capital of the Congo, where Stanley lived. Then climb Mt Cambier (502 metres) for a marvellous view of the Zaïre River, the Yelaba rapids, and the surrounding mountains.

Places to Stay
The 31-room *Le Central* (tel 2687), at 1 Ave Débarcadère, is one hotel, but there are probably cheaper ones. The city's finest is the 63-room *Le Métropole*.

Getting There & Away

Car ferries will take you across the river to Vivi and the huge Inga dam 40 km upriver.

MUANDA

Some 242 km west of Matadi, Muanda is Zaïre's major beach resort. Only about 100 of the 594-km road to Kinshasa remain unpaved. You can get there by bus or plane. The major ocean-front hotel is the 32-room *Mangrove* (tel 9), which has a pool and tennis court.

Eastern Zaïre

BUKAVU

On the southern edge of Lake Kivu, Bukavu (BOU-kah-vou) is one of the most picturesque cities in Zaïre. At 1500 metres altitude, it's also one of the most pleasant. In part for this reason, there are a number of schools as well as the Peace Corps training centre, perched on a hill with a superb view of the lake. Just below the training centre is a good place to take a dip in the lake. It's a beautiful lake and safe for swimming because the mineral ash content in the water kills off not only the fish but also the snails that carry bilharzia.

The city's lay-out is easy to understand because many of the commercial establishments are along two major streets – Ave Président Mobutu, which winds eastward along the lake shore towards Kadutu, a major residential area for the working people, and Ave des Martyrs de la Révolution, which extends from Place du 24 Novembre near the centre southward for two km to Place Major Vangu. Most of the major commercial establishments and pricier hotels plus the cathedral and Peace Corps training centre are along the former, while most of the cheap hotels, bars and restaurants, Marché Maman Mobutu (the main market) and truck parks are along the latter.

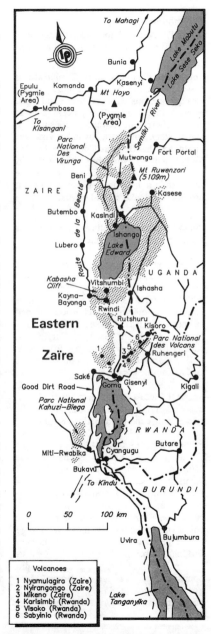

Volcanoes
1 Nyamulagira (Zaïre)
2 Nyirangongo (Zaïre)
3 Mikeno (Zaïre)
4 Karisimbi (Rwanda)
5 Visoko (Rwanda)
6 Sabyinio (Rwanda)

Information

Banks The best bank for changing travellers' cheques is the Bangue Commercial Zaïroise.

Consulates The Burundi Consulate is downtown at 184 Ave Mobutu; they accept visa applications only between 3 and 5 pm, Monday to Thursday. The process takes 24 hours. There's no Rwandan consulate. If you're stuck without a Rwandan visa, you might try the Belgian Consulate on Ave Mobutu a little beyond the cathedral; they're sometimes helpful. Even if they're successful in helping you get a visa, the process could take several weeks.

Photo Supplies Try Bolingo near Amiza on the main road, Ave Mobutu.

Travel Agency The main travel agency is Amiza (tel 2476). It's on Ave Mobutu near the main intersection, as is Tourzaire (tel 3001). Hôtel Résidence, about 150 from Amiza, is where you'll find offices for most airlines and travel agencies, including Zaïre Travel Service and Somaco. For trips to Kahuzi-Biega, Amiza charges from about US$55 per person for a group of four to US$85 for one person alone.

Hospital There's a hospital on the road north out of town staffed by American doctors. The cost of drugs and examinations is minimal.

Places to Stay – bottom end

For the price, it's hard to beat the *Anglican Mission*, with rooms for about US$0.50. Another winner is *Hôtel Canadien*. It's on Ave Mobutu 200 metres beyond the cathedral and opposite the Burundi consulate. Rooms with shared bathrooms cost about US$3; for 50% more, you can get a large room with two beds, private bathroom and lounge chairs.

On the same street and in the centre opposite *Hôtel Résidence* is *Hôtel Keba* – good value at US$5/4 for a double with/without a bathroom. As in many Zaïrois

hotels, they charge more for two men in the same room. The only other cheapie in the commercial centre is *Hôtel Métropole* (tel 2690) on Ave Mobutu, near the main intersection. Poorly managed and not recommended, it has three classes of rooms for US$4 to $6.

Most of the budget hotels, however, are not downtown but along Ave des Martyrs de la Révolution, along with lots of cheap

1	Hôtel Riviera
2	Broussair
3	Kivu Patisserie & Supermarket
4	Club des Anges Noirs
5	Swimming Dock
6	Air Zaïre
7	Lake Ferry Dock
8	Hôtel Métropole
9	Taxi Stand
10	Bank Commercial Zaïroise
11	Peace Corps Training Centre
12	Ferry Ticket Office
13	Amiza Travel Agency, Bolingo Pharmacy
14	Hôtel La Frégate
15	Bank
16	Taxi Stop for Kahuzi-Biega N P
17	Hôtel Tshikoma
18	Hôtel Keba
19	Hôtel Résidence
20	Prison
21	Banque du Peuple & La Pergola Snack Bar
22	Cathedral
23	Restaurant d'Eden
24	National Parks Office
25	Tourist Hotel
26	Belgian Consulate
27	Restaurant Mama na Bana
28	Hôtel Belle-Vue
29	Hôtel Canadien
30	Burundi Consulate
31	Post Office
32	Banque de Zaire
33	Hôtel Jolie Logis
34	Hôtel Moderne
35	Hôtel Taifa
36	Hôtel de la Victoire
37	Ruzizi Border Post
38	Mama Mobutu Market
39	Voix de Zaire
40	Hôtel Nambo
41	Bus Stop for Uvira

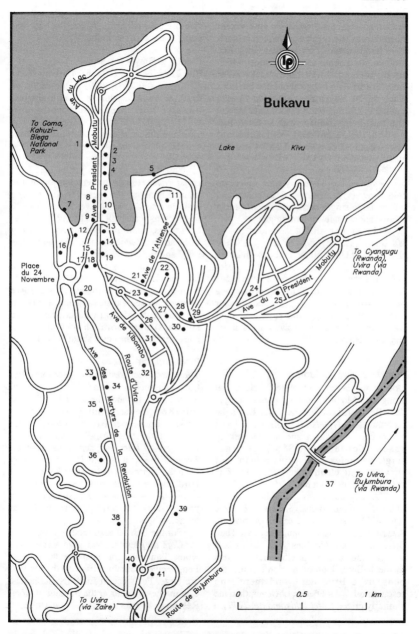

Bukavu

restaurants and bars. It's a lively area, except when the electricity goes out, which is much more frequent in this section than along Ave Mobutu. Two hotels along this street which have received fairly high marks from travellers are *Hôtel Tiafa* about one km from Place du 24 Novembre and *Hôtel Nambo* another km further out at Place Major Vangu. The Taifa is the liveliest, with an active bar, a good restaurant and cold showers; singles/doubles cost about US$3/4 and full meals cost about US$2.

The cozy Nambo charges about US$3.50 per room and has a friendly staff, quiet bar, cold showers, reasonably clean communal toilets, large single beds, and clean, simple rooms that are safe for storing gear.

Another you might consider is the *Mu-Unga* just beyond the marché. They charge about US$2.50 for a room with a bare bed and US$0.50 more for one with a bed, table and two chairs. Not recommended is *Hôtel Mareza* near the Taifa. It's primarily a brothel with a fairly noisy bar and cheaper rooms that are dingy and smelly without windows and more expensive ones that are airy and pleasant.

Places to Stay – middle

One of the better mid-range hotels is not along Ave Mobutu but on Ave des Martyrs de la Révolution before the Taifa. That's the recommended *Hôtel Joli Logis* which has a compound with lawn and ample parking space. For about US$5/7 you get singles/doubles with private bath, hot showers and clean sheets. The staff is friendly and there's a bar.

The only other two places in the centre of town are more expensive. *Hôtel la Frégate* (tel 2823) is in the dead centre of town on Ave Mobutu and has a popular courtyard bar. Spacious singles/doubles with basins and lounge chairs cost about US$9/12. Showers in the hallway bathrooms don't work, the beds are a little hard, and there's no restaurant. It's a lot better, however, than the similarly priced *Hôtel Tshikoma* (tel 2977), a

five-minute walk away. There, you may find there's no electricity before 9 pm.

Places to Stay – top end

The city's best hotel is the 42-room *Hôtel Résidence* (tel 2941/3039) in the centre of town at 89 Ave Mobutu. Large singles/doubles with breakfast cost around US$17/21 (US$24 for an apartment). It has various airline agencies, a boutique, art shop, a nightclub, and the city's best restaurant, the *Bodega*.

You'll get a good view of the lake from *Hôtel Riviera* (tel 2326), which is just off the main drag about 300 metres from the city's main intersection at 67 Ave du Lac. The 22 large rooms cost about US$13 and have clean bathrooms, comfortable chairs, satisfactory beds, and a view of the lake. The lounge has a TV and there is a restaurant.

Hôtel Belle-Vue (tel 2266), as the name implies, has a superb view of the lake. Well-managed with 13 rooms, it's at 143 Ave Mobutu just beyond the cathedral, a km from the dead centre of town. A clean room with a spotless bathroom, hot water and comfortable chairs costs about US$11.

Places to Eat

There are cheap restaurants near the Hôtel Canadien, such as *Mama Na Bana* about 100 metres away towards the cathedral. Open 7 am to 8 pm, they serve full meals for less than US$1. A little closer to town on Ave Mobutu you'll find the equally inexpensive *Restaurant d'Eden* and, across the street, *La Pergola* snackbar. About 100 metres away from the Métropole on the same street you'll find the town's best supermarket, *Alimentation Moderne de Bukavu* and a pastry shop, *Patisserie du Kivu*, a popular breakfast spot.

For the best African food in town, head for *Café du Peuple*, downtown across from Hôtel Tshikoma and near the ferry dock. People rave about this place and the portions are large. For western food, try the hotels. The medieval decor at the *Bodega* in Hôtel Résidence is quite attractive, but it's the food that makes this restaurant special. For about US$10, you can get a scrumptuous three-course meal including drink. For half that amount, you can get the Zaïrois special.

The restaurant at the Riviera has a large menu, with most dishes in the US$3 to $4 range. The restaurant at the Belle-Vue overlooks the lake and is inexpensive, with most main dishes costing around US$3.

Entertainment

Bukavu is full of small bars playing African music all night, especially along Ave des Martyrs de la Révolution. Some of them get pretty wild as the night progresses. As for places in the centre along Ave Mobutu, the Métropole has a lively bar, but the *Club des Anges Noirs* across the street is a much better place for a drink and is highly recommended. It's a bar with good music and lots of tables.

On weekends there's a disco at the Riviera which starts up around 9.30 pm, and the Résidence has the top nightclub in town.

Getting There & Away

Air ACS flies Kinshasa/Bukavu twice a week, departing Bukavu on Mondays and Fridays. Both Amiza and Somaco travel agencies make reservations. If you can't get a seat, fly to Goma. ACS has three flights a week (Monday, Thursday, Friday from Kinshasa) as does Air Zaïre (Wednesday, Friday and Saturday from Goma). The one-way fare to Goma is about US$130. From Goma, try getting one of the two daily flights to Bukavu on VAC (Virunga Air Charters).

A plane leaves Goma every day at 8 am and 4 pm. *Swala* also flies Goma/Bukavu/Goma on Sundays, Wednesdays and Fridays for about US$30. Both Virunga and Swala have offices at Hôtel Résidence. Their schedules could easily change. Broussair is another ailine that flies from Bukavu to Goma, as well as Beni, Bunia, Kisangani and other cities in the region.

Boat Alternatively, you could take the ferry across Lake Kivu. There are two. The *Matadi*

(also called *La Vedette*) takes six hours, leaving Bukavu on Tuesday and Friday at 7 am and leaving Goma on Wednesday and Saturday at the same hour. You must reserve not later than the morning before. You should show up at the docks before 9.30 am and wait in line. Bring your passport as well. The wait in the queue shouldn't take more than half an hour if you make your presence known, otherwise it could take all day. Once you get the ticket you will need to get it validated as well – for a small fee. The cost is about US$4 and seats are numbered. Breakfast and beer is available on board. 'Le grand bateau' (*Karisimbi*) takes cargo as well as passengers and leaves Bukavu on Wednesdays at 7.30 am and Goma on Saturdays at the same hour. The trip takes 10 hours, reservations aren't required, and the price is US$1.50.

Bus & Truck While most traveller's heading north prefer taking the boat, you'll see the scenery at closer range going overland. There is one public bus a week. Minibuses heading north toward Goma usually start from the Place du 24 Novembre, while the BRALIMA brewery two km further north on the edge of Goma is a good place to look for trucks. One public bus departs from Goma on Saturday mornings around 10 or 11 am, and from Bukavu on Sunday mornings around the same time. The trip takes about six hours – more during the rainy season. The road is excellent and the scenery exhilarating.

If you're headed south to Uvira or Bujumbura, you'll find taxis and trucks at the Place Major Vangu at the top of Ave des Martyrs de la Révolution, two km from the city centre. The public bus departs from there every day at around 7 pm. See the introductory chapter Getting Around regarding the visa complications of crossing over into Rwanda on the way to Uvira. Two other places to look for trucks are Marché Maman Mobutu and on Ave de l'Athenée close to the cathedral.

PARC NATIONAL DE KAHUZI-BIEGA

The gorillas in the Parc National de Kahuzi-Biega are the major attraction. Don't miss the opportunity of seeing them. Whatever it costs, the experience will be worth 20 times that – guaranteed. Seeing a lion while you're protected in a vehicle is one thing; crawling through the mountainous bamboo forest for several hours and finding a silver back gorilla standing just a few metres in front of you is quite another. You'll never forget looking into a gorilla's brown, intelligent, curious eyes staring unblinking at you.

Weighing up to 200 kg, one of these gorillas could kill you in seconds. Yet they couldn't care less about humans. After all, gorillas don't eat flesh. Their favourite munchies are young bamboo and stalks of wild celery. All they care about other than food is protecting the young ones, which are accustomed to a lot of body contact. If you get too close, the unpredictable male may pound the ground with his huge fists, stand up and growl, rip down small trees and stare at you in a threatening manner.

A typical family would have anywhere from six to 20 gorillas. The average size in Kahuzi-Biega is one dominant silver-back male, seven adults (males and females), five children and three babies. It is normal for female gorillas to transfer from their natal group into other groups or to join lone silverbacks, but it is rare for males to transfer to a new group. If the dominant silver-back coughs or grunts at the others, he is indicating displeasure or reprimanding them.

The sad thing is that killing by poachers has made them an endangered species. While 5000 to 15,000 were

reportedly surviving in Central Africa in the 1960s, today only about 350 remain.

Unlike in neighbouring Rwanda, you don't need a reservation to see the gorillas, except perhaps on Sundays, but you should arrive there by 8 or 8.30 am (9 am if you have a reservation). For reservations go to the national park office in Bukavu at 185 Ave Mobutu. The office is open weekdays from 8.30 am to 3 pm and Saturdays from 8.30 am to 12 noon. The park is open even on holidays. Children under 15 are not allowed. The park fee is the equivalent of US$20; resident foreigners pay only about US$8. They no longer charge to take photos. There are several families in the park, but only one accustomed to humans is visited. Finding it normally takes one or two hours, so you may be back in Bukavu by early afternoon. Sometimes, however, it takes much longer. Tipping the guide and trackers is customary. Unless you go between June and mid-September, be prepared for rain and bring wet weather gear.

For a very small fee, you can camp at the park headquarters. Some travellers have camped off the road in the jungle several hundred metres before the headquarters and haven't been detected.

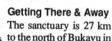

Getting There & Away

The sanctuary is 27 km to the north of Bukavu in a mountainous jungle area. Follow the asphalt road north towards Goma for 20 km until you come to Miti, a tiny village with a sign pointing to the left. The park entrance at Tschivanga Station is seven km up the hill. The cheapest way to get there is to take a truck or bus to Miti and hike from there.

However, plan on taking two days because if you arrive after 9.30 pm, the guide and bushwatchers with machetes will probably have departed. For food, try the small market in Miti. The simplest way is to hire a taxi. If you bargain well, the one-way fare shouldn't be more than US$15. The cost will quadruple if he waits. Getting a ride back is simple; almost anyone returning to Bukavu will take you. Also plenty of trucks pass through.

GOMA/GISENYI

Goma is the starting point for expeditions to Virunga park, which begins only a few km to the north. Unlike Bukavu, Goma is two km from the lake. To get a good view of it, the volcanoes and the nearby lava fields, you must climb Mt Goma nearby – an easy three-hour trip up and down. You can also visit Lac Vert (Green Lake) and the Baie de Saké (Saké Bay), 26 km west of Goma. At 1500 metres altitude, the city's climate is ideal.

There's nothing special about this rundown city itself, so if you have a Rwandan visa and a multiple-entry visa to Zaïre, consider crossing the Rwandan border (open 7 am to 6 pm for foreigners) two km away and spending the night in Gisenyi, about half the size of Goma. It's a delightful town right on the lake, but considerably more expensive. You won't find taxis at the border, but downtown Gisenyi is only a 30-minute walk from the border. Many travellers spend the night there before visiting Rwanda's Volcans park, where you can see gorillas and climb more volcanoes.

Information

Travel Agencies For trips to Virunga National Park, see Zaïre Safari at the Masques Hôtel, Amiza (tel 514), Tourzaire (tel 440) on Ave des Volcans, or Somaco. Most of these places are on or just off Ave Mobutu (the main road). For about US$0.80 a km, you can rent a mini-bus from Zaïre Safari. They also offer package tours but the cost is high. An all-inclusive tour for, say, three days will cost about US$330 a person for a couple and

US$255 a person for groups of four. So the larger the group, the lower the cost per person.

Banks The best bank for changing travellers' cheques is the Banque Commercial Zaïroise.

Gorilla Sanctuary From Goma it is relatively easy to see the mountain gorillas in Virunga park. The starting point is Djomba, 26 km east of Rutshuru. You should book ahead at the Institut Zaïrois pour la Conservation de la Nature, an enormous white compound downtown back of the Bank Commercial Zaïroise, and not easy to find. The fee was recently raised to about US$30 a person but is well worth it. Open daily from 9 to 11 am, they'll radio ahead to reserve accommodation if you wish. Starting time is around 8 or 8.30 am and it's a three-hour drive, so you'll need to leave around 5 am or so. If you're lucky you may be able to arrange a lift with other people booked for that day.

Places to Stay & Eat

Goma The two best places for the money are the *Catholic Mission Guesthouse* and *Hôtel Tuneko* nearby, both about three blocks west of the southernmost roundabout. The clean Mission charges about US$2.50/5 for spotlessly clean singles/doubles with breakfast. There are hot showers, a library, and basins in the rooms, but also two big minuses – a 10 pm curfew and an unappealing *mere* who rules the place with an iron fist. A stone's throw away, the pleasant Tuneko has rooms in the US$3 to US$7 range, a bar (noisy at times) and a tiny restaurant.

For a hole with rock bottom prices, about US$2 to US$3 a room, there's *Hôtel Abki* near the stadium and *Hôtel Haut-Zaïre*, behind the market. The Abki is very friendly, has a small restaurant, bucket showers, and will let you store gear while you climb the volcanoes. The Haut-Zaïre, on the other hand, has cell-like rooms, mosquitoes, intermittent water supply, ineffective locks and is not recommended. Two others in the

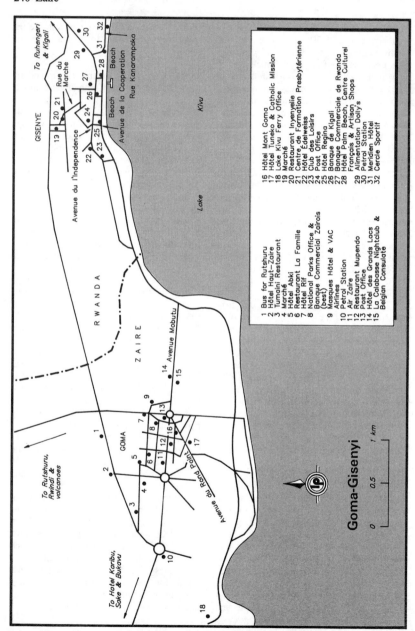

Goma-Gisenyi

0   0.5   1 km

1 Bus for Rutshuru
2 Hôtel Haut-Zaïre
3 Tumaini Restaurant
4 Marché
5 Hôtel Abki
6 Restaurant La Famille
7 Hôtel Rif
8 National Parks Office &
  Banque Commercial Zairois
  (best)
9 Mosques Hôtel & VAC
  Airlines
10 Petrol Station
11 Air Zaïre
12 Restaurant Mupendo
13 Post Office
14 Hôtel des Grands Lacs
15 La Calabasse Nightclub &
  Belgian Consulate

16 Hôtel Mont Goma
17 Hôtel Tuneko & Catholic Mission
18 Lake Kivu Ferry Office
19 Marché
20 Restaurant Inyenyelie
21 Centre de Formation Presbytérienne
22 Hôtel Edelweiss
23 Club des Loisirs
24 Post Office
25 Hôtel Regina
26 Banque de Kigali
27 Banque Commerciale de Rwanda
28 Hôtel Palm Beach, Centre Culturel
  Français & Artisan Shops
29 Alimentation Dolly's
30 Petrol Station
31 Meridien Hôtel
32 Cercle Sportif

same price range that have been recommended by travellers are the *Champres Aspro*, a friendly family-run hotel that allows travellers to use their stove, and *Guest House Mutara* near the market – clean but no electricity.

You can also camp at the *Cercle Sportif* for about US$1.50 per tent. It's filthy, however, and there's only one shower.

For a mid-range hotel there are only two choices. One is the 17-room *Hôtel Mont Goma* (tel 559), which is in the centre of town, one block from the southernmost roundabout. Room prices at the Mont Goma vary between about US$3 and US$10; most are in the US$6 to US$7 range. It, too, has a bar and restaurant. However, if you can get a room, you'll do better staying at the more popular *RIF Hôtel*, on the other side of the circle, near the Masques Hôtel. It has a variety of rooms in the same price range, a reportedly terrible restaurant, but a pleasant street-side terrace for drinks.

Goma's best hotels are *Hôtel Karibu* and *Masques Hôtel* (tel 540), followed by the *Hôtel des Grand Lacs* (tel 306). Most travellers on package tours stay at the Karibu. It's eight km west of town on the lake's edge and has a pool and 100 rooms for about US$22/30. Masques Hôtel is on the main drag in the heart of town near a major circle. It's a pleasant hotel with a popular terrace bar, a clean pool, a travel agency, and 62 singles/doubles for about US$17/21. Even if you're not a guest, they'll change your money.

The 51-room Grand Lac is 200 metres away on the same street, Ave Mobutu. It's a big, older hotel; the pool is unusable. Singles/doubles, which cost about US$9/18, are large and frayed, but the bar and restaurant are attractive and popular, plus the nightclub, *La Calabasse*, is one of the two best in town.

Gisenyi The two hotels closest to the border are *Hôtel Edelweiss* (tel 282), about 400 km off the lake, and *Hôtel Régina* (tel 263) on the water. The Edelweiss, which resembles a Swiss chalet, charges the equivalent of RFr1500/1700 (about US$19/21) for singles/doubles and allows those with vehicles to camp out the back. The restaurant is big on quantity and high on price but low on quality. The Régina nearby is only slightly more expensive. While the atmosphere is a little dreary, the rooms and bathrooms are clean, and the outdoor restaurant serves excellent grilled chicken and fish.

A five-minute walk further along the water will bring you to the heart of town and the *Meridien* (tel 381/2, telex 561 c/o Kigali Meridien, cards AE), by far Gisenyi's best hotel. For US$62/72 a night you get a pool, tennis courts, windsurfers and Hobie cats (for hotel guests only).

The cheap places to stay are a good 10-minute walk from the lake. The *Centre de Formation de l'Eglise Presbytérienne* charges RFr 300 (about US$4) for a bed in a dormitory room. The management is friendly and travellers are welcome. It's across the street from the well-known warehouse OPROVIA and African restaurant *Inyenyeli*, a five-minute walk from the market and a ten-minute walk down the hill to the beach.

For a drink, the most popular watering hole with foreigners is the bar at the *Hôtel Palm Beach*, next to the Meridien and overlooking the lake. At night, there's the popular *Galaxie* discotheque. The more adventurous might try the *Club des Loisirs*, the major night spot for the natives and primarily a bar with, reportedly, an occasional theatrical event. It's only a hundred metres or so from the Hôtel Edelweiss on the dirt road to Goma.

Getting There & Away

Air Both Air Zaïre and ACS have three flights a week from Kinshasa to Goma. Those on ACS leave on Monday, Thursday and Friday, returning on the same days plus Tuesday (connecting with a flight from Kisangani). Air Zaïre flies from Goma to Kinshasa on Wednesdays, Fridays and Saturdays.

Getting to eastern Zaïre is actually easier via Kigali (Rwanda) than via Kinshasa. On

Saturday, Air Rwanda offers a roundtrip flight Kigali/Goma/Kigali.

Between Goma and Bukavu, VAC (next to the Masques Hôtel) has two roundtrip flights a day, leaving Goma at 8 am and again at 4 pm. The cost is about US$30. Swala flies on Sundays, Wednesdays and Fridays. Still another is Broussair on Ave Mobutu, which offers service to Bukavu, Beni, Bunia, Kindu, Isiro and Kisangani.

Bus From Kigali you can take one of the numerous minibuses connecting with Gisenyi, a three-hour trip. There are also daily buses to Rutshuru leaving Goma around 2 pm and Rutshuru at 6.15 am. Get there several hours ahead of time to get a seat. In Goma the bus departs near Hôtel Haut-Zaïre.

There are also up to five buses a week from Goma north to Bunia via Butembo and Beni. The trip takes about 12 hours, longer during periods of heavy rains. Most travellers seem to prefer the company Butembo Safari Bus, which has service out of Goma on Wednesday and Saturday. You must buy your ticket the day before departure at Hôtel Tuneko. If you can't get a seat, you could always hitch. The Texaco station on the main roundabout is the place to look for rides.

While most travellers go by boat to Goma, you can also go by bus most days. One of the buses leaves on Saturday around 10 or 11 am from Hôtel Mont Goma, returning on Sunday. The road is in excellent condition and the scenery is superb.

Boat Travelling to/from Bukavu, most travellers prefer the boat, *Matadi* (also called *La Vedette*), which leaves on Wednesdays and Saturdays around 7 am, returning on Tuesdays and Fridays. You need to buy your ticket the day before departure. Both the Vedette and the bus take six hours and cost about US$4. The slower 'grand bateau' *Karisimbi* leaves on Saturday mornings around 7.30 am, returning on Wednesdays

and costs about US$1.50. Neither boat calls at Rwandan ports.

VIRUNGA NATIONAL PARK

Simply stated, Virunga is the most spectacular park in Central Africa. It's 780,000 hectares stretch some 300 km north from Goma along the borders with Rwanda and Uganda – one of the most geologically active regions in all Africa. Established in 1925 to preserve the mountain gorilla, Virunga is one of the oldest parks in Africa. It is contiguous with the Volcans National Park in Rwanda, Africa's principal gorilla sanctuary. Lake Edward, also called Lake Idi Amin, is in the centre of Virunga, with the world's largest concentration of hippos, an estimated 20,000.

Elsewhere in the park, you'll see volcanoes dominating marshy deltas, cool grassy plateaux and sun-baked plains filled with herds of antelope and other wild animals. Lava plains, deep equatorial forest, high altitude glaciers and snow fields round out the picture. The park's altitude is equally varied, from 798 metres in the south to the huge Ruwenzori mountains north of the lake, Africa's highest range. Along the slopes of Mt Ruwenzori, the tallest peak at 5119 metres, the rainfall measures more than 5000 mm (over 200 inches) annually. Bamboo grows up to a metre a day.

On a bright, fresh morning, the volcanoes may imbue you with a soaring sense of optimism, only to drop you into despair by the afternoon when they are generally masked by clouds. The best time is from December to January when the rains let up and in June, the first month of the dry season. During the rest of the dry season through to September, the skies are dusty, spoiling the views.

The remarkable diversity of habitats is reflected in the fauna and the large variety of animals: lion, buffalo, hippo, antelope, kob, topi, waterbuck, baboon, chimpanzee, the giraffe-like okapi, warthogs, and an occasional gorilla family wandering over from Rwanda.

The tree hyrax, a rabbit-size mammal that some Africans depend on for its meat and pelt, is virtually extinct in the lower valleys, as are the leopard and the duiker, a small antelope.

Until very recently, elephants roamed the Rwindi plains in the thousands; today you're lucky to see one. In the evening when the elephants come out of hiding to feed, the poachers are there waiting. So are the park patrol, over 40 of whom have been killed since 1961 in armed struggles with poachers.

Don't think that purchasing small pieces of ivory jewellery doesn't have an effect. Just between 1969 and the mid-1970s, the price of one kg of ivory soared from around US$8 to US$100. The inevitable happened – an Africa-wide elephant massacre. In neighbouring Uganda, the elephant population went from 30,000 to 2000 in the course of a few years.

Volcano Climbing

The two major volcanoes for climbing – Nyiragongo and Nyamulagira – are both near Goma. Nyiragongo (3470 metres) last erupted in 1977, sending a wall of lava three metres high at 80 km/hour into the valleys, killing 60 or 70 people, but stopping short of Goma, whose inhabitants had fled across the Rwandan border. It could erupt again. Still, people climb it all the time.

The starting point for Nyiragongo is near Kibati (1950 metres), 15 km north of Goma on the Rutshura road. Purchase all your food and charcoal there. You can get guides (compulsory) and porters (about US$5 a day) in Kibati or at the park entrance (the Camp des Guides) nearby. It's an unmarked white building at the foot of the volcano and within walking distance of the road. You can camp there, or if you booze it up with the friendly head guide he may allow you to sleep on his floor. The park fee, about US$10 including the cost of a guide, is good for about seven days and can be used for climbing Nyamulagira as well. Most hikers offer the guide about US$2 extra; for this he'll usually double as a porter.

In spite of the guards, thieves sometimes steal petrol from parked vehicles; so drain your tank. The climb is easy and takes four or five hours up and two to three hours down. No departures after 1 pm are allowed. On the way up you'll pass through jungle forest to two bare tin cabins 25 minutes' below the crater's rim. The cabins have beds and there is water nearby. Most hikers stay overnight, for two reasons: to see the volcano's impressive fires glowing in the dark, and to see the summit in the early morning, the only time it's free of the mist which usually starts moving in around 9 am. Near the top great clouds of sulphurous gas will tower above you and from the crater's lip you'll see the black, smoking platform of volcanic ash below.

The volcano, however, isn't always active, so you could be disappointed. Without a torch, you'll find the trip back at night to the cabin perilous. If you're climbing during the rainy season, be prepared for chilling temperatures. Regardless, it's always cold at night and in the early morning, so bring warm clothing.

The starting point for Nyamulagira (3056 metres), to the north-west of Nyiragongo, is about 40 km up the road from Nyiragongo. It's a three-day trip up and down. Unlike Nyiragongo, it has no boiling lava, but the view is even better and if you're lucky you may see a variety of animals along the way, including forest elephants.

The first day is spent driving or walking 40 km to the base camp; you'll pass through lovely rolling country dominated by towering volcanoes. Bring all your food as well as a tent as the base camp has no accommodation. The nearest water is three km away, so pay a boy to bring you some. The next day's hike takes five or six hours and is fairly gradual most of the way. First, you'll pass through lava fields supporting only lichens and small ferns, with occasional lava pools filled with inviting water. Next come dense forests with hundreds of different birds. You might also spot a herd of buffalo, antelope, buck, maybe even chimpanzees, elephant droppings and, if you're really lucky, a family of elephants.

Eventually, you'll arrive at an enormous rambling cabin with numerous rooms and plenty of beds. There's no stove, but you can cook dinner on top of an oil drum in the centre. If you hear an animal scream it's Bill de Bill, an old guide who died here and still haunts the cabin. The climb to the crater's rim takes another two hours; the views are spectacular. Descending into the crater you'll see lots of yellow sulphur deposits as well as a hut, which is a good place to brew some tea and wait out a possible hail storm. Flowers, shrubs and ferns abound; you may even see a steam-heated orchid. Descending the mountain takes up the rest of the day.

For more information on both climbs see the travel agents in Goma. They can also arrange transport.

Places to Stay

The park is well prepared for tourism. You'll find three government tourist lodges on the main road running north from Goma: *Hôtel de la Rwindi* at km 130, *Hôtel Kikyo* 165 km further north in Butembo, and *l'Auberge du Mont Hoyo*, another 184 km due north at Mt Hoyo.

RUTSHURU & THE PLAINS OF RWINDI

A two-hour drive (73 km) north of Goma on a good road will bring you to Rutshuru. The major tourist attractions are nearby – Rutshuru Falls, the warm springs of May Ya Moto and the gorillas. Ask the locals for the way to the falls and the hot springs.

Places to Stay & Eat

The *Mission Catholique*, which welcomes travellers, charges US$3 for a double and US$1 for meals. If you want to camp, they will probably allow you to do so for free. Cheaper still is a friendly boarding house 50 metres north of the police station on the opposite side of the street. The owner is friendly and charges about US$1.50 for a room with a shower and earth toilet.

The eight-room *Hôtel du Parc* is slightly upmarket, while the *Katata Hôtel* is the town's best and most expensive. Tourists invariably head on to *Hôtel de la Rwindi*, 57 km away to the west in the spectacular plains of Rwindi; it'll set you back about US$25 a person.

Camping around the lodge is illegal, but ask at the nearby village; they might let you camp there even if they don't want to let you use the village guesthouse. If you don't have an all-park entrance fee (about US$35), you'll have to pay another park fee at Rwindi of about US$15. Every morning, there's drama in the plains as kobs clash in trials of strength or in disputes over females. You have a choice of viewing routes, including the Ishasha, Kibirizi, Muhaha and Rwindi tracks.

GORILLA SANCTUARY

The starting point for visits to the gorillas is near Djomba, 26 km to the east of Rutshura. They live on the slopes of Sabinyo and Muside volcanoes bordering Rwanda. The two gorilla families, known as Oscar and Marcel, aren't as tame as those in Rwanda, but contact is likely, the cost is much less and getting a reservation is far easier. Up to eight people a day may visit them – two people is the limit for Oscar and six for Marcel. Usually you can get a reservation for the next day; at worst you may have to wait a day or two.

The only place to make reservations is at the IZCN office (open 9 to 11 am) in Goma; see the Goma section for the location. The fee, which includes a guide (tipping is expected), has risen to US$30, but you won't regret paying. If you don't have a reservation and go to Djomba, you can still join a group if they aren't full. Starting time is 8 or 8.30 am.

The departure point is seven km up the hill from Djomba. You can camp there for US$1.50 or stay in a hut with a stove for about US$4 per person. Villagers will sell you food – cooked if you like. You could also bunk at the *Mission Catholique* in Djomba for about US$6 with full board, or at the

American *Mission Baptiste* in Rwanguba five km up the road.

At a roundabout several km south of Rutshuru you'll see a sign indicating the turn-off for Djomba. The bus from Goma could drop you off there, but travel on this road is very light. The road is rough, requiring four-wheel drive, and may be impassable during heavy rains.

VITSHUMBI

Don't miss taking the 20-km trip north from Rutshuru to Vitshumbi, a fishing village of mud and thatched dwellings at the southern end of Lake Idi Amin – hippo heaven. Even as far away as the Rwindi hotel, you may be awakened by the snorting and wailing of one of these three-tonne nocturnal feeders trying to satisfy its 60-kg a-day eating habit. The lake's greatest concentration of hippos is found in Mwiga Bay, a paradise of aquatic birds, including egrets, white pelicans, and eagles perched on mud banks.

BUTEMBO

As you're travelling north from Rwindi to Butembo (165 km), you'll be passing through the rift valley and along the 'Route de la Beauté', with incredibly spectacular views. This road passes along the Kabasha escarpment and is relatively busy because of all the coffee, tea and banana plantations along the way.

Places to Stay & Eat

In Butembo, population 100,000, three of the better hotels are the Belgian-run *Hôtel Butembo* and *Lodgement Apollo II*, both on on the main road, and *Hôtel Semiliki* near the market. The Semiliki has a good restaurant and charges about US$3.50 for a double with shower, while the Apollo charges about half as much for a room with bucket showers. All have electricity in the evenings. You might also try one of the several missions in town.

A notch up the scale is the pleasant *Hôtel Ambiance*, which charges about US$5 for a double and has showers and washing facilities. Those on group tours invariably stay at the attractive 32-room *Hôtel Kikyo*, which costs at least US$15/20 for singles/doubles.

Getting There & Away

Finding a ride to Beni is no problem; minibuses ply the route constantly. There are also buses running between Goma and Bunia via Butembo at least five times a week. The more popular company, Butembo Bus Safari, departs from Butembo for Bunia on Mondays and Thursdays. If you hitch, the trip will probably take twice as long because of the stops along the way.

BENI

In Beni, 55 km north of Butembo, you'll get your first good view of the snow-capped Ruwenzoris if they're not covered in clouds. If you headed for the Ituri Forest (Pygmy territory), Beni will be the last town of any size you'll see for many days. The dirt roads

from here on can be treacherous, particularly if there is any rain.

Places to Stay & Eat

Tourists stay at the 11-room *Hôtel Beni*, which has the best rooms and serves good meals. To save money, you have a number of choices, many of which are within several hundred metres of the circle at the end of the main drag, such as *Lodge Sina Makosa*, *Hôtel Busa Beni*, which charges about US$2.50 a double, and, cheaper still, the friendly *Jambo Hôtel*, 30 metres from the circle.

The best of the cheapies, however, is *Hôtel Walaba*, about 100 metres east of the roundabout. It costs about US$1 for a twin room and has bucket showers and a cheap restaurant with meat, rice, beans and home-made bread. The staff speaks English and the Somali owner will change money. You can also cook there and store your luggage while you climb the Ruwenzoris. You could also try the mission five km east on the road to Mutwanga and Kasindi.

For a full breakfast costing US$1, try *Restaurant Ronde-Pointe* on the circle; it's highly recommended. There are also numerous small shops in the town centre, mostly Greek-owned, where hikers stock up for the Ruwenzori trek.

Getting There & Away

The road to Kasindi, not the lightly travelled road north from Rutshuru to Ishasha, is the major route to Uganda. If you're headed there or just to the base of Mt Ruwenzori, you'll find a lift more easily on Thursdays when there's a market near the border. Those headed south to Rwindi and Goma can take an early morning bus on Mondays, Thursdays and other days as well. Reserve the day before to be assured of a seat. If you're looking for petrol and it's your lucky day, you may find some here. You'll find minibuses and trucks at the petrol station on the Komanda road near the roundabout.

MT HOYO & BUNIA

Those headed north from Beni should count on the ride taking five or six hours (10 hours in a big truck) to Komanda, the crossroad for Bunia (75 km to the east) and Kisangani (631 km to the west). The route towards Komanda passes through the heart of the equatorial forests. You can see the Balese Pygmies in Oysha, 25 km north of Beni, or at Mt Hoyo, 104 km further north. Half the fun is walking through the amazingly beautiful forests where the Pygmies live. In Oysha, ask at the mission; they have been known to arrange visits with local guides. You can exchange old T-shirts for Pygmy handicrafts.

The turn-off for Mt Hoyo, the northern end of the Ruwenzori chain, is 12 km south of Komanda; the base camp is 13 km to the east. A Porter, if you can find one, will want about US$2 to carry your gear. There, you'll find the 30-room *Auberge du Mont Hoyo*, which has chalets for roughly US$13 as well as rooms for a fifth the price. The restaurant is expensive so bring food or buy it from the Pygmies. Campers will find toilets and showers but not always electricity. The cost is only about US$1 a night per person, plus a little extra to see the Pygmy dance performance. You can exchange old T-shirts and other items for Pygmy handicrafts. Pygmies are just one of the attractions. The others are the many *grottes* (caves), Mt Hoyo, and l'Escaliers de Venus (Venus Staircase) waterfalls where *King Soloman's Mines* was filmed – pictured in many tourist brochures. The park fee for seeing these is US$2 plus another US$1 for a photo permit; you pay at the hotel, not the guide. All except Mt Hoyo are within a short distance of the lodge; a tour takes two hours. Climbing Mt Hoyo takes two days; the trail is apparently overgrown but guides are available at the hotel.

The Balese villagers will gladly act as guides to any of these places. A visit to a Pygmy village costs US$3 per group; they'll charge you for every photograph as well. Tobacco might make a better gift. If you ask, they may even take you on a hunting party – for a small fee of course.

In Komanda, you might be able to stay at a guest house run by two Anglican women.

Bunia nearby is one of the starting points for the trip westward to Kisangani. Since you're this far north you shouldn't pass up the opportunity of seeing nearby Lake Mobutu. The fishing village of Tshoma is the place to head for. Even though you can't swim in the lake because of bilharzia, it's a lively village with 24-hour bars, excellent hospitality and inexpensive fresh fish, so chances are you won't be disappointed.

If you're heading south, there are up to five buses a week, weather permitting. The trip from Goma takes about 12 hours, longer in the heavy rainy season. You could also fly on Broussair to Goma, Bukavu and Kisanga, among other places.

For a place to stay, try the popular *Chez Tout Bunia Hôtel*; it has a restaurant and charges about US$1 a single. Further in the centre there are plenty of other similarly priced hotels. Two that have been recommended are *Hôtel Rubi* on the main street and the friendly *Butembo II*, which serves decent food. Others include hotels *Ituri, Semliki* and *Ngoto*.

MUTWANGA & MT RUWENZORI

What makes the Ruwenzori mountains possibly the most beautiful in Africa is the incredible vegetation. After crossing a grassy savannah plain, you'll pass through dense rainforest, then a rocky area with twisted trees and yellow shrubs, followed by alpine meadows and, if you go high enough, snow. One of the glaciers, Elena Glacier, is almost black, looking like congealed lava, covered with white patches of newly fallen snow.

The proximity of highly contrasting environments produces some unusual, almost mystical sights, with moss entangling yellowish vegetation and snow in the background. Hence, the nickname 'Mountains of the Moon'. Because the humidity is so high, it frequently snows during the night at altitudes of 4500 metres or more. If you climb during the rainy season, from October to May, expect to have a miserable time.

What is most amazing are the huge flowers that literally dwarf humans. Huge primeval trees 10 to 12 metres tall rise up from carpets of brilliantly coloured moss, covering the massive trunks and limbs in dense mounds of crimson, lemon yellow and emerald green, with small clusters of pinkish orchids standing almost a third of a metre high. Heather, which seldom grows more than half a metre in Europe, grows to over six metres here. Blue lobelia plants, the kind that seldom reach a height of more than a few cm in most parts of the world, reach a height of three metres and more.

Because of the cold temperatures high up in the mountains around 4000 metres, plants decay very slowly. The result is a labyrinth of broken trunks, limbs, roots and rock fragments covered with moss. A false move will land you up to your knees in mire. The high elevation of the Ruwenzoris and the high humidity account largely for the size of these plants and the moss-covered environment. Temperatures shift sharply. Every day here is like summer, and every night like winter.

Although Kilimanjaro is almost 850 metres higher, climbing it is a joke compared to climbing the Ruwenzoris. The last 800 metres of the Ruwenzoris is usually all snow, requiring an ice axe, crampons and rope at the least. The park rents none of this equipment. Even if you don't attempt the summit, the weather can be freezing cold and wet. At a minimum, you'll need warm clothing, a good sleeping bag, rain gear, boots (the ground is always wet), warm water-resistant gloves, a hat and cooking utensils. And don't forget cigarettes for the porters; they can get mighty unpleasant if they don't have any to enjoy after a hard day's climb. Some travellers recommend plastic to cover up the huts' open windows – a super idea.

As for food, the widest selection is in

Beni, but many climbers do as the guides and porters do and get theirs at the Mutwanga market where all essentials (meat, vegetables, beer, etc) are available.

Mutwanga, 50 km east of Beni and 13 km of the main Beni-Kasindi road, is at the foot of the mountains and is the starting point for a climb. You can also climb from the Ugandan side starting near Kasese, but you'll have to change over US$100 at the official rate just to get into the country. About one km up and behind the market, you'll find an old historic lodge, *Hôtel Ruwenzori*, alongside a stream. This is the overwhelming choice of travellers on the cheap. Abandoned since the 1964-67 rebellion in the area, this legendary place is unfurnished but it's a great place for a dip in one of the pools. It's free but be sure to tip the friendly caretaker. For a fee he'll bring you firewood.

Other prefer camping at the park entrance in Mutsora, four km up from Mutwanga; the cost is about US$1.50 per person. For about US$4, you can also get a clean, well-furnished double room.

At the park entrance, you'll have to pay a park fee of about US$10, which includes a guide and porter (US$45). The guide will expect a substantial tip. Porters are extra. In addition expect to pay about US$2 a day per person for each of the following: hut, guides, porters and food. Guides and porters bring their own equipment but you pay for their food. If you're with a group, US$75 a person for everything would be typical. The park service rents no equipment except a pair of crampons (about US$3). Realising that guides and porters aren't really necessary, others skip the park headquarters and these fees by heading north from the market, then finding a kid to lead them towards the first hut until the trail becomes easy to follow. From there on, a guide isn't necessary unless you'll be climbing in the snow.

Allow at least five days, preferably six or seven, for the climb – three to five days up and two days down. On the way up, you'll find four unlocked cabins; the hiking time between each is roughly five hours. The climb to Hut 1 is gradual, from 1700 to 2042 metres. Hut 1 (called Kalongi) has dirty mattresses and water nearby. The climb from there to Hut 2 (called Muhungu) is the worst – all uphill to 3333 metres through roots and vines, with wet ground, and it frequently rains even in the dry season. After all, this is one of the two wettest areas in Africa (the other is Mt Cameroun). There are beds here as well but fresh water is two km away. From Hut 2 to Hut 3 (called Kyondo) is another 1000 metres. There are no beds but there is water.

Several trails lead from Hut 3. The one for Hut 4 (called Moraine) starts about 75 metres from the hut. Easy to follow, it leads to Lake Vert and on to the hut and the base of the summit. Hut No 4 is so bad, however, that most hikers avoid it. Also the route is very risky in one area, with only a rope to hang on to. If you plan to stay there the Park Service will make you sign a liability waiver. Instead, most of those attempting the summit (5119 metres) make a direct assault from Hut 3. If successful, they can usually make it down to Hut 1 by the end of the day.

However, most hikers don't attempt the summit; they hike from Hut 3 to some nearby peaks and camp overnight so as to get a view of the higher summits early the next morning, the only time they're free of clouds. The trail to these peaks is obvious.

When you return to Mutwanga, you could check out Ishango, a village 164 km to the south at the northern tip of Lake Idi Amin, which separates Zaïre and Uganda.

Some travellers don't seem to realise how easy it is to combine a trip to Virunga with a trip to the Parc des Volcans in Rwanda. Volcans is merely the Rwandan side of Virunga. The entrance is only about 100 km from Goma via Gisenyi and Ruhengeri. Together, Virunga and Volcans offer the best hiking opportunities in all of Central and East Africa. The really adventurous could hike from one to the other.

Central & Southern Zaïre

ISHANGO

After coming down the Ruwenzoris, you could check out Ishango, a park camping area with most of the animals found around Rwindi, except elephants. It's 164 km to the south of Mutwanga via Kasindi at the northern tip of Lake Idi Amin (Edward), which separates Zaïre from Uganda. You can rent a room at the park entrance or camp (US$3 per tent). Some travellers who have already paid the seven-day registration fee and don't want to pay again simply tell gate officials that they're headed for Kiavinyonge 10 km further down the road and outside the park.

Kiavinyonge is a good place to enjoy fishing and hippo-watching. If you swim in the lake (it's apparently free of Bilharzia like Lake Kivu) watch out for the hippos; they're far more dangerous than they appear. In Kiavinyonge, you can stay at the *Lodgement Special* for US$1 per room, eat at a restaurant on the lake shore and, around 8 am most days, catch a truck hauling fish to Butembo – a four-hour journey over a winding dirt road.

LUBUMBASHI

The capital of the southern, copper-rich Shaba province, Lubumbashi (ex-Elizabethville) and the surrounding area have the best rail connections in the country and the best links with adjacent countries. At an elevation over 1000 metres with cool, dry air, it's also has one of Zaïre's most agreeable climates.

Information

You'll find the US Consulate on Blvd Elisabeth, Avis (tel 223623, telex 41049) at Hôtel Karavia, and a branch of Amiza (tel 3103/7) travel agency. For malachite, there are at least three places within one or two blocks from the central circle in town: Home Comfort at 42 Ave Mwepu, Arts et Cadeaux at the Park hotel, and Artiste Shabien. At least twice a week, there's a train north-bound train.

Places to Stay & Eat

For rooms in the US$8 to US$12 range, you have several choices. At 247 Ave Mwepu in front of the train station and near *Restaurant Zaïre*, you'll find the 34-room *Hôtel du Globe* (tel 3612), with decent rooms, private baths, a restaurant and a bar. *Hôtel Wagenia* (tel 3484), at 535 Ave Mobutu, has 16 rooms that are also comfortable. Others worth trying are *Hôtel Silver Star* and, nearby, *Hôtel Macris*. The latter is Greek-run with a good restaurant. For rock bottom prices, try *Hôtel de la Paix*, a real dive close to the hospital.

The best hotel is *Le Karavia* (tel 4511, telex 41049). Singles/doubles with breakfast cost about US$55/65 (about US$15 more for a room facing the lake). There's only hot water from 6.30 to 8.30 am and 6.30 to 8.30 pm. About two km from the centre of town on Golf Rd, it's a big hotel with a pool, tennis court, and a golf course nearby. The older, 92-room *Park Hôtel* in the centre of town at 107 Ave Kasaï charges about US$40 a room with breakfast. It's not well-maintained, and there is no pool.

The Belgian-run *Hôtel du Shaba* (tel 3617), in the heart of town at 487 Ave Mama-Yemo, is better value for the money. Clean rooms cost about US$20 to US$25 (US$5 extra for a private bath). Only two of the 42 rooms have hot water.

KOLWEZI

The centre of the copper-mining region, Kolwezi made all the world newspapers in 1977/78 when it was captured by rebels from Angola. They killed a number of the 2000 Belgian residents, most of whom were rescued by Belgian paratroopers. Only a few Belgians have returned.

Places to Stay

The city's two best hotels are the 28-room *Hôtel Impala* (tel 2667) and the 10-room *Hôtel Bonne Auberge* (tel 2421) at 30 Ave du

Député Kajama. To save money, try the 11-room *Air-Hôtel* (tel 2697) on Ave Baobab, the *Pax* on Ave Lukal, or the *Zaïre*.

MBUJI-MAYI

A big diamond centre where mining is done both legally and illegally, Mbuji-Mayi is in the centre of the country near Kananga.

The area between Mbuji-Mayi and Tshikapa is full of diamond mines, primarily along the riverbeds. You can get a permit to visit the area from the Ministry of Mines in Mbuji-Mayi or Kinshasa. If you can, it's well worth the visit to watch thousands of families digging for diamonds in the dusty-red, dry riverbeds. However, if there's a government crackdown on diamond smugglers and you don't have an official permit, avoid the area because the local militia doesn't take kindly to strangers who don't have official permission to be there and won't, or can't, offer bribes.

Places to Stay

If you're looking for a good hotel, check out the new *Hôtel Tanko* or the 15-room *Hôtel Impala* (tel 332) on Rue Mwene-Ditu. *Hôtel Mukeba* on Ave Serpent near the post office, *Hôtel Mka-Kazadi* (tel 903) on Rue Kabeya, and the *Guest House* (tel 331) on Ave Tshilomba are others.

KANANGA

With over half a million people, Kananga is one of Zaïre's largest cities. Blessed with a relatively sunny climate, it's in the dead centre of Zaïre, almost equal distance from Kinshasa (1200 km), Lubumbashi (1200 km) and Kisangani (1255 km). Avenues Mobutu and Lumumba, lined with the city's tallest buildings, form the main axes in the commercial and administrative district. The heart of town is the central plaza on Ave Lumumba, the favourite place for promenading. Overlooking the plaza is an old building housing the city museum.

Places to Stay

The 31-room *Hôtel Atlanta* (tel 2828) on Ave

Lumumba is the city's finest hotel. *Moderna Hôtel* (tel 2334) on Ave du 20 Mai, *Hôtel Hocentshi* (tel 2502) on Ave Muhona, and the *Musube* (tel 2438) on Ave du Commerce are less expensive. For a still cheaper room, try *Hôtel Palace* or *Le Cercle* in the heart of town not far from the train station.

ILEBO

One tenth the size of Kananga, Ilebo is nevertheless an important commercial centre because it is at the point where the Kasai River becomes navigable. Consequently, the train from Lubumbashi ends here and the Kinshasa-Ilebo steamers take over. You can reach Kinshasa sooner by hitching a ride in a truck to Kikwit and grabbing a bus from there.

Places to Stay

The *Mission Catholique* three km south of town has rooms and a craft shop which sells carvings at cheap prices. Otherwise there's the the 16-room *SNCZ Hôtel du Palme*, which was built in the early 1920s for the visit of King Albert I of Belgium and is still the best hotel in town, or the cheaper *Hôtel Frefima*. At the Palme, one traveller said he was originally quoted a price of about US$9 for a room with washing facilities (tap and bucket) but ended up paying only US$5.

KIKWIT

The main reference points in Kikwit, population 200,000, are the Kwilu River and Ave Mobutu, which runs from one end of the city to the other. The latter and Ave de la TSF lead to 'Le Plateau' where the market, stadium, most administrative buildings, the Catholic Mission and the finest residences are found. On holidays the stadium and Gungu square are where most folkloric activities, including masked dances are held.

Places to Stay

You'll find the city's major hotel, the 48-room *Hôtel Kwilu*, on Ave Motubu and a cheaper one, *Hôtel Mutashi*, nearby. Every day, there are buses to Kinshasa.

Northern Zaïre

KISANGANI

Kisangani is over 1700 km upstream from Kinshasa and one of Zaïre's largest cities, with over half a million people. The heart of town is the area between the port, Hôtel Zaïre Palace and the post office, which has an efficient Poste Restante. If you see any of Zaïre's tourist brochures, you're sure to see pictures of the city's major tourist attraction – the fishermen of Wagenia, a town just upstream. They catch *capitaine* (perch) by suspending long conical basket traps from wooden scaffolds placed in the river at the falls – don't miss it.

For overland travellers, the former Stanleyville is a major hub. Some take the steamer to Bumba or all the way to Kinshasa; others head north to the Central African Republic or east to Virunga Park, Lake Kivu and East Africa. Because of logistical problems, only a few head south. The steamer stops here because for the next 125 km upstream until Ubundu, there are seven major rapids – the famous Stanley Falls, now called Boyoma Falls. That's also why you'll find a railroad along this stretch of the river. From Ubundu, you can catch another steamer south to Kindu – altogether, a week's journey if connections are good.

Places to Stay & Eat

The Greek-owned *Hôtel Olympia* is the meeting place for overland travellers. Those who can't afford the rooms (roughly US$4 to US$10) often camp there. The cost is about US$1 a person plus US$2 per vehicle. For dirt cheap rooms, try *Hôtel Baninga* in the Zone de Chopo.

The city's major hotels are still the old 100-room *Hôtel Zaïre-Palace* (tel 2664) on Ave de l'Eglise, followed by *Hôtel Kisangani* opposite the Centre Culturel Français, with very decent doubles for about US$17. *Hôtel Wagenia*, has doubles for about US$10, and the pleasant *Hôtel des Chutes* (tel 3498), is a colonial-style hotel on Ave Mobutu near the river which has 40 doubles for roughly US$6 to US$7.

Both the Olympia and the Wagenia have good restaurants. Neither is cheap. The Wagenia, for example, serves steak and chips for about US$3. For cheap rice, beans and beer, try *Restaurant Amical* just around the corner. About halfway between it and the Olympia you'll find the *Transit Café*, a good restaurant and a meeting place for travellers. It has a blackboard with air, boat and train arrivals.

For good pastries try the patisserie very near the Hôtel Kisangani and on the same side of the street. Also Kisangani has one of the few good food markets in this part of Zaïre.

BUMBA

For people travelling between Kisangani and Bangui (CAR), Bumba is a major transit point – where you get on or off the steamer. You can also hop a barge to Kisangani, which will take at least a week (longer if it hits sand) and don't expect to find any food en route except for fruit, bread and beer.

Bumba is a much better place to wait for the steamer and barges than Lisala because it is a more comfortable and less aggressive town. However, beware of a possible scam. Officials have been known to withhold your ticket until the last moment so they can hurry you onto the steamer and ask for more money. Also, the fare for shipping a vehicle to Kisangani is sky high, reportedly US$150.

An interesting Greek who owns the Socam chain of stores lives here. He changes money and is good for information.

Places to Stay

For a cheap hotel with clean rooms, try *Hôtel de la Paix* near the supermarket. There's also a decent reasonably priced campground. The best hotel appears to be *Hôtel Molua* on Ave Manga.

BUTA

Some 321 km north of Kisangani, Buta is on the major route to the Central African

Republic. The town's best hotel appears to be *Hôtel Rubi* on the river's edge near the bridge. To save money, stay at the friendly, Norwegian-run *Protestant Mission* four km out of town.

EPULU

A small town on the route from Kisangani to Virunga park, Epulu Station is definitely worth a stop. This is where you can see Pygmies and the extremely rare okapi (a doe-eyed creature resembling a zebra and a giraffe) discovered only in the early 20th century.

Near the National Park Lodge, you'll find an Efe Pygmy camp of tiny leaf huts where the inhabitants are friendly and enjoy offering travellers a puff on their metre-long pipes. Indeed, the Efe Pygmies are so addicted to tobacco that they will work three or four hours in a villager's fields for a thumb's length of leaf tobacco. The exchange of tobacco for labour is just one component of the complex relationship between the Lese villagers and the Efe Pygmies. The Efe also hunt, fish and gather honey, building materials and medicines from the forest to trade for food, aluminium cooking pots, old clothes, soap, and metal to make knives. The Lese say the Pygmies are lazy, while the Pygmies say the Lese are miserly, and repeatedly cheat them out of their just rewards.

An American Pygmy expert, Patrick Putman, lived and died here in the Ituri forests, studying the Pygmies. Traditionally, they have no chiefs. Instead, each age group has its own sphere of responsibility. The normal blood relationships of an individual family are recognised, but in every respect the 'family' is the whole band. All adults are called 'mother' and 'father' by children and everyone in the child's age groups is his 'brother' or 'sister'. There is an overwhelming impression of very strong bonds existing within Pygmy bands.

In the villages, while the Pygmies may seem happy, they tend to adopt a rather servile attitude towards the Lese. In the forests, however, their servility disappears immediately, which is one reason you should try to go hunting with them. To the Pygmies, hunting is the essence of their traditional livelihood even though gathering food is just as important. Traditionally, a ritual fire is kindled at the start of the hunt; no one must kill more than is needed for food. They use a mixture of leaves, all with magical properties, to create smoke, then pass their bows and arrows over the ritual fire to enhance their chances of success. If a dog is nearby, it too may be passed through the smoke.

You may end up paddling in canoes with them down a jungle river. If the Pygmies catch anything, you'll get to eat it with them. Frequently, however, all they return with is a few mushrooms, some giant snails, honey or wild yams.

Hunting with the Pygmies is neither difficult to arrange nor expensive. The cost is about US$1 a person, US$1 for the guide, US$1 for each camera, plus a US$1 compulsory 'tip'. The camp site in Epulu costs the same. Even if you don't go on a hunt they're used to travellers and will want a tip for sitting and talking.

GARAMBA NATIONAL PARK

In the far north-east corner of the country on the road to Juba (Sudan), Garamba park is noted for having the white rhino as well as elephant and giraffe.

ISIRO

Some 577 km north-east of Kisangani, Isiro is a town of no particular note. If you're looking for the top hotel, try the 19-room *Hôtel Mangbetu* or the 26-room *Hôtel de l'Uélé*. Both have restaurants. For a cheap hotel, try *Hôtel Sport* near the football field but not the *Mission Catholique*, which is reportedly unfriendly.

LISALA

Like Bumba 120 km to the east, Lisala is on the Zaïre River and is a potential transit point for those on the Kisangani-Bangui route who want to take the steamer. If you have to wait for the steamer, go onto Bumba where the accommodation is better, food more plentiful, and the people are not so aggressive. Also, the vehicle loading facilities at Lisala are lousy.

Banks in Lisala will not change money or travellers' cheques. The best place to change money is at the Catholic Mission, but the rates are better in Bumba.

Places to Stay

For a dirt cheap room, try the *Hôtel du Marché*. You'll find more decent accommodation, however, at *Complexe Venus*, close to the river. The rooms cost US$1.50 and are much nicer than *Hôtel Montagne*. The Venus also has cold drinks, which makes a change from the warm beer and smoked fish served elsewhere in Lisala.

Hôtel Zaïre may also be worth checking out. The *Mission Catholique* doesn't take travellers, but the *Mission Protestante* three km down river still lets travellers camp for free and it's much safer than camping in town.

ZONGO

Across the river from Bangui (CAR), Zongo is full of thieves, so don't plan to sleep overnight and don't get caught there on the weekend (immigration offices are closed Saturday afternoon and Sunday, but check this as it may change). There is a bank, but most travellers change money in Bangui or on the black market.

Zongo-Lisala can be done in two or three days and should cost about US$5 to Gemena and the same to Lisala using trucks. Overcharging foreigners is the norm, so ask several locals for the real price. This notoriously muddy route has been improved, with long stretches of new grading. You'll find no restaurants along the way – only sardines, onions, smoked fish and occasionally crocodile in yukky red sauce. Zongo-Gemena takes 10 to 12 hours by truck. Don't be surprised if the driver lets you of two km from town; taking hitchhikers is illegal.

Gemena-Akula is 180 km and a half-day ride. In Akula you must change trucks to cross the river. Then it's another half-day ride to Lisala. If it's getting dark when you arrive at Akula, you'll do better staying overnight at Akuna (12 km north of Akula), which has several decent hotels. The friendly *Bar Madame Hôtel* will give you two excellent mattresses, a grill and hot coals for cooking on, a table and chairs, and even boiled drinking water.

Index

Maps

Temperature

To convert °C to °F multiply by 1.8 and add 32

To convert °F to °C subtract 32 and multiply by ·55

Length, Distance & Area

	multiply by
inches to centimetres	2.54
centimetres to inches	0.39
feet to metres	0.30
metres to feet	3.28
yards to metres	0.91
metres to yards	1.09
miles to kilometres	1.61
kilometres to miles	0.62
acres to hectares	0.40
hectares to acres	2.47

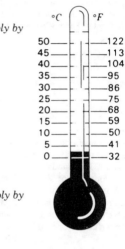

Weight

	multiply by
ounces to grams	28.35
grams to ounces	0.035
pounds to kilograms	0.45
kilograms to pounds	2.21
British tons to kilograms	1016
US tons to kilograms	907

A British ton is 2240 lbs, a US ton is 2000 lbs

Volume

	multiply by
Imperial gallons to litres	4.55
litres to imperial gallons	0.22
US gallons to litres	3.79
litres to US gallons	0.26

5 imperial gallons equals 6 US gallons
a litre is slightly more than a US quart, slightly less
than a British one

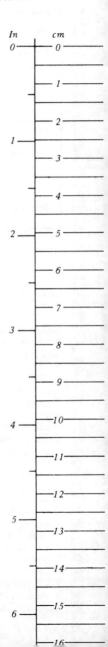

The eastern and southern African countries have always been popular destinations for tourists and foreign workers. The game parks of East Africa draw thousands of visitors each year. In the countries of West and Central Africa, you may not see scenery and wildlife as spectacular as that in East Africa, but you will be able to experience the wealth and colour of African culture, art and music.

Over the past few months, we have received several letters from Central Africa. This section was compiled using information sent to us by the following travellers: A Y Brooks (UK), Suzanne Chapman (NZ), Paul Ferguson (Aus), Michael Nest, Penny & Rachel (UK) and Laura Silvani (Sp).

Visas & Permits

Cameroun You can obtain a visa in Calabar, Nigeria, in 24 hours. You need to fill out two forms and attach two photos. The cost of the visa is incredibly high, having been increased by 300% in May 1989. The Cameroun Embassy is on the Marian Rd Extension.

CAR An Australian traveller tried to obtain a visa at the French Embassy in Lomé, Togo, but had his passport thrown back at him. He finally obtained his visa in Youande by first going to the Consular Affairs Office in the Bastos district and obtaining the text of a telex requesting a visa. He took this telex to Intelcam (which is opposite the post office in town) and sent it to Bangui for CFA 950. A reply was received in less than 48 hours. He then paid CFA 200 to collect the reply and take it to the embassy in Youande. He had to fill out one form, pay CFA 2500, and wait 24 hours. No photos were necessary.

Congo When leaving Congo by plane or ferry to Kinshasa, Zaïre, an exit permit is required. You have to apply for it in the morning at immigration and you can pick it up at 3 pm. It is free. You must show a receipt from a hotel stating that your accommodation has been paid for. One traveller obtained the exit permit and then left Congo via M'Binda on the border with Gabon. No one even asked to see her exit permit!

Equatorial Guinea To obtain a tourist visa from the Embassy of Equatorial Guinea in Madrid, you need two photographs and approximately US$25. Ask for the cheapest type of visa and don't worry if it expires while you're in Equatorial Guinea. Just go to the police station and get an exit visa which is valid for 60 days.

Zaïre Visas are expensive but they are issued in 15 minutes. A one-month single-entry visa costs CFA 18,000, a two-month single-entry visa costs CFA 36,000, and a two-month double-entry visa costs CFA 48,000.

Money

Central Africa remains the most expensive region in Africa. The unit of currency in most Central African countries is the CFA. The current rate of exchange is US$1 to CFA 291.63. In Zaïre, the unit of currency is the zaïre and the exchange rate is US$1 to Z 433.54.

Health

Fansidar should not be used as a prophylaxis. It has many dangerous side effects and is no longer on the market in many countries. Fansidar should only be used as a cure for malaria if Nivaquine (or its equivalent) does not work. One traveller who contracted malaria in Zaïre was taken to the hospital in Buta. She said the hospital was quite modern and that the helpful doctor (no English spoken) was competent and cured her within four days. Apparently, there have been several travellers in Zaïre who contracted malaria even though they were taking the prescribed anti-malarials.

Dangers & Annoyances

One traveller complained that police in Kinshasa, Zaïre, were constantly trying to find some offence to charge her with, obviously hoping for bribe money. The traveller found the best way to deal with this problem was to pretend she didn't understand French and to call local people over to see if they could explain what the police officer wanted. As soon as local people were involved the police officer, realising there might be problems, would call the whole thing off and disappear.

We also received a complaint about Cameroun police and government officials. One traveller claimed that the Cameroun police refused to allow the ferry from Nigeria to dock after 6 pm unless all the passengers paid a huge bribe. Everyone on the boat refused to pay and, consequently, had to spend the night in the mangrove swamp. Apparently, Cameroun and Nigerian police were also asking for bribes on the ferry itself. If you pretend you don't have any naira or CFA, you will probably be left alone.

In Zaïre, immigration officials working at the Zongo border demanded a 'first entry fee' of CFA 5000 from one tourist. Unfortunately, they had to pay or they wouldn't have been allowed to enter the country at all.

CHAD

Chad is slowly recovering from the war. Air Tchad is flying again, but there is only one plane. It flies once a week to various cities from N'djamena to Moundou and Sahr. The flight from N'djamena to Moundou costs about US$80. The plane has around 15 seats and heavy luggage cannot be taken on board.

We received an interesting letter from someone recommending the overland journey from Niger to Chad, north of Lake Chad, as an alternative route for anyone travelling from West Africa to Central Africa. An excerpt follows:

With eight Africans, piles of luggage, jerry cans and grain, we tumbled into the back of a Toyota pick-up. We set off from Nguigmi, the last town in Niger, to Nokou, the first town in Chad, 250 km down the track. The journey was supposed to take one and a half days, but it was three days later when we bounced into Nokou, shaking sand out of every crevice. There are vehicles leaving Nguigmi for Nokou every two to three days. The fare is CFA 7500. Although the driver carries a supply of water, you should carry your own food and water.

The countryside is beautiful. Sahel consists of undulating plains with intermittent sand dunes and a few scattered trees. There are loads of birds. We were lucky enough to be stranded in an isolated nomad's settlement for one day while our pick-up truck went to the aid of a broken down vehicle. Sheltered from the sun by a dwelling made with brush and blankets, we feasted on rice, goat's meat, dates and sweetened camel's milk. The locals were thrilled to have their photos taken, and no one demanded *un petit cadeau* like they did in Niger.

Michael Nest

ZAÏRE

Much to the disappointment of one traveller, Zaïre was not a lush paradise full of tropical fruit and an abundance of food. All they could find for sale were pineapples, bread, bananas, and the occasional fish or animal.

If you want to see the gorillas you have to pay US$100 in hard currency. There is no park entrance fee or camera fee. There are still two viewing groups and a maximum of six people are permitted to view the gorillas at one time. One group is 30 minutes' walk from the starting point and the other group is two to three hours' walk. You can camp cheaply at the starting point.

Travellers' Tips & Comments

A short distance below Brazzaville, Congo, are impressive cataracts on the Congo River. About 60 km further down river its tributary, Lufulakari, falls in a series of very impressive waterfalls into the Congo River. On the Zaïre side of the river there is another waterfall.

To get there from Brazzaville, you have to go very early (before 5 am) to Marché Total Bakongo. From there you take a taxi to Boka via M'Bandza N'Dounga. The taxi will stop at a crossroad about seven km from the waterfalls. To return you have to walk to that crossroad and hitch a ride to Brazzaville.

Jan Kucera – USA

On the Gabon side of the Lekoko border with Congo there were three officers on duty who were just finishing some palm wine. They were drunk and instantly invited me to join them, no doubt hoping that I would pay. I refused. They then quickly discovered that I did not have an inoculation against 'bessaga', a disease they dreamed up themselves, and suggested that I could still cross the border if I paid CFA 3000 for their wine. I readily agreed but insisted on getting a receipt which I claimed was necessary in order to get it refunded from the Gabon Embassy in Washington. They then decided to let me through without paying anything.

Jan Kucera – USA

Guides to Africa

Africa on a shoestring
From Marrakesh to Kampala, Mozambique to Mauritania, Johannesburg to Cairo – this guidebook gives you all the facts on travelling in Africa. It provides comprehensive information on more than 50 African countries – how to get to them, how to get around, where to stay, where to eat, what to see and what to avoid.

East Africa – a travel survival kit
Whether you want to climb Kilimanjaro, visit wildlife reserves, or sail an Arab dhow, East Africa offers a fascinating pastiche of cultures and landscapes. This guide has detailed information on Kenya, Uganda, Rwanda, Burundi, eastern Zaire, Tanzania and the Comoros Islands.

West Africa – a travel survival kit
This book has all the necessary information for independent travel in 16 countries – Benin, Burkino Faso, Cape Verde, Gambia, Ghana, Guinea, Guinea Bissau, Ivory Coast, Liberia, Mali, Mauritania, Niger, Nigeria, Senegal, Sierra Leone and Togo.

Swahili phrasebook
Swahili is widely spoken throughout East Africa – from the coast of Kenya and Tanzania through to Zaire.

Egypt & the Sudan – a travel survival kit
The sights of Egypt and the Sudan have impressed visitors for more than 50 centuries. This guide takes you beyond the spectacular pyramids to discover the villages of the Nile, diving in the Red Sea and many other other attractions.

Morocco, Algeria & Tunisia – a travel survival kit
A blend of African, Islamic, Arab and Berber cultures make this a fascinating region to visit. This book takes you from bustling souks to peaceful oases and is packed with all the information you'll need.

Lonely Planet Guidebooks

Lonely Planet guidebooks cover virtually every accessible part of Asia as well as Australia, the Pacific, Central and South America, Africa, the Middle East and parts of North America. There are four main series: 'travel survival kits', covering a single country for a range of budgets; 'shoestring' guides with compact information for low-budget travel in a major region; trekking guides; and 'phrasebooks'.

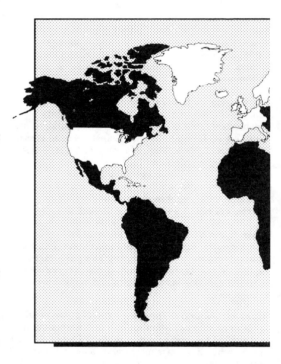

Australia & the Pacific
Australia
Bushwalking in Australia
Papua New Guinea
Papua New Guinea phrasebook
New Zealand
Tramping in New Zealand
Rarotonga & the Cook Islands
Solomon Islands
Tahiti & French Polynesia
Fiji
Micronesia
Tonga
Samoa

South-East Asia
South-East Asia on a shoestring
Malaysia, Singapore & Brunei
Indonesia
Bali & Lombok
Indonesia phrasebook
Burma
Burmese phrasebook
Thailand
Thai phrasebook
Philippines
Pilipino phrasebook

North-East Asia
North-East Asia on a shoestring
China
China phrasebook
Tibet
Tibet phrasebook
Japan
Japanese phrasebook
Korea
Korean phrasebook
Hong Kong, Macau & Canton
Taiwan

West Asia
West Asia on a shoestring
Trekking in Turkey
Turkey
Turkish phrasebook

Indian Ocean
Madagascar & Comoros
Maldives & Islands of the East Indian Ocean
Mauritius, Réunion & Seychelles

Mail Order

Lonely Planet guidebooks are distributed worldwide and are sold by good bookshops everywhere. They are also available by mail order from Lonely Planet, so if you have difficulty finding a title please write to us. US and Canadian residents should write to Embarcadero West, 112 Linden St, Oakland CA 94607, USA and residents of other countries to PO Box 617, Hawthorn, Victoria 3122, Australia.

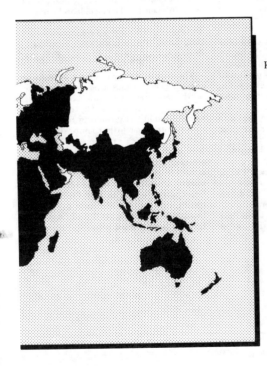

Eastern Europe
Eastern Europe

Indian Subcontinent
India
Hindi/Urdu phrasebook
Kashmir, Ladakh & Zanskar
Trekking in the Indian Himalaya
Pakistan
Kathmandu & the Kingdom of Nepal
Trekking in the Nepal Himalaya
Nepal phrasebook
Sri Lanka
Sri Lanka phrasebook
Bangladesh
Karakoram Highway

Africa
Africa on a shoestring
East Africa
Swahili phrasebook
West Africa
Central Africa
Morocco, Algeria & Tunisia

North America
Canada
Alaska

Mexico
Mexico
Baja California

South America
South America on a shoestring
Ecuador & the Galapagos Islands
Colombia
Chile & Easter Island
Bolivia
Brazil
Brazilian phrasebook
Peru
Argentina
Quechua phrasebook

Middle East
Israel
Egypt & the Sudan
Jordan & Syria
Yemen

Lonely Planet

Lonely Planet published its first book in 1973. Tony and Maureen Wheeler had made a lengthy overland trip from England to Australia and, in response to numerous 'how do you do it?' questions, Tony wrote and they published *Across Asia on the Cheap*. It became an instant local best-seller and inspired thoughts of a second travel guide. A year and a half in South-East Asia resulted in their second book, *South-East Asia on a Shoestring*, which they put together in a backstreet Chinese hotel in Singapore in 1975. The 'yellow book', as it quickly became known, soon became *the* guide to the region and has gone through five editions, always with its familiar yellow cover.

Soon other writers came to them with ideas for similar books – books that went off the beaten track with an adventurous approach to travel, books that 'assumed you knew how to get your luggage off the carousel,' as one reviewer put it. Lonely Planet grew from a kitchen table operation to a spare room and then to its own office. Its international reputation began to grow as the Lonely Planet logo began to appear in more and more countries. In 1982 *India – a travel survival kit* won the Thomas Cook award for the best guidebook of the year.

These days there are over 70 Lonely Planet titles. Over 40 people work at our office in Melbourne, Australia and another half dozen at our US office in Oakland, California.

At first Lonely Planet specialised in the Asia region but these days we are also developing major ranges of guidebooks to the Pacific region, to South America and to Africa. The list of walking guides is growing and Lonely Planet now has a unique series of phrasebooks to 'unusual' languages. The emphasis continues to be on travel for travellers and Tony and Maureen still manage to fit in a number of trips each year and play a very active part in the writing and updating of Lonely Planet's guides.

Keeping guidebooks up to date is a constant battle which requires an ear to the ground and lots of walking, but technology also plays its part. All Lonely Planet guidebooks are now stored and updated on computer, and some authors even take lap-top computers into the field. Lonely Planet is also using computers to draw maps and eventually many of the maps will be stored on disk.

The people at Lonely Planet strongly feel that travellers can make a positive contribution to the countries they visit both by better appreciation of cultures and by the money they spend. In addition the company tries to make a direct contribution to the countries and regions it covers. Since 1986 a percentage of the income from each book has gone to aid groups and associations. This has included donations to famine relief in Africa, to aid projects in India, to agricultural projects in Central America, to Greenpeace's efforts to halt French nuclear testing in the Pacific and to Amnesty International. In 1989 $41,000 was donated by Lonely Planet to these projects.